FUTURE PRACTICE ALTERNATIVES IN MEDICINE,
2nd Edition

FUTURE PRACTICE ALTERNATIVES IN MEDICINE, 2nd Edition

David B. Nash, M.D., M.B.A.
Director of Health Policy and Clinical Outcomes
Jefferson Medical College
Thomas Jefferson University
Philadelphia, PA

 Igaku-Shoin   New York • Tokyo

Published and distributed by

IGAKU-SHOIN Medical Publishers, Inc.
One Madison Avenue, New York, New York 10010

IGAKU-SHOIN Ltd.,
5-24-3 Hongo, Bunkyo-ku, Tokyo

Library of Congress Cataloging-in-Publication Data

Future practice alternatives in medicine / [edited by] David B. Nash —
2nd ed.
    p.   cm.
    Includes bibliographical references and index.
    ISBN 0-89640-236-3
    1. Medicine—Practice—United States. 2. Medicine—United
States—Vocational guidance. 3. Medicine—United States.
I. Nash, David B.
    [DNLM: 1. Delivery of Health Care—trends—United States.
2. Career Choice. W 84 AA1F95 1993]
R728.F88 1993
610.69'52'0973—dc20
DNLM/DLC
for Library of Congress   93-14635
                                       CIP

ISBN: 0-89640-236-3 (New York)
ISBN: 4-260-14236-4 (Tokyo)
Printed and bound in the U.S.A.

10 9 8 7 6 5 4 3 2

To my parents, Al and Charlotte,
who made it possible.

To my mentor and friend, Samuel P. Martin, III, M.D.,
who made it fascinating.

To my children, Leah, Rachel and Jacob,
who made it fun.

And to my physician wife, Esther Jean,
who made it all worthwhile.

PREFACE TO THE SECOND EDITION

This is not a "how-to" book. Rather, I have assembled a broad spectrum of information that will guide physicians as they make important career and professional decisions. Several chapters could stand independently. Taken together, in the order in which they have been assembled, they provide a means for interpreting and benefiting from future developments in medicine. My contention is that the medical school advisory system (and much of the information provided to physicians at each step along their career paths) is woefully inadequate in light of the rapid changes in health care delivery. Most physicians are ill-prepared for a world in which they must commit themselves to and position themselves within the health care system (1). The socialization process of becoming a physician stresses autonomy and independence, leading to a world view that is poorly suited to a corporate culture. It is my hope that this book will enlighten and challenge physicians to reexamine their world view in light of the corporatization of care, increased competition in the marketplace and other forces that are acting inexorably to change forever the way medicine has been practiced. Ideally, physicians can be viewed as agents of positive social change, as educators and as "wellness" promoters. This book will help them reassert their primacy in these important societal roles.

As I reviewed the original chapters in preparing this second edition, I found most of what my colleagues wrote in 1985 to be eerily prophetic. Although some of the actual events are somewhat different, taken as a whole, this book was far out in front of the crowd in discussing the impact of managed care, the growth in group practices, the importance of primary care and the general role of economics within the health care system.

For this second edition, virtually every word has been rereviewed, and many of the chapters have been extensively rewritten. Dozens of new references have been cited and the most currently available information is shared.

The book is divided into an overview chapter and three main sections. The overview reexamines the physician surplus and the current economic environment for young physicians. Advice on approaching the job market, long considered dirty words in medicine, is given with several real-world examples. The overview concludes with a listing of the central forces that are shaping the future practice of medicine. Material presented therein has been distilled from several large, national private-sector studies designed to foretell important trends.

The three main sections were derived by grouping together related contributions from versatile and talented experts.

Section I, "Social Concerns," explores such important issues as physician collectivism, the role of women in medicine and a plan for reforming undergraduate medical education. Like the other main sections, it is preceded by a brief commentary that summarizes the main arguments.

Section II, "Emerging Career Trends," explores six career pathways that I believe will be increasingly important as the delivery of health-care services is restructured. Hopefully, readers will integrate the information about the physician surplus presented in the overview and explore further some of the viable career alternatives described in detail in this section. Most of the emerging fields described herein are currently undersubscribed and are forecasted to be booming in the near future.

Section III, "Future Directions," consists of chapters on the role of computers in medicine, the changing face of continuing medical education and a guide to technology assessment. This section serves as a final springboard or platform to propel readers headlong into the future.

I hope that I have fulfilled the challenge laid down by Dr. Frank Rhodes, then the President of Cornell University, at the second Cornell Medical Conference on Health Policy. As articulated by Eli Ginzberg (2), the conference concluded that medical school applicants (and residents and fellows) need to be forewarned about the "immensity of changes" that are under way and those that are still to come. We should strive to cultivate "realistic anticipations and thus avoid later regrets and frustrations" on the part of all physicians.

It is the Editor's responsibility to articulate the purpose, audience and scope of any assembled work. Many chapters have ample references, provided more for the reader's further exploration and reading than for academic rigor. No doubt, the chapters could have been arranged differently. Some opinions presented in this book are unorthodox, perhaps even irreverent. Hopefully, readers will be challenged to rethink their current view of medicine and, as a result, become well prepared to assume an important role in helping to shape the future of the profession.

Who should read this book? The intended audience is diverse— medical students, residents, fellows, attending physicians, residency-program directors, chiefs of service, hospital directors and other persons who are interested in the future practice of medicine. Although written primarily by physicians for physicians, professional educators and other members of the lay public may find the unique perspective presented herein to be a fascinating insight into the world of doctors.

REFERENCES

1. Ottensmeyer DJ, Smith HL: Patterns of medical practice in an era of change. *Front Health Serv Manage* 3(1):3–30, 1986.
2. Ginzberg E (ed): *From Physician Shortage to Patient Shortage, the Uncertain Future of Medical Practice*. Boulder, Colorado, Westview Press, 1986.

FOREWORD

Nash and colleagues in their second edition of *Future Practice Alternatives in Medicine* have challenged the readers to expand their visions as to the obligation and responsibilities of physicians to the medical profession and to society. The authors have raised a number of issues ranging from the education students receive in medical school, the growing influence of women in medicine, the future of continuing medical education, the use of new and costly technology, and the ways which society will evaluate and pay for the care physicians give to patients. The chapters within the sections Social Concerns, Emerging Career Trends, and Future Directions, will stimulate the readers to reassess their beliefs in light of societal perceptions and expectations.

Physicians' many responsibilities have always been difficult to discharge and to balance. Given the new societal demands and expectations, they will require more attention by all, including medical schools, teaching hospitals, professional groups, third-party payers, and society.

Physicians need to behave as clinicians, as teachers for their patients, and as managers of resources. Which of these competencies should receive the highest priority in medical school is a source of debate, as it is impossible to meet every expectation in four years. What is needed is linkages between medical school, residency programs, and practice so that strengths and gaps or deficiencies can be recognized early. The physician's final degree should be received only with retirement from practice.

This book can benefit students, residents, faculty, practicing physicians, and hospital administrators. The students and residents who are considering career choices will be challenged to weigh the options within the traditional fields of medicine in addition to exciting new opportunities in health care management, quality assurance, and health policy. Young physicians will soon appreciate that the complexities and demands posed by the basic and clinical science curricula and postgraduate training are rather minor issues compared to the requirements and expectations that society has for the medical profession.

Medicine is an exciting profession. The new technologies, the many demands (some of which are unreasonable), and the legal and ethical issues should prompt physicians to introduce reforms within the profession as well as to make society recognize its obligations.

Cost/benefits analyses should include the contributions of the patients, third-party payers, regulators and legal profession, as well as the medical profession. This writer hopes that the reader will see that the 21st century will provide the physician opportunities to discover new worlds even though the waters will be choppy: this book will open new vistas for physicians.

Joseph S. Gonnella, M.D.
Professor of Medicine
Senior Vice President for
Academic Affairs and Dean
Jefferson Medical College
Thomas Jefferson University

CONTENTS

CONTRIBUTORS

David J. Brailer, M.D., Ph.D.
Assistant Professor of Health Care
  Systems
Director Health Care Reform Project
The Wharton School of the University
  of Pennsylvania
Ralston House, Room 322
3615 Chestnut Street
Philadelphia, Pennsylvania

James B. Couch, M.D., J.D.
Vice President
Managed Care and Employee Benefits
Operations—Quality
The Traveler's Corporation
One Tower Square
Two Main South
Hartford, Connecticut

Allen Douma, M.D.
Former Vice President and Medical
  Director
Traveler's Managed Disability Ser-
  vices,
Traveler's Insurance Corporation
13604 Soft Breeze Court
Herndon, Virginia

A. Mark Fendrick, M.D.
University of Pennsylvania School of
  Medicine
Clinical Scholars Program
3615 Chestnut Street
Philadelphia, Pennsylvania

David Gluck, M.D.
Medical Director
Metropolitan Life Insurance Com-
  pany, Inc.
One Madison Avenue
Area 16R
New York, New York

Alan L. Hillman, M.D., M.B.A.
Director Center for Health Policy
University of Pennsylvania
Leonard Davis Institute of Health
  Economics
3641 Locust Walk
Philadelphia, Pennsylvania

Robert H. Hodge, Jr., M.D.
Vice President
Commonwealth Health Alliance, Inc.
1650 State Farm Boulevard
Charlottesville, Virginia

Thomas James III, M.D.
Medical Director
Traveler's Managed Care Systems,
  Inc.
100 West Plume Street
Suite 400
Norfolk, Virginia

Jay B. Krasner, M.D.
Private Practice, General Internal
  Medicine
111 Boston Post Road
Suite 107
Sudbury, Massachusetts

Lila Stein Kroser, M.D.
Clinical Instructor, Community and
  Preventive Medicine
Medical College of Pennsylvania
c/o 2855 Welsh Road
Philadelphia, Pennsylvania

Risa Lavizzo-Mourey, M.D., M.B.A.
Deputy Administrator
Agency for Health Care Policy and
  Research
Executive Office Center
Suite 600

2101 East Jefferson Avenue
Rockville, Maryland

Barry L. Liebowitz, M.D.
President
Doctors Council
21 East 40th Street
New York, New York

Donald C. Meyer, D.D.S. (deceased)
Executive Director
Doctors Council
21 East 40th Street
New York, New York

David B. Nash, M.D., M.B.A.
Director, Office of Health Policy and
   Clinical Outcomes
Thomas Jefferson University
621 Curtis Building
1015 Walnut Street
Philadelphia, Pennsylvania

Alan S. Rosenthal, M.D., Ph.D.
Vice President, Research and Devel-
   opment
Boehringer Ingelheim
900 Ridgebury Road
Ridgefield, Connecticut

Seth Allen Rudnick, M.D.
President and Chief Executive Officer
CytoTherapeutics, Inc.
Two Richmond Square
Providence, Rhode Island

Robert B. Taylor, M.D.
Professor and Chairman
Department of Family Medicine
School of Medicine
The Oregon Health Sciences Uni-
   versity
3181 Southwest Sam Jackson Park
   Road
Portland, Oregon

ACKNOWLEDGMENT TO THE SECOND EDITION

As my mentor, Samuel P. Martin II, M.D., was fond of telling the following anecdote: "How do you make silk purses out of a sow's ear?" "Start with silk sows!" In editing this book, I have had the privilege of assembling 13 sows who are experts in their fields. They have each chosen a path in medicine that grants them license, literary and otherwise, to comment authoritatively about the future. I recruited them individually, with a combination of cajoling and arm-twisting, to participate in this project and to revise their chapters for this second edition.

Other persons as well, long before this "gang of 13," had an important role in the genesis of this book. I thank Dr. Leighton Cluff (a past president), and Annie Lea Schuster of the Robert Wood Johnson Foundation for generously supporting the best two years of my professional development as a Clinical Scholar at the University of Pennsylvania School of Medicine.

At Penn, Dr. Sam Martin, now the program's emeritus director, continued in his two decade-long role as my confidant, mentor and, hopefully, friend. He only opened the doors of opportunity—it was my job to stumble across the threshold. Dr. Sankey Williams, Section Chief of General Medicine, supervised my first attempts at publishable original research with patience and a quiet sense of humor. I am grateful to them and to Dr. John Eisenberg, now Chairman of Medicine at Georgetown, for his early support.

Dr. Edward J. Huth, for more than 25 years serving as editor of *Annals of Internal Medicine,* saw fit to hire me as his deputy from 1985 to 1989. His expressed confidence in my abilities, his attention to editorial detail and his sheer intellectual prowess made my work at the *Annals* stimulating and fun.

Art Fulton and George Longshore, of Fulton, Longshore and Associates, helped focus my thinking about private-sector issues, and they often challenged my ivory-tower outlook. Their early support enabled me to read widely in health policy, economics and health-services research.

George Schall, Vice-President and General Manager of Igaku-

Shoin, shepherded me through the publishing field, with all its ravines and crevices. He is an inspiring and enthusiastic editor, a fine teacher and a good friend.

I owe a special debt of gratitude to the best two "bosses" any physician maverick could hope for—Joseph S. Gonnella, M.D., Dean of Jefferson Medical College, and Thomas J. Lewis, Chief Executive Officer of Thomas Jefferson University Hospital. They hired me nearly three years ago to help build a unique office at Thomas Jefferson University composed of physicians, pharmacists, researchers and analysts dedicated to improving the quality of care while trying to contain runaway costs. Our work continues.

Elizabeth Brown, my administrative assistant and expert organizer, newsletter designer, travel agent and helper, continues in her role as all of the above. Susan Howell, social worker cum health-policy analyst, really kept every contributor in line and every piece of paper on track. Don't cross her.

Finally, my physician wife, Dr. Esther Jean Nash, has been supportive of the book's central concept, and she tolerated many lonely evenings with good graces. My young children, Leah, Rachel and Jacob, don't really understand what Daddy does in his office at home, but I know they will appreciate it all one day soon.

Like all honest authors, I take full responsibility for any errors of commission or omission throughout the text.

David B. Nash, M.D., M.B.A.
Philadelphia

OVERVIEW

WHITE COAT OR BLUE COLLAR?

David B. Nash

Why do nearly 40 percent of young physicians claim that on reflection, they would not have chosen a career in medicine?[1] I believe this disconcerting finding speaks to some deeper problems in the continuum of medical education from medical school through residency and practice. Although these problems are gaining increased attention in the medical literature, my view is that little real reform of medical education has occurred. To prepare better for the alternatives available in the future, we need to understand our current challenges.

The structure of modern medical education, established 80 years ago and manifested in a science-based research mission, has "crowded out its social responsibility to train physicians for society's most basic health care delivery needs."[2] The locus of curriculum control in most schools is very diffuse and may explain, in part, the paradox of why there appears to be broad consensus on the need for change and, at the same time, why so little change has occurred.[3] Indeed, a clear majority of medical school deans feel a need for fundamental change, but they disagree as to its direction and scope.

The president of Johns Hopkins University noted that perhaps medical educators need to realize they have more influence on the health-care system than they care to admit, "through what we teach, through the role models and mentors that we provide, and through the kind of clinical sites in which we educate our students."[4] The question remains: Are we

1

teaching our future leaders what they need to know and does this explain their current malaise?

I review some answers to this question and then discuss several potential reforms to lay the foundation for the predictions appearing at the end of this chapter and throughout the book.

Overall, medical students and residents believe that the primary objections of training—developing skills through an understanding of bedside data collection, the natural history of disease, the use of diagnostic tools and the effect of therapy as these tools apply to specific patients—are readily met. However, they yearn for much more.

For example, at Jefferson Medical College, in Philadelphia, Pennsylvania, the nation's largest private medical school, graduating senior students rate their global satisfaction of their preparation for a career in medicine as an 8.04 (10 = extremely well prepared).[5] On closer inspection of the returns, one notices, however, that more than half were dissatisfied with their preparation in understanding the economics of health care, and more than two thirds were dissatisfied with their grasp of practice management issues.

The attitudes of chief residents closely mirrors those of graduating students. In a widely reported study conducted by the Internal Medicine Center to Advance Research and Education (a foundation established by the American Society of Internal Medicine), 49 percent of chief residents rated training in providing cost-effective care as a top priority, whereas only 15 percent of the residency programs provided such instruction.[6] Furthermore, 74 percent of the chief residents rated patient-physician communication as a top priority, and a paltry 9 percent of training programs offered any formal instruction in this vital area.

In addition, some observers[7] have noted "to date, higher [medical] education does not offer adequate programs to prepare health care professionals to assume their emerging roles and fulfill requirements to regulate their practice through new mechanisms of quality assurance, utilization review, infection control, risk management and professional credentialing." In another study, Jacobs and Mott[8] determined that "the curriculum areas [in medical schools] rated as needing much greater or somewhat greater emphasis by 90% or more of the respondents included utilization review and/or quality assurance."

Finally, and perhaps most disquieting, is recent evidence[9] that although house officers make mistakes in training, with adverse outcomes for patients, only 54 percent discussed the mistake with their attending physician. In my view, this lack of communication just serves to perpetuate the ills in the system and breaks a "feedback loop" that would improve teaching, improve the quality of patient care and ultimately benefit everyone. This is educational malpractice.[10] Thus, although trainees at all levels recognize that they need broader vision and training to cope with future changes, what reforms are being advocated to address these needs?

The American College of Physicians (ACP), headquartered in Philadelphia, Pennsylvania, has been among the leaders in organized medicine working toward residency curriculum reform. In the report of an important conference, co-sponsored by the Association of Professors of Medicine and the Association of American Medical Colleges (June 15, 1992; special supplement to *Annals of Internal Medicine*)[11], a variety of educators laid out their plans for reform. Participants called for more experimental learning, a greater emphasis on primary care, improved integration with undergraduate medical education and more attention to training in procedural skills. At this conference, little was said that addressed the aforementioned nonclinical concerns such as health economics.

Others have directly tackled these nonclinical curriculum needs. Greenlick[12] advocates educating physicians for "population-based clinical practice," with a renewed emphasis on epidemiology and the social and preventive functions of medicine. Boyer and colleagues,[13] at Tufts Medical School, have just such a program in place.

Swartz and colleagues[14] believe we ought to educate a new group of physician-scholars for leadership roles in the health care system. They tackle nonclinical curriculum head-on by noting that "we can also point out the potential for improving the efficiency of existing and proposed federally supported health care programs by increasing the availability of physician scholars educated in non-traditional areas; for example, physician scholars who could measure and improve quality of care in Medicaid and Medicare."

Finally, as we move away from the notion of the hospital as the doctor's workshop, we must educate the future generation of physicians to understand better their new role. Borondess,[15] Stoeckle and Reiser[16] and others have admirably called for physicians to lead the effortsto resolve the access to care dilemma, to design new delivery systems and to make consideration of public policy in health an academic endeavor of importance.

In summary, although university presidents, medical school deans and other leaders call for changes in the medical education continuum, the ultimate responsibility for change rests with you, the reader. You must prepare yourself to wisely choose among many future practice alternatives. To help you make these choices, read on.

THE ECONOMIC ENVIRONMENT

As early as 1979 and 1983, the American Medical Association (AMA) completed two surveys of resident physicians[17] that contained questions on many areas, including residents' personal characteristics, income, fringe benefits, hours and kinds of activities performed, extent of moonlighting and perceived problems with the residency program. The response rates were an impressive 35 percent of all residents in all fields in 1979 and 45 percent in 1983.

Although residents' salaries had increased an average of 7.5 percent/year since 1978, the annual growth in the consumer price index during the same period was approximately 9.4 percent. Thus, when adjusted for inflation, median annual salaries actually decreased for all categories of residents from 1978 to 1983. In other words, the standard of living for most residents had not kept pace with inflation, and their buying power had been eroded. This disturbing trend has continued into the 1990s. Although median physician income increased 4 percent in 1990, less than inflation (5.4 percent), this marked the second consecutive year that earnings did not keep pace with inflation. Over the longer 1981 to 1990 period, median earnings for doctors in practice (in all settings, excluding residency) grew at a rate of only 2.1 percent when adjusted for overall price level changes.[18]

In addition to the salary stagnation, educational debt during the same period skyrocketed. A 1984 AMA report[19] showed that the average indebtedness of medical residents was $18,200 in 1983, compared with "only" $13,300 in 1979. Under the former Reagan administration policies, special low-cost, long-term loans for health-care professionals were no longer available, further exacerbating the situation. The Association of American Medical Colleges (AAMC) maintains that the average debt burden of 1985 graduates from medical school was $30,256, an increase of approximately 96 percent over 1980 levels.[20] By 1990, according to the AAMC,[21] indebted graduates had a mean debt of $46,224, compared with $42,374 for 1989 graduates. By 1990, 78.8 percent of *all* graduates had some level of educational debt. The impact of indebtedness on specialty choice is a controversial topic with equally compelling evidence on both sides of the issue.

One thing is clear: Cohen and colleagues[1] revealed some warning signs for particular segments of the physician population when they observe "With incomes generally below the median income for all young physicians, many more primary care physicians (especially black physicians) may be in danger of encountering economic stress in the near future." Potential reform of physician payment systems, such as the recently adopted Medicare method, would likely benefit these physicians. However, implementation of this system is likely to take some time, and it is unclear whether higher Medicare payments to physicians will be sufficient to offset the demands of an increasing debt burden for young physicians.

Perhaps most alarming is the finding that the youngest cohorts of young physicians (i.e., the most recent graduates) have higher proportions of individuals with real debt in excess of $25,000 than older cohorts.

This finding suggests that unless potential remedies are devised (e.g., enhanced financial aid packages, reduced medical school expenses), the increasing concentration of real educational debt may prove to be a barrier to entry into the profession."[1]

Although their economic environment was harsh, residents did not voice major concerns about their salaries when they were asked to evaluate their training programs. As a testament to their true character, most residents listed problems that were primarily educational in nature when evaluating their programs. Residents wanted a greater degree of participation in the planning process for their training, as well as more direct faculty instruction time.

In general, they felt that their "service" component, the care they delivered to the indigent, entitled them to a certain minimal amount of teaching time from private attending physicians and faculty. It was clear from both surveys that "despite economic problems," the residents seemed willing to accept these temporary hardships to achieve their long-sought educational goals.

Astute observers of medical education contend that free-market forces cannot be relied on to distribute residents efficiently to the appropriate subspecialties. The distribution of residency positions is insensitive to the relative demand for practitioners in various fields within medicine.[22]

After completing residency, a young physician is currently faced with another economic crisis of greater proportion, the physician surplus. It is the author's contention that this surplus has fundamentally altered each physician's relationship to the market for their services. How does it impact on career choice and practice patterns, and what are its future consequences?

THE PHYSICIAN SURPLUS REVISITED

Throughout this book there are several recurrent themes appearing like a dominant color or design within a thickly woven fabric. One theme concerns the impending physician surplus as it affects educational goals (Chapter 3), choice of a specialty (Chapters 5–10) and, possibly, the need to unionize (Chapter 1). Paul Lairson, the physician liaison at the giant Kaiser-Permanente Health Maintenance Organization (HMO) in California, told the *Wall Street Journal* in a front-page story that recruiting physicians had become "markedly easier" in the past five years.[23] It appears as though there is certainly a buyer's market, and a bullish one at that, for the purchasers of physicians' services. How did physicians get into this predicament? Does everyone agree on the scope and intensity of the problem? What about more recent evidence, because of the manpower demands of acquired immunodeficiency syndrome (AIDS) and the like, that the earlier reports might be wrong?

Perhaps the current controversy about the supply of physicians is the result of social planning gone amuck. In 1968, the Health Manpower Act authorized federal support to construct new medical schools and to increase the number of primary-care physicians. There was a widespread perception that the nation was faced with a shortage of medical manpower and that under the Great Society's programs, access to health care would be markedly improved. Also, private-sector studies, such as those reported by the Carnegie Commission in 1970 and by the Macy Foundation in 1976, all concurred with the increase in the size of the physician pool. Unfortunately, as with many of the programs in our pluralistic society, there was no long-range plan. What target population of physicians were we aiming for? Would the mixture of specialists and primary-care providers be appropriate by the mid 1980s? These questions were never adequately addressed.

Under former President Carter, Joseph A. Califano, the then secretary of Health and Human Services (HHS), authorized the formation of a blue-ribbon research panel to advise HHS on the future need for physicians' services. In September 1980, the committee, known then as the Graduate Medical Education National Advisory Committee (GMENAC), released its first seven-volume report. The recommendations to Secretary Califano had the effect of several bombshells dropping on the medical-education hierarchy. The enthusiastic government-sponsored growth in the supply of physicians during the early 1970s had become the dire predictions of the 1990s.

The GMENAC forecasted that by 1990, there would be 536,000 physicians trained to practice, a staggering 70,000 more than the perceived requirement. By 2000, approximately 643,000 physicians would be in practice, representing 145,000 more than the forecasted requirement.[24-26] There would be especially crowded conditions in many surgical subspecialties, radiology and such medical fields as pulmonary medicine and cardiology. Alvin Tarlov, the former chairman of the GMENAC and now a professor at the Tufts New England Medical Center, reviewed and updated his committee's findings. Most of the original assertions were reaffirmed.[27]

In addition, Tarlov characterized a new dimension of the GMENAC analysis, the so called third compartment. When the report by the GMENAC was first released, there were really only two "compartments" for practicing medicine: the fee-for-service compartment, which comprised approximately 95 percent of all practicing physicians in 1980, and the federal compartment, which was composed of approximately 19,000 government-employed physicians, such as those in the Veterans Administration system. Tarlov's third compartment includes all physicians who provide prepaid care on a capitated basis to patients enrolled in HMOs (see also Chapter 8). If current growth rates continue, this newly formed third compartment will be dominant by the turn of the century.

The third compartment "can be considered a circumscribed market employing a relatively fixed number of physicians that varies only according to enrollment growth. Remaining physicians, those not practicing in prepaid systems, must be absorbed into the first compartment which can take on physicians more readily than either the second or third compartments.[27]

Tarlov reworked the GMENAC model using certain assumptions about this third compartment. He found that by 2000, there will be only 120 physicians for each 100,000/population in the third compartment. This ratio is in contrast to the 323 physicians (per 100,000/population) in the federal and nonfederal compartments. There will be three times as many physicians per patient in the first two compartments, consequently worsening the competition in the fee-for-service sector. In fact, Steinwachs and associates[28] studied the staffing patterns at only three HMOs and concluded that because of the proliferation of HMOs, 20 percent fewer primary-care physicians will be needed for children and 50 percent fewer for adults than had been projected in the original GMENAC report.

More recently, authors of new studies[29] concluded that the threat of a future surplus was greatly exaggerated. The authors recalculated all of the GMENAC predictions, factoring in such disparate concepts as the intensified level of care necessary for patients with AIDS and the increasing numbers of women in medicine (who generally work fewer hours than their male counterparts), and concluded that we may face a slight shortage of doctors by the year 2000. I think it is fair to say that *no* methodology exists in 1993 to accurately predict a surplus or a shortage for the next 10 years.

Some facts remain clear, however. New technologies, the aging of the population, the growth in HMOs and the ascendancy of the flower children to adulthood (don't trust anyone over 40!) will conspire to vary the need for physician services in the coming decade.

Also, our lopsided reliance on the skills of the subspecialist is surely contributing to the "induced demand" for physician services. In virtually all developed nations, primary-care physicians predominate. Yet, in Australia, 73 percent of physicians are primary-care providers, in Canada 52 percent, in Germany 45 percent, in Great Britain 70 percent and in the United States 33 percent and decreasing.[30] National medical spokespersons like C. Everett Koop, M.D., have called for new financial incentives for medical students interested in primary-care careers to partially redress these inequities. It is likely that the federal government will stimulate the system, by manipulating funds to medical schools and hospitals, toward production of more generalists.[31] Interested readers should see Chapter 10.

If we accept the possibility of surplus, or at least a maldistribution, what then are the direct consequences for the individual clinician? Some authors contend that the net result of the surplus will be "a steady decline in the demand for the time of individual physicians."[27] In other words, there will be so many more physicians that each one will have more unoccupied professional time. Perhaps with this increase in available professional time, physicians will spend more of it with their patients. Surely, many people would prefer to have more time to ask their doctors relevant health questions.

Perhaps physicians will devote more time to continuing medical education (see Chapter 12) in an attempt to personally contain the explosion in medical information. Maybe faculty members and attending physicians will have more time to teach. Maybe physicians will take some unoccupied time to help care for the indigent and patients without health insurance. Maybe they will take time to smell flowers and be with their families, too. Unfortunately, the author is much less sanguine about the future.

The physician surplus has fueled the corporatization of health care, and it is clearly the rate-limiting reaction to the proliferation of HMOs. More younger physicians will join large group practices with fixed patient schedules, regulated hours and good benefits, but lower salaries. Physicians will rapidly move into Tarlov's third compartment because that is where the jobs will be, not because the efficient market is allocating resources appropriately.

Nearly 40 percent of physicians under age 36 are currently working as employees in large medical bureaucracies,[23] surrendering some of their autonomy for a guaranteed livelihood.

More pernicious aspects of these social trends, according to Light,[32] include increased competition between hospitals and physicians in the ambulatory-care marketplace. Hospitals will seek to align themselves with a cadre of physicians to control markets and to increase hospital bargaining power. Hospitals and HMOs will be in a position to choose among many physicians with the aid of "market-relevant criteria." They will choose physician employees who appreciate the changes in health-care delivery systems, who can practice cost-effectiveness and who are comfortable with stringent peer-review systems.

Physicians of the future will be able to practice because they hold a "job," according to the respected historian Rosemary Stevens.[33] This job will be sought by means of advertisements, a recruitment firm or formal and informal networks. Stevens believes that physicians of the future will be assessed "not only on technical and behavioral skills but on conformance to the prevailing corporate style, corporate goals and corporate ethos. Medical students and residents will need to be sophisticated readers of the job market and be aware of divergent corporate expectations."

This situation might widen the generation gap between established physicians and new competitors. Physicians will be forced to seek out new niches, such as adolescent medicine and geriatrics (see Chapter 5). Physicians' "turf" will be divided into ever-smaller lots. Consultation and referral patterns among physicians will certainly be disrupted by the surplus as "collegial interaction is . . . replaced . . . by systematized formats and limited choice protocols. Some of these factors have the potential of interfering with patient welfare and pose situations that may push practicing physicians into ethical and financial conflicts of interest."[34]

By means of traditional economic analysis, one could argue that the possibility of an increasing supply of physicians will (1) force down costs as physicians compete for providing services, and (2) that the market will distribute newly trained physicians into areas of high patient demand and low physician supply. Unfortunately, many leading economists have shown repeatedly that these traditional arguments do not apply.[35] Enlarging the physician supply produces increased utilization of services without a commensurate reduction in costs.[36] Tarlov's notion of "unencumbered time" (meaning more physician free time) by 2000 may completely backfire as underutilized physicians create business by scheduling more office visits, performing more procedures per visit and ordering more laboratory tests and surgical procedures.

Future-thinking young physicians should study the evidence and all of the aforementioned predictions carefully before considering a specific subspecialty. They should pay close attention to the chapters in this book on such burgeoning fields as geriatrics, occupational medicine, primary care and medical management.

THE REAL WORLD

The preceding text highlighted some important consequences of a possible physician surplus on a societal scale. What about individual young physicians? What can they do to prepare for a fruitful medical career without necessarily mortgaging the future? How can clinicians approach the job market and be prepared to make important career decisions?

Most residents, in almost all fields of medicine, approach the "job search" in a haphazard fashion. Residents have followed a lock-step educational system (see Chapter 3) from college through medical school. Time was measured in several-year increments until the next application process arrived. By the end of residency, most young physicians probably have not thought about assembling an appropriate resume! Unfortunately, most university-based training programs provide substantial help to the fellowship-bound but little assistance to those interested in entering practice.

It is important to develop a personal plan for getting that first job. Consider which specific aspects of medicine are personally enjoyable and which environment is comfortable. Is a large group practice too threatening? Is peer review annoying? Is locale crucial?

Senior residents in almost all fields tend to make decisions based on little information. They are accustomed to the highly structured world of the medical-school curriculum, the residency match and the on-call schedule. Some residents even accept their first job offer without examining all the possible options.

It is therefore important that young clinicians learn how to market their skills. Many old physicians are taken aback by these terms, but students in other professional schools are expert in this area. At the Wharton business school in Philadelphia, Pennsylvania, for example, the names of eager Master of Business Administration graduates are programmed into a large job-searching computer that matches potential employers with the skills and attributes of each graduate. There is a formal interview system that incorporates published rules and penalties for graduates who are noncompliant. Representatives of many employers visit the campus and are part of this formalized system. Although the author does not necessarily advocate exporting the Wharton model to residencies, he does believe that young physicians can learn to improve their resumes and personal presentations to allow them to function better in an increasingly competitive world. It will not be long before large health-care corporations, such as Hospital Corporation of America and Kaiser, come to the readers' hospital to recruit physicians in much the same way that IBM comes to Wharton. The key to success is to be prepared early for this eventuality.

Young physicians should practice interviewing with a videotape to review their performance and to have it critiqued by colleagues. They should get residency program directors to support seminars with local consulting and management firms. One hospital conference per month should be dedicated to these types of "real-world" issues in place of yet another clinicopathologic conference (see Chapter 3). Program directors should be reminded that the quality of offers made to graduating senior residents is in large part a reflection of their training programs.

The California House Office Medical Society (CHOMS), for example, sponsors an annual conference titled "How to Find a Job After Residency." Members of the society recently assembled practice consultants, attorneys and state medical authorities in an all-day program to advise young physicians about employment opportunities. Their conference objectives[37] included teaching residents "standardized techniques for evaluating available opportunities." Many local employers that specialize in physician-practice contracts gladly participate in such programs as a way to expand their business. Such an effort could be called a "win-win" negotiating position because both parties gain something in the exchange of information. Similar programs have been held at Jefferson Medical College in Philadelphia, to an enthusiastic response from interns and residents.

Young physicians need to be well informed about changes within the health-care delivery system, especially if they expect to participate fully in it. The author would urge all physicians to become more familiar with the jargon of "alternative" delivery systems, including HMOs, independent-practice associations (IPAs) and preferred-provider organizations (PPOs). This book provides a solid framework that readers can use to make sense of their observations and aspirations.

For physicians who are definitely fellowship-bound after residency, there are important general guidelines to follow. Lind[38] analyzed the fellowship application process and concluded that "all too often, applicants seem to move on to fellowship training simply because it is there. They have played the game so well for so long that they do not realize that there may in fact be an end of the long stream of certificates and so [they] instinctively sign up for the next available diploma." He contends that the most important step in the process is a critical self-appraisal. This contention may sound hackneyed to some readers, but it is not a trivial task to honestly evaluate one's goals, objectives and motivations. Lind calls for better career counseling, elective time spent in the proposed area of specialization and short-term seminar series, or "reality rounds," with current practitioners to aid potential fellows in making the transition to subspecialty practice.

Young physicians should explore programs offered by the private sector, such as the KRON Scholars Program,[39] which enables senior residents to enhance their career development through a one year, paid fellowship in "real world" medicine. KRON is a well-known, national locum tenens firm that places physicians in temporary practice positions throughout the country. Alan Kronhaus, M.D., the physician-entrepreneur president of KRON, has written an engaging book,[40] entitled *Choosing Your Practice,* that focuses on how to evaluate the job market, negotiate a contract and better understand the intricacies of professional liability insurance.

Somehow, "job searching" has become a kind of sullied topic in the medical lexicon. It cannot be sanitized with medical jargon or with a word only physicians can pronounce. Within five years, only physicians with market-relevant knowledge will be successful at obtaining any job. Physicians should not turn up their collective noses at colleagues in other professional schools. After all, one of them may be the reader's future boss in some large HMO or health-care conglomerate.

Although individual efforts to improve competitive standing are necessary, they are not sufficient to solve these real-world problems. There are efforts by organized medicine and other groups to improve the job-searching and market awareness of residents in many fields. Some of the

most important programs are highlighted herein. A little-known organization outside internal medicine circles is the Association of Program Directors in Internal Medicine (APDIM). The APDIM was fully incorporated
in 1977 and is a member of the Federated Council for Internal Medicine
(FCIM), which also includes the American Board of Internal Medicine
(ABIM), the American College of Physicians (ACP) and the Association
of Professors of Medicine (APM). Of the 440 accredited training programs
in internal medicine in the United States, 412 are APDIM constituents.
The ADPIM's official goals include sharing information about training,
financial support and relationships with certifying bodies and defining
criteria for affiliation of medical schools with various types of hospitals.
More importantly, however, the APDIM publishes an official journal,
Careers in Internal Medicine. According to James Bernene of the Good
Samaritan Medical Center in Phoenix,[41] "Among the new features being
developed for coming issues of *Careers* is a guidance column on career
opportunities in the field, which is especially important in view of the
ever shrinking job market for graduating medical residents. We may also
include a classified listing of job opportunities throughout the country."

A quick perusal through several issues of *Careers* reinforces the
author's impression that such a listing would be extremely useful for any
thoughtfully planned job search. Articles in this journal discuss graduate
medical education, cost containment, residency stress management and
other relevant topics. In addition to *Careers,* the APDIM sponsors a
national meeting of chief residents in medicine. These yearly meetings
are an excellent forum to develop innovative programs for teaching and
guiding residents through the employment and fellowship maze.

The ACP, headquartered in Philadelphia, Pennsylvania, has received grant support to develop an in-house program on "Practice Management for Medical Residents." It is gratifying to note how organized
medicine at the national level is responding to the unique needs of its
youngest constituents.[42]

Often, local, state and county medical societies sponsor some form
of a job matching program. For example, the Pennsylvania Medical Society (PMS) has a physician placement service. Resident physicians register with the program for a discounted fee and then periodically receive
a private listing of employment opportunities in many fields. The PMS
circulates an applicant's resume to designated advertisers seeking new
associates. The PMS also has in-house publications on marketplace analysis, conducts practice-management seminars and provides a practice-
opportunity assessment document that is specific for a given community.
In researching this book, the author used the PMS placement service
and, unfortunately, found that many "private listings" were unappealing
because of locale, salary, specialty or other reasons. However, the author's opinion should serve as a damper on expectations rather than as
a blanket condemnation.

Although advertisements in medical journals for positions are widespread and widely read (sometimes to the exclusion of journal articles!), the author believes that such advertising is a low-yield procedure. Unfortunately, many advertised positions have already been tacitly promised to certain persons. Programs in academic centers often advertise simply to satisfy legal statutes regarding antidiscriminatory hiring policies.

In retrospect, perhaps the best time to educate young physicians about the medical marketplace is before they finish training—before they have made important career decisions. The School of Medicine of the University of Pennsylvania, for example, has sponsored a yearly careers and life-styles colloquium for medical students. A recent two-day colloquium[43] covered such topics as coping with residency stress, living with debt, losing out to inflation, living in a two-career household and interviewing for residency. The colloquium sent a clear message to the student body: The medical school administration recognizes the exigencies of the marketplace and is willing to set aside precious curriculum time to help the students. Jefferson Medical College sponsors an annual Alumni Day where recent graduates return to discuss their own practice arrangements, life-styles and personal challenges.

Workshops on specialty choice, women in medicine, the Match and other relevant topics are important forums, as important as the basic-science lectures that they supplant for one day.

As if to mirror some of these real-world deficiencies in the training and job-search process, the Pennsylvania Society of Internal Medicine (a component arm of the American Society of Internal Medicine [ASIM]) published results of a survey of their young members.[44] Only 5 percent of the associate members surveyed reported that residency programs provided enough information concerning diagnosis-related groups and prospective payment. Only 15 percent believed that they adequately understood the operation and ramifications of diagnosis-related groups. Eighty-five percent of the associates expressed an intense interest in learning more about joining an HMO or a PPO; all the respondents needed help with financial planning. The author's guess is that a survey of most residencies would yield strikingly similar results.

This book provides answers to some of these questions; however, one volume cannot possibly cover the entire spectrum of medical practices and opportunities. One might be well advised to start with asking the right questions of a professional "search" firm. Such companies, although often unjustifiably maligned, can provide a useful service. For example, Fulton, Longshore and Associates in Plymouth Meeting, Pennsylvania, published a helpful three-part series titled "Planning Your Medical Career."[45] Sections on choosing a career path, life planning and the "end game"—an evaluation of job offers—provide details about writing resumes and negotiating salaries. Surely these important skills are ignored by the traditional medical school curriculum. However, as the author hopes to have convinced readers by now, these skills can no longer be ignored in light of current competitive market forces.

There are other full-length textbooks that provide more "how-to" information for young physicians. Some of the best ones are briefly reviewed.

Anita Taylor's book, *How to Choose a Medical Specialty,* now in its second edition,[46] is geared primarily to senior medical students. Many specialties are described in detail, and current practitioners provide helpful insights into the demands and rewards of their work. An entire section is devoted to choosing a residency, and it includes information for physician couples and those who fail to match. The decision-making process is analyzed, and wise counsel is offered with regard to honest self-evaluation and career planning.

Stephen Lock, the highly respected former editor of the *British Medical Journal,* has compiled an interesting book appropriately called, *How to Do It*[47] from articles in the journal. More than 50 topics are included: how to run a medical meeting, give a press conference and be a dictator (using a dictating machine skillfully!). Although not directly relevant to the career search, these topics certainly are important real-world skills that one can always improve. The book is thoroughly entertaining and could help cement the readers' first posttraining position in almost any field.

A more ambitious and highly focused work is the *Handbook for the Academic Physician*[48] by William McGaghie and John Frey, both at the University of North Carolina School of Medicine in Chapel Hill. This book deals with the science and literature relating to academic administration, medical education and the process of conducting research. The book provides detailed guidelines on improving professional communication, improving the quality of teaching and advancing up the academic ladder. It grew out of course work developed expressly for family physicians who were participating in a faculty fellowship. The generic chapters on professional development have the broadest applicability for young physicians recently out of training.

Two related books by John Aluise, also at Chapel Hill, are particularly useful guides to the future. The *Physician as Manager*[49] is a primer on basic management philosophy for physicians. We finish our residencies well prepared to manage medical problems, but poorly prepared to function in the many other roles required. This book fills that void. Also, *The Art of Leadership and the Science of Management*[50] explores the role of stress that sometimes accompanies a physician's wearing of several hats. Tips on conflict management, performance appraisal of employees and time management are helpful.

The University of Utah School of Medicine, Salt Lake City, seems to be a hotbed of activity in this area. Neal Whitman and colleagues authored two manuals that deserve special mention. *The Chief Resident* as Manager[51] and *Executive Skills for Medical Faculty*[52] are easy-to-read guides to the everyday challenges faced by medical leaders. Developing a career plan, giving feedback and resolving conflicts are among the highlighted areas.

Probably the strongest book in the career-guidance genre for physicians (next to the one you are reading of course), is Patricia Hoffmeir's and Jean Bohner's book, *From Residency to Reality*.[53] Written from the perspective of a professional recruiter, this book highlights the nuts and bolts of the job search with chapters such as "Marketing Yourself" and "Surviving the Interview" to "Getting the Offer and Negotiating the Contract." This is a no-nonsense guide for skeptical, first-time job-hunting, young physicians.

Finally, a soon-to-be-released monograph from the Association of American Medical Colleges (AAMC) in Washington, D.C., entitled *A Guide to Success in the Premedical Years for Minority Students*,[54] may prove very useful for a certain segment of readers. We have to recognize the special needs of minorities in medicine at the earliest possible stage in their training.

Although not really part of the career-guidance genre, Edward Huth's book *How to Write and Publish Papers in the Medical Sciences*[55] is useful in developing a clear and concise written argument. Huth, the retired editor of *Annals of Internal Medicine,* draws on his experience to sharpen the writing skills of would-be journal contributors. The author's contention is that all physicians need improvement in this area, and this book is singularly helpful.

Another series that may prove useful, especially to young physicians entering directly into practice, are the "how to be successful in practice" books. For example, *Medical Practice Management*,[56] by Horace Cotton, describes office-management skills, hiring ancillary staff and developing a functioning appointment schedule. Again, these issues are rarely covered in the medical school residency curriculum. *The Physician Guide to Professional and Personal Advisers*,[57] by Warren Boroson, adds a new dimension to a young physician's repertoire. This book explains how to judge advice—whether from accountants, attorneys or interior designers—and act on it. Finally, *Competing for Clients*,[58] by Bruce Marcus, is a standout in the crowd of recent books that portray the increased competitiveness in the marketplace. This marketing textbook is really focused on the needs of professionals, and it succeeds. The author does not advocate buying all the aforementioned books; however, if a reader had enough foresight to buy and read this unorthodox book, some of these other titles might provide additional useful information to help cope with real-world issues.

The author discussed a major force that is reshaping the practice of medicine, the physician surplus. The reader has traveled the uneven road to obtaining that first posttraining job. Now, what of the future? What are the professional soothsayers and other pundits saying about the shape and substance of medicine in 1998 and beyond?

FUTURE TRENDS IN MEDICINE

Alvin Toffler introduced the term "future shock" into our lexicon when he described events deemed likely to take place in the future. John Naisbitt amplified this theory in Megatrends (and Megatrends 2000) of the important social forces that are acting to shape our future. Predicting trends is a risky, yet growing, business. Consulting companies and insurance firms spend large sums to predict the future investment climate for clients. Even Henry Kissinger operates a company whose objectives include a hefty dose of forecasting the political fortunes of unstable regimes around the world. Forecasting has become a big business with many facets. At some risk, the author will add to the fray by focusing on the future of medicine based on informed speculation, expert opinions, futurist writings and guesswork. We may expect to see:

- Emphasis on the practice of medicine by protocol
- A shift in professional relationships
- Changes in the doctor-patient relationship
- Increased technologic vulnerability of specialties
- Continued growth of organized group practices
- Changes in the way society funds graduate medical education
- Continued shift of political power from providers to payers of health care

Practice by Protocol

Young physicians will be asked—compelled—to practice according to protocols. They will have to meet work-load standards and observe predefined criteria for use of resources.[59] The hiring of new physicians will be conducted according to market-relevant criteria. Capitation programs will persist in some altered form. Diagnosis-related groups will be continuously changed, and schemes that are more clinically relevant will be introduced. Some form of severity-of-illness adjustment factor will be applied nationwide to every diagnosis.

Coupling these capitation schemes, severity adjustments and sophisticated management-information systems will create a powerful new administrative tool. Hospital and practice directors will increasingly be able to identify "atypical practitioners," physicians who use too many resources, order too many tests and keep their patients in the hospital too long. How will this information be used, and who will have access to it? Will clinical privileges be tied to some measure of economic efficiency?

Protocols will create a leveling effect in two important spheres.

First, third-party payers, leaning on established protocols, will no longer tolerate marked geographic variations in practice patterns. As Caper and associates[60] have convincingly shown, current surgical and hospitalization rates vary tremendously across markets. These rates will plateau at some agreed-upon level. Second, there will be a leveling of practice incomes, especially a flattening of the income peaks associated with procedurally oriented specialties. This leveling will be driven by reform of the Medicare payment process, known as the Resource-based Relative Value Scale.

Utilization-control programs will begin to ask detailed questions about why physicians provided certain services. Prior-approval programs will become more widespread, and physicians will be called on increasingly to judge the decision of their peers. Many physicians will live their professional lives in a kind of fishbowl.

Some physicians will view practice by protocol as a threat to their professional autonomy[61] and disparage them as examples of "cookbook medicine." Others recognize that if guidelines are absent we keep to our own track, safe, yet perpetually ignorant. The nationwide efforts and energies being expended to write guidelines are well documented elsewhere[62] for interested readers.

A Shift in Professional Relationships

Camaraderie among physicians and physician groups will diminish markedly.[63] There will be a shift from collegial to contractual relationships. In managed-care settings, such as HMOs, primary-care physicians, or "gatekeepers," will become increasingly important. Specialists will witness a decrease in their influence in hospitals. Institutional programs will continue to pursue patient referrals as part of a marketing strategy to attract new patients, who then become attached to the institution rather than to a physician. This changing professional interaction will raise major new ethical dilemmas concerning professional sovereignty and potential conflicts of interest. When year-end bonuses are based in part on a residual dollar pool from under utilization of resources, who will chastise the partner who is a heavy "utilizer" of consultants?

The traditional town-versus-gown antagonism will worsen as the competition for a dwindling number of unattached patients increases. Some hospitals have been using Medicare funds as kickbacks to physicians to encourage them to admit certain patients.[64] As community hospitals absorb the increasing number of specialists, often graduates of nearby university fellowship programs, they will not want to surrender difficult cases to their mentors and to senior faculty from academic centers.[65] This situation will create a new set of competitive pressures on medical school faculty, possibly threatening their research commitments. When academic and clinical faculty have been studied,[66] no appreciable differences between the two groups relating to job satisfaction, total stress, anxiety or depression scores could be found. However, academic faculty reported working longer hours and taking less vacation time, and they experienced more conflict between work and their personal lives than clinical faculty. These stresses will continue to exacerbate town and gown relationships.

Development of hospital-physician joint ventures will create bed-fellows out of previously cool relations. Indeed, certain hospitals will survive only if the armed camps represented by the administration and the medical staff can build new communication lines. As the scope and prevalence of these joint ventures becomes more apparent, Congress will clamor to have a role in their ongoing review and regulation. It is important to point out that the proportion of referring physicians involved in direct patient care who participate in joint ventures is much higher than previous estimates suggest.[67]

The pressure on individual practitioners to produce may threaten the idealism that many young physicians bring to medical practice.[68] Another aspect of changing professional relationships revolves around physicians and containment of costs. Some observers have commented that physicians should not ration resources; rather, they should identify and curtail unnecessary health care.[69]

Changes in the Doctor-Patient Relationship

Well-regarded futurists believe that in our emerging information society, the public will become better-informed consumers of care.[70,71] Preventive practices, such as dieting, stopping smoking and exercise, will be widely adopted. Self-care will become increasingly important. Sophisticated home diagnostic kits and the availability of on-line computer expert systems will create a generation of well-informed, critical health-care consumers. The workplace will be recognized as a rich setting for health-promotion activities, and many corporations have already learned about the benefits of a healthier and therefore happier and more productive work force. Patients will demand a voice in medical policy discussions. The public has strong convictions about living wills and right-to-die issues. They will make their mandates known. Jensen[72] believes that further deterioration in doctor-patient rapport may be due to increased consumerism, advances in medical technology and a societal trend toward deprofessionalization. He calls for greater patient involvement in the doctor-patient relationship, which will subsequently lead to greater satisfaction and improved health care.

Prepaid entitlement programs, however, may create a new generation of angry "bureaucratic clients" who bring to HMO physicians demands and expectations that they consider a kind of enforceable, legal contract. One physician group has already outlined its plan to deal with this eventuality:[73] (1) review marketing efforts of the practice to foster realistic expectations, (2) develop a physician-generated, prospective internal policy for dealing with dissatisfied patients, (3) appoint a strong central administrative physician to serve as a "lightning rod" and counselor, and (4) continue physician orientation and education to improve judgment and attitudes.

Yet, unsettling issues remain. Will physicians continue to act as unfettered patient advocates or will the "bottom-line" mentality prevail? Newspapers[74] are filled with stories about pediatric patients being denied access to critical procedures such as bone marrow transplants as the underwriting health plans cry economic foul. Physicians have not hesitated to go public when they feel their abilities to deliver high-quality care have been undermined.

These changes in the doctor-patient relationship will be stressful. Some physicians will turn to professional medical anthropologists, such as John-Henry Pfifferling, at the Center for Professional Well-Being in Durham, North Carolina, for ongoing counseling as well as crisis intervention. Pfifferling visits physician groups and helps get derailed practitioners back on track toward productive, professional lives. Physicians will increasingly rely on these kinds of services as the complex issues in their relationships with patients are slowly sorted out.

Technologic Vulnerability of Specialties

Physicians will continue to witness many advances in medical technology. Such advances will have two dramatic effects on the practice of medicine. "New diagnostic imaging technologies, less invasive therapeutic technologies, new drugs, improved home-care services, and other similar developments will accelerate the flight from the hospital."[75] As a result of this flight, hospitals may become the providers of last resort care, essentially huge intensive care units catering to supersubspecialists and their critically ill patients. Also, this change will mean that most routine procedures will be relegated to outpatient facilities, or surgicenters, as many of them are now called.

The second dramatic impact of accelerating medical technology will be its role in shaping residency and fellowship training. With recent advances in molecular biology, it will not be long before specific anticancer drugs will be able to seek out and destroy malignant cells selectively. Perhaps future oncologists will be experts in the pharmacodynamics of a host of new, clonally derived therapeutic agents.

With the advent of magnetic resonance imaging and new antiplaque medication for atherosclerotic disease, physicians may be able to locate and dissolve occlusions of the coronary arteries.[76] Currently, coronary artery bypass grafting is the most frequently performed surgical procedure in the United States, with a societal cost in the billions. What will happen if this procedure is obviated by technologic advances? The implications for training programs are worrisome (see Chapter 13). Physicians must collectively begin to give serious consideration to limiting the number of specialty positions available. Physicians must act to enforce strict certification of all fellowship programs and, in so doing, close down the weaker ones. When physicians contemplate career choices, they must consider the technologic vulnerability of their sought-after skills. As the pace of change accelerates, specialists could be forced to retrain or, more ominously, surrender their already obsolete technical prowess to other specialists. Blind reliance on one technical skill, such as cardiac catheterization, could severely limit future options should technologic change continue so rapidly.

Finally, what of our ethical responsibilities to patients and the inherent learning curve attached to mastering a new technology? New York State is scrutinizing the outcomes from laparoscopic gallbladder surgery as hundreds of reports of botched cases were reported in Albany and the State Health Department. It certainly appears as though strong economic pressures compelled some surgeons to quickly adopt new techniques with less-than-thorough training.[77]

Growth of Organized Group Practices

"Because the development of new practices will be expensive, the competition for patients intense, the chances if failure high, and the debts from medical training heavy, . . . physicians may opt to join institutions with quite different objectives, sacrificing their independence for security and predictable hours, and for social goals more compatible with their own. These younger physicians may become the salaried employees of HMOs, groups, public hospitals, or clinics that are working to make more restrained and discriminating use of technology, personnel and social support systems."[75] The recent growth of HMOs is a case in point, and this topic is thoroughly discussed by James in Chapter 8.

In early survey work done by the AMA[78] titled "Medical Groups in the United States," the number of group practices (defined as three or more physicians) grew 143 percent between 1969 and 1984. Other important findings of this survey were:

- Approximately one fourth to one third of all nonfederal physicians now practice in groups.
- Seventy percent of all groups are single-specialty groups (up from 49.7 percent in 1969).
- The average size of groups increased to 9.1 positions (due mainly to the growth in size of multispecialty groups).
- The proportion of multispecialty groups dropped from 38 percent of all groups in 1969 to 18.3 percent in 1984, but the average number of positions in multispecialty groups grew, from 10.1 in 1969 to 26.6 in 1984.

By 1988, 30 percent of all physicians practiced in group settings.[79] Expert panels of physicians and health-care administrators are predicting that the percentage of physicians in medical group practices will increase by one third between 1990 and 1996.[80] Finally, William M. Mercer, Inc., New York-based employee benefits consultants,[81] noted that salaries for physicians working in group practices and HMOs are now often comparable to net earnings of physicians in private practice. Certainly, physicians trade some autonomy for security and must be willing to practice in a fishbowl to be comfortable in a group. The author's contention is that most physicians will not have much of a choice in the matter—the "cottage industry" of the solo practitioner will soon be extinct.

Groups are now struggling to develop appropriate productivity measures and incentive plans. This will continue to be a creative area for further work by specially trained physician-managers. To prevent the primary-care group practitioner from "burning out," a whole host of incentives, bonuses, special continuing medical education programs and other practice-enhancing modalities will need to be implemented.

Stephen Schoenbaum, the deputy medical director of the Harvard Community Health Plan (HCHP), a large HMO in Boston, has been developing "work expectations" for his medical staff.[82] Also, staff physicians are periodically reviewed by departmental chiefs, and such reviews cover practice-management skills, cost-effectiveness of practice style, participation in nonclinical activities in the plan, continuing education and participation in teaching or research. HCHP has established a "performance fund," which is generated from achievement of targeted objectives for average panel size, patient satisfaction levels, out-of-office and hospital-utilization costs and quality-of-care indicators. This fund is distributed on the basis of a merit review of physician staff.

Researchers have also been studying some issues surrounding physicians' decisions to join group practices. Freund and Allen[83] found that physicians with relatively low incomes and relatively few patient visits and those who were newly established in the community were more likely to join than were other physicians. Apparently, peer pressure also played a part in the decision-making process to sign up with an HMO, whereas presentations from marketing representatives had little or no effect.

Kralewski and colleagues[84] determined that large group practices, especially multispecialty practices, appear to engage in a highly organized corporate style of medical practice. In fact, within such groups, many important professional decisions are shifted from clinicians to the administration.

Researchers at the University of North Carolina at Chapel Hill are now analyzing the findings of their project entitled "The Salaried Physician: Medical Practice in Transition."[85] They documented that physician group practice and HMOs have become larger, more complex, more tightly administered and more strategically oriented than their antecedents. Such developments affect how physician-employees understand the nature of their work and assess their professional autonomy. Beyond this, however, large medical organizations with varying orientations toward the health-care market and diverse beliefs about how medical practice should be organized may have a substantial impact on future health-care arrangements in the United States and the professional culture of medicine.

Thus, the primary-care gatekeeper, discussed in detail by Taylor in Chapter 10, is at risk of becoming a glorified technical expert working on an assembly line of new patients. Physicians must develop creative solutions to this dark side of HMO practice if they are to forestall the white coat/blue collar syndrome.

Changes in the Way Society Funds Graduate
Medical Education

Currently, the Medicare diagnosis-related group system provides separate payments for indirect and direct costs of medical education. Reimbursement for direct costs, such as house-officer salaries, is geared as a "pass-through" to Medicare. The government simply picks up the tab. Indirect costs, such as expenses associated with teaching and research, are paid according to a complex formula based on geographic location, ratio of number of residents to number of hospital beds and number of Medicare beneficiaries treated. However, it will not be long before the $3 billion federal support of graduate medical education (GME) dries up. It is inconsistent with federal policy to continue to support physicians in training while simultaneously facing a surplus of specialists and geographic maldistribution of practitioners.[86] As deficit-cutting fever worsens, GME subsidies will decrease—it is only a matter of degree. Also, other third-party payers, such as Blue Cross and Blue Shield, will be increasingly unwilling to fund GME because they view house staff as inefficient and wasteful of health-care resources. Researchers[87] have found that health care in a teaching hospital may be nearly three times as expensive for the same diagnosis as care in a community hospital that does not have residents. No one wants to subsidize this difference.

This situation will create a ripple effect in the educational system. The author is afraid that physicians will see many restrictions placed on what insurance companies are willing to reimburse. As funding for GME dwindles, and as the true costs are identified, fellows may have to take unsalaried positions or, worse yet, pay a hefty tuition for training. Again, if specialty societies can police their own backyards and begin to limit their own numbers, some of these problems will be ameliorated. The author is not optimistic.

In an internal memorandum, prepared for its long range planning committee, entitled "An Assessment of the Environment of the American College of Physicians (ACP)," it was predicted that there will be an increase in the voluntary accreditation of residency and fellowship programs.[88] There will be attempts by the public sector to control accreditation in response to the perceived failure of the private sector to deal with such issues as program quality, manpower imbalances and costs. The college document also predicts a reduction of the number of accredited programs as standards are strengthened, a decrease in public funding for subspecialty training to cut costs and to address manpower imbalances and a withdrawal of funding for graduates of nonapproved programs.

Finally, to redress the imbalance between specialists and generalists and to prepare a new generation of practitioners for work in the ambulatory setting, how will we pay for GME outside of the hospital? Experts[89] contend that we could redistribute the dollars currently available for GME to "stimulate rather than discourage other essential aspects of training." Furthermore, those who pay for medical care should be required to pay for education as part of the cost of care.

Shift of Political Power from Providers to Payers

Employers will begin to manage actively their health-care benefits and will use as leverage their market power for preferred rates, discounts and special arrangements with HMOs. Such private-company purchasers of care (for many other potential consumers) will demand reasonable cost, quality and accountability in the system. Many employers may become directly involved in health care for their employees by providing workplace health facilities[90] (see Chapter 6). Corporations that spend millions of dollars on health care will negotiate purchasing agreements with physicians and hospitals—they may even decide to own the various systems involved. Improved utilization-review data provided by insurers and buttressed with employee demographic information can document and verify improvement in employee health. This process will create a strong demand for physicians with skills in chart auditing, utilization review and quality assurance. Hopefully, physicians will work in concert with large employers to develop soundly managed health-care plans with potential benefits for employees, providers and payers.

A dark side of the increased clout of payers may be their insistence on packaging physicians' services. There is a groundswell of support to develop physician diagnosis-related groups (MD-DRGs) that would transfer some of the financial burden from payer to provider. Physicians would receive a set fee for taking care of a particular patient (or diagnosis), regardless of the number of resources used, procedures ordered or specialty referrals made. It is believed that this MD-DRG system would promote integrated patient care and encourage physicians to shop around for the best price on certain services (e.g., radiographic procedures).[91] However, the author believes that this system would be impossible to administer and that there would be a strong financial incentive for physicians to skimp on necessary tests, limit referrals and spuriously upgrade certain DRGs to receive higher payments (so called diagnosis-related group creep). One thing is clear from this shift of political power: "Physicians will never again have the same level of independence or the ability to work in an environment where there is neither a marketplace discipline nor government regulation such as we have had in the past."[92]

As the purchasers of care shift from being passive consumers to savvy shoppers, they too will follow guidelines—rules that will enable them to obtain the best care at the most affordable price.[93]

SUMMARY AND CONCLUSION

The seven scenarios described herein are the author's view of the future. An attempt has been made to outline the major forces that are shaping the profession. Are the predictions too dire? As the most recent past president of the Robert Wood Johnson Foundation, headquartered in Princeton, New Jersey, David Rogers occupied an enviable position in the world of health-care policy formation. The dollars funneled from Princeton under his stewardship have helped shape health-care delivery systems nationwide. His perspectives about the future are decidedly upbeat, and the author presents them in an attempt to balance the scales on both sides of the issues. Rogers' "final projections" include:[75]

1.   . . . the structural, organizational and governmental changes in medicine now underway will be successful in bringing medical care costs under control . . . .
2.   . . . as costs come under control, I believe that the practice of medicine will become somewhat less economically attractive than it is at present; this will lead the profession to attract once again more young men and women whose fundamental interests are predominantly both social and scientific . . . .
3.   . . . the organizational revolution—the striking changes in how medicine is practiced and its increasingly competitive nature—will lead it to become once again much more responsive to the needs and wishes of patients.
4.   . . . medical education will turn more attention to the humanistic, caring, compassionate skills, which are so critical to the therapeutic potential and capacity of the fully-informed physician.
5.   . . . the greatest hope for the future welfare of society is the remarkable potential of new biological science.

The American College of Healthcare Executives (ACHE) outlined a future strategy for physicians, including:[80]

1.   Physicians must be knowledgeable of the policy and payment system changes that are under way, including their causes and their likely effects.

TABLE 1

HEALTH PROFESSIONALS' RATINGS OF THEIR TRAINING IN EACH
OF THE PEW HEALTH PROFESSIONS COMMISSION'S
COMPETENCIES (n = 1501)[1,2]

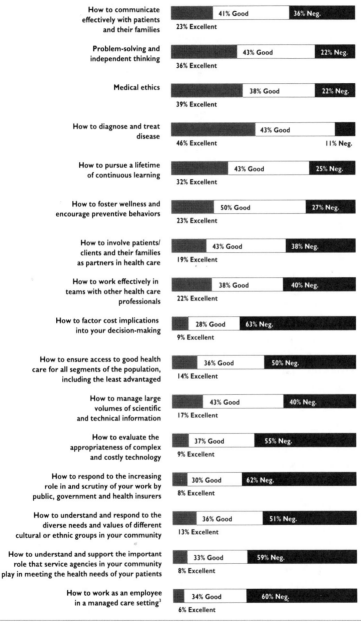

Competency	Excellent	Good	Neg.
How to communicate effectively with patients and their families	23% Excellent	41% Good	36% Neg.
Problem-solving and independent thinking	36% Excellent	43% Good	22% Neg.
Medical ethics	39% Excellent	38% Good	22% Neg.
How to diagnose and treat disease	46% Excellent	43% Good	11% Neg.
How to pursue a lifetime of continuous learning	32% Excellent	43% Good	25% Neg.
How to foster wellness and encourage preventive behaviors	23% Excellent	50% Good	27% Neg.
How to involve patients/clients and their families as partners in health care	19% Excellent	43% Good	38% Neg.
How to work effectively in teams with other health care professionals	22% Excellent	38% Good	40% Neg.
How to factor cost implications into your decision-making	9% Excellent	28% Good	63% Neg.
How to ensure access to good health care for all segments of the population, including the least advantaged	14% Excellent	36% Good	50% Neg.
How to manage large volumes of scientific and technical information	17% Excellent	43% Good	40% Neg.
How to evaluate the appropriateness of complex and costly technology	9% Excellent	37% Good	55% Neg.
How to respond to the increasing role in and scrutiny of your work by public, government and health insurers	8% Excellent	30% Good	62% Neg.
How to understand and respond to the diverse needs and values of different cultural or ethnic groups in your community	13% Excellent	36% Good	51% Neg.
How to understand and support the important role that service agencies in your community play in meeting the health needs of your patients	8% Excellent	33% Good	59% Neg.
How to work as an employee in a managed care setting[3]	6% Excellent	34% Good	60% Neg.

Source: Pew Health Professions Commission (Reprinted with permission.)
[1]Competencies ordered according to importance ranking in Table 3
[2]Fair and poor responses are combined and reported in the negative category
[3]Results are reported only for human health professionals who graduated from professional school between 1980 and 1990

25

2. Physicians must plan for leadership roles.
3. Physicians must determine the level of practice productivity that will be required to be competitive.
4. Physicians must improve their hospital relationships.
5. Physicians must strengthen their commitment to the measurement and improvement of patient care quality and be prepared to disclose information about quality to the payors.

Compare then, if you will, the projections by Rogers and the ACHE to the *current* state of affairs in medical education as documented by the PEW Health Professions Commissions survey findings in Table 1.[79] As educators, our pedagogic challenges are clear and the need for immediate action is pressing. The author hopes that the following Chapters will help you to be better prepared.

The author hopes to forestall the development of the white coat/blue collar syndrome. He too, bemoans the "loss of opportunity" and the "failure of medical leadership"[94] but hopes that the chapters in this book will provide young physicians with new ideas. The erosion of professional autonomy may continue as the forces within the health-care system remain in flux.

The remainder of the book explores many of these issues in greater depth, taking into account the point of view of experts in each field. As well-informed and motivated readers, your task will be to sort through the information and necessarily draw conclusions about future practice alternatives in medicine.

REFERENCES

1. Cohen AB, Cantor JC, Barker DC, et al: Data watch—Young physicians and the future of the medical profession. *Health Affairs* Winter 138–148, 1990.
2. Bloom SW: Structure and ideology in medical education: An analysis of resistance to change. *J Health Soc Behav* 29:294–306, 1988.
3. Cantor JC, Cohen AB, Barker DC, et al: Medical educators' views on medical education reform. *JAMA* 265:1002–1006, 1991.
4. Richardson W: Educating leaders who can resolve the health-care crisis. *The Chronicle of Higher Education* June 3, 1992.
5. Hojat M: Personal communication. May 1, 1992.
6. Tuteur P: Internal medicine chief residents want changes in education. *JAMA* 264:175, 1990.
7. Norman DK, Randall RS, Hornsby BJ: Critical features of a curriculum in health care quality and resource management. *QRB* 16:317–336, 1990.
8. Jacobs MO, Mott P: Physician characteristics and training emphasis considered desirable by teachers and HMOs. *J Med Educ* 262:725–731, 1987.
9. Wu AW, Folkmar S, McPhee SJ, et al: Do house officers learn from their mistakes? *JAMA* 265:2089–2094, 1991.

10. Stitham S: Educational malpractice. *JAMA* 266:905–906, 1991.
11. Inui TS, Nolan JP (eds): Internal medicine curriculum deform. Part 2. *Ann Intern Med* 116:1041–1045, 1992.
12. Greenlick MR: Educating physicians for population-based clinical practice. *JAMA* 267:1645–1648, 1992.
13. Boyer MH, Madoff MA, Bennett A, et al: Tufts' four year combined-MD-MPH program: A training model for population based medicine. *Acad Med* 67:363–365, 1992.
14. Swartz HM, Gottheil DL: The need to educate physician-scholars for leadership in the health care system. *Ann Intern Med* 114:333–334, 1991.
15. Barondess JA: The academic health center and the public agenda: Whose three-legged stool? *Ann Intern Med* 115:962–967, 1991.
16. Stoeckle JD, Reiser SJ: The corporate organization of hospital work: Balancing professional and administrative responsibilities. *Ann Intern Med* 116:407–413, 1992.
17. Hough DE, Buzzoli GJ: The economic environment of resident physicians. *JAMA* 253:1758–1762, 1985.
18. Gonzaley ML (ed): *Socioeconomic Characteristics of Medical Practice 1992*. Am Med Assoc Center for Health Policy Research, 1992.
19. Geertsma RH, Romano J: Relationship between expected indebtedness and career choice of medical students. *J Med Educ* 61:555–559, 1986.
20. AAMC Legislative Update. July 17, 1986.
21. Jolin LD, Jolly P, Krakower JY, et al: US medical school finances. *JAMA* 266:985–990, 1991.
22. Whitcomb ME, Caswell J: The market structure of residency training. *N Engl J Med* 314:710–712, 1986.
23. Wessel D: More young doctors shun private practice work as employees. *The Wall Street Journal* Jan 13, 1986:1.
24. Stelmach WJ: Is there really a doctor glut? *New Physician* Sept, 8–11, 1984.
25. Iglehart JK: How many doctors do we need? *JAMA* 254:1785–1788, 1985.
26. Iglehart JK: The future supply of physicians. *N Engl J Med* 314:860–864, 1986.
27. Tarlov A: HMO enrollment growth and physicians: The third compartment. *Health Affairs* Spring, 24–35, 1986.
28. Steinwachs DM, Weiner JP, Shapiro S, et al: A comparison of the requirements for primary care physicians in HMOs with projections made by the GMENAC. *N Engl J Med* 314:217–222, 1986.
29. Schwartz WB, Sloan FA, Mendelson DN: Why there will be little or no physician surplus between now and the year 2000. *N Engl J Med* 318:892–897, 1988.
30. Marwick C: Medical news and perspectives: Trend to specialization reversing? *JAMA* 268:11, 1992.
31. Page L: Federal committee recommends privacy care quotas. *Am Med News* July 27, 1992:8.
32. Light DW: The growing physician supply: Implications for hospitals and doctors. Unpublished manuscript. The Leonard Davis Institute of Health Economics, U of Penn, 1984.
33. Sevens RA: The future of the medical profession. In Ginzberg E (ed): *From Physician Shortage to Patient Shortage: The Uncertain Future of Medical Practice*. Boulder, CO, Westview Press, 75–95, 1986.
34. Shaffer WA, Holloman FC: Consultation and referral between physicians in new medical practice environments. *Ann Intern Med* 103:600–605, 1985.

35. Ginzberg E, Ostow M: *The Coming Physicians Surplus, in Search of a Public Policy.* Totowa, NJ, Rowman and Allanheld, 1984.
36. Marmor TR: The more there are, the more we pay. *The New York Times* June 29, 1986, sec F:2.
37. The California Medical Association's 114th Annual Session: How to find a job after residency. Pamphlet, Mar 9, 1985.
38. Lind SE: The fellowship application process. *JAMA* 252:3409–3410, 1984.
39. Shulkin D, Kronhaus A, Nash DB: A privately financed fellowship model for management training of physicians. *Acad Med* 67:266–270, 1992.
40. Kronhaus AK: *Choosing Your Practice.* New York, Springer-Verlag, 1990.
41. Bernene J: Message from the editor. *Careers Intern Med* 1:3, 1985.
42. Deutsch S: Personal communication. Aug 2, 1992.
43. Careers and Lifestyles Colloquium. Program and resource book available from the dean's office. U of Penn School of Med, 1985.
44. PSIM Reports: Oct 1985. Newsletter, p 3.
45. Longshore G, Fulton A: *Planning Your Medical Career.* Available from Fulton, Longshore and Assoc, 527 Plymouth Road, Suite 410, Plymouth Meeting, PA.
46. Taylor A: *How to Choose a Medical Specialty.* Philadelphia, WB Saunders, 1986.
47. Locks S: *How to Do It.* London, British Med Assoc, 1985.
48. McGaghie W, Frey J: *Handbook for the Academic Physician.* New York, Springer Verlag, 1986.
49. Aluise J: *The Physician as Manager, 2nd ed.* New York, Springer Verlag, 1987.
50. Aluise J: *The Art of Leadership and the Science of Management.* Raleigh, NC, Apollo Med Systems, 1989.
51. Whitman N, Weiss E, Lutz L: *The Chief Resident as Manager.* Salt Lake City, Utah, Univ of Utah School of Medicine, 1988.
52. Whitman N, Weiss E, Bishop F: *Executive Skills for Medical Faculty.* Salt Lake City, Utah, Univ of Utah School of Medicine, 1988.
53. Hoffmeir P, Bohner J: *From Residency to Reality.* New York, McGraw Hill, 1988.
54. James E (ed): A guide to success in the premedical years for minority students. Available from the U of Penn School of Medicine, Dean's Office, Phila, PA 19104.
55. Huth EJ: *How to Write and Publish Papers in the Medical Sciences.* Philadelphia, ISI Press, 1982.
56. Cotton H: *Medical Practice Management.* Oradell, NJ, Medical Economics, 1985.
57. Boroson W: *The Physician's Guide to Professional and Personal Advisers.* Oradell, NJ, Medical Economics, 1986.
58. Marcus B: *Competing for Clients.* Chicago, Probus, 1986.
59. Chassin MR: Get ready for more review and standardization. *Internist* May-Jun 11–14, 1986.
60. Caper P, Keller R, Rohlf P: Tracking physician practice patterns for quality care. *Bus Health* 3:7–9, 1986.
61. Berwick DM: Practice guidelines: Promise or threat? *HMO Practice* 5:174–177, 1991.
62. Nash DB: Practice guidelines and outcomes: Where are we headed? *Arch Pathol Lab Med* 114:1122–1125, 1990.
63. Ginzberg E: 1990s and beyond—personal economics. *New Physician* Sept, 15, 1985.

64. McIlrath S: Hospital kickbacks to physicians assailed by GAO. *Am Med Assoc News* Aug 15, 1986:7.
65. Thompson BL: The influence of medical practice competition on the academic medical center's educational mission. *J Med Educ* 59:605–606, 1984.
66. Linn LS, Yager J, Cope D, et al: Health status, job satisfaction, job stress and life satisfaction among academic and clinical faculty. *JAMA* 254:2775–2782, 1985.
67. Mitchell JM, Scott E: New evidence of the prevalence and scope of physician joint ventures. *JAMA* 268:80–84, 1992.
68. Stifford D: When idealism meets business. *The Philadelphia Inquirer* Aug 25, 1985.
69. Angell M: Cost containment and the physician. *JAMA* 254:1203–1207, 1985.
70. Bezold C: Medical megatrends reshaping delivery and evaluation of care. *Med Healthcare* July 165–167, 1984.
71. Bezold C, Carlson R, Peck J: *The Future of Work and Health.* Auburn, MA, Auburn House, 1986.
72. Jensen PS: The doctor-patient relationship: Headed for impasse or improvement. *Ann Intern Med* 95:769–771, 1981.
73. Schroeder JL, Clarke JT, Webster JR: Prepaid entitlements: A new challenge for physician-patient relations. *JAMA* 254:3080–3082, 1985.
74. Kolata G: Increasingly, life and death issues become money matters. *New York Times* March 20, 1988:6e.
75. Rogers DE: *Where Have We Been? Where Are We Going?* Boston, Daedalus, 115: 208–229.
76. Giggins CB: The potential role of magnetic resonance imaging in ischemic vascular disease (editorial). *N Engl J Med* 326:1624–1625, 1992.
77. Altman LK: When a patient's life is price of learning new kind of surgery. *New York Times* June 23, 1992:C3.
78. The trend is toward group practice. *Internist* May-Jun, 9, 1986.
79. Shugars DA, O'Neil EH, Bader JD (eds): *Healthy America: Practitioners for 2005, an Agenda for Action for U.S. Health Professional Schools.* San Francisco, CA, The Pew Health Professions Commission, 1991.
80. Arthur Anderson and the American College of Healthcare Executives: *The Future of Healthcare: Physician and Hospital Relationships.* New York, Arthur Anderson, 1991.
81. Larkin H: Employee doctor pay found comparable to private practice. *Am Med News* July 20, 1992:11.
82. Schoenbaum SC: Employment of physicians at Havard Community Health Plan. In: Ginzberg E (ed): *From Physician Shortage to Patient Shortage: The Uncertain Future of Medical Practice.* Boulder, CO, Westview Press, 95–118, 1986.
83. Freund DA, Allen KS: Factors affecting physicians' choice to practice in a fee-for-service setting versus an individual practice association. *Med Care* 23:799–808, 1985.
84. Kralewski JE, Pitt L, Shatin D: Structure characteristics of medical group practice. *Admin Sci* 30:34–45, 1985.
85. Konrad TR, Kory WP, Madison DL, et al: The salaried physician: Medical practice in transition (Executive Summary). UNC Chapel Hill, Dec 1989.
86. Politzer RM, Harris DL, Gaston MH, et al: Primary care physician supply and the medically underserved. *JAMA* 266:104–109, 1991.
87. Cameron J: The indirect costs of graduate medical education. *N Engl J Med* 312:1233–1238, 1985.

88. Tab D, Board of Regents: An assessment of the environment of the ACP: Trends forecasted between 1987–1992. ACP, Nov 5, 1985.
89. Eisenberg JM: How can we pay for graduate medical education in ambulatory care? *N Engl J Med* 320:1525–1531, 1989.
90. Frishman ME: Future roles for purchasers of care. *Internist* May-June, 28–30, 1986.
91. Mitchell JB: Packaging services: More responsibility, more risk, more savings. *Internist* May-Jun, 15–16, 1985.
92. Fox PD: Practicing medicine in the year 2000. *Internist* May-Jun, 7–10, 1986.
93. Nash DB: Medical purchasing guidelines for the business community: How to ask the questions and get the answers we need. *QRB* 16:98–100, 1990.
94. Golden WE, Olive DA, Friedlander IR: Megatrends in medical education. *Am J Med* 81:112–116, 1986.

SECTION
I

SOCIAL
CONCERNS

COMMENTARY

David B. Nash

The first section of this book consists of four chapters on physician collectivism, the public-spirited physician, changes in medical education and the growing influence of women in medicine.

In the first chapter, Dr. Barry L. Liebowitz and Dr. Donald C. Meyer of Doctors Council of New York trace the history of physician collectivism using their own union as a paradigm. Sadly, Dr. Meyer passed away unexpectedly this past October.

As the corporatization of health care continues, economic and business decisions might take precedence over decisions regarding quality of care. Drs. Liebowitz and Meyer believe that a union gives physicians a collective voice to represent their concerns to the owners of health-care delivery systems. Perhaps a doctors' union even helps maintain high quality-of-care standards. This chapter is provocative and no doubt will create strong feelings on both sides of the issue. As more physicians join organized, managed-care settings, it is axiomatic that doctors' unions will continue to proliferate. The work of Drs. Liebowitz and Meyer continues to make national news since publication of the first edition.

In the second chapter, Dr. David J. Brailer traces the development of physicians in organized medicine. His thesis is that physicians can act as agents of positive social change. Indeed, physicians should take an active part in the political process, and they should help influence the development of policies that are beneficial for patient care. He uses some real-world vignettes, taking examples of physicians who he feels are public spirited from several different settings, including organized medicine, politics, academia and the private sector. He challenges physicians to become more involved in the national political process and gives practical advice on how to accomplish this objective.

According to Dr. James B. Couch, an attorney as well as a physician, physicians will not be able to participate in the political process unless medical school curricula undergo major changes. He describes in detail the curricular innovations that will be necessary to educate physicians for the 21st century, following some of the recommendations from the famous Association of American Medical College's report on graduating physicians for the future. Dr. Couch outlines five specific types of physician, including what he calls the "new breed" of physician, who will shape the future of medical practice. His chapter will be of particular interest to medical educators, deans and directors of medical school admissions committees.

Perhaps no force is as powerful in medicine today as the growing number of women among the ranks of physicians (1,2). Dr. Lila Stein Kroser, as past president of both the American Medical Women's Association and the Alumnae Association of the Medical College of Pennsylvania, is in a key position to comment on women physicians. She skillfully uses the history of the American Medical Women's Association as her historical backdrop. She, too, offers practical advice on styles of practice, organization and the balancing of home and work commitments.

Section I lays the groundwork for the second section, Emerging Career Trends. By understanding the political, educational and economic forces that are helping shape the future practice of medicine, we can begin to examine specific career pathways in detail.

REFERENCES

1. Angier N: Bedside manners improve as more women enter medicine. *New York Times,* June 21, 1992.
2. Cotton P: Women scientists explore more ways to smash through the glass cieling. *JAMA* 268:173, 1992.

CHAPTER 1

DOCTORS' UNIONS

Barry L. Liebowitz
Donald C. Meyer

A physician employed by a municipal hospital is told after ten years that his services are no longer required. To whom can he turn to correct this professional affront? Will his local medical society step in to help? He might get sympathy, but little else. What if he belonged to a doctors' union that had a grievance procedure that provided a mechanism for dealing with this situation? The answer is as real as the case is authentic. In 1986, after a series of grievance steps led to a binding decision by an arbitrator, this union member received a $78,000 settlement for all the time not worked and has resumed his regular schedule at the hospital.

A labor union is an organization that seeks to represent the interests of its members through a collective voice. Although doctors are professionals, the fact that they have been turning to union representation is not particularly surprising. Unions of professionals have been an integral part of the labor movement for quite some time, and more doctors are identifying with the "union label."

HISTORY OF UNIONS IN THE UNITED STATES

Many lengthy books have been written about the development of unions in the United States. It is impossible to document the progress of unions in a single book, let alone a chapter. Yet, a basic understanding of the subject is necessary to assess the growth of doctors unions. Briefly, the first permanent labor unions were organized in the 1790s by the printers and the shoemakers in the Northeast. In the early days, the focus was on maintaining the professional integrity of these highly skilled craftsmen against the competition they faced from untrained workers who were willing to work for lower wages. Collective bargaining with an employer was a local affair, and the usual demands were for a wage scale and an assurance that underqualified employees would not be hired.

The labor movement gained strength in 1827, with the push for the ten-hour workday. This movement was important in that it proved that with adequate resources and support, employees could achieve victory in their fight for improved conditions. As a result of the "ten-hour movement" in Philadelphia, the first city federation of labor in the nation, the Philadelphia Mechanics Union of Trade Associations, was created. It eventually was transformed into a political party.

The Noble and Holy Order of the Knights of Labor was perhaps the first *national* organization of workers with a wide-reaching effect. The order was founded in 1869 in response to the radical changes that were occurring in manufacturing and the economy as a whole. Corporate capitalism was threatening the traditional crafts and trades. Monopolies and great aggregates of wealth were developing, and the individual worker was virtually powerless to defend his interests. The knights were formed as a "monopoly against monopolies" and attempted to include all trades and callings within its ranks, the only exceptions being "bankers, stockbrokers, professional gamblers, lawyers, and those who derived their living from the sale of intoxicating liquors."[1]

Terence V. Powderly, the leader of the organization with the title of Grand Master Workman, was a strict enforcer of the order's two basic tenets, membership secrecy and no striking. Membership in the knights was kept secret, and cryptic signs on sidewalks and fences alerted members as to when and where meetings were to be held. This reluctance to affirm involvement in the federation publicly is understandable, especially in light of the fact that many known union activists of the day found themselves on employer blacklists. It served the additional purpose of giving members a sense of power, a vocabulary of coded messages and signs that hinted at mysticism, while giving the organization a misleading aura of power.

The knights had a strong aversion to strikes, favoring what they called "arbitration." They defined arbitration as the peaceful settlement of disputes, which is not the same as today's understanding of the term (to mean the submission of disagreements to a neutral third party). Powderly wanted to educate the workers in the methods of peaceful settlement, and his aversion to strikes was not unwarranted. The strike was, and is, an explosive weapon and often not necessarily the best way of addressing a problem. Strikes and lockouts did take place, however, and the knights, although unprepared, were forced to deal with them. The refusal of the order to recognize the conflictual nature of labor relations contributed to its downfall, as did the organization's inability to integrate its various factions. The membership was diverse, encompassing everyone from farmers and entrepreneurs to laborers, all with different, or possibly conflicting, interests.

The incredible success and staggering downfall of the Knights of Labor is reflected in its membership statistics. In 1879, the national membership stood at 9,287, and within one year it had increased to 20,000. At its peak, in 1886, there were an impressive 729,677 members in the organization.[1] By 1890, membership had dropped to 100,000, and before the end of the century, the order was virtually extinct.

As the order went into decline, another organization developed to fill the vacuum. The American Federation of Labor (AFL) was formed in 1886, an offshoot of the Federation of Organized Trades and Labor Unions (FOTLU), which was formed by a dissident group of knights. The AFL learned an important lesson from the failing knights: they organized along craft lines. Organizing along craft lines means that the federation did not attempt to unite people from all walks of life but instead focused on unionizing only skilled craftsmen.

The AFL was exclusive, whereas the knights had been inclusive. The AFL was also a loose organization, in that it was composed of autonomous national unions, and the federation had little power. The power rested in the component unions, and the AFL served as a kind of umbrella under which they organized. There were no mysteries in the AFL, no secret codes or cryptic signs. In fact, the federation was straightforward in its practices and policies. The AFL practiced what came to be known as "bread-and-butter" unionism, focusing on economic gains for its members, as opposed to idealistic goals.

Samuel Gompers was the driving force behind the AFL from its birth in 1886 until his death in 1924. An immigrant from the slums of London, Gompers moved at age 13 to America, where he worked as an apprentice cigar maker. Legend has it that the young Gompers read Marx to his co-workers as they rolled cigars, although his later attitudes did not reflect any Marxist tendencies. As a labor leader, Gompers had no interest in the unskilled and unfortunate masses. He was not willing to suffer or martyr himself for the cause, as were many activists of the time, such as Eugene Debs. Gompers sought respectability for workers and epitomized the concept of bread-and-butter unionism.

This brief review of labor history gives us the means by which to understand how and why unions have evolved to their current status. It is important to separate history from the present and to avoid allowing traditional perspectives to color our current perceptions. For instance, ask a person what industries a labor union operates in and the reply will commonly be automobile manufacturing, transportation and textiles. The real picture, the fact that unions also protect airline pilots, engineers and attorneys, all professional employees, is unknown and unacknowledged by the public. It is, after all, more comfortable to think of the world as static, instead of recognizing the constant and sometimes unsettling changes that are occurring around us.

It is crucial to recognize that as the composition of our country's economy shifts, unions are moving into new areas, particularly sectors that were once considered inviolate. Office workers, hi-tech craftsmen and government employees in large numbers are now being brought into union ranks.

The layman has a stereotypical image of physicians and unions, images that, although rooted in historical fact, result in beliefs that are inaccurate in today's world. Many people still view a physician as that kindly old fellow depicted in Norman Rockwell's paintings—a private practitioner, with a comfortable office in a corner of his white colonial house, in some lazy American suburb. Some people still view unions as communist-dominated radical groups bent on overthrowing the U.S. government.

Needless to say, neither of these extreme perceptions is accurate, and it is doubtful as to whether they ever were. Doctors are still thought of as privileged, an untouchable group removed from the troubles of everyday life, protected by their professional expertise. Americans have a tendency to elevate the status of all "professionals," to regard them with awe, believing that the label somehow makes a worker invincible. Yet, it is important to realize that a professional may be in a situation that renders him or her an employee, just as a coal miner or an assembly-line worker. Even the small-town doctor down the street, who may appear independent and secure, is forced to defend his or her interests against the arbitrary decisions of the government and other third parties.

When asked what he wanted for his union, Samuel Gompers gave a simple answer, "More!" This one word has come to represent the simplistic belief that all that unions stand for is the greedy self-interest of workers. In considering the concept of professional unions, it is important to recognize that a union has much more to offer than improvement of the economic status of its members. Simply being a "professional" does not protect an employee from the whims of management. All too often, professionals sneer at the idea of union representation. Parents raise their children to be doctors, teachers, engineers, but rarely does a father clap his son on the back and say, "Boy, I want you to make me proud . . . be a union member." However, are unions and professions like oil and water? Does a profession necessarily rise to the top, or can the two mix to create something better? It is these questions, and others, that this chapter seeks to resolve.

The chapter examines the goals of unions, the history of the legislation that protects unions (specifically those in the health-care sector) and the various issues surrounding the unionization of doctors. Many differing opinions exist as to whether salaried doctors may unionize, if nonsalaried physicians are eligible to join labor unions and whether medical societies could function as labor unions. The reasons for unionizing are also examined, along with the threat of strikes and the alternative forms of collective action that are available to doctors.

GOALS OF UNIONS

The primary reasons workers join unions are improved wages, fringe benefits and working conditions, as well as job security. However, unions also organize employees in a manner that makes it possible to negotiate other issues. Teachers, for example, are renowned for the focus of their negotiations and upgrading of the educational system. A doctors' union has the power and ability to influence the quality and availability of health care. By collectivizing, employees try to eliminate the weaknesses that individuals have in negotiating with a more affluent and powerful employer.

Legislative History

President Franklin D. Roosevelt and his New Deal administration made the first attempt to legislate a protective umbrella under which employees could organize. In 1933, the National Industrial Recovery Act (NIRA) was passed. It contained section 7(a), providing certain safeguards for labor. The act met with much resistance from industry, and its administrative body, the National Recovery Administration, was declared unconstitutional by the Supreme Court in 1935. This decision was based on the grounds that Congress did not have the same power to regulate intrastate business as it did to control interstate commerce.

In the 1934 elections, a labor supported the New Dealers, despite the failure of the NIRA, and politicians, surprised and pleased by this show of faith, resolved to address the issue once again. Senator Robert Wagner (D–N.Y.) proposed a bill to strengthen and alter the provisions of section 7(a), and it was passed in 1935 as the National Labor Relations Act (NLRA). In 1937, the Supreme Court supported Congress' power to pass such a law protecting the right of employees to organize and seek representation. The NLRA is the base on which all current labor legislation has been built, and it is fundamental to an understanding of the laws that pertain to unions.

The Wagner Act of 1935 did not exempt charitable, religious or educational institutions from its coverage, although it clearly excluded all public employees. Thus, it was unclear as to whether employees of nonprofit hospitals were protected by the new law until 1942, when the U.S. district court and the court of appeals both held that the act included such institutions, in an historic case known as *Central Dispensary and Emergency Hospitals.* In 1947, this decision was, in effect, reversed by the passage of the Taft-Hartley Act, another major piece of labor legislation that amended the NLRA and excluded the health-care industry with the argument that it was essentially noncommercial.

In 1947, when the Taft-Hartley change was instituted, there was no prolonged discussion over this exclusion, and the exemption of nonprofit hospitals did not receive much attention. Over the ensuing years, however, it became a topic of intense debate. Nearly every Congress subsequent to 1947 proposed amendments to repeal the exclusion. These appeals met with resistance because there was widespread apprehension that an attempted alteration of a section of the Taft-Hartley Act would result in a reopening of the entire law.

In 1974, the issue was finally addressed by Congress, and the result was an amendment to include nonprofit hospitals under the labor laws, known as Public Law (PL) 93–360. The change was made for a number of reasons, including a shift in the economy toward the service sector, a surge of union activity in the federal and state sectors and a rise in government and private insurance programs financing health-care systems. There were also alterations in pertinent laws, such as the Social Security Act. In 1950, the act was updated to permit the voluntary participation of employees of nonprofit and public institutions, and the Fair Labor Standards Act of 1966 was extended to include hospital employees.

CAN SALARIED DOCTORS JOIN UNIONS?

Thousands of employed doctors currently belong to unions.[2] Salaried physicians are represented by various types of unions. For example, some state and municipally employed doctors belong to unions that represent large, diverse blocks of civil servants, not doctors alone. Some physicians employed at state-supported medical schools are represented as part of a union that includes all the professors in the university system. The United University Professions (UUP) union represents physicians at Downstate Medical College, for example. A number of housestaff doctors are represented by independent unions, as are thousands of attending physicians.

In general, salaried physicians in the public sector can be organized under the protection of the labor laws that are applicable to the area in which they are employed. Private-sector physicians are usually permitted to organize under the protection of the NLRA.

According to labor laws, employees who have duties that are considered "managerial" or "supervisory" are denied the right to form a labor union. In the landmark case involving Yeshiva University, the Supreme Court, in a 5-to-4 decision, ruled that salaried professors who had a voice in granting tenure to their colleagues could not join a union because the granting of tenure is a supervisory function.

In 1985, the National Labor Relations Board (NLRB), in a similar case, ruled that doctors who either sat on or were eligible to sit on certain committees of a health-maintenance organization (HMO) could not be union members (*Family Health Plan* v. *Union of American Physicians and Dentists*). As in the Yeshiva case, the NLRB ruled that as long as these doctors had the right to participate in policy making, they had managerial power.[3]

Determining which doctors perform supervisory or managerial roles comes up whenever doctors' unions organize. Titles mean nothing in many cases. A director of medical education may supervise no one, and a physician with no particular title may actually supervise a number of colleagues in a clinic or a department. The majority of employed physicians perform duties that permit them to join unions.

In organizing doctors, one of the principal aspects of negotiation is often the determination of the unit. The unit is the group of employees the union will represent. If the employer and the union cannot reach an accord, the NLRB undertakes to settle the issue.

CAN NONSALARIED DOCTORS JOIN UNIONS?

Many unions in the United States claim that they can represent both salaried and "private-practice" doctors. This declaration has produced a wide range of reactions and is the topic of heated debate. The point in question is whether privately practicing doctors can be considered "employees," in the commen sense of the word. The NLRA protects only workers who are participants in an employee-employer relationship, as are salaried doctors. A physician who has his or her own practice, however, is considered by many experts to be a private contractor, not an employee. The right of a nonsalaried doctor to join a labor union is still under discussion. The real issue is not whether nonsalaried doctors may form a union but, rather, what the union can do for such doctors who have no visible employer-employee relationship and still be protected under the law. Labor unions, under the NLRA, are protected from prosecution under antitrust legislation that might be applicable to their wage-setting techniques. At one time, these activities were seen as conspiracies in restraint of trade. Technically, any organization may label itself a "union," but whether it is protected by the laws that are applicable to labor unions is a distinctly different matter.

WHY UNIONIZE?

Since the passage of the 1974 amendments to the Taft-Hartley Act, many experts have predicted that hospital unions would boom and that health care would be the new union frontier. This prophecy has yet to be fulfilled because many groups of hospital employees are skilled professionals and, as was mentioned previously, professionals and unions have not always been perceived as complementary.

In addition to the problem of unionizing professionals, doctors face another barrier to unionizing. No matter how poor the pay or how bad the conditions, they are somehow expected to perform not for financial security but for the intrinsic rewards they gain from the care of those in need. Opponents of doctors' unions argue that a union is merely a manifestation of the baser desires of doctors to obtain greater compensation for their services. Many clinicians believe that a union will surely interfere with the sacred doctor-patient relationship.

Patient care represents the "bottom line" in the health-care industry. It is the primary concern of doctors and should be the primary concern of hospitals as well. All too often, however, economics are of first importance to hospital administrators, and to a certain extent this situation is understandable. The health-care field has undergone a massive change in the past two decades. Health care has become a commodity; it has been corporatized. It seems that profit, not health care, has become the motivating factor.

There is a growing trend toward corporate ownership of hospital chains. Large companies, such as Dow Chemical and Standard Oil, have acquired health-care facilities across the nation, merging into giant conglomerates and erasing the distinctions between the once discrete function of medical supplier and health-care provider. Corporate and business health-care spending was $186.2 billion in 1990, and 75 percent of that spending was comprised of employer contributions to health insurance premiums, to the tune of $139.1 billion.[4] In terms of gross national product, in 1990 the United States spent 12.2 percent of our $666.2-billion gross national product on health care.[5]

Physicians have been placed in a vulnerable position, owing to the expense of setting up a private practice, to the oversupply of physicians and to the increased focus on profit-making in health care. It is becoming increasingly likely that physicians will be working in a hospital or an HMO and that they will be salaried employees. The emphasis on profit will inspire employers to pass the burden of cost cutting down to doctors in the form of decreased wages and a stronger control over the types, amounts and duration of services they may render.

The changes in the health-care system that place doctors in an employee status put them in situations where they must often choose between being pro-patient or pro-institution. The aims and objectives of doctors, institutions and patients are not necessarily congruent. Institutions are concerned with containment of costs and offering inexpensive, adequate care. Patients want top-quality health care, regardless of the expense, because third parties often foot the bill. Doctors are caught between the two parties, wanting to minimize costs according to employers' wishes, yet bound to offer the best (and possibly the most expensive) care.

Lone doctors are powerless in fighting the effects of cost cutting on health care. They have no voice and can be fired at will if they protest a hospital's policies. Often, doctors are forced to administer care that they feel is inappropriate or inadequate, and the person dictating these policies may be a hospital administrator, bureaucrat or other lay party. To protect their professional autonomy, doctors must be able to voice their opinions without fear of retribution. A union gives doctors security and the vehicle with which to speak out.

A union is formed to assure doctors of financial stability, due processes, a voice in health care and protection from reimbursement agencies. The traditional alliance between doctors, hospitals, business and insurers has been broken. Doctors stand alone against their former allies, and unless they unite, forming a collective front, they will be crushed beneath the growing might of industrialized medicine.

UNIONS AND PROFESSIONAL ASSOCIATIONS: ARE THEY IN CONFLICT?

Many lay people regard such organizations as the American Medical Association and its components as the voice of organized medicine, the equivalent of a "doctors' union." It is, however, the belief of most doctors active in the union movement that professional associations, despite numerous attempts to exert their influence, have had relatively little success in dealing with socioeconomic issues in American health care. It is the feeling of many union leaders that such issues as standard setting, accreditation and dissemination of scientific information properly rest with the societies and their associated groups. Despite this, employers, government, insurance companies and health-care conglomerates are the concern of professional associations as physician autonomy is lost.

Medical societies have been generally inaccessible to doctors with a parochial complaint or problems and traditionally did not deal with bargaining issues. The focus of a medical society is more general than that of a union. The needs of doctors are secondary to the interests of the entire profession. Despite this, the two areas are destined to converge because the American Medical Association (AMA) has begun to recognize the need for collective input as health-care is transformed. Legislative action is still their most successful weapon, and they have made great progress in that area.

Many doctors in positions of union leadership have been or are still active in their professional organizations. The two are not mutually exclusive, and because they focus on different issues in the medical field they have the potential to be complementary.

In the United States, on a national level, both the AMA and the American Dental Association (ADA) have expressed opposition to "self-employed" doctors joining unions. Some people have suggested that these associations, which are experiencing a decline in membership, are concerned that doctors wishing to limit their expenditures will opt for joining a union at the expense of association membership.

CAN UNIONS ESCAPE THE ANTITRUST LAWS THAT LIMIT PROFESSIONAL ASSOCIATIONS' ACTIONS?

Where employed doctors are concerned, unions generally are regulated by federal, state and local labor laws and are usually afforded the same protection as other collective-bargaining units. In the nonsalaried sector, labeling a group a "union" does not automatically remove it from antitrust regulation. Unions have been successful in negotiating for nonsalaried doctors on an individual or group basis and in dealing with many third parties, such as government, insurance companies and hospitals. They have, for the most part, been careful to stay within the law, but there is no guarantee that they can continue to do so.

Could professional societies enter the field of direct negotiation? The traditional aims, abilities and general orientation of the societies have prevented them from making a serious effort to get actively involved in this kind of negotiation.

The difference between a union and a professional association is well illustrated by a case history that involved the Indiana Federation of Dentists (IFD), a union, and both the ADA and the AMA.

The IFD objected to the insurance companies' use of nondentist employees to screen radiographs, and the union claimed that any type of lay review amounted to the unlawful practice of dentistry. Furthermore, the IFD protested that proper diagnosis and treatment planning required an evaluation of *all* diagnostic aids and not just radiographs.

In support of its protest, the union asked its members and other dentists not to submit patients' radiographs routinely with "prior-approval" insurance claims forms. The Indiana Dental Association initially supported the position of the IFD on this issue.

The Federal Trade Commission (FTC), however, thought that this act restrained trade and in 1978 issued a "cease-and-desist" order on the IFD policy. The Indiana Dental Association promptly acceded to the order. The IFD did not comply with the order and began the long and costly process of appeal. In a 1983 ruling that reiterated its original complaints, the FTC said that the IFD substantially limited competition among dentists in their willingness to cooperate with dental-insurance cost-containment programs. The IFD proceeded to appeal the FTC decision to the U.S. Court of Appeals for the Seventh Circuit.

The court, in 1984, ruled in favor of the IFD. It found that the evidence did not indicate any anticompetitive effect and that the FTC ruling harmed consumers by preventing dentists from joining together to promote professional standards as represented in the code of ethics of the ADA.

The FTC appealed this landmark decision to the U.S. Supreme Court. Of particular interest is the belated filing of a"friend-of-the-court" brief with the Supreme Court by both the ADA and the AMA in support of the IFD. This last-minute support by organized medicine and dentistry demonstrates clearly that a union will undertake projects for which a professional association is not willing to take the risk.

In June 1986, the Supreme Court ruled unanimously that the decision of the FTC was appropriate. Even though this case was lost, it must be understood that a small group of dentists, united as a labor union, fought for important professional issues while the professional associations remained disinterested.

IS A STRIKE THE ULTIMATE WEAPON
OF DOCTORS' UNIONS?

Perhaps the greatest fear concerning doctors' unions is the possibility that they might decide to strike. Such a thought is particularly disturbing to many people because physicians' services are considered essential. Yet, the same argument has been used throughout recent history when "essential" groups exercised their perceived right to concerted action. Coal strikes in the middle of this century spurred government action, yet they proved to be less debilitating than had previously been believed. Sanitation strikes have been endured without any long-term consequence, as have teaching, nursing, prison-guard and transportation strikes. This is not to say that a strike by doctors would be without mishap or that doctors would necessarily find it morally acceptable to strike, but that the effects of such a strike would probably not be as serious as many people believe, assuming that sufficient precautions were taken.

A strike may be broadly defined as the withholding of services. When doctors refuse to render nonemergency care to a patient who cannot afford to pay the fee, are they striking? When doctors cut office hours substantially or refuse to accept new patients, are they striking? When doctors locate their office in an affluent suburb and have nothing to do with an innercity slum just a few miles away, are they striking? If doctors refuse to work in a salaried position or to continue caring for a hospitalized patient, is that not a clear case of striking? Suppose the institution in which a doctor works is so inferior in terms of supplies, sanitary conditions and ancillary personnel that patients' health is in jeopardy. It is reasonable to assume that the doctor's conscience may no longer permit him or her to function as usual in such a facility. Is the doctor striking?

Many people would answer the aforementioned questions with a resounding no. Some people, however, might concur that there was some kind of "withholding of services," although the word "strike" might not be applicable.

Most doctors' unions have taken the position that they will never strike against patients. They have indicated that they will always make provisions for emergency care and that no currently ill patients would be abandoned. Refusal to fill out charts and forms required for institutional reimbursement and refusal to sit on hospital committees are more common ways of doctors collectively taking "strike" action. Most strikes of active doctors in the United States have involved house-staff organizations. In such instances, the attending staff have always been available to render the needed care.

For the first time, attending physicians at a municipal facility in Brooklyn, New York, walked out in November 1991. The physicians at Woodhull Medical and Mental Health Center and Cumberland Neighborhood Family Care Center took to the picket line with the support of the community, their fellow union members and colleagues for quality patient care.

The doctors conducted a legal strike that was not over money, but was a last desperate attempt by the staff to focus attention on a community's right to quality patient care. The employer threatened laying off physicians while callously admitting that these layoffs would be at the expense of patient care.

The doctors had tremendous support from the various health-care and employees' unions. The entire staff reinforced the message by attending mass demonstrations. Meetings were held with community leaders to discuss how the community would be affected. The community was gratified to see the doctors' taking such a stance on behalf of the patients they serve.

The media reported the story to cities and communities across the country. The doctors were not only supported by the community, but also by the media, who reinforced the doctors' concern for patients.

The strike ended after two days of picketing. The doctors and the community told the employer that there was a responsibility to the staff as well as to the community it serves. Patients have the right to quality patient care and they do not have to settle for inadequate patient care. The doctors did not have to stand by and watch it happen any longer.

Doctors' unions hope that, through collective negotiation, such drastic actions as strikes may be avoided. Recent refusals by substantial numbers of private-practice obstetricians and orthopedic surgeons in Massachusetts and New York to accept new patients due to oppressive malpractice insurance costs are the result of doctors acting on an individual basis. Had these physicians been joined together in a professional union that engaged in negotiation with the governors and state legislature leaders, such actions might have been avoided. The force of thousands of doctors collectivized to form a union might have persuaded the states' leaders to address the situation.

RECENT HISTORY OF DOCTORS' UNIONS

New York City's Committee of Interns and Residents and the Doctors Association of the Department of Health of the City of New York, which date from the late 1950s and early 1960s, respectively, were pioneers in the doctors' union movement.

In the early 1970s, the nationwide spread of doctors' unions commenced with the creation of the California-based Union of American Physicians and Dentists (UAPD), led by Sanford Marcus,[6] and the Missouri-headquartered American Federation of Physicians and Dentists (AFPD). This upsurge reflected the concern of many private practitioners that the creation of national health insurance was imminent and that professional unions rather than associations were best equipped to deal with this threat to traditional fee-for-service practice. As this threat decreased, so did the growth of doctors' unions among self-employed practitioners. In the 1980s, a resurgence of the doctors' union movement began as a rapid proliferation of alternative health-care delivery systems, such as HMOs and independent-practice associations (IPAs), threatened traditional private practitioners. This issue is dealt with later in the chapter.

Salaried doctors have increasingly looked to unions for help in improving their economic status and in bettering care for their patients. House-staff unionization trends have been stymied to a large degree by a 1976 ruling by the NLRB that interns and residents were "students" rather than "employees" and that they had no collective bargaining rights under federal law. Many doctors working for state governments have been unionized under the umbrella of large "professional" units, where they are usually at the top of the heap economically but among the smallest number of autonomous professionals.

The largest number of salaried attending doctors represented by a strictly doctors' union is the 3,000 members of the Doctors Council of New York City. Next is the UADP, which represents a large number of state- and city-employed doctors in California.

ACCOMPLISHMENTS OF DOCTORS' UNIONS

Unions that represent salaried doctors have been able to increase earnings of doctors and improve health care to a startling degree in many cases. One union, Doctors Council, has been able to raise salaries and benefits of attending doctors to the point where they are finally competitive with the private sector. Through its efforts with the community, the city government and the state legislatures, many public clinics and hospitals have been spared closure. When severe budget cuts were gutting health-care services throughout New York City in the hot summer of 1991, the city proposed shutting down the dental clinics throughout the city. Lobby days were heating up the state's capitol as community and organized labor attended, helping to prevent scores of layoffs across the city.

Doctors Council has found victory in its coalition with various communities across the city. One area of recent victory has been in the area of school health. The Department of Health was removing doctors from the schools, thus avoiding its public responsibility to provide legally mandated services to the children of New York City. Most recently, as a direct result of a Doctors Council lawsuit, the city has been forced to hire new staff for the school program. Again, the community and the unions were able to work together and build a coalition to help secure and maintain the public health for the residents of New York City.

The membership as well has been protected under the union's grievance procedure; doctors' positions have been retained, proper pay has been issued and due process for doctors has been revived.

The UAPD, whose members are primarily private practitioners, has had great success lobbying in the California state legislature, aiding the medical staffs of hospitals to protect the rights of physicians to control health-care matters and helping its members individually and collectively to deal with third parties trying to influence practice. The insurance grievance department of the UAPD has been particularly successful in dealing collectively with large insurance companies on behalf of doctors or patients. Millions of dollars in claims payments have been made owing to the existence and use of this important service.

Doctors Council has been able to assure its members that any work done "out-of-title," meaning tasks that should be performed by a physician in a higher title, are paid as such. Take, for example, one case in which the Department of Health hired a large number of pediatricians for the child-health stations and pediatric centers operated by New York City. Some of the pediatricians were hired as "medical specialists," whereas others were hired as "clinicians," a title that entitles them to substantially lower salaries. No rationale for the discrepancy was offered. After a grievance was filed and offers to settle amicably were rejected by the health department, the case was submitted to arbitration, the final step in the dispute-resolution process. The arbitrator, a neutral third party who reaches a final and binding decision, ruled in favor of the union. All the pediatricians who were Board certified or Board eligible were given the higher title. As a result of the city's delaying tactics, the 30 doctors were owed more than $350,000 in retroactive compensation, which was paid to them after resolution of the case in their favor.

Another example of the union's defense of doctors' rights is exemplified by the rule of New York City's Health and Hospitals Corporation

(HHC) concerning financial disclosure. The HHC runs 16 hospitals as well as neighborhood family-care centers and clinics in the metropolitan area and is a semipublic corporation. It has the power to promulgate a number of rules for its employees, and in this case it was concerned about employees being tempted by kickbacks and gifts. As a result, a strict financial disclosure rule was put into effect. All managerial personnel were affected, as were all employees earning more than $42,000 annually. The rule stipulated that all such employees fill out a yearly statement detailing all income and assets for doctor and spouse, without any guarantee of confidentiality.

Doctors Council urged the HHC to reconsider the requirement and who it affected. The rationale was that the type of job one performs, rather than yearly income, is the source of possible temptation. A secretary who has access to information concerning contractors' bids and earns only $10,000 annually has knowledge of a more confidential and valuable nature than does a pediatrician who deals only with patients and earns $60,000 annually. The HHC ignored the union's arguments, and the matter was taken to court. The financial disclosure regulation has remained in effect, but doctors are the only HHC employees who are not required to fill out the forms.

Another example of the union's function beyond that of bargaining over wages is the institution by Doctors Council, with support from the president of the New York City Council, of a hot line for members to report instances in which patient care has been jeopardized. The 24-hour-a-day "incident line" was advertised by eye-catching red and white stickers, which were distributed to the members to put in appropriate places. By calling a special telephone number, doctors, health-care personnel and patients can report incidents or conditions in city medical facilities that threaten patient care. The calls are verified and referred to the appropriate facility for corrective action. If the matter is not resolved, the complaint will be made public and will be provided to the appropriate governmental agencies, community boards and consumer advocacy groups. Information received on the incident line will be compiled and used by the president of the City Council and other officials to assess the quality of care in the city's health-care system.

DOCTORS UNIONS AS VIEWED BY PATIENTS AND THE COMMUNITY

Uninformed members of the public usually react to the thought of doctors' unions as follows: "Don't they make enough money now?" "Why do they want more?" or "They already have the AMA; isn't it a union?"

Once the public begins to understand the functions of a doctors' union, these questions will be answered. For example, when community leaders and citizens of New York City realized that the Committee of Interns and Residents and Doctors Council supported them in their demands for better health care, they recognized the union as a powerful, pro-patient organization with the resources to effect change. In California, when the UAPD fought for proper patient reimbursement rates (as supposedly guaranteed by health-insurance companies) the patients, with the cooperation of the doctors' union, were fully reimbursed. Union endorsement of the public's right to quality health care is demonstrated by its continuing attempts to protect both professionalism and patient interests.

The following two examples illustrate how Doctors Council has successfully worked within New York City communities on patient care issues that transcend bargaining over salaries and working conditions.

In central Brooklyn, the community, joined by Doctors Council and other labor unions, successfully opposed a fuller affiliation contract between SUNY Health Science Center at Brooklyn Medical School and Kings County Hospital Center. An expanded affiliation between the two organizations would have meant a loss in seniority, job security and other rights enjoyed by the physicians represented by Doctors Council at Kings County Hospital Center. For the community, the medical school had a long history of insensitivity to the needs of the local residents, many of whom lacked health insurance or were Medicaid recipients. There were also questions concerning the mission of Downstate Medical Center, which as a medical school emphasized teaching and research rather than primary care.

At public hearings concerning this proposed affiliation, the unions and the community successfully focused attention on the pitfalls of such an arrangement, and, as of this writing, the affiliation agreement is being reworked to meet the needs of the community and the Doctors Council.

Another example of Doctors Council working with the community concerned a Department of Health child-health station in one of New York City's large public-housing projects that was in danger of being shut down. It was the city's plan that all patients displaced from the child-health station could be absorbed by a new, federally-funded center in the area. The underlying motive, however, was to boost the census of the federal center, for which the city's expense was minimal.

Community residents were irate. They appreciated the quality care rendered by pediatricians at the child-health station, which they had come to rely on during its 13 years of existence, and they were distrustful of the new center. One resident described her feelings to a reporter, saying, "We have our doctors, and we don't trust the new ones coming in."[7]

As a result of this concern, the pediatricians spoke to members of Doctors Council, and a meeting with community leaders was arranged. An agreement was made whereby the union would provide the community with the financial resources to carry out a protest demonstration. Mothers, children and infants became involved, and at one point they took possession of the health station, patrolling its borders with picket signs and posters. A sit-in was staged by 40 residents, who held out for 36 hours before a New York Supreme Court injunction forced them to vacate the premises. One woman camped in front of the station for two weeks, taking breaks only to cook meals and catch a few hours sleep. In the face of such opposition, the city admitted defeat quickly and reopened the health station, which is currently flourishing.

DOCTORS' UNIONS AND FUTURE PRACTICE PATTERNS

As costs for health insurance continue to increase, there is a renewed emphasis on the part of government, insurance companies, large labor unions and other special interest groups (e.g., senior citizens) to cut costs. Managed care and other related practice plans, such as preferred provider organizations (PPOs) and HMOs, are looked on as a way to promote ambulatory primary care, and to reduce the need for inpatient care and hopefully reduce reliance on emergency room visits. New York State, for example, has mandated that its Medicaid recipients be enrolled in a managed care plan.

While the demand for primary care physicians is increasing, recent studies show that fewer graduating medical school students are choosing to concentrate in general family practice, internal medicine or pediatrics. In 1992 only 14.6 percent of medical school graduates entered primary care fields, down from 30 percent in 1987.[8]

This growing trend toward third-party influence on physicians will continue relatively unabated. Restrictions on practice by government, insurance companies, managed care networks, PPOs and HMOs not only will increase and expand but also will affect income as well as practice patterns. As physicians are forced to join together in large consortiums of one kind or another to survive, collective concern leading to collective action will become commonplace.

In this regard, an increasing number of doctors find themselves in a true employer-employee relationship, and the traditional union role of collective bargaining takes place. As the certified representative of employees, a union is able to bargain regarding wages and conditions of employment. A doctors' union is thus empowered to negotiate salary scales, pay increases, working conditions and issues that impact on the quality of health care on behalf of its members. The thousands of doctors now represented by unions will be joined by many colleagues as economic pressures on physician-employees and independent physicians increase.

It is wishful thinking to believe that the era of high incomes and domination of the health-care field by doctors will ever be repeated. If quality health care and professionalism are to survive, collective action is essential.

"SUMMING IT ALL UP"

Doctors are people. Doctors are citizens. Doctors are workers—highly educated and skilled workers with awesome responsibilities—but workers nevertheless.

Even though physicians clearly earn a living as a result of their labors, they have traditionally not been considered by the public (or by themselves for the most part) to be members of the U.S. labor force. Perhaps the most prominent reason for this misconception has been doctors' respected "professional" status as well as their traditional image of being strictly "private practice."

Increasingly, doctors are accepting full-time and part-time salaried positions in hospitals, medical and dental schools and HMOs. With the growing intrusion of third parties, such as health-insurance companies, hospitals and government, is there any doctor who can truthfully say that he or she and all his or her patients still enjoy a strictly two-party, completely confidential doctor-patient relationship?

The merits and drawbacks of changing the present system of health-care delivery will continue to be debated. In the heated rhetoric about health-care "rights" (right of consumer to participate and even control, right of government to inspect and regulate, right of each citizen to quality health care) what has been overlooked is the right of doctors to have the final determination in all facets of medical practice that affect the health and well-being of patients.

Under *any* health-care delivery system, if a patient is to receive the best care available, only the doctor—by virtue of education, skill and experience—can practice his or her profession. Computers do not practice medicine. Government, health-insurance companies, hospitals, nurses, assistants and all categories of ancillary personnel may aid doctors, but if they are allowed to control or take over medicine, the idealists' dream of "high-quality health care for all" will never materialize.

Clearly, in the interest of protecting patients from forces—political, financial or otherwise—that would destroy quality health care, doctors must assert another of their rights. As the skilled dispensers of disease prevention and management, they have every ethical, moral, legal and human right (perhaps obligation rather than right would be more appropriate) to fight for how their skills can be utilized most effectively.

This advocacy on behalf of patients and doctors in dealing with hospitals, health-insurance companies and other third parties is called "bargaining" in labor jargon. If two, four, five or 500,000 physicians band together and demand input into the rules, regulations and legislation that affect their professional lives, this activity is called "collective bargaining."

There can be no question of the right of doctors to bargain, individually or collectively. The only question is whether this right will be exercised fully before it is too late to prevent the abuses that have occurred in so many other countries from taking place here.

U.S. doctors and their patients have no such alternatives—there is nowhere else to go. The bargaining for quality health care, delivered in a safe environment, by properly paid professionals, must continue unimpeded in this country.

ACKNOWLEDGMENT

Dr. Liebowitz and Dr. Meyer wish to acknowledge the assistance of Maya Crone, Thomas Shpetner and Renee Campion in the research, coordination and writing of this chapter. Their contributions have been invaluable in this venture.

REFERENCES

1. Brooks TR: *Toil and Trouble: A History of American Labor,* ed 2. New York, Dell Publishing Co, 1971, p 59.
2. Sandrick K: Doctors turn to unions. *Private Pract,* November 39, 1985.
3. NLRB ruling clouds union participation. *Am Med News,* August 16, 1985.
4. Levit K, Cowan C: Business, households, and governments: Health care costs, 1990. *Health Care Financing Review* 13:83, 1991.
5. Peden E, Lee M: Output and inflation components of medical care and other spending changes. *Health Care Financing Review* 13:75, 1991.
6. Marcus S: Trade unionism for doctors: An idea whose time has come. *N Engl J Med* 311:1508–1511, 1984.
7. Smolowe J: 2 Pediatric units in Harlem given reprieve by city. *The New York Times,* July 24, 1980.
8. Weissenstein J: Studies show woe in primary-care supply. *Modern Healthcare,* October 12, 12, 1992.

CHAPTER 2

THE PUBLIC-SPIRITED PHYSICIAN

David J. Brailer

Active involvement of physicians in public affairs draws little attention. Indeed, the traditional view of physicians focuses largely on their role in patient care. The doctor-patient relationship has been portrayed by numerous authors,[1-3] by painters ranging from Daumier in the 1850s to Rockwell and even by popular television shows, such as "Ben Casey," "Marcus Welby" and "St. Elsewhere." Rarely shown or described, however, is the other side of physicianhood, the public spirit of physicians. From the time of Hippocrates, as described in his First Aphorism, the responsibility of physicians was viewed to extend beyond patient care to the community and society at large. This public-mindedness still exists, benefiting both ill and healthy persons and influencing numerous local, state and federal policies. It is the contemporary physician's expression of leadership.

Patient care is directly supported by physicians' interest in the general public. It is clear that medicine is different from other professions because its subject matter is human life. More importantly, however, medicine is unlike traditional service economies, in which highly informed buyers choose for themselves in a free market of sellers. In medicine, patients passively consume services provided by physicians or other health-care professionals. Physicians cannot enter the medical marketplace without the haunting potential for conflict of interest and self-dealing. Therefore, physicians must approach their market in a different manner from other professionals. That difference is public-mindedness.

This chapter is written both for physicians and medical students who believe in public service and for those who do not. "Public-spirited physicians" will use this chapter as a guide to public service, including professional careers and such part-time activities as organized medicine. For them, it will be a call to arms. Conversely, traditional patient-care physicians, or medical students or residents planning to enter private practice, will be introduced to the methods and components of public service by this chapter. They will find tolerance for, if not understanding of, the larger context of medicine. For all physicians and medical students, this chapter will complement other chapters in the book by reasserting the need for public service despite changes in the health-care delivery system, such as corporatization and competition. It strives to close the gap between public affairs and patient care.

Historical Considerations

More than a century ago, pathologist Rudolph Virchow gave the cardinal challenge of social leadership to physicians: ". . . if medicine is the science of the healthy as well as of the ill human being (as it ought to be), what other science is better suited to propose laws as the basis of the social structure. . . ."[4] Virchow was indeed a gifted futurist, but only for the distant future; the years following his admonition were grievous for physicians. Many physicians of his time were seduced by or became purveyors of turn-of-the-century nostrums; "quacks" were rampant. Other physicians died in and were distracted by wars and civil strife. Health and social concerns were unheard of as policy agendas during the economic upheaval and industrial explosion of the nineteenth and early twentieth centuries. In fact, by giving physicians the mandate to regulate themselves in the late 1800s, society isolated them from public affairs. That isolation continues today.

The prospect of imminent health reform necessitates a reexamination of the relationship between physicians and society. Few people are unaware of the dramatic change in the professional and personal lives of physicians since 1963, when Medicare took its roots. The complex dynamics of these changes have been tirelessly documented. Paul Starr, in his landmark book, *The Social Transformation of American Medicine,*[5] revolutionized the way medicine is viewed as a social institution by all people, including physicians. Early visionary accounts[3,6] of the extensive change facing professional practices still ring true today. There is no absence of evidence proving the changing role of physicians as professional and economic entities. Few writers, however, have addressed the equally extensive change in the roles of physicians as social leaders.

Physicians have been active leaders in American social and political affairs since Colonial times. In recent decades, however, the number of physicians holding congressional and gubernatorial offices has fallen substantially.[7] Beyond elected office, physicians' involvement in local charities and municipal activities was jealously sought in the past. More well educated and rational than most people, and acting frequently from professionally borne human compassion, physicians enjoyed a respect in social settings matched only by their autonomy in medical practice—they were arbiters, judges and sage advisers. However, soon-to-be-adopted landmark legislation—Medicare—permanently altered the course of medicine, and with it the role of physicians in society.

Medicare, although originally vigorously opposed by physicians and organized medicine, was an economic windfall. It was a transfer of wealth, in the form of health-care benefits, from thriving workers to the poor elderly. A new, less healthy segment of the population had access to physicians and made extensive use of health care. Unable to keep up with high and growing demand for their services, physicians fell quickly into relative undersupply. Perhaps driven by high educational debts, physicians aggressively cared for underprivileged and elderly patients and enjoyed the financial rewards that Medicare policies were intended to provide. Medicare's tax-subsidized payments also stimulated rapid advances in run-away medical technology, allowing physicians to do more for patients than ever before. As a result, physicians worked unprecedented long hours, leaving less time in their schedules for civic and individual political activities. Perhaps physicians were originally correct in opposing Medicare: Current negative public attitudes about physicians and harsh public policies concerning health care may have resulted from the social abrogation and economic fulfillment brought on by that law.

Present Decisions, Future Challenges

In a time of health care crisis, physicians may once again be tapped for involvement in public service. What is the current state of physicians' leadership? Transition in the life-styles and work ethics of young physicians, the presence of formerly unforeseen risks in medical practice[8] and renewed social conservatism permit and encourage physicians to regain their social callings. Revolutions in health-care reimbursement and the introduction of managed care are changing the doctor-patient relationship and may rekindle the public spirit of physicians who seek to save that relationship. However, can physicians return to formerly held levels of influence and be balanced, enlightened leaders?

The essence of their leadership is the challenge, unchanged in a century, for all physicians to work for the collective benefit of society as vigorously as they do for the individuals who constitute it. There is a special calling as well for a select few physicians to become full-time leaders and managers. Such physicians will be able to promote the public health socially, rather than clinically or biologically. They will work with corporate physician-executives in the health-care industrial complex.[9] They will be the torchbearers for all other physicians.

The leadership of physicians is expressed in two ways. Many physicians and medical students, interested exclusively in public health and health policy, enter organized medicine to deliberate among physicians. Other physicians, of more secular intentions, enter general politics or civic affairs to influence broader issues within society. Both organized medical activism and civic activism are legitimate forms of leadership by physicians.

This chapter is divided into two major sections. The first section, "Physicians in Public Service," is about just that: public service. Within it, running for public office and professional careers in public service are discussed. The second section, "Organizational Physicians," is about organized medicine, the most common outlet for public service that physicians choose. It focuses on the dramatically changing roles and functions of organized medicine and the new opportunities for young physicians created by this transition. Emphasis is placed on understanding the process of involvement in public affairs, the benefits to be gained from investment of time in such activities and the pitfalls that have troubled many physicians in the past. The chapter closes with a discussion of political will, the single most important component in public policy.

THE PHYSICIAN IN PUBLIC SERVICE

The classical triad of medicine is patient care, teaching and research. One aspect of teaching that is often overlooked is public education—the instillation in the public of a belief in worldly values, aesthetics and social institutions. For physician leaders, it means involvement with the traditional leaders of society, such as elected officials, civil servants and other key public decision-makers. Public-minded physicians will be mediators for the interests of physicians and the public and will be immersed in political affairs; some such physicians may choose to become policymakers themselves. By their actions, physician leaders may redefine the medical triad as it is needed for a future in which social policy is of key importance to the public health.

The antecedent to involvement in political affairs is the belief that benefit can come from investment of time and effort. Regardless of one's political ideology on compelling issues, a belief in and understanding of the political process is the key to a successful outcome. The political system—whether federal, state or local, public or private—can be viewed as a conduit that is blind to the outcome. It is driven by a set of tacit rules that govern the interaction between individuals and groups with competing or even collinear goals. Knowledge of this system is a prerequisite for physicians in public service.

If each physician and medical student is not sensitive to the importance of policy debates that affect health care, these debates will not reflect the unique and valuable views of physicians. It is thus the responsibility of physicians to read daily newspapers, talk to local experts, form interest groups and take other steps to combat the ignorance that results from highly focused professional interests. More important in this context is that physician leaders must gain an in-depth understanding of issues to rally other physicians to higher levels of political effort.

Several skills benefit putative physician leaders. A habit of reading a national newspaper every day is the most accessible and least costly option; it is one goal for which all physicians should strive. Reading a respected newspaper, such as the *New York Times* or the *Washington Post,* or any other reputable periodical as critically as one would read a medical journal is a strong step towards political self-sufficiency. Further steps would include visits to state capitals or Washington, D.C., regular contact with elected officials, membership and active participation in organized medicine and supplementary readings. Many physicians are now choosing advanced education—in business, economics or policy—as a tool to maximize their contributions to policy debates.

Visits to state capitals and Washington, D.C. may be both foreboding and inspiring for beginners. While there, visits to policymakers and elected officials may be informative. Lobbying will instruct the uninitiated about the events and persons who form legislative and executive decisions. Interest groups other than physicians abound, each extolling their priorities with alacrity. The legitimate role of physicians is to provide credible information about the need for and human consequences of policies. Whether about drug-abuse laws, nutrition funding, humane fiscal policy or health-care financing, no lobbyist commands more respect from policymakers than a physician or a medical student who has taken time to become involved. The dynamics of lobbying go far beyond this chapter, but two essential points should be remembered by beginners.

First, policymaking is the result of interactions between persons who know and trust each other, despite having different opinions or vested interests. All such persons know that the next decision may team them with today's adversaries. Outsiders and newcomers must enter this group and become insiders themselves to become effective. Lobbying arduously for a single important issue—"This is the issue that was important enough for me to come to see you about, Senator"—is a common mistake that prevents otherwise reasonable persons from influencing policymaking decisions. It is a mistake commonly made by physicians. The solution is to visit state capitals and Washington, D.C., meeting all the appropriate persons—elected officials and key health (or other) policy makers—and to maintain contact with them occasionally. When an important issue surfaces, prepared lobbyists will be poised for action, for they, just as any trusted medical consultant, will be known to be thoughtful and fair. Many policymakers come to rely on such physician-advisers and frequently call on them for advice.

Second, physicians and medical students may encounter ambivalence or outright resistance when confronting policymakers and elected officials. It has been widely believed among such officials that physicians act generally out of self-interest. They expect physicians to lobby for higher payment schedules, malpractice relief or trade protection. These issues may well be legitimate and ones in which physicians should be interested. Policymakers, however, who frequently communicate with businessmen and employers who are strapped by health-care costs, believe that physicians' incomes are too high and that physicians are simply greedy in asking for more economic support. One solution to this problem, as espoused earlier, is for physicians to become known to officials and to let them understand the practice of medicine before any issue of substance arises. Another solution is to discuss both public-health issues and inevitable economic issues with policymakers.

Organized medicine has an important role in representing professional aspects of medicine, but physicians cannot rely on mediation for resolving important health-care issues. Organized medicine's credibility emanates from the physicians for whom it directly speaks. The key steps to success in policy circles are belief in the process, desire for an outcome and direct, active involvement. These virtues have seen many difficult issues through to fruition.

The Physician Candidate

A small number of practicing physicians, residents or medical students choose full-time public service. For such persons, the oversupply of physicians provides a comfortable release from traditional medical obligations in favor of broader public service. Some analysts speculate that current advances in the health-care delivery system are as important to the public as was basic-science research during the 1970s. Physician leaders will gain credibility for their bold actions if they enter full-time public service to bring about change.

Many physicians will continue, as they have in the past, to work as analysts or managers of health-care delivery organizations or insurance companies; a few other physicians will have a higher calling. Some such physicians will become health-care delivery analysts and researchers in government and academia. Other such physicians—the ones who will make a difference—will "throw their hats in the ring" and become candidates for public office. Perhaps someday, the chief executive will be addressed as "Dr. President."

Young physicians can train early to become elected officials. One must first know how to get elected and then what to do when in office. Medical students and residents will find organized medicine a fertile training ground for cultivating political gamesmanship. Otherwise, local student-body activities and house-officer organizations are less stringent but, nonetheless, available practice fields. Role models for shaping oneself as a full-time physician and public servant are lacking.

Physicians who enter the political arena must begin early and expect few results for several years. Some political-action committees sentimental to physicians unofficially acknowledge that they frequently do not support physicians for public office. Many physicians, they charge, over-confidently run for Congress or governor as a first office and are unabash-edly slaughtered at the polls. Physicians must follow the same rules of the game as other nascent politicians—work hard, start small and carry victories forward. Laying groundwork cannot be emphasized enough for physician candidates, particularly because they will likely not give up clinical practices during the early years of stumping.

Physician candidates will be at their best when their races are the end point of years of preparation. Some physicians will call on organized medicine to support their candidacies. Such physicians will be best ad-vised to have been supportive of organized medicine prior to solicitations. Physicians who are elected to representative bodies, particularly Con-gress, will find that they are generally treated as nonphysicians by most people (including fellow physicians and members of medical organiza-tions). Physicians in such capacities will usually not be called on for their expertise in medical practice; no special preference will be given to seat them on health committees. They will be expected to be conversant with numerous issues outside health care and medicine. On health-related is-sues, organized medicine, speaking from the collective voices of many physicians, will try to sway physician leaders as expert policymakers. Clearly physician candidates have much to do in preparation for their role as public servants.

Physician Civil Servants

Physicians who seek full-time public service without the distraction of elected office may choose to work in voluntary activities, such as community committees or charitable organizations. Others may elect to serve in the capacity of a federal or state executive. Physicians who enter full-time public service, unlike physician candidates or voluntary civil servants, will be expected to focus nearly exclusively on health care.

There are numerous opportunities for physician-policy analysts. Health care is a costly, economically complex activity, and its develop-ment and coordination require informed administration. As changes in the health-care marketplace occur with increasing rapidity, the need for policy development will increase. Physicians who are committed to pub-lic service will work with their counterparts in the private sectors, physi-cian-executives,[9] in managing the social side of the medical-industrial complex. Some physicians seek advanced research and analysis skills to deal with the complex issues on either side.

Public-oriented physicians will find a growing need for their direct involvement as candidates for office or as full-time civil servants. There are clearly several roads that they can travel toward important positions in public service. Physician leaders will not likely plan to pursue elected office or full-time public service but by interest and ability will find oppor-tunities numerous and compelling. Their highest service to patients, fellow physicians and the public is to follow their yearning and enter an undersupplied medical specialty, human development.

Final Notes on Public Service

Physicians can no longer expect continued goodwill from American society. That has been depleted by two decades of extraction from society by physicians without commensurate returns. Physicians in the past followed the incentives offered by public policies, but the near future will bring much more stringent controls, which further erode physician professionalism. This will change only if complacency is edged out by visionary opportunism, and physician activism is reborn.

Employed physicians may be best poised to follow alternative pathways that lead to public service. Reason and empiric data confirm that direct, fixed-salary employment reduces physicians' working hours and frees them from the administrative burdens of solo practice. More importantly, however, a new kind of physician is being cultivated: one who sees reduction rather than expansion in health care, one who is reorienting toward the public. This environment will clearly not turn every physician into an activist and a leader. Practicing physicians will, however, quickly grow supportive of physicians who surface as leaders. The professional flexibility of employed physicians may allow them to become the vanguard of politically active physicians.

Physicians have a special contribution to make to the deliberations in which they participate. Good judgment, thoughtfulness, impartiality and many other virtues lacking in most public proceedings are the products of clinical training. Likewise, critical analysis and rationality, the results of good education and professional discipline, are desirable characteristics of public policymakers. Physicians are, in fact, an important public resource, as clinicians and leaders.

Public-spirited physicians will encounter laymen who have not had the rigorous training or the imperative of physicians. Such persons constitute the political world that we prefer to ignore. In aggressively countering them, physicians will learn their most important skill: the balance of substance and style. There is no doubt that a physician's education is steeped in substance, but style—conversational ease, poise and appropriateness to surroundings—is often lacking. Although physicians serve society by investing time in public service, they can be effective only by being part of society's leadership. This is the only conduit through which the abilities of physicians can be manifest as impartial policy.

THE ORGANIZATIONAL PHYSICIAN

Involvement in organized medicine is the expression of public service that many physicians choose. Called the "federation" to insiders, it has been the fabric of medicine for most of the twentieth century. It is not just the American Medical Association (AMA), the American College of Surgeons, the local county or state medical society or any highly differentiated research or specialty society, but *all* medical organizations, working together within a vast network of members, staffs and competing priorities. Its influence affects decisions of state, local or the federal government, medical schools and teaching hospitals, foundations and universities, journalists and, of greater consequence, practicing physicians. Use of heroin for relief of pain in terminally ill patients, payment for physicians' services, restrictions on tobacco advertising and funding for graduate medical education are a few of the recent public-policy issues that have been woven in the "house of medicine."

Organized medicine has been in existence for more than 150 years; it entered its modern phase about 1900. At that time, the power of the elite scientists running the AMA, one of the few national medical organizations then, was consolidated, and organized medicine began growing and has not stopped growing since. One of the events that resulted in that consolidation of authority over the profession was brought about by the Carnegie Foundation, which studied the medical profession and medical education in unprecedented detail and produced the Flexner Report. Although that report is still both praised and criticized,[10] it unquestionably changed a fragmented, ineffective organization into the omniscient oligarchy that we currently know. Many other changes have ensued since that time. To name a few, medical education has become sophisticated and systematized; equitable-access ("health care is a right") legislation, such as the Hill-Burton Act, community health centers and Medicare have been adopted; technology has proliferated; and alternative health-care delivery systems have become commonplace. As medicine changed, an internal fabric that went beyond managerial lines, organizational boundaries and provincial interests to coordinate growth and change was needed. Organized medicine's course was set.

Organized medicine is a leviathan; more than 450,000 physicians belong to one or more of the several dozen component organizations. Although attitudinal surveys show that many physicians do not understand or agree with every activity of organized medicine, they support its operation. Dues paid to the organizations amount to hundreds of millions of dollars per year. This money is used to hire and support the activities of staff members who develop policies that guide clinicians, publish scientific articles, lobby policymakers and, of course, solicit new members. Nondues income—from advertisements, investments, endowments and for-profit activities conducted outside the nonprofit corporate veil—supplements the activities of the organizations. Organized medicine also raises substantial political action committee (PAC) funds; medical PACs were the second largest contributor in the 1992 Presidential election. Staff members of medical societies—specialty, local, county, state and national—number in the thousands.

Committed leaders, talented staff resources, finances and an important product—the delivery of health care to the citizens of the United States—carried organized medicine and U.S. physicians to historically unparalleled heights of income, prestige and autonomy. However, some physicians say that organized medicine is an anachronism, that, in a time of pluralism in health policy, autocratic style and power-brokering are useless; organized medicine has no future.

Other physicians say the future of organized medicine may not be so bleak. Many physicians believe that organized medicine remains resourceful, waiting for the proper time to strike, as it has in the past. For instance, the formation of Blue Cross can be traced to actions taken decades ago by the American Hospital Association, California Medical Association, Oregon State Medical Association and AMA.[11] Although originally intended to protect the physicians' market from outside control (which was introduced in the form of primitive employer preferred-provider organizations), the market power and coverage benefits of the Blue Cross/Blue Shield plan still have a strong impact on the health-care marketplace. If organized medicine takes such bold steps in the current environment, it could easily resume its position of domination.

If doomsayers are wrong and organized medicine survives, its form will undoubtedly change. The federation has been unquestionably weakened by internal conflict, power changes and waning influence in Washington, D.C. It appears that a new guard of medical leaders is taking its place. One organization in particular, the American College of Physicians, has been among the first to change its chief executive from a well-respected academic physician to an aggressive physician-manager, John Ball.

> John Ball was the first graduate from Duke University's conjoined physician-attorney program. When he graduated with both degrees, Ball, a grinning Southern gentleman, entered residency at Duke University Medical Center and became Board certified in internal medicine and was later a Robert Wood Johnson Clinical Scholar at Johns Hopkins University. After a brief stint with the federal Office of Technology Assessment, he joined the staff of the American College of Physicians, directing its then-new Washington, D.C. office. He proved himself to be a thinker and a clever strategist, someone with ability and style. He became executive vice-president of the American College of Physicians in midsummer 1986, a post he currently holds. Ball has become widely known and respected for leading physicians toward cooperative relations with employers, insurers and the federal government.

Young Physicians and Organized Medicine
Young physicians have not long been drawn to, or welcomed at, the tables of organized medicine. Medical students in particular have found difficulty in breaking ranks and influencing the decisions of the

AMA, for example. Medical students, according to lore, are not vested physicians and, as such, should not be given fiduciary responsibility for making decisions that affect the practice of medicine. Nor should they be involved in passing judgment on physicians because they have not been in clinical practice. Both of these arguments were, and still are, reasonable. As late as the 1950s, organized medicine was the sole regulator of the practice of medicine; only members could gain hospital privileges. The policy of the AMA then was commensurate with the health-care policy of the U.S. government. Over the past two decades, direct authority of organized medicine over health-care policy has been supplanted by federal authority and, to a lesser extent, by state policies. As the impact of the decisions of organized medicine diminished, opportunities for medical students grew. By the late 1960s, medical students had gained a solid foothold in organized medicine.

The "erosion of professional autonomy"[5] was not the sole factor that prompted organized medicine to yield to medical students. When practicing physicians were obliged to be members of organized medicine, membership penetration was obviously high. The AMA, for example, dropped from a 1950 market share exceeding 90 percent to a respectable 40 percent of all practicing physicians at present. This decline was accelerated by the proliferation of specialty societies, which competed with general organizations for dues dollars and interest. As membership dropped, medical students and residents were allowed to apply for membership. They brought with them some occasionally turbulent times.

The meetings of the AMA's house of delegates are majestic events. Filling a grand ballroom, flags, state-delegation tables, the press and hundreds of participants surround the speaker's platform, at which is seated the executive committee of the board of trustees. Eloquent speakers address the group, and hot debate fills the room. However, in New York City several years ago, the grandeur was interrupted by a march—across the speaker's platform. Medical students and residents, and even a few older physicians, captured the speaker's dais and burned their membership cards in protest;[12] there is still disagreement about *what* was being protested. As unrest in the general society eased, young members of organized medicine became more integrated and now can frequently be distinguished from their elders only by the absence of gray hair.

The entry of medical students and residents into organized medicine was certainly facilitated by the opening of organizational affairs to them. However, the changing attitudes of medical students and residents were probably of greater importance. In the past, a small number of physicians in training attended federation meetings, but most of them were oblivious to the proceedings or sneered at their conduct. They were not unlike most young antiestablishment adults of their time. It is reasonable to conclude that medical students and residents followed their peers in general society as they changed from liberal, antiorganizational militants to cooperative, integrated participants. In the AMA, medical students and residents now sit on the board of trustees and on all councils.*

Essentials of the "House of Medicine"

The federation is a loose conglomeration of medical organizations, each with its special interests and expertise. The cooperation that emanates from the federation is a result of extensive deliberations, deference and occasional infighting. Progress is made slowly and sometimes with difficulty. Each member organization must develop internal policy on a given issue—a process that can take years—before the federation will give full consideration to the issue. Some large organizations tend to dominate discussions, but smaller, more focused organizations occasionally are victorious. The process and players in organized medicine are not unlike those in the United Nations and its member countries.

Organizational Structure

There are four types of medical organization: general, specialty, geographic and restricted. General organizations are those that are open to all physicians—whether in research, practice or residency—and usually to medical students. The AMA, with 270,000 members, is a prime example of a general organization. Although perceived as having a predominance of private practitioners in its ranks, it attracts physicians from all specialties and practice settings. There are more medical students in the AMA than in any other medical organization; they comprise more than 10 percent of the AMA's membership.

There are more than 200 specialty societies, ranging from the well known (e.g., the American College of Surgeons) to the more obscure (e.g., the American Academy of Bariatric [Obesity] Physicians). Organizations exist for every imaginable specialty. Such organizations only need to incorporate and have members to form; some are surely bogus. Several specialty societies are highly respected by the press and the public; an example is the American Dermatologic Association ("Nine out of ten dermatologists recommend . . ."). Specialty organizations frequently ally themselves with such organizations as the American Cancer Society, the American Heart Association and the American Diabetes Association (so called disease-of-the-month-club organizations) to formulate public-oriented health-care recommendations. Scientific proceedings are an important part of the life of specialty organizations.

Geographic divisions have given rise to many organizations. There

---

*The AMA has seven councils that advise the board of trustees and the house of delegates. The councils consist of long-range planning and development, medical service, scientific affairs, constitution and bylaws, legislation, medical education and ethical and judicial affairs. Medical students and residents are represented on all seven councils. A medical student and a resident were added to the council on ethical and judicial affairs in December 1986.

are medical societies in every state and in most countries that are affiliated with the AMA. Most state medical societies are members of one or more regional interest groups, which are alliances formed frequently for the promotion of political candidates in elections in organized medicine. Many specialty societies have regional or state districts; some have county units. Most medical student and resident organizations are divided into units on the basis of medical school and hospital, respectively. State units of organizations, whether specialty or general, work together and with other state organizations on political agendas, such as with state legislatures, for business management and to elect members from their states to offices in national organizations. Geographic units are financially, politically and philosophically distinct from their national mother organizations. This situation multiplies by 50 the number of interested parties that are involved in policy-making decisions.

Membership in some organizations is restricted, but not on the basis of specialty or geographic area. Medical student, resident and women's organizations have obvious membership restrictions. Other organizations with membership restrictions include those for foreign medical graduates (a powerful faction within organized medicine), physician-attorneys, medical-society executives (nonphysicians), physicians' wives and several organizations for physicians in research. Such organizations tend to be aloof from organizations in the mainstream of medicine. An example of such organizations is the American Medical Women's Association, which was formed during a time when the AMA would not allow women physicians to hold membership cards. Another interesting example is the American Medical Student Association, which split off from the AMA more than a decade ago, forming a sanctioned and funded autonomous organization. Two years after the American Medical Student Association was formed, several medical students approached the AMA to ask for membership, and the student business section (later to become the medical student section) came into being. In general, membership-restricted organizations have a legitimate purpose and serve their members and society well.

One aspect of the structure of organized medicine with which all participants should be familiar is the web of semi-independent organizations that surround the organized medicine federation. Semi-independent organizations were established out of necessity to provide apparently autonomous activities, such as hospital licensing, certification of graduate medical education, licensure of medical schools and physicians and peer review. In most instances, these organizations have representatives from the big three—the AMA, the American College of Surgeons and the Association of American Medical Colleges—and several representatives from other societies. Organizations such as the Joint Commission on the Accreditation of Health Care Organizations (JCAHCO) and the Accreditation Commission for Graduate Medical Education (ACGME) are derivations of organized medicine and other groups (e.g., hospitals). Many decisions that are made are not pro forma policy of the member organizations. This situation permits flexible formation of policies, and concentrates much authority in a few hands. The importance of the committees is often forgotten by persons who scrutinize or attempt to influence the behavior of organized medicine.

Policy Formation

Formation of policy by the federation is achieved through a complex interaction of organizational might, personalities, compromise and respect for tradition. In the AMA, for example, policy deliberations can be initiated by state components, specialty societies or the AMA's board of trustees, councils (introduced as reports) or staff (usually introduced through the board of trustees). Ideas undergo detailed research, and background materials are prepared. Many issues first come to the attention of the AMA's reference committees, where testimony is heard in an open forum, and finally end up in its house of delegates, where all physicians and all legitimate medical organizations are represented. Final decisions are implemented by the AMA's staff. It is indeed a complex process, usually lasting two years for a given issue.

Despite the complexity of the decision-making process in organized medicine and the many subtle variations that further complicate it, there are some characteristics that are important landmarks for beginners to observe. It is not true that one must be an old physician to be of great influence. It does help, however, to behave like one. Medical students, residents and young physicians frequently do not influence important issues for three reasons: their failure to give the required commitment of time, lack of jurisdiction and inability to use their strength effectively. The most important of these reasons is the time commitment: issues move through organized medicine slowly because of the need for a consensus.

The first observations of organized medicine by beginners will be accompanied by surprise at the disdain for its slow progress toward policy decisions. Medical students or residents frequently matriculate and graduate from medical school or complete residency before a developing issue is resolved. Many of them leave in frustration after one or two years of seemingly fruitless effort. Medical students and residents who are particularly frustrated tend to be deeply involved in one or two issues that they wish to see become policy. They frequently leave without success. Medical students and residents who quit have forgotten one key to long-term effectiveness: successful young physicians always begin by training other young physicians about issues that they believe to be important. Further, many experienced young participants in organized medicine develop several alternative methods by which they can implement their ideas. Alliances shift as frequently as issues, and determined young physicians are prepared for the changes that take place. Medical students and residents can be successful in influencing organized medicine if they commit themselves to being active participants in a lifelong endeavor.

The Changing Face of Organized Medicine

Traditionally, the AMA has been the center of organized medicine. Specialty societies, such as those discussed previously, strive to gain representation in the AMA's house of delegates to acquire access to the vast network of medical societies, associations and other organizations. The largest and most well financed of all the legitimate organizations, the AMA has undergone dramatic change during the past decade. Clues for future changes in the AMA, and for organized medicine in general, lie in a brief examination of recent changes in the AMA.

There was a time, the 1950s, when all physicians belonged to the AMA. The AMA unknowingly had a brilliant marketing ploy for membership: physicians had to be members to obtain admitting privileges at many hospitals. Early antitrust regulations loosened the AMA's grip on hospital staff membership. A series of popular liberalizing legislative decisions followed (many of which were vehemently opposed by the AMA:[13] at one point, actor Ronald Reagan was hired to promote public support of the AMA's actions). Some studies indicate that although the AMA maintained a conservative philosophy, it liberalized its thinking[14] in the early 1970s. For whatever reason, membership in the AMA fell, hitting a low point in the mid 1970s of 45 percent of the nation's physicians. The AMA has not recovered from this membership loss, and 1974–75 saw the AMA in crisis—the organization had to borrow millions of dollars to stay afloat. Inquiry panels pursued detailed investigations into the finances and operations of the AMA. Some physicians believe that this upheaval ended at the 1975 annual meeting, when the executive vice-president of the AMA and his heir apparent were overthrown on the 14th ballot by a little-known Texan, Jim Sammons. Sammons, the new executive vice-president, fired one fourth the AMA's staff members on the spot ("Black Friday" as it has come to be called) and began establishing a new political order. The centerpiece of that order was financial solvency into perpetuity.

Financial solvency took precedence over nearly all other goals. Dues were raised and, as expected, some members quit. The AMA refused to sell its stocks in tobacco companies because they were "good investments" (they were quietly liquidated shortly thereafter). Within a few years, all programs—international medicine, public-health issues and medical student support—had to be striving toward self-sufficiency; some programs are subsidized to this day, however. Many scientific activities of the AMA, including wet-bench research, drug analysis and scientific sessions at meetings of its house of delegates, were curtailed. Liquid investments and real estate were accumulated. The goal was apparent and remains unchanged: to make the AMA free of financial concerns. The ingenious financial buildup of the AMA will be legendary for decades, but it was only the first step of a master plan.

Membership marketing is a complex social, computer and business science. It is the key to the legitimacy and solvency of any organization. It has always been known that some physicians and medical students are philosophically opposed to joining any organization, the AMA in particular. Marketing experts believe that such physicians and medical students, who could comprise 20 percent of all physicians and medical students in the United States, will be attracted to membership by benefits that are unattainable elsewhere at the same price. This marketing strategy may be of great benefit, for it is believed that a number of the physicians and medical students who join for economic reasons will learn and support the mission of organized medicine. Another important consideration in relation to commercial membership benefits, including computer equipment, patient billing, credit cards, car rentals, investments and retirement plans, is that the AMA makes millions of dollars each year from them. High-finance activities have changed the orientation and abilities of organized medicine in ways that are of great importance to future physician leaders.

Staff members of organized medicine tend to be trained in public health, public policy and other social sciences. Hard-core business talent has until recently been noticeably absent. Management of profit-making ventures and the acquisition of multimillion dollar reserves over the past five years at the AMA has necessitated the hiring of business specialists. Their solutions to problems involving physicians' practices are business-oriented; likewise the policies they develop are business-oriented. The impact of their thinking will be a dramatic shift in the way organized medicine serves the needs of physicians in the United States. Instead of developing lame-model legislation for a public-health problem, or lobbying in Washington, D.C. for cost-of-living increases in physicians' fee schedules, innovative, direct business solutions are being developed. Such solutions may, for example, link private physicians into an independent-practice association managed by the federation. Another example of the unique view of business specialists is that rather than constantly shore up Medicare funds, they recommend the creation of health-care individual retirement accounts into which people would accumulate savings for retirement health care. Such dramatic departures from traditional approaches could hold the key to a new role for organized medicine. Shedding its past role as a passive mediator for other national organizations, other professions and government, organized medicine is poised to be an aggressive trade organization for, and business partner with, physicians. The future will see a new role for organized medicine as a network tying together financial resources and market power rather than spreading political philosophy and professional development.

An important question for future physician leaders to ask is what long-term effect the transition to the business imperative will have on the practice of medicine. Social dynamics indicate that the current state of medical practice in the United States is an equilibrium of complex, opposing forces. If organized medicine changes, secondary changes will occur, resulting in a new equilibrium point. Some people predict the following scenario. The market share for physicians is declining as other health-care professionals gain a larger share each year. Physicians in increasing numbers are becoming employees of a shrinking number of employers. Organized medicine is evolving into a trade-support group and is creating a financial link between tens of thousands of otherwise independent physicians. Simply stated, a consolidation of the physician market is occurring. Organized medicine's primary role after this consolidation will be to expand the profession's total market share and to act as an advocate for its members with their employers. It will be, in other words, a union (see Chapter 1).

If organized medicine is functionally a union in the future, will physicians maintain credibility with the public and with policymakers to effect change on such issues as public safety, preventive medicine, scientific policy and access to care? Some physicians argue that their influence has already begun to wane—physicians have had diminishing success in influencing Congress on such key issues.

The reality of the influence of organized medicine is that physicians are credible when they lobby for things of benefit to their patients but not when they lobby in their own behalf. Physicians, like any other component of the economy, know their profession well and, in working hard at it, believe that better remuneration is always in order. Regardless of if this is true, clinical expertise does not constitute expertise in payment for health-care services or in alternative delivery systems. Physicians' concerns, some people say, should not be the basis of all public policy relating to health care. Likewise, expertise in public finance does not bestow knowledge of appropriate patient-care protocols or public health on policymakers. A sharing should be effected between physicians and society as represented by elected officials. Organized medicine's greatest impact is achieved in mediating for physicians on *appropriate* issues.

As public sentiment reverses and physicians come into favor once again, exciting new policy opportunities will open. New policy ground is now being broken within organized medicine; its business side is not the only scion of change. Organized medicine has rediscovered the American public, has redirected many activities away from policymaking bodies toward television promotion and public-relations ventures. Medical students and young physicians who have entered practice during this stale period in organized medicine's public-relations image must strive to reacquaint themselves with the public.

Making Organized Medicine Work for You

The challenge for medical students, residents and young physicians is clear. Each must become involved in organized medicine in some comfortable way. Physician leaders, however, have greater challenges: not only to become involved and get others involved but, more importantly, to ensure that thoughtful, socially productive actions emanate from organized medicine. Regardless of whether a medical student or resident is destined to become a leader or a supporter, the first step is the same—getting involved.

Medical students and young physicians will enter a world of older men and women who are dramatically different in style, stature and outlook. Many of them will encounter deans or residency program directors in political settings through organized medicine. It is important that all medical students and young physicians remember that, in health-care politics and in policy debates, all physicians are peers, regardless of age or station.

The bond that allows the development of policy is trust. Affecting organized medicine requires beginners to master details of policies, bylaws and strategy and, more importantly, to identify important elements in discussions and debates. The guidelines set forth in the form of bylaws and conventions inculcate trust among their users. Young physicians will benefit greatly by working and learning alongside elder statesman physicians; such physicians should be sought out. One can only shape the outcome of policy in organized medicine as a trusted insider, regardless of one's view of an issue.

Medical Students

Medical students have numerous organizations from which to choose to express their activism. Each organization has a peculiar history and role in representing the ideologies, nationalities or special needs of medical students. Membership in one or more of these organizations should be a goal for every medical student. Respected organizations for medical students include the following:

Medical Student Section of the AMA
American Medical Student Association
Organization of Student Representatives of the Association of
    American Medical Colleges
National Conference of Student Affiliate Members of the American Academy of Family Practitioners
Boricua National Medical Association
Student National Medical Association
American Medical Women's Association
Association of Native American Medical Students
Student Osteopathic Medical Association

Some of the preceding organizations work within their respective mother groups; other organizations are autonomous entities. All of them are financed in whole or in part by dues from medical students, placing them in direct competition for dues dollars. The elected officials of these organizations meet three times a year in the Consortium of Medical Student Organizations, a loosely organized discussion group.

The consortium was an early attempt to consolidate medical student organizations by providing a forum for regular communication. Some medical students believe that the consortium should serve medical students throughout the country by becoming an energetic activist organization. This view was held by a majority of participating leaders, for example, when the consortium attempted to produce a joint statement about the need for guaranteed student loans before an important congressional vote was to take place. The effort went awash, and Congress voted for the measure despite the absence of advice from medical students. (It is noteworthy that the AMA's medical student section conducted a nationwide letter-writing campaign asking all medical students to write to their congressmen to garner their support for guaranteed student loans.) If the situation within the consortium does not change, its future will be short-lived.

For medical students who will not commit the time to become leaders of their national organizations, there are other options. Whereas the number of national leaders is expectedly limited, other positions are bountiful. Nationally, the AMA's medical student and resident physicians sections, the American Medical Student Association, the American Academy of Family Practitioners, the Organization of Student Representatives and many other organizations have annual or biennial national meetings to which students may, and should, come. Officially, medical students may be elected to represent a school or a region (each organization has separate rules). Attendance at national meetings, whether as elected representatives or as observers, is educational and interesting and frequently leads to further involvement. Only general organizations offer leadership positions for medical students; specialty societies rarely allow medical students to become involved to this extent.

Local or state activity is available through the AMA's federation. Each state has a medical society, and most countries have component chapters. Nearly all state and county medical societies welcome medical students. Many such societies have positions on councils or committees available to medical students. Outside the traditional federation, the American Medical Student Association has regional divisions and strong school affiliates that are also fulfilling for some medical students. Many high-quality projects are conducted each year by local chapters of the American Medical Student Association. Regardless of the size or style of an organization, a small investment of time and talent will return much in training, camaraderie and satisfaction for most medical students.

Resident Physicians

Resident physicians and young practicing physicians have far fewer opportunities for activism than medical students. Residents have had a special section in the AMA (the resident physicians section) since the mid-1970s. The American College of Physicians makes associate membership available to some residents entering internal medicine and associated fields. In fact, associate members comprise the largest percentage of its membership. Few other general organizations have sanctioned involvement by residents, although many organizations have considered doing so. Residents are caught between medical students, for whom membership is considered gratuitous by many organizations, and young practicing physicians, for whom gaining leadership footholds in many organizations has been difficult. Residents and young physicians have a "separate but equal" status that keeps them on the periphery of effectiveness but, as some of them have observed, "within watch." Breaking these barriers is an important goal for future residents and young physicians.

Specialty societies have relatively few resident members. Such societies have fallen far behind general organizations in attracting residents and giving them key positions of influence. Some highly progressive organizations, such as the American Society of Internal Medicine, have taken initial steps toward involving residents. The society opened its resident section in December 1986.

Membership in specialty societies will become an important prerequisite for professional affiliation for residents in the future. Specialty societies have always been more tightly knit and focused than general organizations. Unlike the mosaic of interests that constitute general organizations, specialty societies are the strongholds of discrete professions with trade-oriented agendas. One tacit item on their agendas, unfortunately, is protection of specialties from oversupply. This objective may explain the halfhearted efforts of specialty societies to attract resident members. Economic upheaval in specialties will force specialty societies to rely on resident members for size and future growth, if for no other reason. Unprecedented membership opportunities will open in specialty societies in the future.

Final Notes on Organized Medicine

Beginners becoming involved in organized medicine should come to early terms with a paradox: it is a great bastion of a powerful profession—the mightiest lobbying force in the United States, some people say—and at the same time a weak proprietor of divergent interests. There is no question that beginners have much to learn from organized medicine. Many leaders in medicine and health-care policy began their careers in organized medicine. The social context and historical perspective of medicine will become evident to medical students, residents and young physicians as they fully assume their professional charge by becoming involved. Other skills, such as leadership development and policy analysis, can be learned as well. However, beginners must know the limits of organized medicine and should learn to employ its assets as one would any tool.

The policies of organized medicine represent the least common denominator of physicians' opinions and expectations. A nagging feature of organized medicine is its paternalistic treatment of physicians and medical students who are not involved. If no other reason is persuasive, being involved in organized medicine to prevent being spoken for should be incentive enough. The birth of self-determination—as medicine becomes fragmented in the health-care industrial complex—will alter permanently the conduct of affairs of organized medicine and, therefore, its content and outcome.

Organized medicine is anachronistic in current society, not for what it is or who it represents but for its central control of the decision-making process. It will eventually be forced to open itself to the numerous stakeholders in medicine. Young physicians and physicians in training are stakeholders and are obliged to be present when change occurs, or, moreover, to ensure that it does. Future physician leaders must be prepared to respond to this challenge. Their response will determine the future of organized medicine and, in large part, the practice of medicine in the turbulent environment of the future.

THE LESSON OF POLITICAL WILL

Everett McKinley Dirksen, the great statesman for whom the U.S. Senate office building is named, turned to the Senate galleries as he voted for the Civil Rights Act after a series of negative votes and recanted, quoting Victor Hugo, "Nothing is as powerful as an idea whose time has come." For today's young physicians, residents and medical students, the time has come. Physicians have fallen from the pedestal where they had been placed by an American public that romanticized little-known technology and desired a magnificent health-care system. The labor of physicians to build that health-care dream has placed them in professional chaos and at odds with the public, the press and policymakers. Young physicians are now being tapped by older physicians and the public to lead the repositioning of physicians in society and to restore a balance in health care. Young physicians must be prepared for that challenge.

The lesson that Senator Dirksen invoked as he broke the dam of social consciousness in 1961 was the lesson of political will. This is a lesson which must be mastered by all physicians, particularly those just entering practice. Physicians must believe that legislative victories— generous payment systems for their services, for example—inevitably erode with the political tide or the downturn of popularity ratings. Stability is derived only from the social value of medicine, not from short-lived windfalls. All of medicine's stakeholders—physicians, the public, policy-makers, employers and many others—must be involved in open deliberations about health: physicians are only one component of America's pluralistic health-care system. Physicians are the center of health care, however, and that gives them special responsibility.

Medicine is clearly made different from other professions by its very subject matter—human life. Economically speaking, however, medicine is unlike traditional service professions, in which highly informed buyers choose for themselves in a free market of sellers. In medicine, patients passively consume services provided by a physician or other licensed health professionals. Physicians cannot enter the medical marketplace—alone or as a profession—without the haunting potential for conflict of interest and self-dealing. Therefore, physicians must approach their market differently than other professionals. That difference is public-mindedness.

The public has a legitimate role in the macroallocation of resources into medicine. Physicians, facing declining control over the microallocation of resources—how to care for a given patient, for example—are fully acquainted with the resolve of a society determined to be a stakeholder in health-care deliberations. Public officials have the will to change the course of medicine and shall do so with or without medical advice. This challenge necessitates change among physicians. Young physicians must consider themselves leaders of this change because of its implications for the future of health care and the medical profession.

Rudolph Virchow admonished young physicians by claiming that "medicine is a social science in its very bone and marrow." Perhaps not since that time, when nature-philosophy in medical thought was being replaced by experimental science, have his lessons been important to physicians more than today. Virchow's marriage of statesmanship with medical practice and research has affected many facets of modern medicine and public health, and should be the mold in which the professional development of contemporary physicians is cast. Society is anxious for young physicians to regain the calling of public leadership.

Virchow above all things taught the larger role and responsibility of physicians. All young physicians must always demonstrate excellence in their primary skill, caring for patients, and should always be concerned with the social context of that care. Some will step beyond their clinical roles to become mediators, and will be widely regarded as physician leaders. They will represent medicine in policy deliberations to balance current fiscal conservatism with human and social value. Society will quickly recognize and seek out the value a physician leader brings to his endeavors. Not all physicians will respond to this calling; not all should. All, however, will benefit by the outcome. Medicine itself will change by such efforts.

REFERENCES

1. Blum S: *The Doctor and His Patient.* New York, Russel Sage Foundation, 1963.
2. Mechanic D: *Medical Sociology.* New York, The Free Press, 1968, chap 5.
3. Fox R: *Experiments Perilous: Physicians and Patients Facing the Unknown.* Glencoe, Ill, The Free Press, 1959; Philadelphia, University of Pennsylvania Press, 1974 (paperback).
4. Virchow R: *Disease, Life, and Man,* Rather LJ (trans). New York, Collier Books, 1962.
5. Starr P: *The Social Transformation of American Medicine.* New York, Basic Books, 1982.
6. Stevens R: *American Medicine and the Public Interest.* New Haven, CT, Yale University Press, 1971.
7. Jameson MG: Physicians and American political leadership. *J Am Med Assoc* 249:929–930, 1983.
8. Brailer DJ, Nash DB: Uncertainty and the future of young physicians. *J Am Med Assoc* 256:3391–3392, 1986.
9. Hillman AL, Nash DB, Kissick WL, et al: Managing the medical-industrial complex. *N Engl J Med* 315:511–513, 1986.
10. Ludmerer K: *Learning to Heal: The Development of American Medical Education.* New York, Basic Books, 1985.
11. Rejda GE: *Principles of Insurance.* 2nd edition, chapter 2. Glenwood, CA, Scott Foresman & Co. 1986.
12. Campion FD: *The AMA and Health Policy Since 1940.* Chicago, Chicago Review Press, 1984.
13. Hume E: The AMA is laboring to regain dominance over nation's doctors. *The Wall Street Journal,* June 13, 1986.
14. National Center for Health Services Research: *Physicians View Social Change in Medicine.* PB86-174240, November 30, 1984.

CHAPTER 3

EDUCATING PHYSICIANS FOR THE TWENTY-FIRST CENTURY

James B. Couch

This chapter evaluates how adequately (or inadequately) the current educational system is preparing physicians for the unprecedented changes to be expected in how medicine will be practiced in the 1990s and early twenty-first century and provides suggestions for improvement. The chapter is intended for physicians and aspiring physicians at all levels of their preparatory and continuing training. It is directed especially toward innovative medical educators, deans, associate and assistant deans and admissions and curriculum-committee members intimately involved in selecting and preparing the next generation of physicians.

The first part of the chapter examines the traditional preparation of physicians to follow conventional career paths. The second part illustrates why, in light of current political and socioeconomic trends, this type of preparation is rapidly becoming obsolete. The third part outlines various proposals for appropriately responsive educational changes and curricular innovations to prepare the next generation of physicians for the rapidly emerging, new health-care system. Finally, the fourth part illustrates five types of physician that are evolving from this socioeconomic transformation in American medicine.

TRADITIONAL MEDICAL CAREER PATHS

Premedical Study

In the recent past, the route to becoming a physician was fairly well traveled. In general, persons who chose to pursue careers as physicians would make their decisions early in the educational process. Given the intense competition for medical-school admittance, this early self-selection process was borne of necessity. Taking a rigorous load of preparatory courses in the biologic, physical and chemical sciences in high school became a prerequisite for achieving a high enough cumulative premedical science grade-point average at a prestigious college or university for admission to a U.S. medical school. At the peak of the competition for medical-school admission in the 1970s, it was not unusual to see this degree of scientific preparation and competition traceable back to the junior-high and even grade-school level. Surely, this was the case in the private preparatory schools, especially for the fledgling students who were heirs to a multigenerational legacy of physicians from the same "prestigious institution."

Regardless of protestations to the contrary, the "bottom line" for medical school admittance was performance in the required premedical sciences and the science portion of the medical college admissions test (MCAT). Although medical school admissions committees looked favorably on "nonscience" majors, even a "budding da Vinci" would have had difficulty explaining away a C in organic chemistry at his interview.

In all fairness, there were attempts by some medical schools to liberalize their admissions procedures. Cooperative programs between medical schools and other schools within or outside universities were developed. A few such programs promoted "nontraditional" premedical students (usually postbaccalaureate students in nonscience fields wishing to fulfill the necessary premedical requirements).

Nevertheless, consistent with the presumed national health-manpower priorities of the 1970s, many cooperative programs became vehicles for condensing the time from high-school graduation to doctor of medicine degree to six and even five years. Although such "fast-track" programs were marketed as combining the "best attributes of a medical and liberal arts education," they had the effect of turning out an even greater supply of physicians in their early twenties with little world perspective beyond cadavers, petri dishes and pathologic "fascinomas." Moreover, the fast-track programs pushed the requisite medical career decision-making process even further back into the adolescent and preadolescent years for its eager aspirants.

Medical School

In most medical schools, the "rote memorization/regurgitation" pedagogy (which premedical students have down pat) serves students well during the first two years of formal medical training. Although several medical schools in the 1960s and 1970s experimented with innovative, condensed, organ systems-oriented and/or interdigitated curricula with early exposure to clinical medicine, the rapid (and vapid) assimilation/disgorgement methods have continued to constitute the predominant pedagogy during the basic-science years.

At the beginning of the third year, medical students trained in the traditional manner may respond to the change from academic to clinical medicine by falling into one of three reactive typologies:

1. Students who appropriately adjust by shifting their focus from that of primarily accumulating knowledge to that of selectively applying it to diagnose and manage disease;
2. Students who remain in the obsessive/compulsive academic mindset, regarding each new patient primarily as another experiment on whom to test the latest technology as part of an ongoing, randomized, double-blind clinical trial; or
3. Students who suffer a severe professional identity crisis, not being adequately prepared to follow the first path and unwilling, in good conscience, to follow the second path.

Students of this last typology have been the most severely shortchanged by the current medical education system. It is this large group of otherwise competent, caring and compassionate professionals who have become the most cynical and coldly clinical in their approach to patient care to cope emotionally.

With its current methods of selection, evaluation and promotion of students, basic science and clinical teachers, the current medical education system is perpetuating the following types of physicians, who will not fit into the health-care system of the twenty-first century:

1. Physicians who feel compelled to consume all available medical resources in diagnosing and managing disease;
2. Those who are technologically (rather than humanistically) oriented;
3. Those who are paternalistic (rather than participative) in the clinical treatment of patients;
4. Those who are oriented to diagnosing and managing disease, instead of teaching prevention; and
5. Those who cannot appreciate the socioeconomic and sociopolitical interactions that affect health-care delivery in the macrocosm of society, generally, and in the microcosm of individual patients, specifically.[1]

Lately, creation of such "misfit physicians" has become even more accentuated as growing competition for "desirable residency positions" has moved the senior year of medical school away from being a last chance to broaden medical-training experience to being a "preresidency warm-up." Medical schools are not nearly so much to blame as is the economically perverted reimbursement system of the past 28 years.

Residency and Fellowship Years

The postgraduate years, especially the first one, mark the transition from student to physician. Undergraduate medical education has been relegated, in many ways, to the status of a four-year preparatory course for the first year of residency. That first year is when student physicians suddenly find themselves exercising independent medical judgment and being held accountable for it, perhaps for the first time. Were undergraduate medical education currently structured to foster development of broad-minded, independent medical judgment, self-learning and an appreciation of the role of medicine in society as a whole,[2] this transitional year would not need to be nearly so traumatic. Unfortunately, currently, it still is.

Perhaps the most traumatic aspect of the first year of residency is the feeling of powerlessness: powerlessness to reverse the ravages of patients' advanced diseases and disorders; to meet impossible time constraints; to satisfy the expectations of superiors, family and friends; and to come to terms with one's inadequacies without losing the outwardly calm air of professional competence so painstakingly difficult to acquire. The continued division of resident physicians into the three typologies described may be accentuated during the first year of residency and then perpetuated into subsequent years of residency and fellowship training.

Transition to Practice

In the recent past, assuming that young physicians either avoided or escaped the typology of the professional identity crisis, they in the later years of residency may have begun to ask the proverbial question: "Is there life after residency?" The choices were fairly well defined as solo practice, small partnership and subspecialty training or a chief residency at an academic center.

During the later training years, to the extent that it was deemed necessary, residents would attempt to cultivate relationships with established practitioners with the hope of becoming either junior partners or, in some cases, of taking over the practices of retiring physicians. In lieu of these options, a resident generally would pursue some type of postresidency training (a fellowship, a chief residency or some research or academic post). Still, it seemed that there would always be a place for rugged individualists, who could hang out a shingle and strike out on their own. With hard work and perseverance, such physicians could build a medical practice beholden to nobody except themselves and patients. To many physicians, this kind of independence remained the ideal. Hopefully, the ideas presented throughout this book will clearly demonstrate that this is no longer a realistic scenario.

HEALTH-CARE MEGATRENDS

Changing Health-Policy Priorities

The clarion call emerging from the Great Society of Lyndon Johnson in the 1960s was to create the greatest, most technologically sophisticated health-care delivery system in the world, accessible to all without regard to ability to pay. The vehicles by which this goal would be accomplished were the Medicare and Medicaid programs. These programs were originally intended primarily as a form of social insurance for elderly and indigent. However, they rapidly became the financial engine behind an unprecedented growth in medical school number and size, hospital-bed number and capital expansion of facilities, graduate medical education offerings and program lengths and development of sophisticated medical technologies. It was not until the projection of near-term bankruptcy of the Medicare trust fund (publicized widely for the first time in the early 1980s) that a bipartisan consensus began to realize that something had to be done to curb this runaway growth. However, the difficult questions remainted: What? By whom? How fast? How much?

Since the widespread proliferation of health insurance in the 1930s and 1940s, accentuated in the 1960s by the Medicare and Medicaid programs, health-care services had become almost totally protected from the usual economic supply-and-demand cycles incumbent on all other major industries. The health-care industry became artificially supported by a change and cost-plus-based reimbursement system. This system prevented the usual incentives in the marketplace from working, where, to remain competitive, products had to be delivered with the highest possible value (i.e., the best quality at the lowest possible price). Rather than bring down the price or increase the quality of care, the more physicians and hospital beds there were in an area, the greater the per capita health-care expenditures that resulted.

This topsy-turvy world of medical economics has persisted into the 1980s and 1990s, resulting in an increase in the number of medical schools over a 30-year period from 94 to 127, an increase in the number of graduating physicians annually from 9,000 to almost 17,000 and a total bed complement among 6,000 U.S. hospitals of more than 1 million. The net effect of this unprecedented growth has been an increase in health-care expenditures from $40 billion in 1965 to a projected $900 billion in 1993. This represents an increase in the total U.S. gross national product from six percent to almost 15 percent. Moreover, total expenditures are now doubling every five years.

The industry is ripe for continued revolutionary change. It has been a combination of these building forces and outlandish expenditures, a dwindling Medicare trust fund, a growing federal deficit and trade imbalance, a postindustrial economy, a growing oversupply of specialist physicians and acute care hospital beds and the cost-cutting sociopolitical fervor of the Reagan and Bush administrations that has produced the initial policy changes that has provided the spark for this revolution, which is continuing to grow.

Hidden in a tax bill known as TEFRA (Tax Equity and Fiscal Responsibility Act of 1982) was an initial spark (known as prospective pricing systems [PPS], or diagnosis-related groups). This monumental change has affected the health-care industry more profoundly than anything else since the passage of Medicare.

With these profound changes in the public-sector method of health-care financing, the private sector (potentially an even greater source of financing and policy development) began to awaken from a long slumber. In 1984, for the first time, employers paid out more for their employees' health-benefits premiums than what they had left to return to their stockholders in the way of dividends. In addition, the mounting federal deficit, by increasing the value of the U.S. dollar, had made U.S. goods much less competitive relative to their Japanese and West European counterparts. The combination of these two forces (in no small part the result of rapidly escalating health-care expenditures) resulted in a lower corporate profit margin in 1985 than in any year since the worst recession after World War II hit its peak in 1982. This situation has been aggravated further during the economic downturn of the early 1990s.

In the early 1990s, virtually all chief executive officers of Fortune 500 companies have become intimately involved in the choice of alternative health-care delivery plans for their employees. The days of the open checkbook or charge-based reimbursement in such employee-benefits plans are over forever.

Changes in Medical-Manpower Requirements

There are currently approximately 230 physicians for every 100,000 population. By the year 2000, there should be at least 260. Several well-respected health-policy analysts, most notably Walter McClure, have postulated that the "ideal" number of physicians per 100,000 population in a modern postindustrial society is approximately 150. On the basis of this estimate, it is clear that society is already absorbing a 55 percent surplus of physicians. By the year 2000 this surplus will be approximately 75 percent. Even more importantly, in some of the nation's major metropolitan areas, there are already as many as 300 physicians for every 100,000 population, or twice the number needed according to McClure's projections.

This substantial physician surplus (especially of nonprimary care physicians) should be aggravated even further by the rapid move toward a market-driven, highly competitive health-care industry in which the bulk purchasers of services (i.e., the public and private sectors) may take economic advantage of the situation through competitive bidding practices. Health care had been largely protected from the effects of their largesse in the past through the artificial supports of charge and cost-plus-based reimbursement. Although burdensome, many regulations of health planning and fee schedules also protected the industry from the strong competitive forces ordinarily present in markedly oversupplied industries (e.g., the airlines and financial-services industries).

With the slow removal of these protective subsidies from a $900 billion per year industry, what has occurred in the past ten years in the airlines and financial-services industries should occur in the health-care industry in the 1990s. It is clear that the next generation of physicians must be trained to be much more business- and systems-oriented.

Changes in Health-Care Technology

The past 20 years have produced an unprecedented explosion in sophisticated medical technology. However, to an appreciable degree, this explosion has added greatly to the escalating costs of health care. The investment in sophisticated technologies (especially by academic medical centers) carries with it the expectation that such technologies will be utilized sufficiently so that they "pay for themselves." Whereas this expectation made sense and was easily satisfied in the bygone area of charge and cost-plus-based reimbursement, this will not be the case in the tightly managed, prospectively reimbursed, capitated-payment systems toward which this nation is rapidly moving.

Many health-care professionals (particularly at academic medical centers) claim that this new type of financing mechanism will adversely curtail development and implementation of new technologies. This is not necessarily the case. The technologies that will be employed in a more cost-conscious environment will be those that should decrease (rather than increase) health-care costs for diagnosis and management of disease.

Technologies that are only partially developed result in the greatest costs to the system. This is especially true of the super-specialized technologies, which (although permitting high-resolution diagnostic and therapeutic support) end up increasing costs by narrowing clinical perspective. Indeed, such "high-resolution" technologies (often used due to underlying anxiety or defensiveness of physicians) may trigger "clinical decision-making cascades" that result in million-dollar work-ups. Such work-ups may result in false leads; the performance of unnecessary, costly and hazardous invasive procedures; and continual delays and aggravation to patients and their families, the very results (i.e., patient harm or litigation) sought to be minimized by such ill-conceived, defensive medical practices in the first place.[3] Learning how to evaluate new technologies is an important skill (see Chapter 13).

Technologies that can be applied readily, cost-effectively and safely in the broadest possible context of health-care settings will be at the cutting edge of the health-care industry in the 1990s and early twenty-first century. Perhaps the best example of such a technology is the use of lasers. Lasers can already be applied cost-effectively and safely for diagnosis and management of a wide variety of diseases in at least 15 different medical and surgical specialties and subspecialties.[4] The research and development of new laser applications will be greatly facilitated by innovative ventures between academic medical centers and industry in the next five to ten years. However, the "warp and woof" of medical education must be changed dramatically, with considerably more attention being paid to outpatient practice before this tremendous uptapped potential may be realized.

Another area with overwhelming potential for transforming the delivery of health care is the use of computer-facilitated clinical decision support systems (see Chapter 11). As knowledge-based expert consulting systems in many specialties and subspecialties continue to evolve and be refined, the delivery of health care may be completely revolutionized. Already there are clinical decision support systems operating on a par with leading medical experts in terms of diagnostic accuracy and precision. As various statistical, rule-based and cognitive models continue to be refined into second- and third-generation systems, the potential for application on a widespread scale should begin to be realized.

Knowledge-based clinical decision support systems that are "downloadable" to personal computer systems are already commercially available. In a growing age of capitated-payment systems, the amount of specialist fees that could be saved through the judicious use of such a system by primary-care practitioners is incredible. Consider the following possible scenario.

A group of ten primary-care physicians who have formed an independent practice association (IPA) purchase a knowledge-based expert consulting system for $25,000. Assume that each physician in the IPA receives from its major payer $20 per patient per month and that half of this amount is earmarked for specialist care, with the balance returnable to each physician for funds not expended on specialty care.

By coupling patient information with an international medical-knowledge base, this system may suggest further historical questions to ask, records to check, prioritized diagnosis to rule out and specific tests and treatments with their costs and efficacies to try. Use of this system could dramatically reduce expenditures for consultations with specialists (often obtained because of anxiety or defensiveness, with their potentially adverse results discussed previously). By reducing the need for such consultations by 50 percent each month, for example, this IPA could pocket an additional $5 per patient per month from the payer. In this scenario, a capitated-patient base of only 6,000 patients (or 500 patients per practitioner per month) would be required for this expert consulting system to pay for itself in one month. Granted, the quality of the results of the system would have to be monitored closely. Nevertheless, there are already reports of the quality and cost-effectiveness of such systems rivaling those of leading medical experts, and it is probable that most payers will accept such a system readily on behalf of their patients by the late 1990s.

Changes in Patients' Expectations

Changes in patients' expectations are the final event (brought about in no small part by the "information age") that has contributed greatly to the health-care revolution of the 1980s and 1990s. In other words, the expectations of patients (consumers) have risen, as the result of increasing technologic sophistication in the health-care industry. Americans have become very "wellness-oriented" in the past few years. This movement has become a major thrust in corporate health-policy efforts to contain employee-benefits costs. Nutrition counseling, stop-smoking programs, fitness/aerobics sessions, weight-reduction seminars and other preventive programs have become integral parts of progressive companies.

As health plans continue to require larger copayments, deductibles and coinsurance premiums, employees will have a vested interest in using the health-care system as little as possible. To the extent that employees must use the health-care system, their expectations of receiving adequate medical attention and a satisfactory result would be directly proportional to their out-of-pocket expenditures for necessary care. The greater the out-of-pocket expenditure, the greater the expectation of high-quality health care in a convenient and accessible format. Failure to meet these expectations, coupled with a less than satisfactory medical outcome or "service without a smile," will greatly increase the chances of litigation. The probability of litigation is also greatly increased as soon as a physician begins to regard a patient in a potentially adversarial role and practices "defensive medicine." This response by physicians represents, perhaps, the chief underlying cause of the current medical-malpractice crisis and lies at the source of a self-fulfilling prophecy of increasing litigation in the health-care industry.

Need for Educational Change

These "health-care megatrends" are making traditional medical career paths and the educational process that prepares students and resident physicians for them rapidly obsolete. The Association of American Medical Colleges, the Liaison Committee for Medical Education, the Accreditation Council for Graduate and Continuing Medical Education and other medical-education accreditation agencies are beginning to accept this situation, however slowly. Nevertheless, most academic medical associations, agencies and institutions will likely lag in this process by several years. However, progressive academic medical centers will rise to meet the challenges posed by the new (often harsh) economic environment by integrating health-care management; medical economics; corporate, legal and policy analysis; and computer education into their curricular offerings. Such institutions will provide the type of training for their students, residents and fellows that will adequately prepare them as both clinicians and astute business managers in the coming years.

NEW MEDICAL CAREER PREPARATION

Preparatory Education

With the prospect that physicians of the future will be part of large corporate systems, the decision to embark on a medical career must be carefully measured. It would be preferable for aspiring physicians to look for guidance to much younger role models than to their parents' generation of physicians, as they have in the past. Young physicians may provide a more realistic and less cynical outlook on what it will mean to be a physician in a very different economic climate.

Given those caveats, what kind of advice should be given not only to aspiring premedical students, but also to the admissions officials of the nation's medical schools? The operative word must be "Change!"

Most medical school admissions officials (and premedical students reacting to them) have continued to emphasize narrow mastery of the premedical sciences and performance on the science portions of the MCAT as the keys to gaining entrance into medical school. Premedical students have been forced to slant their concentration heavily in favor of achieving top-notch science preparation at the expense of a broad liberal-arts education.

Admissions officials should not continue to gravitate toward "ace science students" for at least two good reasons:

1. We are entering an age in medicine in which scientific technology must further the ends of patients and not vice versa; and
2. A broad liberal-arts education, combined with training in economics and business management, will be essential to compete in the new consumer-oriented and intensely market-driven corporate health-care system.

This is not to suggest that students who are generally interested in science should major in French literature to fit into "the new mold." On the other hand, premedical students should not feel inhibited to take virtually any type of college curriculum that most appeals to them, provided that the minimal premedical science requirements are completed. Indeed, liberal training in the humanities, social and behavioral sciences, economics and management disciplines should be viewed as an important enhancement to a student's overall preparation, sufficient to offset even a less than stellar performance in certain of the more traditional premedical sciences.

The main priority for students must be that they not feel *compelled* to choose an undesirable (and ultimately less than optimal) course in preparing for medical training. The "premed pressure cooker" must be dismantled. It has produced many overly narrow, socially stunted, obsessively compulsive, pompous and arrogant physicians not in touch with their patients' needs, much less with the highly interdependent societal context in which they must ply their trade. The fact that the practice of medicine "suddenly" is not nearly such a "desirable" calling may well provide the window of opportunity for dismantling the premed pressure cooker. From this new, less urgent preparatory route to a medical career (contrary to the lamentations of many a current medical educator), there could well emerge new physicians who are more humane, compassionate and equally (if not more) competent in the new ways of practicing medicine than were their more traditionally predecessors.

Undergraduate Medical Training

All is still not lost if the selection process for the "new type of medical student" is slow in coming. With several changes in the current undergraduate medical curriculum, the "new breed" of physician may still emerge. However, to have any impact, curricular changes must be substantial, introduced in the first year of medical school, reintroduced and reinforced through the basic-science and clinical years, required for graduation and tightly integrated with the socialization process of becoming a physician.

Accounting for the social, behavioral, financial, legal, ethical and philosophic factors in diagnosing and managing disease must be as highly integrated in an aspiring physician's thought processes as are the biologic, chemical and physiologic factors. The failure to impress this way of thinking on the next generation of physicians will relegate medical schools to the status of trade schools. More importantly, the next generation of physicians will be poorly trained to perform adequately within the new system of health care, which is experiencing rapid changes.

To change the traditional medical school curriculum so drastically is clearly no small task. However, the logistic elements are not nearly so imposing as are the political aspects of effecting such a metamorphosis. There is only so much time and there are only so many resources at an academic medical center's disposal. Moreover, time and resources are being whittled down as these words are being written. To the extent that the foregoing educational elements are integrated into the curriculum, the more traditional (but perhaps obsolescent) features must be pared back. Indeed, the whole educational period involved in becoming a physician may have to be reduced. This period would not be reduced to crank out more physicians faster (since there are already too many). It would be necessary to accommodate for shrinking financial support, the increasing complexities of society and the increasing commitment on the part of those medical students to their families, friends and themselves in pursuits outside medicine.

Given these assumptions, the growing surplus of physicians could be the best thing that has ever happened to the medical profession and the society it serves. Through professional time-sharing arrangements and other patient-care distribution devices, perhaps physicians once again may lead something closer to the more balanced existences to which most people have become accustomed. This change would dramatically improve the overall doctor-patient relationship. The increasing influx of women into the medical profession in the years ahead should accelerate this humanization of medical practice.

This humanization of the practice of medicine and the hours physicians and physicians-in-training could do more for resolving the current professional liability crisis and career frustrations to which so many physicians are subject than anything else. Perhaps the leading underlying reason that patients file malpractice suits is that they feel that their physicians did not make enough time for them, acted superior to them or could not relate to them as equal human beings.

Physicians are human beings, too. Unfortunately, because their training in the past has not been sufficiently humane, many physicians display a martyred, arrogant and condescending attitude to their patients as well as to their families and friends. Perhaps more than any other single factor, it is this shortcoming, this dehumanizing/desensitizing process in the training of physicians, that must be addressed most urgently. With the growing oversupply of physicians and the unprecedented need for good consumer relations in health-care delivery, now is the best time to address this critical issue.

Clearly, the "down side" of all this is that physicians will make substantially less money (relatively speaking), perhaps 20 to 30 percent less, when adjusted for inflation. This downward trend in income will be fought most vigorously by physicians who are currently 45 to 55 years of age. Physicians in this age group have had a chance to grow accustomed to medical practice as it was. Indeed, they probably have made many long-term financial commitments on the assumption that their incomes would continue to grow substantially throughout their careers.

Tomorrow's medical students must fully appreciate how different the financial and organizational aspects of practicing medicine will be for them. This awareness must be an integral and ongoing part of their education from the start. The sooner they realize the manner by which the ineluctable societal forces are molding their future practice settings, the easier shall be their passage into this new health-care system. Medical students who are not amenable need to come to that conclusion as early as possible in the long educational pipeline of becoming physicians.

Although outlining a detailed undergraduate medical curriculum is beyond the scope of this chapter, some suggestions concerning how the curriculum could be sufficiently liberalized to reflect current and projected socioeconomic realities are offered.

During the first two years, the standard basic-sciences courses should be retained, but the time allowed for them could be pared back by approximately 50 percent to provide time for the following courses.

Clinical epidemiology and biostatistics
Computers in medicine
Preventive medicine and public health
Medical ethics and humanities (including philosophy and history
    of medicine)
Medical sociology and social work
Health policy and the political/legislative process
How to find and read the medical literature
Medical grantsmanship
Legal aspects of medical practice
Economic and business aspects of medical practice
Health-care systems and financing
Cooperative work/study in a health-care facility
Free elective time in other professional schools of the university

The "introduction to clinical medicine" course should be begun near the beginning of the first year and extended throughout the first two years so that all the foregoing disciplines could become tightly interwoven into a student's nascent clinical decision-making process.

Many physicians could call the foregoing course list revolutionary and far too great of an encroachment of the time required for basic-sciences courses. Nevertheless, the opening wedge for this revolutionary readjustment of curricular priorities has already been set in place by the *General Professional Education of the Physician* (GPEP) report.[2] Perhaps the most important recommendation coming from that landmark report is that after their undergraduate medical years, aspiring physicians should possess an adequate ability to engage in a lifetime of continuing medical education through the acquisition of self-learning skills.

Computers have the potential to effect this recommended and sorely needed revolutionary change in a relatively brief period. As is occurring in many undergraduate engineering and business schools throughout the country, access to a computer should now be at least as important for a medical student as has been access to a microscope in the past. Although the applications of computers in health care are covered in Chapter 11, a few words about their primary potential for revolutionizing undergraduate medical education may be useful at this point.

Primarily, ready access to computers will provide medical students with the ability to engage in the type of "self-directed learning" that the previously cited report[2] extols as a major educational virtue. Computer-assisted instruction through authoring systems being developed in all the various basic medical sciences (even gross anatomy) should obviate the need for a substantial amount of classroom instruction time, notetaking and textbook and journal reading.

Computer-assisted instruction should be part and parcel of any "introduction to clinical medicine" course as well. Authoring systems tailormade for such courses now exist. Such systems may permit a medical educator to incorporate many different elements and levels of branching analysis into a neophyte's clinical decision-making calculus. The elements may include the relative certainty of a patient's signs and symptoms, the sensitivity and specificity of various tests and procedures and their costs and safety with different patient groups.

Learning by this method will produce much more well-rounded and well-grounded clinical decision-makers. Even more importantly, ready access to computers will permit students to practice their clinical decision making on simulated patients, before being unleashed on the genuine article! The potential for savings in preventing litigation from this approach alone should justify the cost of such a system, independent of its educational benefits.

During the third and fourth clinical years, although there may be less time for the broad-minded interdisciplinary pursuits, the "nonmedical" aspects of becoming a physician must continue to be emphasized. If anything has been learned by medical educators in the past in teaching nonmedical courses, it is that to be effective, such courses cannot be optional, piecemeal, sporadic or isolated from the clinical curriculum as a whole. The ethical, legal and economic aspects of medical practice must be integrated into the practical learning experience in each major clinical specialty during the third and fourth years.

It is to be hoped that the stage for this integrated interdisciplinary clinical education process has already been set during the "introduction to clinical medicine" course, as well as in the other parts of the modified preclinical curriculum discussed previously. Assuming that all students entering the "clinically intensive" third year have been properly indoctrinated, it should be relatively easy to continue this process with such innovations as weekly clinicolegal and clinicoeconomic case-management correlations conferences with backup, computer-assisted, clinical-simulation exercises.

The fourth year of medical school is becoming an increasingly troublesome one. As a result of the increasing competition for the perceived "desirable" residency positions, the fourth year is progressively becoming a "preresidency" year. During this year, when students have their last real opportunity to indulge in the multidisciplinary pursuit with which the practice of medicine is inextricably bound, an increasing percentage of students are pursuing progressively narrow, specialized and subspecialized courses in an effort to optimize their chances for acceptance into those narrow subspecialty residencies. Ironically, revolutionary changes in the health-care system have not deterred, but have apparently increased, the efforts of students to pursue this narrow range of subspecialties. These changes in the health-care system almost surely will render such subspecialties as highly undesirable career choices (at least from a cost-benefit standpoint) by the time students finally complete their lengthy training.

Clearly, the fourth year should be a time for refinement of the well-rounded clinical skills hopefully acquired during the third year in preparation for the residency years to follow. However, the scope of clinical activities must be much broader than has become the norm of late. In addition, there must be new opportunities for fourth-year students to work in the myriad of ambulatory-care settings emerging on the medical landscape (e.g., ambulatory-care centers, surgicenters, urgicenters and emergicenters, birthing centers, "medical malls," health maintenance organizations [HMOs] and IPAs). Part of the training of fourth-year students in such centers should involve learning about the practical economic, business and legal aspects involved in running and financing them, and in their delivery of health care to increasingly diverse populations. Inpatient subinternships will become unnecessary, and even undesirable, if they reinforce profligacy in the consumption of health-care resources under the guise of "academic medical practice."

Having received such exposure to the medical world in which they will be practicing in the 1990s and beyond, fourth-year students should be in a much better position to choose their specialties. This career decision-making process may be further facilitated by means of a readily available medical career counseling/development office coordinated by the university hospital's director of medical education. Adequate time must be alloted to fourth-year students (particularly in the first half of that year, when residency decisions must be made) so they can sample the foregoing and discuss their career development with house officers, young physicians and wise, older advisors. To provide less to them at that critical time in their professional lives is a grave disservice to them and their future patients.

Graduate Medical Training

Residency training in the first year is strikingly similar across different specialties, hospitals and geographic areas nationwide. A first-year resident physician is truly on the "front line" of acute inpatient care. As such, first-year residents have extremely limited flexibility in their schedule.

This may be the only time in the medical education process during which young physicians may not have much time to learn further (at least in a didactic sense) about how the rest of the world interacts with the delivery of health care in this country. However, if young physicians' premedical and medical education has followed the program outlined, the first year of residency training should permit them to appreciate fully in a practical sense the dynamics of such interactions. If this understanding is forthcoming, young physicians may truly come to appreciate (even at this early stage) the art as well as the science of practicing medicine.

During the later years of residency and fellowship training, however, there should be allotted an increasing amount of time for residents to acquire some of the business-management skills that will be as essential for them as their clinical abilities in the emerging corporate medical system. An increasing portion of the later residency and fellowship years should also be devoted to practicing in ambulatory-care settings, including HMOs, IPAs, preferred-provider organizations, ambulatory-care centers, surgicenters, urgicenters and emergicenters. The advent of prospective-pricing systems (discussed in the section "Health-Care Megatrends") has accelerated the transition from inpatient to outpatient care dramatically.

By the final year in their residency or fellowship programs, physicians should be spending perhaps 25 to 50 percent of their time in ambulatory-care settings. They should be learning how to practice in them not only as physicians but also as eventual leaders of such health-care organizations. This point has been stressed for physicians entering training programs in general internal medicine.[5] This landmark article by Schroeder and colleagues should be read carefully by all aspiring internists, internal medicine program directors and physician-educators in other departments.

Perhaps an even more important transformation of graduate medical education must take place to prepare young physicians for a different economic environment. This transformation relates to a continuation of the instruction in cost-effective medical decision making begun during medical school.

Even during the first year, resident physicians should be given continual instruction and practical training in the techniques of cost-effective clinical decision making. If there is any conclusion that may be drawn from the literature of teaching clinical decision analysis, it is that to have a major beneficial effect, it must be provided on an ongoing basis with relevant clinical material.

This type of instruction may be provided in a number of formats. Perhaps a good way to present this information to house staff initially is by means of a series of open discussions about the rapidly changing economic environment in the health-care industry. The discussions could proceed from the more general economic areas to how physicians can and must change their practice patterns to respond to this changed environment. After this initial series, there could be a short series concerning new systems that assess how the relative levels of utilization of health-care resources may be adjusted without compromising the quality of care through the use of clinical epidemiologic techniques involving testing thresholds and the like.

With that background, then, grand rounds in medical economics could be transformed into more practical, clinicoeconomic correlation case-management conferences. Such conferences could center around the presentation of simulated clinical cases, from which decision-analysis trees, or algorithms, could be constructed. At each decision node concerning whether to test the sensitivity, specificity and predictive positive and negative values of a test result (given the likelihood of the underlying problem sought to be elucidated) could be assessed. The clinical-utility function of different outcomes in the diagnostic and therapeutic process could also be assigned, as could the costs and risks of various tests and procedures that could be employed to achieve a given outcome.

Applying basic statistical analysis to decision-making exercises would permit a continuous assessment of how cost and safety factors aid physicians in arriving at desired outcomes (i.e., appropriate diagnosis with safe and beneficial treatment that maximizes overall utility with the least consumption of scarce health-care resources). The foregoing "nuts and bolts" instruction in cost-effective medical decision making lends itself readily to computer-assisted instruction. Authoring systems exist that permit the development of special case files to integrate the relevant clinical, financial and risk factors into cases that are constructed for ultimate use by students, residents and practicing physicians. The Society for Research and Education in Primary Care Internal Medicine (SREPCIM) and the Society for Medical Decision Making are at the vanguard of this emerging revolution in computer-assisted instruction.

After the initial grand rounds in medical economics and clinicoeconomic correlation case-management conference series, a more self-directed continuing computer-assisted course in cost-effective clinical decision making may take place. This course may be implemented through a type of clinicoeconomic "case-of-the-week" series accessible through computer terminals throughout a teaching hospital. Cases could be developed through the authoring system and would permit evaluation of examinees individually and jointly concerning their clinical and cost effectiveness in diagnosing and treating the simulated patients whose cases were presented. Completion of the cases should be required on a weekly, or at least a monthly, basis, as an academic condition of continuing in the residency program. "Clinicoeconomic scores" could be determined and stored, so that comparisons between residents, services, departments and, eventually, hospitals could be made at any given time to assess improvement trends. These evaluative analyses would permit educational interventions for different groups and physicians on a prospective basis so that improvements in cost-effectiveness techniques could be taught or reinforced, which, hopefully could be applied in the care and treatment of actual patients.

Such a program would carry substantial benefits for all participants. Most importantly, a hospital would benefit through training resident physicians who are much more efficient at selecting only the resources that are necessary for optimizing the quality of health care. Residents would benefit by becoming more cost-effective and therefore more competitive participants in the burgeoning number of tightly managed alternative health-care delivery systems.

Although implementation of the foregoing curricular innovations may be highly flexible, according to the constraints of a particular graduate training program, they might be introduced along the following lines:

Year One

Month 1:   Effect of growing health-care expenditures on
           the U.S. economy
Month 2:   Health-care financing: how it is changing
Month 3:   The brave new world of alternative
           health-care delivery systems
Month 4:   Physicians responses to changing economics:
           managed competition
Month 5:   The new health-care paradigm: continuous
           quality improvement
Month 6:   Application of clinical epidemiology to the
           decision-making process in medicine
Month 7:   Medical record review/clinicoeconomic
           case-management conference no. 1
Month 8:   Disease tracers and staging/clinicoeconomic
           correlation case-management conference
           no. 2
Month 9:   Severity-of-illness adjusted clinical
           benchmarking/clinicoeconomic correlation
           case-management conference no. 3
Month 10: Computer-assisted medical decision making:
           statistical models/clinicoeconomic correlation
           case-management conference no. 4
Month 11: Computer-assisted medical decision making:
           rule-based inference systems/clinicoeconomic
           correlation case-management conference
           no. 5
Month 12: Computer-assisted medical decision making:
           heuristic and cognitive models/
           clinicoeconomic correlation case-management
           conference no. 6

Years Two and Beyond
>   Required clinicoeconomic case-of-the-week
>   series in particular specialties

Continuing Medical Education (CME)

This area is covered in detail in Chapter 12. There are more than 500,000 practicing physicians who are finding themselves ill-equipped to respond in an effective manner to the rapidly changing economic environment in health care. Their training to become experts in the clinical management of patients has left them little time or wherewithal to become experts in the business management of organizations, or even of their financial affairs, to a great extent. As such, they have found themselves increasingly dependent on other persons for this assistance, as their patients depend on them for their clinical expertise. This is a bitter pill for most physicians to swallow.

There is hope, however, for physicians who are secure enough in their practices and themselves to recognize this rather gaping deficiency in their overall training. Especially in the past three to five years, there has been an unprecedented proliferation of seminars targeted toward physicians relating to practice enhancement, medical economics, marketing, legal and financial aspects of practice management and negotiation with alternative health-care delivery systems and other contractual health plans. Not a day goes by that the average physician's office is not inundated with such "course announcements."

There is a major problem, however. These half-day to two-week "courses," to a great extent, are commercially sponsored. As such, the "faculty" is understandably involved in self-marketing campaigns. Competition for the services that such courses can provide to physicians is heating up. It is no surprise that every group imaginable is seizing on this "built-in deficiency" in physicians' training to fill this current and projected demand by addressing as many physician gatherings as possible.

There is currently little quality management of these myriad seminars. What such seminars or courses seek to convey to physician audiences is that with the economic environment changing so rapidly, physicians must be protected (as they always have been) from such forces so that they can concentrate on what they do best: practice medicine. The thinly veiled message is that although it might be all right for physicians to be "enlightened" about all the nonmedical aspects of practicing medicine, they should continue to rely primarily on nonphysicians to rescue them from the regulatory and competitive jungle. Sponsors of such seminars and courses try to convey to physicians just enough information so that they know they must continue to seek professional assistance in many new areas for their practices to survive. However, the sponsors do not (and cannot) convey enough information so that physicians or their office staff could begin to solve such problems by themselves. This approach has the effect of shifting more funds away from "in-house education" toward "practice consultants" and similar "professionals," thus increasing overhead and, ultimately, the fees passed on for reimbursement from third- and fourth-party payers as well as patients.

What is needed is more "in-house" or "on-site" training of physicians and office staff in the various "nonmedical" aspects of practice, rather than further proliferation of seminars and courses in exotic locations at exorbitant prices. "On-the-job training sessions" should include faculty professors of business, finance and law from nearby business and law schools, administrative representatives from local medical societies and associations and physician and office staff "alumnai" of previous in-house practice-management seminars. Although it may be unrealistic to expect that on-site training sessions would not be expensive, the amount of time and money saved by being able to stay put and appreciate the direct practical and customized application of management expertise to everyday operations of a physician's practice should more than compensate.

Physicians' participation in such sessions would be indispensable. Moreover, with the academic credentials of the faculty above reproach and the content of the program immediately implementable, the quality of such continuing medical education would be assured. As further evidence of this contention, category I continuing medical education credit toward the AMA Physician's Recognition Award for such educational sessions should be a prerequisite before they are marketed to physicians.

These "nuts-and-bolts" in-house training sessions could easily be extended and modified to apply to myriad other practice situations, including multispecialty groups, HMOs, IPAs, urgicenters and academic medical (or hospital-based) practices. The American College of Physicians Executives (a national organization of physician-executives) has taken the lead in developing and implementing in-house training sessions for physicians and their institutional facilities. Training programs customized to individual centers' needs, capabilities and financial and time constraints are provided on site by appropriate financial, legal, organizational, computing and systems specialists on behalf of the college (see Chapter 9).

PHYSICIANS: PAST, PRESENT AND FUTURE

In general, both medical and nonmedical CME of the future must be based on a continuing assessment of needs by physicians and their patients. How well CME meets these needs must be continuously evaluated and improved through reliable subjective and objective measurement methods, including clinical outcome assessment systems. The pages that follow outline the different types of physicians beginning to emerge from the transformation of the health-care delivery system. The examples are by no means meant to exhaust the growing list of niches that future physicians may carve out for themselves. Moreover, the examples do not presume to be mutually exclusive. It is expected that physicians will derive their livelihood and ultimate income by following a variety of the following career typologies. It is also assumed that physicians will have to be flexible in moving between and among the various options in the coming years to maintain something even approximating the level of income that they have enjoyed in the past. This further underscores the need for continuing on-site education in the practical aspects of optimizing one's practice opportunities while adopting one of the career typologies that are discussed in the text that follows.

"Diehards"

Diehards who choose to remain even partially in traditional fee-for-service practice in the future will have to do one of two things to survive: carve out a unique specialization in an underserved field or have access to some of the best practice-marketing skills available. With the growing surplus of physicians, to remain outside a large preferred or managed capitated system or network will require such a practitioner to become continually involved with positioning (and repositioning) in the marketplace. To that end, such physicians should have access to annual market-demand forecasts for their services and extensive competitor analyses to confirm that a projected demand for such services could not be met just as well and more economically elsewhere.

Physicians who currently have well-established practices might scoff at the notion that this effort would ever be necessary for them. However, if the projected explosion in alternative health-care delivery systems and the projected surplus of physicians and decrease in office visits is even close to that indicated by a Wall Street investment banking firm[6] or a Johns Hopkins study,[7] such a scenario for diehards would seem to be inevitable, at least in metropolitan areas by the mid-1990s.

"Groupies"

This category of physician is most closely associated with the "Big Chill" or the "Woodstock Generation." Such physicians, largely in their late thirties to mid-forties, received their medical training in the early 1970s in the land of plenty. Still, some of them had enough foresight to realize that once the open faucet of reimbursement gradually closed, there would be some safety in numbers. This category of physician (many of whom include family practitioners) was among the first to realize that there was a dubious future in store for solo practitioners, who must run a small business in the face of rapidly growing competition and regulatory constraints.

Physicians who developed their practices in large multispecialty groups should be better prepared for the tumultuous changes that will take place in the health-care industry in the years ahead. Large multispecialty groups will be in a good bargaining position to negotiate the details of fee schedules and utilization-review programs in proposals from alternative health-care delivery systems and other payers of health care.

To continue to be viable entities in the new health-care delivery system, however, they must remain cohesive and flexible, yet tightly managed. Each group should have at least one primary-care case manager, who can coordinate the flow of patients among specialists and available technologies, because such groups will be capitated by many payers.

Physicians in such groups must also be attuned to the future posibilities of being acquired or merged into progressively larger health-care delivery systems. Although this reorganization may further diffuse the autonomy of medical practice, it should expand the range of opportunities for multispecialty group practices.

Physicians in multispecialty group practices should realize that becoming an attractive acquisition to one of the emerging health-care superpowers may be a testimonial to their having succeeded in the new system.

Entrepreneurs

Because of the tremendous financial success of some for-profit alternative health-care delivery systems, an increasing segment of the physician population is embarking on diversified ventures in the health-care field among themselves, with hospitals and sometimes with businesses already in existence or of their own making. Revolutionary changes in the health-care industry have spawned a new type of physician—the physician-entrepreneur—to take advantage of new opportunities. Nonphysician-entrepreneurs in the health-care field may scoff at such physicians and refer to them as frustrated, "would-be" masters of business administration.

As the health-care industry continues its inexorable trend toward corporatization, the number of such physicians will likely increase dramatically. Physicians (with some degree of credence) still regard themselves as the leaders of the health-care industry. As the United States becomes much more of a professional meritocracy in the days ahead, physician-entrepreneurs can expect to become the health-care industry's representatives in this new class.

Physician-entrepreneurs (despite the naysayings of some academic physicians) should find themselves in an enviable position in the emerging health-care delivery system. In a $900 billion a year industry, there should be no shortage of rewarding opportunities to mix capitalism and health care creatively.

Other physicians may venture out with colleagues to develop out-patient facilities (surgicenters, urgicenters or emergicenters) that actively compete with hospitals and other institutions for patients. Still other physicians may forge alliances with corporations and other payers of health care to provide consultative services concerning methods of containing health-care costs without compromising the quality of care. They may conduct such activities as a part-time adjunct to their clinical practices or may pursue them on a full-time basis as a new line of business. Functioning as consultants full time might alleviate some of the inherent ethical concerns raised by people who believe that providing health-care services while also pursuing profit-making enterprises makes for a precarious, and sometimes conflicting, set of professional motivations.

Reaganites

This emerging group of physicians, although somewhat similar in mindset to the entrepreneurs, may be distinguished in two important ways:

1. They are usually relatively young; and
2. They are not yet financially secure enough to embark on profit-making ventures in the health-care field.

Reaganite physicians are creatures of the 1980s financing revolution. They are ardent advocates of cuts in government health-care spending. They believe that the health-care industry is at least as bloated as the defense establishment. They are convinced that health care can be delivered for much less than its current cost with no decrease (and a probable increase) in its overall quality.

The group of physicians is not in the health-care field to make big money—most of them are, or will be, salaried. However, they *are* in the field to make sure that other people do not make big money at the expense of the system as a whole or of patients in particular. As such, these physicians expect that they will become corporate medical directors of large health-care provider/insurer organizations and Fortune 500 companies in the coming years, making use of their special talents of squeezing every last unnecessary test, procedure, consultation and hospitalization out of the system.

It is likely that this group of physicians will be rewarded handsomely for their talents in the new health-care delivery system, just as efficient executives in other large businesses and organizations who improve bottom lines currently are. However, it is not their raison d'être to make money for themselves. They may be intrapreneurs, but they are not entrepreneurs. Nevertheless, the demand for this type of physician (still a small but growing minority in the young ranks) should be great in the next 20 to 30 years.

The "New Breed"

This type of physician currently is fairly rare—hence the name new breed. They are the kind who could best be described as eclectic, assimilating the most appropriate aspects of the previous four groups in response to a rapidly changing environment. The new breed of physicians will combine the compassionate aspects of the doctor-patient relationship touted so highly by the diehards with the cooperative spirit of the groupies, the boldness and wits of the entrepreneurs and the cost-effectiveness ethic of the Reaganites.

The new breed of physicians will become the "one-minute clinical case manager" of the future. Such physicians will learn how to assess clinical situations rapidly, yet compassionately, and will cooperate with all involved in a patient's care (including institutional providers and payers), take many calculated risks based on rapidly assessed objective and subjective data and integrate cost to the patient and the overall system as an important factor in all clinical decision making.

The new breed of physicians will be well educated with regard to organizational dynamics and politics. Such lessons are currently glossed over in the teaching programs of academic medical centers. This situation is ironic because such venerable institutions are some of the most politically charged organizations with which physicians, residents and students will ever make extended contact.

The new breed of physicians will understand power structures in the evolving health-care system. This knowledge will be necessary for such physicians to circumvent their more noxious aspects. This must be done for the good of their patients (or clients) as well as for their careers. Physicians must carve out a unique niche over time with the flexibility to change rapidly in response to a constantly changing health-care environment.

The substantial oversupply of physicians will soon tip the power balance away from physicians toward multi-institutional providers, payers and consumers of health care. Without a substantial redirection, the consequence of this power shift will be to identify physicians increasingly as commodities to be bought and sold to meet the aggregate demands of patient populations affected by large employer/insurer contract plans. To avoid this characterization, the new breed of physicians must become proactive in uniquely identifying themselves, their services and their markets. However, this should not be interpreted as a call for even greater specialization and market segmentation. Regrettably, many physicians will blindly follow this route, bypassing the real opportunities in the changing health-care marketplace.

However, the new breed of physicians will have the foresight not to narrow their focus by concentrating on increasingly more discrete parts of the body, more exotic diseases or discrete organ systems in a misguided effort at carving out new niches. The new breed of physicians will bring to bear *all* their professional training (especially their nonmedical training) in carving out niches.

It is not progressive narrowing but broadening of one's repertoire of skills that makes any person (including any physician) unique. This realization at most medical schools and residency programs, unfortunately, has been lost as a result of the mountains of data that accreditation and curriculum committees and program directors have determined to be "essential information" for fledgling physicians to absorb and regurgitate. This didactic process, however, does not identify and nurture a student's uniqueness. The current pedagogy does not, in the words of Plato, "bring out that which is within," as true education can and must do. Rather, it often stifles creativity in favor of producing overinformed medical clones. This is not wholly the fault of medical educators, inhibited as they are by such regulatory forces as the external accreditation agencies, licensing and certifying authorities and the professional-liability specter.

The new breed of physicians (despite the overwhelming forces of tradition to the contrary) must overcome these strong undercurrents to emerge as the future leaders in health care. They must be "street smart" but not cynical, well versed in scientific advances but not obsessed with them and skillful in negotiation and facilitation techniques, with a broad sense of perspective and advocacy for responsive change.

The new breed of physicians will probably be alumnai (if not faculty members) of the preparatory, undergraduate, graduate medical and continuing medical education series outlined previously in this chapter. The depth and breadth of the educational process required to produce the new breed of physicians make early enrollment in the foregoing education-training system mandatory.

This is not to say, of course, "that you can't teach an old dog new tricks." Students, residents and practicing physicians at all levels of their training may take advantage of these educational series and thereby become more prepared for the future of health care in the United States.

SUMMARY AND RECOMMENDATIONS

Summary

As a result of revolutionary changes in the financing and delivery of health care, the traditional methods and pathways of medical career development must be radically redirected to prepare physicians for the future.

Health-care megatrends that necessitate this redirection are changes in health-policy priorities, in medical-manpower requirements, in health-care technology and in patients' expectations.

Medical career preparation for the emerging health-care system must be substantially redirected to be responsive to the rapidly changing environmental forces. This redirection should include:

- Preparatory education: a much more prodigious effort by medical school admissions officials to seek out applicants with the most well-rounded liberal-arts educations;
- Undergraduate medical education: a splitting of the first two years between medical-sciences and health-policy training (in its broadest sense), with continuing integration of this "nonbiomedical" training (as it relates to clinical practice) during the third and fourth years;
- Graduate medical training: an integration of the economic, business and legal aspects of practicing medicine early in the second year of residency, with cooperative "on-the-job" training in alternative outpatient settings by the final year; and
- Continuing medical education: an increasing amount of in-house training sessions of physicians and office staff in the nonmedical aspects of their practices, as opposed to more commercial "canned" seminars.

Out of the tumultuous changes in the health-care delivery system should emerge five physician typologies:

1. Diehards: a few physicians (usually older) who hold onto the rapidly obsolescent creed of independent, unmanaged fee-for-service medicine;
2. Groupies: an increasing number of "Woodstock-generation" physicians who choose to "circle the wagons" and "huddle around the campfire" as their means of coping with external pressures;
3. Entrepreneurs: also an increasing segment of the physician population who see no inherent incompatibility between practicing medicine (or "in medically related enterprises") and taking advantage of the capitalistic opportunities arising from the privatization of the health-care industry;
4. Reaganites: generally physicians who are younger than the entrepreneurs but who have less financial security, and are not as much interested in making money in medicine as they are in making sure nobody else makes too much money at the expense of patients, the health-care industry and society as a whole; and
5. The New Breed: the new "Renaissance persons" in medicine who are thoroughly eclectic and flexible situational leaders, extensively educated in the new medical career development processes introduced in this chapter.

Recommendations

As urgent as the need is for substantial changes in medical school curricula, it cannot be emphasized too strongly that such changes must be accomplished gradually through "grass-roots" coalition building, which, ultimately, will facilitate the revolution.

As an initial foray into these ambitious projects, the author would suggest implementing a medical economics grand rounds/clinicoeconomic case-management conference series as part of a continuing-education program for resident physicians. This conference series should be introduced in as innocuous a manner as is possible, accommodating the extremely busy schedules of residents. Perhaps a good method to ensure participation is to make the series part of a larger effort to help senior residents make the transition into clinical practice.

After some initial success, the educational process may become more specific in its intent (i.e., to improve the cost effectiveness of physicians' decision making through patient-simulation exercises). At this point, the potential audience may be broadened by inviting students, junior residents as well as practicing physicians, who may receive continuing medical education credits. Ultimately, the interaction among these groups will be essential if there is any hope that the lessons learned may be applied in the care of patients.

After further acceptance, the most imposing obstacle of all (yet the area in which there lies the greatest potential for effecting change) may be approached—the traditional medical school curriculum. By gradually implementing the educational changes recommended into this final academic bastion, further implementation at the levels of resident and practicing physicians will be greatly facilitated.

It will be an incredible challenge for progressive medical educators to achieve these goals. Nonetheless, some of these recommended changes should be implemented before it is too late. These changes are consistent with and will likely presage the recommendations soon to emanate from the national accreditation agencies. It will be bold medical educators who take these initial steps now, those who will be at the vanguard in producing the new breed of physicians, who, in turn, will shape and lead the development of health-care policy and the delivery of health care well into the twenty-first century.

ACKNOWLEDGMENTS

The author extends special thanks to two outstanding visionaries in medical education, who have provided inspiration for this chapter. Samuel P. Martin, M.D., formerly director of the Robert Wood Johnson Foundation Clinical Scholars Program at the University of Pennsylvania, and John G. Freymann, M.D., past president of the National Fund for Medical Education.

The author also expresses sincere appreciation to Patricia B. Kalita for her invaluable assistance in preparing and typing this chapter.

REFERENCES

1. Couch J: Forum: A remedy for outmoded medical education. *Health Cost Manage* 2:1–2, 1985.
2. Muller S, Gerberding W, Alexander D, et al: Physicians for the twenty-first century: Report of the project panel on the general professional education of the physician and college preparation for medicine. Part 2. *J Med Educ* 59:1–208, 1984.
3. Mold J, Stein H: Sounding board: The cascade effect in the clinical care of patients. *N Engl J Med* 314:512–514, 1986.
4. Kirschner R, Unger M: Symposium on laser surgery. *Surg Clin North Am* 64:837–1024, 1984.
5. Schroeder S, Showstack JA, Gerbert B: Residency training in internal medicine: time for a change? *Ann Intern Med* 104:554–561, 1986.
6. Abramowitz K: *The Future of Health Care Delivery in America*. New York, Sanford C Bernstein & Co, 1985.
7. Steinwachs D, Weiner J, Shapiro S, et al: A comparison of the requirements for primary care physicians in HMOs with projections made by the GMENAC. *N Engl J Med* 314:217–222, 1986.

CHAPTER 4

THE GROWING INFLUENCE OF WOMEN IN MEDICINE

Lila Stein Kroser

My first patient in my newly established office in my heavily mortgaged twin home in northeast Philadelphia, a vivacious girl of seven, told me as she hopped from one foot to another, that I could not be the doctor because doctors were men and women could only be nurses. My four-year-old daughter, when identifying her parents' occupations in nursery-school class, was told that her mommy could not be a doctor because mommies were only mommies and only daddies were doctors. My own image of a doctor had been forged by the friendly, competent "doc" on the corner, in whose footsteps I was determined to walk, when at the age of five, caring for my dolls, I decided being a doctor was special.

This chapter deals with the growing influence of women in medicine. Influence must stem from previous experience, just as the future, we are taught, is always rooted in the past. I trace my path as a physician for 35 years, and women physicians in the United States trace their footsteps for 300 years. The momentum of the woman physician's role in health care for the future is gathering, has been growing and will be better understood as we reflect on our past.

In recent times, women physicians have all traveled the same path, namely, high standards in schooling, premedical education, medical college admissions tests and, finally, acceptance to medical school in numbers greater than ever before. Interestingly enough, in reviewing the work of historian Ruth Abram, *Women Doctors in America 1835–1920,* we learn that a golden age of women in medicine existed and was lost.[1] How that came about and what historic events affect our future will be explored in this chapter.

HISTORIC OVERVIEW

Perhaps one of the most succinct yet comprehensive accounts of the history of women physicians in the United States can be found in the book *In Her Own Words* by Regina Morantz Sanchez and Cynthia Pomerleau.[2] The author recommends that readers take time to read this book from cover to cover. For the sake of brevity and perhaps to whet the reader's appetite to delve more deeply, the author will only provide a brief historic account that helps review the history of women in medicine and speculate about the future.

The struggle for women to be admitted to medical schools in this country started when the first U.S. medical school was established in 1767, but it was not until 1847 that the first woman was admitted.[2] Women were excluded from the "gentlemanly" profession of medicine, denied access to education and relegated to domesticity or "woman's place" in the scheme of family life.

Although women long practiced the "healing" art of midwifery, by the middle of the eighteenth century, owing to technical improvements in the use of forceps, women were again relegated to the sidelines, "not to be able to understand the mechanics of labor since they did not understand thoroughly the profession of medicine as a whole."[3]

Perhaps the road would have been easier had American women physicians opted for the road taken by the first woman to practice medicine in Canada, James Miranda Stuart Barry, who lived and dressed as a man, attained the rank of Inspector General for Upper and Lower Canada and was found to be a woman only at her death. Our women physicians were unable to follow this eccentric pattern and, instead, "wanted to be accepted on their own terms; women they maintained were needed as physicians and it was high time this fact was recognized. So they dressed as women wearing long Victorian skirts and respectable Victorian hats and respectable Victorian men looked at them and went into shock."[4]

Emergence of the Victorian prudery and delicacy that made it difficult for physicians to treat or examine their female patients at all caused the movement to train women in medicine to move forward. Nineteenth century professional ideas were shaped by the social structure, values and technical capabilities of the age. By 1846, the rise of medical quackery and sectarian medicine (which formed their own schools, journals and societies and educated women) led to easy access to a medical degree and abandonment of restrictive licensing.[1,2] The roles of women physicians in Victorian America were confined largely to the treatment of women and children. Victorian women physicians were viewed as social and physical healers and were sought after as lecturers for women's groups and for medical and nursing students. They promoted good health, nutrition, hygiene, sanitation and temperance. They struggled to eradicate the ignorance they believed to be the cause of social and moral ills.[1] In addition, they served as important role models for young women. The health reform movement, with emphasis on the central role of women in domestic medicine, led women physicians into the field of preventive medicine, and hundreds of women believing "that medical science needed the leaven of tender humanity that women represent" sought medical training in the decades following Elizabeth Blackwell's graduation from Geneva Medical College.[2]

Neither the absence of a college education nor the lack of a medical degree prevented anyone from practicing medicine in the United States in the nineteenth century.[2] Whether missionaries, suffragettes, war heroines, welfare workers, researchers or family practitioners, women physicians began to make noteworthy contributions to the country as well as the medical profession by the late 1800s. The only medical degree Harriot Hunt possessed was an honorary one from the Women's Medical College of Pennsylvania. Yet, because she devoted her life from the earliest days of her medical practice in 1835 to her death in 1875 to the cause of women in medicine, she earned the title of "Mother of the American woman physician."[5]

It was not until 1850 that the first medical college for women was created, when the Woman's Medical College of Pennsylvania opened in the back of a rented house on Arch Street in Philadelphia. The college promised to confer a medical degree that would "not be inferior to those of the graduates of any other medical institution of this country or Europe."[1] Throughout the nineteenth century, aware that the entire concept of the medical education of women was on trial and anxious to distinguish itself, the college did offer a superior course.

Not satisfied with coeducation and not easily admitted to regular medical schools, female pioneers founded regular and sectarian women's medical colleges. Edwin Fussell, professor of anatomy and histology at the Woman's Medical College, was an avid supporter of women's medical education; in 1861, he asked the schools new graduates, "Ladies, why are you here?"[1,5] "Ladies could you not be content to do nothing and to be nothing?" Fortunately, a resounding no is once more echoing through the sterile halls.[1,6]

Ann Preston, a dean of the Woman's Medical College of Pennsylvania, who had been a member of its first graduating class in 1851, addressed the class of 1879 with these words: "From towns and cities we are frequently receiving the inquiry, 'Can you not send us a reliable lady physician?' "[1] Women physicians then created their own hospitals to provide training for the college graduates who were refused postgraduate positions at male-controlled institutions. In the late nineteenth century, medical practices were conducted from the home primarily so women could readily combine marriage, career and child rearing. In a not yet technocratic profession, women were considered well suited as nurturers and could focus on family, prevention and hygiene. "The purpose of the women's medical movement is for the purpose of occupying positions which men cannot fully occupy and exercising an influence which men cannot wield at all," said Elizabeth Blackwell.[1]

Women's medical colleges provided academic training and emotional support via mostly female professors serving as important role models. As women made a place for themselves in medicine, prestigious medical schools were made available to them. Hospitals offered women staff positions; state and local medical societies invited them to join. (The American Medical Association seated a female delegate from Chicago at its annual meeting in 1876 but did not elect a woman to membership until 1915.) With the decline of sectarian medicine, women physicians matriculated and graduated in increasing numbers from regular medical schools, had reports published in scientific journals and took steps to formalize networks among themselves.[2]

In Philadelphia, the Alumnae Association of the Woman's Medical College of Pennsylvania had 219 members in 1900. They met for several days annually discussing cases, scientific papers and interests common to women in the profession. They recognized by honorary memberships distinguished female graduates of other medical schools. Indeed, when the Blackwells closed the Woman's Medical College of the New York Infirmary (thinking that it was no longer needed), only two women's medical colleges survived at the turn of the twentieth century, one of which was the Woman's Medical College of Pennsylvania.[2]

More problems beset women physicians in the mainstream of medicine in the early 1900s, when the actual number of female students declined from 1,280 to 992. By 1920, women were students in many of the nation's prestigious universities and medical schools. Sometimes, "creative philanthropy" opened doors, according to Rossiter writing in *Women Scientists in America: Struggles and Strategies to 1940*. Johns Hopkins University, for example, allowed women into its medical school in 1893 only after Mary Garrett, heiress to the Baltimore and Ohio Railroad fortune, raised $307,000 to build the school on the condition that women be admitted.[6]

However, the struggles of women were far from over. Ironically, the very institutions that had educated women would not hire them for positions on their faculties. The changing nature of the professions also created a double standard, one that was higher for women aspirants.[1,6] Many women's colleges closed in the 1920s, and enrollment of women plummeted as the women's rights movement also began to wane. Enrollments did not substantially climb again for 50 years.[2]

The gains of the women's medical movement in the late 1800s were steadily eroded. In searching for reasons, several explanations are offered, including the fact that as the practice of medicine evolved, it became more attractive and respected as a male profession. Women, more interested in nurturing, chose alternative fields, such as nursing, teaching and social work. Coeducational medical schools used quotas to keep out all but a handful of women so that a lack of female faculty deprived apiring women physicians their role models. Medical education fees increased, but fellowships for women decreased as the medical profession became more respected, prestigious and lucrative.[1]

Because the formal and most visible barriers to women's entrance into the profession had appeared to have dissolved by 1920, female medical leaders who still supported separate women's institutions were hard pressed to justify their continued existence. In 1909, Abraham Flexner had concluded that women's choices in medical education were "free and varied." He editorialized that "now that women are freely admitted to the medical profession, it is clear that they show a decreasing inclination to enter it." Flexner speculated that either women were not interested in medicine, or there was no strong demand for women physicians. Moreover, he believed that women's medical schools had served their purpose and were no longer necessary.[7,8] Ruth Abram, author of *Send Us a Lady Physician,* produced a powerful exhibit that documented the history of women physicians in the United States from 1835 to 1920 and assailed readers with a number of questions regarding the decline in the number of women physicians at that time.[1]

Was the setback due to the collapse of the nineteenth century women's movement and its supportive networks, along with the demise of women's medical colleges, which, in turn, diminished the number of professional role models? Did the change in the concept of medicine, from a healing art to a scientific solution, or the change in the image of the ideal physician, from healer to scientist, drive out women who continued to think of themselves as nurturers? Did the new careers in social work and teaching offer preferable alternatives? Was the rising cost of medical education, coupled with a dearth of scholarships for women, responsible for the demise? Or, was it a matter of discrimination on the part of medical schools and medical institutions? Was it the "new woman's" rejection of the older generation's ideology of "virtuous womanhood" that undercut the rationale that once supported women's advances in the profession? Did the new emphasis on the psychologic development of the child convince more women to devote themselves exclusively to mothering? Was the Flexner report on medical education, sponsored by the Carnegie Foundation in 1910, the final nail in the coffin?

Chronically short of funds, the Woman's Medical College of Pennsylvania was plagued by problems. The school's small budget meant that it could not grow easily and that it would concentrate on clinical education rather than on research. Katherine Sturgis, emeritus professor of preventive medicine, when seeking a medical education in the mid-1930s and not being interested in research, was advised, "Go up on the hill to Woman's Medical. They'll train you to be a good general practitioner." It seems all the more remarkable that this college trained brilliant women practitioners when several studies have indicated that the wealthier the school, the greater the success of its student body.[7]

The American Medical Women's Association (AMWA) valued the Woman's Medical College as "a bulwark of the future." "I have no quarrel with them for going to other medical schools," wrote Ellen Potter, of women who preferred coeducation, "but our continued existence is essential to them." The AMWA developed a close relationship with this school in the years after 1920, giving it financial support and featuring the school in its newsletter.[7]

By 1944, nearly a century after the first female medical student was admitted, 9 percent of U.S. medical schools still excluded women. The last school to exclude women admitted them in 1960. The 1970s brought the first major increase in the number and percentage of women admitted. This change in policy was initiated by the enactment of federal antidiscrimination legislation, the adoption of a resolution by the assembly of the Association of American Medical Colleges in 1970 that assured equal opportunity and, finally, changes in women's attitudes in seeking their full potential spurred on by the feminist movement. The Women's Medical College of Pennsylvania became coeducational in 1970, and women physicians evermore would struggle to capture that professional identity that only a single-gender education could afford them.[7]

The current influx of women into medicine forces a closer look at local and national trends of women in all levels of medical career development.

CAREER TRENDS

In sheer numbers, women in medicine have come a long way. Women comprise approximately 37 percent of the medical-school graduates of 1991. Let us examine other statistics. From 1970 to 1990 the number of women physicians has quadrupled, from 25,401 to more than 100,000; the proportion of physicians who are women more than doubled, from 7.6 to 16.9 percent; the number of women in office-based practice increased almost five-fold; and the proportion of women who are office-based has increased, whereas those in hospitals has decreased. By the year 2010, women physicians are projected to represent 30 percent of all physicians.[9] There are currently more women physicians than were total physicians in 1870.[10]

In addition to differences in age and specialty distribution, there are differences in the socioeconomic practice characteristics of men and women physicians. The following data, reviewed in the American Medical Association's publication *In the Mainstream,* reveal that women physicians were less likely to be self-employed and, on average, practiced fewer hours and had fewer patient visits per week than did their male counterparts.[10] This difference has remained a constant, and in 1991, we see the same.[9] Physicians age 40 or younger were more likely to be self-employed, whereas those over age 55 were less likely to be self-employed.[10] For women physicians, there is a greater potential for career interruptions, such as childbearing, and because of high investment costs for individual practice, young women may prefer to practice medicine as employees.

Earning potential is influenced by hours practiced, specialty, age and employment status. Women physicians earn less than their male counterparts. In 1982, the average net income of women physicians was $65,200; men earned an average of $102,000. In 1990, the unadjusted net income among women nonfederal patient care physicians was $101,500 and for men, $164,300. Thus the unadjusted income for women physicians has averaged 62 to 63 percent of male incomes consistently.[9] One recent survey reported that women physicians worked an average of 54 hours per week, as compared with 59 hours worked for all physicians. Female/male income differences are smaller in the per visit category, indicating that women may schedule fewer patients per hour than men. For the year 1991, total visits per week were 123.6 for men physicians and 99.6 for women physicians. The difference between men and women physician incomes increases by approximately 3 percent as years of experience increase.[11]

From 1970 to 1983, the proportion of women physicians increased to one eighth of all physicians, representing nearly a 175 percent jump. The proportion of women in residency training tripled in that 13-year period, whereas the proportion of women in research more than doubled. The proportion of women in residency training rose from 10.7 percent in 1970 to 24.5 percent in 1983, whereas their patient-care load increased from 6.6 percent in 1970 to 13 percent 13 years later.[12]

The total number of women physicians in 1991 is 104,194, an increase from 21,404 in 1967. The most popular specialties of women physicians in this year were, in descending order, pediatrics, internal medicine, psychiatry, family medicine and anesthesia.[9] Almost 60 percent of all women physicians are in these five specialties. The number of women has increased in each, whereas the rank order has remained unchanged since 1980.[9]

Women physicians are a steadily growing part of the work force; they account for 17 percent of the total physician population and 29 percent of residents. The greatest percentage of women are under 35 (37%), whereas the remaining 72 percent are 44 and under. The largest number and percentage of women physicians are in office-based practices; namely, 49,249 (50%).[9] In addition, women have not yet reached equality with their male counterparts in Board certification. Half as many women as men in family practice are not Board certified.[10] In 1970, women comprised 4.45 of all Board-certified physicians, whereas they were 7.6 percent of all physicians. In 1988, women were 12.3 percent of all Board-certified physicians, which was still below their 16.4 percent representation but, overall, proportionately higher than in 1970.[11]

Where do women physicians practice? In 1983, there were more women physicians in New York than in any other state, 14.4 percent of all women physicians. In descending order, women physicians chose California, Illinois, Pennsylvania, Texas, Massachusetts, New Jersey and Ohio; these seven states accounted for 56 percent of women physicians in 1983. The distribution of physicians according to age reveals that a higher percentage of women than men are under age 35. In 1983, a listing of all women physicians according to state and type of practice showed that more than 43 percent were office-based, 37 percent were hospital-based and 20 percent were in other professional activities within the eight states noted previously.[10] Women have been traditionally less likely to practice in rural areas. In 1988, only 7 percent practiced in nonmetropolitan counties, not much higher than in 1970.[11]

What do the preceding statistics say about women physicians and their male counterparts? Women have come to medical schools in increasing numbers, with good qualifications, and have been doing well in school and training, but their professional attainments in practice and in the power structure (of health care) lag dangerously behind. The politicians have recognized the position of women in health care just recently by naming the first female director of the National Institutes of Research and the Surgeon General of the United States, but have yet to appoint a woman physician as Secretary of Health and Human Services. Lifestyles, career choices and medical economics are changing. We are in an era when technology is advancing rapidly, but the challenges of health care lead to fierce competition in the marketplace. Women are faced with the tough decisions of how, when, where and what type of medicine to practice and how best to blend a medical practice with a personal life. Although these questions pertain to all physicians, they are especially unique to women physicians, who are expected by society to perform well and to integrate career, family and personal needs much more so than are their male counterparts.

The vast majority of women practitioners have been choosing office-based practices because such an arrangement allows them to enjoy the advantages of personally controlling work hours, service hours, teaching or research commitments, fees and other aspects of practice. Decisions regarding whether to participate in publicly funded health care programs, such as Medicare and Medicaid, are virtually mandatory if not in a legal sense, certainly in an ethical and moral sense. The managed care options facing new women graduates are similar to those facing men graduates (e.g., employee versus participant, capitation versus fee for service or even discounting medical care costs).

Unfortunately, because of financial, personal and legal responsibilities, a solo private practice is becoming extremely difficult in many areas of the country. Regular hours of practice and much of family life must be sacrificed. Marketing chores and personal appointments are hard to fit in with medical meetings, school meetings and other community activities. It is difficult to escape from the responsibilities of a neighborhood practice when one's neighbors and patients are one and the same. Shopping excursions become mutual information sessions when one is approached by patients in food markets, hairdressing salons and shopping malls.[13]

The solution for me, while I was practicing family medicine, was to maintain a private practice in my home. I alternated my hours to suit my children's growing needs and never to "cover" for my physician husband on off hours. I insisted that work time and playtime were taken together and not alternately. Total organization to create an adequate coverage system for greater time off and vacation flexibility is imperative for a successful combination of marriage and career. The main requirements for a private practitioner in a dual role are organization, motivation, an insatiable need to be your own boss, true love for what you are doing, flexibility, optimism, love of people, a gregarious nature, good humor, self-reliance and a degree of egotism.[14]

All things being equal, this was my choice and still is for the best type of medical practice for this doctor. Physicians are currently faced with the encroachment of third-party medicine well described elsewhere in this book. Decisions regarding styles of practice are broadened for women physicians as more women integrate their professional identities as women and thereby confront more problems and conflicts.

Successful physicians have participated in the "golden era of medical practice." That period witnessed an explosive growth of new diagnostic capabilities, curative therapies and dramatic procedures that made the practice of medicine intellectually demanding and exciting. Good physicians had an overwhelming supply of patients and succeeded both professionally and financially despite their lack of business expertise. Physicians acted as the captains of health care, being respected both in the hospital and in the office.[15] Perhaps physicians in that period were victims of a system that drove them in one dimension characterized by long hours and few personal rewards.

With the advent of third-party medicine and the creation of a multibillion dollar health-care industry, medical times are "a changin." The health care industry is in constant transition and upheaval. New systems, new technologies, new alliances of providers and new incentives for improvement have and are continuing to reshape the health-care delivery system for Americans. Young physicians will enter the health-care environment with a different view of medicine, a different view of life, and, within the foreseeable future, a government-mandated plan of managed care for all Americans.

The future of medical practice has been somewhat shaped by the Graduate Medical Education National Advisory Committee (GMENAC), organized by the Department of Health and Human Services, whose report was made public in September 1980. The committee's goals were (1) to determine the number of physicians required in each specialty to maintain a balance between supply and demand, (2) to find methods to improve the geographic distribution of physicians and (3) to improve mechanisms to finance graduate medical education. The committee developed strategies and made recommendations regarding physician-manpower planning.

The GMENAC reported that there would be 70,000 surplus physicians in the United States by 1990. It was recommended that medical school enrollments be decreased by 17 percent and that the number of foreign medical graduates entering the country be drastically curtailed. Furthermore, the presence of nonphysician personnel, such as nurse-practitioners, physicians' assistants and nurse-midwives, creates another area of concern with respect to public-policy decisions. The GMENAC recommended that the numbers of such personnel be stabilized until a complete study of their effect has been completed. This projected surplus is expected to affect most medical specialties. The supply and demand of family practitioners, internists, osteopathic practitioners and pediatricians are expected to remain in or near balance. Shortages are predicted in psychiatry, emergency medicine and physiatrics. The report recommends increasing the supply in the specialties with projected shortfalls and channeling the residual surplus into the basic primary-care areas, namely, pediatrics, family practice and internal medicine.[16] (See Overview section.)

The report recognized that the inequality in the geographic distribution of physicians represented a major health-care problem for this country. It also noted the difficulty in solving the problem because of the lack of well-demarcated geographic areas. The study stressed the need to develop functional medical-service areas within which most of the population receives such services. It was suggested that to alter the geographic distribution, financial incentives could be offered in graduate and undergraduate medical education. Also, professional-service reimbursement plans could be used as leverage. Financial incentives were touted as being able to influence the distribution of specialties. There is legislation currently being contemplated in Congress to mandate via the medical school admission policies the number of physicians to be directed to primary-care practice in rural, inner city or underserved areas.

The recommendations of the GMENAC report have affected women physicians to the same extent as they have affected physicians in general.

The GMENAC addressed the concern that in reducing the entire physician work force, there might be a disproportionate decrease in the number of women physicians. According to the report, "care should be taken to assure that programs to increase the representation of minority groups are not thwarted."[16]

The report recommended that greater diversity among medical students be accomplished by promoting more flexibility in the requirements for admission; by broadening the characteristics of the applicant pool with respect to socioeconomic status, age, sex and race; by providing loans and scholarships to help achieve the goals; and by emphasizing, as role models, women and underrepresented minority faculty members. There is no doubt that this has had a profound impact on the future of all physicians, especially women physicians.

CAREER DEVELOPMENT

The current evolution of medicine will probably lead women physicians to work harder, provide less direct care and receive less remuneration.[17] As we have seen, women physicians who became successful had to have not only outstanding intellectual capabilities but also extraordinary dedication and a kind of spiritual armor to deflect the "slings and arrows" sent their way by male classmates.

The "Women's Movement" has, of course, changed much of the past situation. Women have spoken out boldly and refused to accept the patterns of discrimination, have gained access to most of the "old boy's" residency programs and, to the surprise of some of the old boys, have done well.

The nurturing qualities of women physicians are self-evident, special and a boon for patients. Women physicians have to ask themselves, now that their number has increased again so dramatically, What is the relationship of gender to doctor-patient choices? Judith Lorber found that women patients do not strongly prefer physicians of the same sex and furthermore that "male and female physicians like most medical workers prefer patients who allow them to carry out their tasks with a minimum of fuss, make little trouble and are cooperative, trusting, and appreciative of their care. . . ".[18] In general, the gender composition of most practices depends on the specialty. General practitioners have more women than men patients, regardless of whether they are men or women, because more women than men seek health care in this country. The gap between men and women physicians in number of patients treated and hours worked over the course of a career is narrowing because men physicians are seeking fewer patients and working fewer hours per week than are women physicians.[18]

The lag of professional women in career development is conventionally attributed to their family responsibilities. There is much evidence to the contrary. Heins' study of women physicians in Detroit demonstrated that despite family responsibilities, such physicians were as productive as their male counterparts,[10] and others found that perceptions and commitments were more important variables in the career persistence of women physicians than was the actual extent of family responsibilities. Women physicians devote more practice time to administrative chores and continuing medical education than do men physicians, especially during childbearing and child-rearing years.[19]

The medical work place has enlarged to accommodate ancillary and paramedical personnel. In actuality, such personnel have encroached on the real practice of medicine. We are in an era of entrepreneurship in which nurse-practitioners diagnose, treat and prescribe; physical therapists in many jurisdictions are licensed to perform the same functions as physiatrists; psychologists are practicing psychiatry with or without the use of drugs; ophthalmic technicians perform functions formerly allocated only to ophthalmologists; and nurse-midwives practice obstetrics and routine gynecologic care. In fact, in at least one state, pharmacists are permitted to diagnose and prescribe for a number of human illnesses. Physicians, especially women physicians, must organize and develop their skills as physician-managers. What better way to protect the future than to enlarge on the 75-year-old AMWA.

WOMEN AND ORGANIZED MEDICINE

As our brief look at the historic aspects of women in medicine has already shown, women physicians in the early part of the twentieth century found their number declining and their previous gain of recognition steadily eroding. Realizing the need to provide emotional support to pioneering professionals, Bertha Van Hoosen (in 1915 a noted Midwest surgeon) founded the National Medical Women's Association, later renamed the American Medical Women's Association. Legend has it that Van Hoosen organized the AMWA after a meeting of the American Medical Association (AMA), during which a handful of women, attending as members, sat isolated, ignored and unable to participate in the proceedings.[20] The pioneers of that day looked to each other for professional and personal support and paved the way for the advance of women in medicine. Since 1915, the AMWA has had uninterrupted growth and meetings despite two world wars and several depressions. It has been the voice of women physicians in American medicine, the only organized group with this intent and responsibility. It has been the custodian, but not the only one, of the history and legacy, both cultural and scientific, of women in medicine. The AMWA is a forum for issues of concern and an advocate for womens' equality. It has exerted a major influence in transforming the place of women in medicine and the profession itself, representing a tradition of progress, while still pioneering for the future.

The collection of most of the important history books on and by women in medicine originally begun by Van Hoosen, together with other papers and memorabilia, is now in the Archives and Special Collection on Women in Medicine, part of the library at the Medical College of Pennsylvania. The efforts of all members of the AMWA are responsible for this achievement. The archives and special collection, located at what was the first and is the only extant school organized for the education of women physicians, is a resource for information about women in medicine. It helps women understand the social and cultural aspects of how they have influenced medicine and society. All women physicians and every medical organization founded by women must interact to foster better understanding and to perpetuate the history of women in medicine.[21]

Esther Lovejoy, the leader of the AMWA, along with other foreign physicians, jointly founded in 1919 the Medical Women's International Association, the first international medical association.[20] This association has members from 39 countries, placing all of the AMWA in communication with the medical world at large.

The aims of the AMWA are (1) to promote the interests common to women physicians, (2) to provide a support network to enable women physicians to speak candidly and share their concerns, (3) to encourage all aspects of medical training, (4) to position women to make a positive impact and advance in medicine and medical academia, (5) to solidify gains toward equal rights for women in medical training and practice and (6) to cooperate with other organizations that have similar interests.[22] In having these goals, the AMWA is rare among professional organizations. By granting full voting privileges to its student members (because, as the author noted in her inaugural address in 1983 as president of the AMWA, "our students are our lifeline to the future,"[23] the AMWA has taken a leadership initiative.

Perhaps no organization is better suited than the AMWA to advance the cause, position and posture of women physicians in this country and, through its affiliation with the Medical Women's International Association, throughout the world. Women physicians have all suffered the same traumas and have had to deal with the same problems of being women in a male-dominated profession. Women physicians need to share their successes and communicate their concerns. They need representation for their growing numbers, and they need to reach out to women who will follow to make the road smoother for them. Women physicians have been addressing the problems they share in expanding career options, in gaining leadership positions, in promoting women's health-care needs and in balancing their demanding careers with their personal lives.

Networking helps women physicians to become known, recognized and elected to various committees of the "coed" specialty societies and to other professional organizations. Membership in such institutions can help prevent feelings of isolation and depression, unfortunately common in the high-pressure profession of medicine. The cumulative microinequities of the daily lives of women physicians add to existing pressures and result in a higher risk for depression and suicide. The moral support of a network may prevent such tragedies.

Throughout the year, the AMWA offers opportunities to obtain continuing medical education credits through interesting and relevant educational programs. Such programs focus primarily on women's health-care issues and serve to educate women physicians as well as the public. Workshops teach women physicians behavioral and decision-making skills that facilitate their upward mobility in academic or practice settings.

Perhaps no function typifies the AMWA's dedication to providing health care to the indigent and the elderly more than its hospital service work. The committee that provides this service conducts a fund-raising effort to support and staff clinics in parts of the country where such care is scarce as well as to provide day care for children, care for the indigent and the elderly, medication and basic treatment supplies, counseling, mobile multiuse clinics, visiting-nurse programs and home health-care programs.[24] The American Women's Hospital Service Committee is now a part of the recently established Foundation of AMWA, which consolidates philanthropic, research and educational programs and promotes endowment activities.

I believe that women physicians are privileged to be members of the medical profession because they have special abilities and talents, and therefore it behooves them to form a local and national network for all women in medicine. Branch activities, annual meetings and workshops provide opportunities for women physicians to share their experiences in career and practice development. On a professional or career level, such activities provide a network of contact referrals and advice for women in medicine. Networking on this level has stimulated research and the growth of innovative teaching methods. Meeting women from a variety of specialty areas facilitates referrals that benefit both physicians and patients. Participation in the AMWA encourages mentor-protégé relationships that benefit both parties and that are important in providing access for women to informal information channels so crucial to careers in the academic, research and clinical settings. The AMWA's bimonthly journal publishes scientific articles and also includes information on women in medicine. It also serves as a means of communication among the AMWA's many branches and encourages women physicians to submit articles geared to issues relating to women physicians as well as to health care. Being part of a national organization helps women physicians be role models for students in their own areas as well as in other parts of the country.[22]

The power of group purchasing can provide members of an organization with the benefits of low-cost life and disability insurance, group rates for travel, discount buying services, a national directory for ease of referral and low-cost loans. Serving as a collective voice for women in medicine, the AMWA can have an impact on legislative and political developments. The AMWA can help women physicians learn how to develop political skills, run meetings, keep agendas, argue effectively and influence health-care policies.

Women must join associations to expand their career options, to secure acceptance of innovative styles of practice suited to their diverse needs and to address the problems they share in balancing their social roles and roles as physicians.

Women physicians will gain more visibility if they link with one another and other professional organizations to battle large societal issues. They must remember that medicine does not stand apart from life. They must review the past and return order to the present. "It is only as we see how it has come to be that we can appreciate what it is; it is only as we can direct its growth that we can control its future."[25]

If women physicians are to be successful in facing the impact of changes in the field, both men and women physicians will need to stand together and make use of all the organizational entities available. To this end, it is gratifying to note the election in several specialty organizations of women presidents and, of even greater importance, establishment of the Women in Medicine Advisory Panel of the AMA. The panel provides direction and coordination for the AMAs activities that address the needs of women physicians. The goal is to mainstream women physicians into organized medicine, defined as when the proportion of women physicians joining the AMA is the same as the proportion of men physicians joining and when the number of women in leadership positions in the AMA is proportional to their number in organized medicine.[26] Currently, there are two woman serving on the board of trustees of the AMA.

The AMA maintains a data bank of women physician leaders that contains information on more than 600 women leaders, including their specialties, locations and areas of expertise. The women-in-medicine advisory panel, an outgrowth of an ad hoc committee formed to study women in organized medicine, provides support services and consultation to component societies of the AMA. The panel strives to identify areas for greater involvement for women physicians and students. The data bank is considered to be a resource and an asset in promoting women physician leaders. As the first observer-delegate from the AMWA to the AMA's house of delegates during her presidency, the author participated in networking workshops and leadership conferences to enable women physicians to accept positions of leadership in their local branches. In these critical times, it is imperative that women physicians be sponsored for advancement and be given recognition for their abilities and commitment to a better health-care system.

Within the past five years, the American Academy of Family Physicians (AAFP) has established a committee for women in family medicine. The author has been privileged to serve on this committee and has recently been named Chair. This group promotes women physician's involvement at local, state and national levels via a "how to get involved" packet; a data base of speakers as role models; a membership recruitment program; and vignettes on videotape portraying personal and professional problems experienced by women in their careers. In May 1992, there were 16,639 women members of the AAFP, representing 23.1 percent of the total membership, a 15-percent increase in growth from 9.7 percent in 1982.[27]

Too often, women physicians have cited the problems of their dual roles in society, the scarcity of role models, their lack of leadership skills, their lack of financial resources and competition in the work place for their apathy and failed commitment to organized medicine. No longer can these objections be voiced if women physicians are to assume, as their growing number dictates they must assume, leadership positions in the major medical organizations of this country. They must stand up and be counted, and they must do so at the grassroots level by attending meetings and serving on committees. They must act as knowledgeable, assertive and articulate members of a team. With the growing acceptance of women physicians as full partners in health care, they shall prove not only that they are capable and caring but that they are also eminently capable and qualified to assume leadership positions in organized medicine in this country.

Historically, by banding together, physicians have been able to secure legislation to protect their professional interests within the health-care delivery system. As was noted previously, women physicians were forced to unite under the banner of the AMWA for similar reasons and to protect against sex discrimination. Perhaps the time has come when physicians of both sexes will have to accommodate one another under the banner of trade unionism, as exists in other countries, and some states to protect economic and professional gains and to secure future advantages (see Chapter 1). Perhaps more important is that all physicians must band together to ensure quality health care for all while protecting their professional gains, independence and interdependence.

Government statistics indicate that 13 percent of the gross national product is spent on health care. Steinwachs and coworkers,[28] in reviewing staffing patterns in three large health maintenance organizations, found that by 1990, 20 percent fewer primary-care physicians for children and 50 percent fewer for adults will be needed. Respect, honor and fair compensation as the rewards for quality health care may not be sufficient to guarantee that deserving women physicians will all be gainfully employed in the future.

As an analogy, the author is reminded of the dinosaurs, which are extinct not because of their small amount of brain tissue in relation to body mass, as was suspected, but because of their inability to adapt to environmental changes.

Joint ventures, surgicenters, emergicenters, "docs-in-a-box," health maintenance organizations, independent-practice associations and preferred-provider organizations will lead to physicians competing for diminishing health-care resources. Women residents, already debt ridden, will be overburdened and most likely will become salaried physicians or unemployed ones. Doctor bashing is part of the overall plan by which our adversaries in government and the "for-profit" sector of the hospital industry try to reduce physicians to serfdom. Because women physicians are not dinosaurs and have good brains, they will adapt and avoid extinction. Women physicians who do not adapt will perish financially and end their careers in disillusionment. Physician involvement in public issues will be a key to a successful future because a health access and/or managed care plan for all Americans looms on the horizon.

RESIDENCY AND BEYOND

Every resident's goal is to seek out the residency training program that will equip him or her in a chosen specialty and also give added prestige from peers and the public. However, because there are so few of the most desirable residencies and because women are fighting harder for them, those who do not get their preferred choices must succeed as best they can in lesser environments but not as "lesser physicians."

Match Day during the fourth year of medical school takes on the aura of both the beginning and the end of a student's world. On the one hand, students have completed general medical training, having focused on a field that they wish to enter; on the other, students begin to qualify to practice medicine, something for which a degree alone is not adequate preparation. A residency program is designed to prevent new physicians from overreaching their experience while at the same time allowing them to become more comfortable with greater responsibility.[29]

Learning how to avoid roadblocks, to sustain a vision and to follow through on an idea that will lead to becoming a medical entrepreneur *can* be accomplished.

The following tips and tactics for senior women residents appear in a new publication, *America's New Women Entrepreneurs,* as a possible road map for success in the field of medicine to be pursued with vim, vigor, vitality and perservance:

1. Know your heritage, who and what you are and how you can contribute to society's needs.
2. Have faith in your ability to succeed, and balance your personal needs with your professional requirements.

3. Seek a broad-based educational program that encourages educational curiosity in areas other than science.
4. Seek a relationship with a role model that can provide guidance in your chosen field.
5. Join organizations that can provide personal support and be a springboard to major professional and community involvement.
6. Take advantage of shared experiences in career and practice development.
7. Attend workshops available across the country and around the world.
8. Learn managerial and decision-making skills to facilitate an upward mobility in academia and in practice.
9. Be a positive advocate for yourself, your profession and the health of all.
10. And remember always the following quote: "The woman physician, daughter or science pioneer, thy tenderness hath banished fear. Woman and leader in the blend, Physician, Surgeon, Student, Friend."[30]

    As the turn of this century beckons, women physicians will need to be the judge of past experience to see what lies on the horizon. As listed in the 1991 JAMA medical education issue, approximately 24,500 women resident physicians, 29.5 percent of all residents, were on duty as of September 1990. More than one third of women residents were training in pediatrics or internal medicine, and another 26 percent were training in obstetrics, family practice or psychiatry.[11] One method for increasing prestige and personal growth will be for resident physicians to seek an academic appointment soon after residency. Women in academic medicine have had a slow but steady increase in number. Eleanor Shore, associate dean for faculty at Harvard Medical School, stated that the proportion of women in academia increased from 9.6 percent in 1967 to 13.7 percent in 1981.[30] Charles Seashore, an organization consultant, comments that only 13 percent of associate professors and 20 percent of assistant professors on school faculties are women. Seashore encourages women in medicine who do not think of a faculty or a management position as the pinnacle of their career to reconsider and seek such positions "to make improvements in the system."[31] Even though the percentage of women medical school graduates joining medical faculties has been consistently higher than that of men, in 1991, although 21 percent of full-time faculty were women, only 9 percent were professors and there were no women medical school deans.[9]

    From experiences in the AMWA, AMA, AAFP and from meeting residents from all over the country, the author has found that advancement in medicine in the future will depend largely on not only one's ambitions and medical judgment but also being part of the established power structure.

Women must not isolate themselves in medicine, Estelle Ramey, professor of physiology and biophysics at Georgetown University School of Medicine, admonishes residents. She encourages women to be interested in the power structure of medicine, reminding them that "the two things that will determine your fate in this society are money and power."[32]

Women physicians need to prioritize their lives not only as doctors but also as human beings. Where one goes in one's residency will depend on a multitude of personal choices and needs. This will be a time in one's professional life when one will reach to the depths of all the knowledge and wisdom from all the roots and sources one can summon. As a newly educated physician, one faces questions that are as unsettled as they are unsettling.

The previous generation of physicians came to medicine facing different issues. Social and economic forces that affect the methods of medical practice and the incentives under which physicians work have changed. Instead of one physician serving the health-care needs of patients, specialists of many varieties are needed. Practices replete with complex technologic advances that require special facilities, usually a hospital, and the complex of organized health care complete for patients and health-care dollars. The major societal variables that will affect the decisions that face all physicians include:

- Cost of medical care;
- Increasing high-tech capabilities; and
- The increasing number of physicians.

To the foregoing items must be added the special variables that affect women residents:

- Meshing within male-female medical partnerships;
- Keeping the "high touch" needed to maintain society's attention on human needs; and
- Maintaining sensitivity, nurturing and caring ways.

Women physicians will need to be the architects of their destinies. They must maintain their importance in medicine by embracing, along with their own problems, major societal problems, such as economics, peace, resolution of conflicts, disarmament, worldwide hunger and ecologic issues. When women physicians are in the forefront of major issues, as they have been in the past, they will maintain a major presence in the medical power structure.

Before a new woman physician can seek to function in the lofty halls of power, as has been suggested, she must establish a practice. Three thousand years ago, according to the Bible (Lev. 27:1–4), it was written that "when a man explicitly vows to the Lord, the equivalent for a human being, the following scale shall apply: if it is a male 20 to 60 years of age, the equivalent is 50 shekels of silver by sanctuary weight; if it is a female, the equivalent is 30 shekels." In modern times, the same ratio of values continued to exist; the average hourly wage for women is 63 percent of that paid to men.[33] Sex-related differences in remuneration have been ascribed to differences in productivity, whether inborn, acquired or socially imposed; differences in the nonmonetary characteristics of male-dominated and female-dominated jobs (e.g., risk for injury on the job or job site); and discrimination by employers, employees and consumers. With the Equal Pay Act, which made it illegal to have separate pay scales for men and women performing similar jobs, women's remuneration has come more into line, but total equality has not been achieved. Women physicians are overrepresented in the lower paid specialties, are more often salaried, work fewer hours, see fewer patients and are younger.[11] Equality depends greatly on income sharing within households. The feminist movement can be credited with making women question traditional sex differentials with respect to work and family.[34]

The disparity in earnings between men and women physicians may be offset by the satisfaction gained in the practice of medicine. A ten-year study of graduates from Case Western Reserve University School of Medicine found that although women graduates did not reach the same academic or economic levels as did their male counterparts, women were more satisfied with their careers and tended to work fewer hours than men. A major reason for the greater degree of happiness among women physicians was that many of them took time off to have children and to take care of families. Women physicians worked an average of 35 hours per week compared with 53 hours per week for men. Almost unanimously, women physicians in the Case Western Reserve study said that they would choose a career in medicine if they were starting over.[35]

PRACTICE STYLES

Some decisions that must be made are much more difficult for women than for men residents. Marriage, childbearing, life-style, location and type of practice are most pertinent in this regard. Dual-career choices will surely increase in the future, regardless of whether a woman resident has a physician spouse. Personal needs should dictate the location of a practice. "Physicians ought to decide where they want to live before they accept any offers," says health-care consultant George Longshore.[36] To illustrate his view that physicians often approach career decisions backward, Longshore, a partner of Fulton, Longshore and Associates in Haverford, Pennsylvania, cites the opinion of Philadelphian David Rich, an expert in life and career planning: "Because physicians usually have some latitude in selecting where and under what circumstances they will practice they should look carefully at the relationships between work and leisure, work and environment. Many people," he observes, "including new doctors are inclined to let the job offer dictate the move—and the consequent lifestyle. The life planning process turns that around. You begin with the ideal and work toward the real."[36]

According to Longshore, as a physician, one begins with perceptions of what medical and social environments are most suitable and then pursues opportunities in those environments. The quality of one's practice in this perspective is inseparable from the quality of one's life. "You need to be personally satisfied and very comfortable with what you are doing in order to be successful at it. Many people are not comfortable or happy regardless of how much money they are making. Physicians who are caught up in their effort to emulate their role models may not realize that success in other people's terms may not spell out satisfaction for themselves."[36]

Among the criteria that a new resident must consider when choosing the location of a practice will be climate, terrain, housing availability, health-care facilities, transportation, educational and cultural assets, recreational facilities and regional economic health. A useful reference that discusses these variables is *Places Rated Almanac,* by Richard Boyer and David Savageau. Physicians will find this book especially helpful in assessing medical as well as life-style variables. The chapter on health care includes specific breakdowns of each metropolitan area's resources.[37]

Although it is important to stress life-style, the author would be remiss if she did not stress the importance of purely professional considerations. Any physician considering where to practice needs to learn where the competition is and where the need is. The extramedical demands of private life greatly influence a woman physician's choices. The role of homemaker is surely unique and one of the most demanding. In the author's opinion, and based on experience as a wife, physician and mother of three, there are certain traditions of homemaking, as opposed to house-keeping, that are the sole domain of the woman of the house. Sharing of child care, attention to household chores and "taking out the garbage" can be allocated between spouses, but the balancing of family life, a difficult work load and role conflicts are mainly those of a woman physician. In a study from West Virginia University Medical School, the responses of 108 of 142 women physicians who graduated between 1962 and 1982 showed that most women physicians are married, hold full-time jobs and do not rely on domestic help. More than half the respondents with children paid for child-care help. Forty-four of the respondents said that they were unhappy with their work and complained that their jobs demanded too much time, 17 said that they were completely happy and

47 made no comment. The 100 women who responded to a question relating to income reported that their earnings were two thirds that earned by men physicians, but this discrepancy was not a cause of great concern. Their dissatisfaction was not related to their work; it arose from emotional and physical fatigue, yet was not reason enough to consider changing careers.[38]

The primary-care specialties will put the greatest demands on a woman physician's time but will give her less structured time than a woman physician in academia or a management position will have. The private practice of primary care affords greater flexibility than the delivery of primary care, whether a woman physician is an employee or a nonentrepreneurial member of a group.

THE UPS AND DOWNS OF PRIVATE PRACTICE

Until recently, virtually all that a new physician had to do was hang out a shingle to build up a practice. Physicians must now struggle with high office-operating expenses, low net income, a small number of patients and long hours. Interviews of new women physicians reveal that start-up equipment costs range from $20,000 to in excess of $50,000, depending on the specialty.[39]

In 1984, the AMA's Council on Long Range Planning and Development found that practice expenses had been rising by an average of 10.4 percent per year and that the share of revenue allotted had increased from 40 percent. This study also revealed that office visits had dropped by 2 percent. Although women physicians spend six hours less per week seeing patients than men physicians, this difference has decreased between 1982 and 1988.[11] The addition of Cinical Laboratory Improvements Act (CLIA) and Occupational Safety and Health Act (OSHA) regulations will further increase practice expenditures and decrease revenues.

To remain economically viable, a physician's practice may have to be relocated several times during his or her career. This situation, again, poses greater difficulty for women than for men physicians because it affects their extramedical lives. It might be wise for women physicians to consider joining respectable practices where they will benefit from having office procedures and equipment already in place. In this way, women physicians will also benefit from inheriting the trust and the "good name" of their more experienced partners.

Medical marketing practices have become increasingly important, especially for services of new women physicians as more patients elect to have women doctors. Many established practices are looking to enhance their position and productivity by adding women associates. This possibility was not readily available 30 years ago.

Young women physicians need to survive the "lean years," and this need in some ways dictates the choice of specialty. Overburdened with loan-repayment problems, many of them will choose the highest paying specialties. However, such a decision is not always the best one because time spent in longer residencies can worsen the financial burden. Income for new physicians is considerably lower than for physicians who have been practicing for 10 to 20 years and is even lower for women.

Important courses not included in current medical school curricula are those relating to business management and the day-to-day nonmedical demands of practice economics. Graduates are not prepared for the loss of income that results from mistakes made in billing, collection and completion of insurance forms.

To improve cash flow, women physicians might supplement their early income by (1) covering for vacationing colleagues, which the author did for several years; (2) by working in emergency rooms; (3) by examining for insurance companies; or (4) by taking hourly paid jobs in local health-department clinics. In addition, keeping the office open for a few extra hours at night or on weekends, creating an extended-payment plan for low-income patients and hiring an accountant who helps budget properly will help new women physicians.

I remember having office hours between the 8 pm and 1 am feedings just after my first child was born. I never thought that patients would come to the office during the intervening hours, but my working patients were delighted to have a physician see them after the end of their work days, and I was available for those "late-night emergencies."

LIFE-STYLES

Women residents and new women physicians must realize that not only can they combine career and family but they are advised to do both to be fulfilled.

Judith Lorber has described medicine and marriage as "greedy institutions" in that they both require strong commitments of time, energy, thought and emotions. There is evidence that being married, especially to another physician, is advantageous to a woman physician's professional life. The advantages of a two-physician marriage are compatibility of interests, understanding of problems, encouragement of career commitments and expansion of professional networks.[40]

For me, all the above are true and, in addition, my husband has always been there to encourage my career development. We married during medical school, and both of us chose family medicine. My husband has advised me and has been my biggest booster. Professionally, he is proud of my accomplishments and directs patients to me when their problems fall into areas where I may have greater expertise. We share office space, not as competitors but as independent entrepreneurs, but we work at marriage as a team.

Due to my traditional background, I was more conscious of trying to be in charge of the household chores, concerned with children's needs and being the primary caretaker of an extended family. My husband and I consult professionally, giving our patients the benefit of a second opinion at no extra cost. We have mutually decided what is right for us as medical contemporaries as well as what is right for us as husband, wife and parents. We are often frustrated by the lack of free time together and have partially solved this problem by sharing the organizational aspects of medicine and making continuing medical education conferences and conventions times to be together. Medicine-and-marriage partnerships require compromise. There are times when one spouse or the other suffers and both partners are stressed. As in everything, communication is the key, and simply being able to ventilate and share one's feelings does protect one's identity in a demanding setting. The intellectual advantages of sharing "this magnificent obsession" with a spouse can be magnified if both partners are in the same specialty—a sort of built-in continuing medical education course. Our 30-year partnership has been, and still is, the best of all worlds.

Unfortunately, this is just one side of the coin. For many two-physician marriages, there are the questions of whose priorities come first, whose career should be put on hold for children, where should training take place and what type of practice should be developed. The competition that can arise from one spouse being the overachiever, especially if that spouse is the wife, and the shortchanging that can occur to either partner's career or family life are serious problems in dual-career families.

Esther and David Nash, cognizant of the changing roles of physicians professionally and personally knowledgeable regarding the impact of dual careers, organized a dual-doctor families group that grew to more than 1,500 members before disbanding in late 1985 to gather information on practice patterns, residencies and training. They exchanged information on maternity leave, children, family growth and services for working fathers and mothers via newsletters and meetings.[41]

In the March 1982 issue of the *Journal of the American Medical Association,* an article cites a 1975 survey of 87 women physicians living in Detroit. The survey revealed that "nearly all the women accepted total responsibility for household tasks, that is for seeing that they got done by somebody, however at least three quarters of the women said that they did everything themselves." The modern woman physician in dual capacity has a different solution to the common problems that all working couples face. Marilyn Grayson, a member of the dual-doctor families group, faces these challenges, she says, with "compromise based on simple courtesy. Whoever has the time, does the work." There has been an evolution in the thinking of physicians with families. Thirty years ago, most physicians let their careers be the measure of their worth. Today, however, they are placing just as great a value on their spouses and their children.[41] There is recent recognition that professionalism has been at odds with a healthy family life, not only for women physicians but also for their male counterparts. In 1982, Brodkin and colleagues cited the results of a new program at the University of Medicine and Dentistry of New Jersey. A course titled "Parenting and Professionalism" was developed to aid students in solving crises relating to work, career and personal life.[19]

The AMA, ACP and AAFP medical specialty societies have responded to the feminization of medicine by recognizing key issues affecting women in medicine. Maternity leave is one such issue. Women who have just started out in practice are reluctant to take time off, and women medical students are hesitant to interrupt their studies. Carol Nadelson, the current president of the American Psychiatric Association, states: "The current economic situation really hurts women's futures as mothers. If a woman takes time off, who will hold her job, who will pay her? If she works part-time will she lose her academic appointment?"[42] This country lags behind other industrialized nations in providing maternity leave with job protection and child-care benefits.

A ten-year review of women physicians in Harvard-affiliated residencies revealed that although pregnancy during residency was common and generally planned, most institutions were unprepared and had no maternity-leave policy. Pregnancy in residency, a naturally occurring event, causes stress in an already high-pressure environment. It can occur comfortably with the cooperation of fellow residents, a supportive program director and an institutional policy geared to meet the "time" needs of family and career. Much depends on how pregnancy is approached by a resident and her program coordinator.[43] The AMA advisory panel found in late 1989 that 75 percent of residency programs had policies granting from one to three months leave. Many programs now stress paternity leave as well. There is a wide variety of policies, often not published or formally made available. The need for time to take Board examinations is a major factor in these policies. All programs should be encouraged to develop and publish a policy in an effort to model humane values.

With the number of women residents increasing, policies should be forged that ensure not only three months of maternity leave, if desired, but also alternative means of hospital coverage during this leave and sensitivity during training to issues that are an integral part of all women's lives.

Child care is the next problem residents or young physicians face after maternity leave. The AMA's Women in Medicine Panel conducted a study in 1989 of child care in hospitals and found just under 17 percent of the community hospitals surveyed and 35 percent of teaching hospitals currently offer such service. Where such services do exist, medical students and residents were least likely to be eligible to utilize them. In 1989, the AAFP surveyed and found that only 32 percent of programs for family practice residencies had child care available; therefore, a position paper has been developed by the Committee on Women in Family Medicine recommending that such facilities respond to the special needs of women family practitioners.

There is an overwhelming demand by women professionals to reverse the situation in which women barter career advancement for time to raise children and time to care for their families. One solution of coparenting requires that husbands share such responsibilities on an equal basis and "be open [about them] with . . . colleagues at work."[7] When asked what men physicians can do to help their women colleagues, Marilyn Heins, in 1983, stated that they can

1. Recognize the biologic imperative;
2. Help eliminate barriers put in the way of pregnant physicians or those with young children;
3. Acknowledge that slower career tracks to not indicate lower intelligence, lack of true worth or a lesser commitment to the profession but, rather, may result from the choice a woman made to spend more time at home;
4. Learn how to be a mentor to women with slower career tracks;
5. Learn to be comfortable doing household tasks and taking responsibility for them.[7]

Shared or part-time residency positions in medicine are available in 14 percent of residency programs, according to a graduate medical education survey; 50 percent were in family practice, internal medicine, pediatrics, psychiatrics or child psychiatry. In addition, more flexible practice options are becoming available for women physicians with family obligations who wish to limit their practice hours during child-rearing years. Although not yet accepted practice, women are nevertheless foregoing their own alternative practice relationships, such as part-time positions, flexible hours or job splitting and sharing.[9]

Although there is an apparent social bonus to a dual-physician marriage that imparts a certain standing in the community, what about the unmarried woman physician who no longer wishes her career to be paramount in her life? Is she not fulfilled? Not so, says a survey article in the *Medica Newsletter* of January 1986. Many unmarried women physicians who were interviewed demonstrated that young unmarried residents, once they have established themselves in practice, endeavor to develop interests outside medicine that will open up satisfying social avenues, new groups of friends and new sources of interest.[44]

It must be recognized, however, that most women physicians are overachievers, highly motivated and competitive; otherwise, they would not have succeeded in medical school and residency. It is hard, when the biologic clock ticks by at age 35, to ignore the issue of personal life and family. There is a delicate balance between career and personal life, but marriage and a family are not the answer for all women physicians. When interviewers start asking men physician applicants for residencies or jobs when *they* expect to marry or have children, as is so often asked of women applicants, perhaps we will have reached humanistic parity.

I recall with some enduring chagrin when, at the start of my career in private practice, I interviewed for staff privileges at two local hospitals and was told that I could not be a wife, mother and physician and still be productive enough to be a useful member of their staffs. Four other hospitals did not see me in the same light, and my ability to practice fully was not impaired by a few threatened old fogies with tunnel vision.

Perhaps one of the best assertive messages for now and the future comes from Natalie Shainess, author, psychiatrist and lecturer, who tells women physicians, "Don't doubt yourself—overreach yourself."[45] We can all agree that within the framework of our dynamic society, satisfying professional life-styles that emphasize completeness of life, commitment to quality and service and aversion to personal and financial risk will bring a sense of well-being and inner fulfillment.

ORGANIZED MEDICINE AND THE FUTURE

The AMWA has been redirecting itself and searching for a mission that will appeal to the growing number of women physicians. It is said that in unity, there is strength and power. Women physicians now have a communications network dedicated to helping one another but still suffer from the "queen bee" syndrome and often do not unselfishly help their sister physicians. Women physicians have tried too hard to shine independently in the past, whereas as a minority in medicine, they could have shone more forcefully as a beacon by focusing their light collectively. Once women physicians have this collective, powerful sense of being, they can integrate with their male colleagues in all specialty groups so that all physicians can together examine their future in medicine.

Women physicians must not remain isolated; they must integrate themselves completely into the medical profession. This integration will require that all women physicians take their rightful places in the hierarchies of all the major medical organizations and assume policy and decision-making positions. All women physicians should be aware of medical school admissions policies, residency-program choices and all decisions made at the medical-school and hospital-staff levels. They need to address political issues concerning health care. This requires much hard committee work at local and state levels. One must be physically present to influence health-care policies.

Organizations frequently overlooked by too many women physicians are the alumni associations of medical schools. The voices of women must be heard at the sources of their training if they are to exert an influence on the women who come after them. They should stand out as loyal beneficiaries of the institutions that granted their degrees. Time and financial generosity are required.

According to a survey conducted by the AMA's Committee on Women Physicians, most women physicians said that they did not encounter obstacles to attaining a leadership position in organized medicine. However, approximately two thirds of the women felt that women physicians in general encountered obstacles because of their sex, citing the unwillingness of men physicians to accept female leaders.[46] With women now making up one third of medical school graduates and with a large number of women consumers ready to accept their health rights, only the failure of *women* physicians (to recognize their potential power and to join with male and female colleagues who stand ready to share their goals) will interfere with their accession to positions of leadership. As Nancy Dickey, M.D., a member of the board of trustees of the AMA, says "there are still barriers but there are few hurdles that can't be leaped by women who are energetic and dedicated."[9]

Women are currently widely accepted and respected in medicine. They are represented at key levels in public health, science, administration, research and academia. Despite this representation, reports of sexual discrimination and harassment are not uncommon, especially in medical school, residency and the initial practice setting. Eighty-one percent of women surveyed in a 1988 medical school third-year class reported sexist slurs, sexual advances, denied opportunities or other forms of gender discrimination.[9] Policies to prevent sexual harassment and to rapidly respond to grievance charges have clearly been urged and established at most medical schools, training programs and the workplace.

The last 50 years have witnessed phenomenal advances in medicine, the growth of specialty societies and the growing influence of women in medicine, much of which has subsumed some of women's original commitments, changed the face of medicine and altered the way in which it is now practiced. Arnold Relman, M.D., Editor-in-Chief of *The New England Journal of Medicine,* wrote in 1989 that "a changing younger profession, more broadly representative of American society, with more moderate income expectations and a greater commitment to primary care specialties, will be in a better position to meet the needs for health care in the next century.[9] The increasing numbers of women in medicine, with their special dedication and involvement, will create that future.

All future physicians will need to master the technology of medicine as well as learn the business of medicine; otherwise, they will no longer control themselves or their profession. For women physicians, this represents an additional challenge. Women have traditionally placed the care of their finances in the hands of a man—father, husband or financial advisor. Good judgment dictates that intelligent women master the knowledge and techniques required for business and financial management. The author envisions the time when women physicians will carry their expertise and their attaché cases into the boardrooms of every major medical organization (see Chapter 9).

The best marketing tool, whether in business or medicine, is the delivery of an excellent product. What better product can women physicians offer than themselves, well-trained managers. Women physicians embody optimism, persistence, knowledge of hard facts, a social conscience, courage and know-how. They handle the overwhelming responsibility of life and death. They shape and direct personal and family lives and will, by natural inclination, be advocates for health issues.

Women physicians need to demand and assume their places in the policymaking bodies of organized medicine and in the community commensurate with their number and their abilities. The author was fortunate, by virtue of being president of the AMWA, to be an ad hoc member of the board of directors of the Medical College of Pennsylvania and to observe and participate in the workings of "the boardroom." Women physicians must hold such positions in every national, state and county society and association as well as in industry and government, particularly in institutions where health policies are formulated.

The barriers are giving way. In the past five years, the author has served and is continuing to serve on the boards of her county medical society, her state specialty society and as the newly elected president of the Family Health Foundation of Pennsylvania, the philanthropic arm of the PAFP. I am the incumbent chair of the Women in Family Medicine Committee of the AAFP and a delegate to the state medical society and AMWA. We must, as women and physicians, be a part of our societies, our communities and our profession. The American medical system is good but is changing and can be improved as women physicians challenge the issues and cause prejudices to be cast aside.

In the words of C. Everett Koop, former Surgeon General of the United States, "I envy those starting a career in medicine. I regret some things that are going on—the lack of good doctor-patient relationships . . . the growth of regulation, and so on. But, I also know that medicine still offers the individual one of the most satisfying ways to make a life that I have ever encountered."[47]

I, too, envy the woman physician starting her career today, for she embarks on an exciting voyage despite bleak predictions about changes in the health-care delivery system. Clearly, the influx of women in medicine causes women physicians to examine the issues unsolved in the past, to resolve those applicable to the present and to hope collegiality and improved health care will be the way of the future.

As I have reflected on my career in medicine, I see myself as a member of a profession whose opportunities go beyond our mothers' wildest dreams, whose struggles have no precedent in history, and I know future women physicians will bring more humaneness, more idealistic striving, more tender loving care to their patients, their communities and themselves.[48]

ACKNOWLEDGMENTS

This chapter would not have been possible without the combined efforts of my family, who researched, typed, proofread, criticized and helped crystallize my thoughts and ideas. This was truly a labor of love, and I acknowledge their help with grateful thanks.

REFERENCES

1. Abram R (ed): *Send Us a Lady Physician: Women Doctors in America 1835–1920,* ed 1. New York, WW Norton & Company, 1985.
2. Sanchez RM, Pomerleau CS, Fenichel CH (eds): *In Her Own Words.* Westport, Greenwood Press, 1982, pp 3–35.
3. Ware J: *Remarks on the Employment of Females as Practitioners in Midwifery, by a Physician.* Boston, 1820, p 6.
4. Hacker C: *The Indomitable Lady Doctors.* Toronto, Clarke, Irwin and Company Ltd, 1974, p 16.
5. Riddle J: Women in medicine, the early days. *The Washington Post,* March 26, 1986, p 23.
6. Jacobs M: Science: Pioneering women's role in field. *The Los Angeles Times,* March 23, 1986, p 26.
7. Sanchez RM: *Sympathy and Science.* New York, Oxford University Press, 1985, pp 343, 347, 348, 350.
8. Flexner A: *Medical Education in the United States and Canada.* New York, The Carnegie Foundation for Advancement of Teaching, 1910, Bulletin No. 4.
9. Kopriva P (ed): *In the Mainstream. Women in Medicine in America.* AMA, 1991.
10. Heins M: Women in medicine, a historical perspective. *Internist* 28(3):7, 1986.
11. Women in Medicine, DATA source, AMA, 1992.
12. *AMA Women in Medicine Project—In the Marketplace.* Chicago, American Medical Association, September 1985, pp 5, 10–12, 15, 20, 46.
13. Davis K: How do practice styles of women and men differ? *Internist* 27(3): 11–12, 1986.
14. Carlson B: What makes a good doctor? *Practice 84,* March, pp 55–58, 1984.
15. Practice management. *Pa Med* 89(5):41, 1986.
16. GMENAC Report—Review for Strategic Planning. American Medical Women's Association Strategic Planning Committee, November 1984.
17. International Medical News Service. *Fam Pract News,* February 1–4, 1984, p 12.
18. Lorber J: Mothers or M.D.'s, women physicians and doctor-patient relationships. Read at Eastern Sociological Society meeting, Philadelphia, March 1985.

19. Brodkin A, Shriver D, Buxton M: Parenting and professionalism—A medical school elective. *J Am Med Women's Assoc* 37(7):227–230, 1982.
20. Nemir R: Six decades of progress in the service of women in medicine. *J Am Med Women's Assoc* 29(11):486–487, 1974.
21. Chaff S: Archives and special collections in women in medicine. *J Am Med Women's Assoc* 38(3):73–74, 1983.
22. Kroser LS: A look back at AMWA. Read during Hahnemann University Women's Week, Philadelphia, March 9, 1983.
23. Kroser LS: Inaugural presidential address. Read before 68th Annual Meeting of the American Medical Women's Association, Dearborn, Mich, November 11, 1983.
24. *American Women's Hospital Service Brochure.* Dearborn, Mich, American Medical Women's Association, 1986.
25. Motto of the College of Physicians of Philadelphia, 19 South 22nd Street, Philadelphia, Pa.
26. Formica P, Ruddwyn S, Warren LD: Report of ad hoc women in medicine project of AMA. Read before the Annual Meeting, Chicago, June 16, 1984.
27. Committee on Women in Family Medicine, White Paper. Kansas City, MO, American Academy of Family Physicians, Revised July 1992.
28. Steinwachs DM, Weiner JP, Shapiro S: A Comparison of the requirements for primary care physicians in HMOs with projections made by the GMENAC. *N Engl J Med* 314(4):217–222, 1986.
29. Klass P: Now we're all going to be doctors. *Discover* 7(6):14–16, 1986.
30. Kroser LS: How to succeed as a woman doctor, in Harrison P (ed): *America's New Women Entrepreneurs.* Washington, DC, Acropolis Books Ltd, 1986, p 121–126.
31. Seashore C: Commentary, in Proceedings of Third Regional Conference for Women in Medicine. New York, Cornell University Medical College, April 8–10, 1983.
32. Ramey E: Making a difference in research. *J Am Med Women's Assoc* 39(3):74–76, 1984.
33. Fuchs VR: Sex difference in economic well-being. *Science* 232:459–464, 1986.
34. Editorial: *On the Issues of Women in Medicine.* New York County Medical Society, August 1983, p 11.
35. Phillips R: Women M.D.'s happier. *Fam Pract News* 5(23):32, 1985.
36. Longshore GF: Life planning for the new physician. *Hosp Physician,* March 1985, pp 2–94.
37. Boyer R, Savageau D (eds): *Places Rated Almanac,* ed 2. Chicago, New York and San Francisco, Rand McNally, 1985.
38. Curry J: Work hours and female general practitioners. *Med World News,* January 9, 1984, p 80.
39. Todd J: Medical practice the next 15 years. *Physicians Manage* 25:10, 1985 (special issue).
40. Lorber J: What makes or breaks a medical career. *Medica,* September/October 1985, pp 29–32.
41. Murphy K: Dual doctor families. *Private Pract,* October 1982, pp 2–22.
42. Nadelson C: Read before Acceptance Speech for Elizabeth Blackwell Award, 70th Annual Meeting of American Medical Women's Association, San Francisco, November 9, 1985.
43. Sayres M, Whyshak G, Denterlein G, et al: Pregnancy during residency. *N Engl J Med* 314(7):418–423, 1986.

44. Bensley L: Wanted: Career protection for doctors on maternity leave. *Med Obstet Gynecol FP Newsletter,* April 1986, p 1.
45. Shainess N: The problem of assertiveness. *J Am Med Women's Assoc* 38(2):42, 1983.
46. Kroser LS: Women in organized medicine. Read before Second Midwest Regional Conference on Women in Medicine, University of Kansas, Kansas City, September 28, 1985.
47. Koop CE: *Vocation in Medicine Challenges and Satisfies.* Editorial: *Pa Med* 88(12):28–31, 1985.
48. Kroser LS: My daughter, the doctor. Read before Congregation Beth Shalom, Elkins Park, PA, April 11, 1984.

SECTION

II
EMERGING
CAREER
TRENDS

COMMENTARY

David B. Nash

This section draws on the expertise of physicians in academia, industry and the private sector. I have deliberately focused on six potential career pathways that I believe will continue to undergo explosive growth into the next century. Each chapter is written by an expert or practitioner in the field.

With the "graying" of America, geriatrics will certainly become a growth industry in the next century. Dr. Risa Lavizzo-Mourey is a nationally recognized health-policy expert and a practicing geriatrician. She gives a personal reflection on the development of geriatricians. How are geriatricians different from internists or other primary-care givers? She describes practical steps toward approaching a career in geriatrics, including a career in research.

With the growth of corporate medicine, not only will physicians be employees of large organizations, but some physicians will be directors of corporate medical affairs. Dr. David Gluck, corporate medical director at Metropolitan Life, is in an excellent position to comment on the development of occupational health. This subspecialty within preventive medicine is a long-neglected field in medical-school curricula. Dr. Gluck describes corporate medical directors as accomplished "gatekeepers"—physicians who are able to take advantage of the lack of competition from private practice and use all the resources of a large organization to practice high-quality preventive medicine. He handily describes some of the potential conflicts between physicians and companies in the areas of individual privacy and the doctor-patient relationship. Dr. Gluck provides appropriate references and resources for developing a career in occupational health.

Dr. Seth Allen Rudnick and Dr. Alan S. Rosenthal, vice-presidents of research and development at major pharmaceutical firms, discuss the development of physician-executives in the pharmaceutical industry. They trace the budgetary and decision-making processes that are necessary in large, scientifically oriented organizations. Clearly, more physicians will be joining their ranks, lured by the challenges, set hours and lack of headaches encountered in private practice.

Dr. Thomas James is in an excellent position to describe the growth of health maintenance organizations and their impact on individual clinicians' practices. As a regional medical director for a major national health maintenance organization, he has recruited physicians to join medical centers across the southeastern United States. He provides an insider's view of this health-care setting, comparing the advantages and disadvantages of a managed-care environment. In addition, the second part of this chapter, which is coauthored by myself, traces the historical development of health maintenance organizations and puts their current explosive growth into perspective. Some observers have predicted that as many as 60 million Americans will be members of such organizations by the late 1990s. Many young physicians will be drawn to practice in this exciting environment.

Dr. Robert H. Hodge, Jr., is a physician-executive. He provides insights into managing a large health-care delivery system in an academic environment. He traces his decision-making process to join the growing ranks of physician-executives. The second part of this chapter, which is an expansion of a report by myself and colleagues that appeared in the *New England Journal of Medicine,* describes the national phenomenon of the growth of physician-managers. This chapter points out that medical administration has become virtually a Board certifiable specialty. It also describes in detail programs that enable physicians to obtain the skills needed to become managers. Last, the chapter outlines many organizations that certify and provide continuing medical education for physician-executives.

As managed-care settings proliferate, and as more Americans join health maintenance organizations, primary-care physicians will probably be at the forefront of the health-care delivery system. They will continue to act as the "gatekeepers" or points of entry into the health-care system and will influence the use of all health-care services. Dr. Robert B. Taylor, as chairman of the department of family medicine at Oregon Health Sciences University School of Medicine, is an expert in primary care. He has authored one of the leading textbooks in family practice. He discusses in detail the survival skills necessary for primary-care givers, provides excellent tips on developing styles of practice and describes current opportunities in the field.

In light of the physician surplus and the report of the Graduate Medical Education National Advisory Council, which was discussed in detail in the Overview chapter, I would recommend that physicians who are contemplating career changes pay particular attention to the second section of the book. Because there are few role models of established physicians in health maintenance organizations or in health-care management, this section may also provide needed advice on career selection.

CHAPTER 5

GERIATRICS: TOWARD THE FUTURE

Risa Lavizzo-Mourey

Dr. Jones is a geriatrician. She is in the business of caring for elderly people. Because the major consumers of medical care are elderly, such a statement could refer to many, if not most, physicians. Yet, most physicians are not geriatricians; in fact, most physicians do not even know what a geriatrician is or does.

Dr. Jones is a typical geriatrician of the 1990s. She is Board certified in internal medicine, has pursued additional fellowship training in geriatrics and has earned a certificate of added qualification in Geriatric Medicine. The team she works with is composed of other young, specially trained health-care professionals who chose geriatrics because it is unique within medicine. It offers not only a body of knowledge but also an approach to the care of the elderly. It is the approach or philosophy of geriatrics that links geriatricians. Some geriatricians are gerontologists, some are ethicists, some are primary-care physicians, some are nursing-home physicians, some are health promoters and others are health analysts and policymakers. Some geriatricians are all the above. Unlike other areas of medicine, the pathways to geriatrics and the roads a geriatrician may follow are marked by their diversity. This chapter will provide a perspective on geriatrics. It will explain the content and art of geriatric medicine and will also describe the many roles of a geriatrician. The next section looks at the various practice settings and job opportunities. An answer to the question, "Why geriatrics?" is attempted before the training process is addressed. The last section offers educated speculation regarding the future of geriatric medicine and advice to the young or would-be geriatrician. What, then, is geriatrics?

WHAT IS GERIATRICS?

Geriatricians treat elderly people. This answer is enough for readers who know what is involved in treatment and understand who elderly people are. Saying "elderly people are over 65 years old" is meaningless. Mrs. Kelly, who is over age 65, recently moved into a life-care community and, in her own words, spends her day "driving the old people places." The founder of the Gray Panthers is over age 65, as is Mr. Mills. Mr. Mills is not a fiery spokesperson. He is mute as a result of Alzheimer's disease and totally dependent on his daughter for his every need. More than half of all patients admitted to acute-care hospitals are over age 65, but do they all need the same kind of care? Indeed, the elderly are more heterogeneous than any other age group. To refer to the elderly as one group is misleading. Some authorities have divided the elderly according to age, defining those between ages 65 and 75 as the "young-old," those between ages 76 and 85 as the "old" and those over age 85 as the "old-old." Even this classification, while an improvement, assumes that people of a similar age have similar characteristics. Not so. As people age, the differences between them become more pronounced.

At conception, all human beings look alike. By the time they are born, they no longer look alike, but their physical capabilities are virtually identical. With each year, the differences outgrow the similarities.

After ages 50 to 75, the stakeholders in geriatrics are richly diverse but can be categorized according to their medical needs into four groups. There are the elderly who have escaped illness and remain well—Mrs. Kelly. There are those with acute illnesses—the ones physicians and other health-care professionals in hospitals know best. There are the chronically ill elderly who live in the community—Mr. Mills. Unfortunately, there are also chronically ill elderly whose diseases have made them totally dependent to the point of institutionalization. Geriatrics addresses the health-care needs of each of these groups and, as such, has a different focus than most other areas of medicine.

In a seminal essay, Robert Kane and associates defined five goals for geriatric clinicians.[1] First, maximize the independence of a patient. Optimizing the physical, mental and social functioning of the elderly is the core of geriatric medicine. Second, ensure a maximal level of "comfort." In other words, alleviate physical discomfort and also reduce the emotional stress of being sick, functionally limited or having suffered the many other losses of old age. Third, promote a sense of well-being. Even the chronically ill can experience a sense of well-being if their symptoms are relieved and if they have adapted physically and mentally. Fourth, prevent premature death. The goal here is not longevity at any cost;

rather, it is avoiding the causes of death that are easily manageable. Fifth, minimize the cost of care without compromising the outcome of care.

Physicians who view the maintenance of health as medicine's ultimate goal might argue that the goals of geriatric medicine and the goals of medicine as a whole are congruent. The World Health Organization defines health as not merely the absence of disease but as the presence of physical and mental well-being. Both sets of goals sound similar, yet the process of achieving those goals is usually different.

The difference lies in the means to the end. Medicine as a whole seeks the cure of disease as the ultimate means to maximize well-being. Geriatrics, on the other hand, views the cure as something to be considered, or as an unlikely alternative, but not the most important path. Almost any physician would subject a young patient with Hodgkin's disease or testicular cancer to surgical intervention, chemotherapy, radiation therapy and a seemingly endless number of hospital days, examinations, radiographic studies and venipunctures. The cure is the accepted way to maximize long-term well-being. Similarly, a robust 50-year-old patient with a solitary pulmonary nodule is almost certain to get a "tissue" diagnosis. In other words, much care would be taken to evaluate the extent and nature of the disease to assess the possibility of a cure. In both examples, the focus is the disease and the curing of that disease. The presumption is that once the disease is cured, health is restored.

The elderly usually do not have a single disease. They often suffer from five to ten diseases, and only one or two of them may be curable. Fixing the fixable might avoid premature death, but it does not restore health or maximize well-being. The means of achieving Kane's five goals are the heart and science of geriatric medicine and represent the work— past, present and future—of geriatricians and their basic-science counterparts, gerontologists.

Geriatrics, like other clinical disciplines, is based on a defined body of knowledge as well as on an approach to the practice. In the real world, the two overlap, and each is dependent on the other. However, considering them separately—the body of knowledge first and the approach, or art, of geriatrics second—may help clarify the picture.

THE BODY OF KNOWLEDGE AND THE ART

Geriatricians are by necessity generalists. Their base of knowledge is rooted in internal medicine or family practice but has grown to include seven additional areas that are essential to the practice of geriatric medicine. These seven areas—normal aging, nonspecific presentations of disease, atypical presentations of disease, diseases and medical problems seen most commonly in the elderly, geriatric pharmacology, rehabilitation and multidimensional assessment—broaden rather than narrow one's medical view. Furthermore, the art or practice of geriatric medicine, which focuses on the whole person, the environment and the family, and the team approach, emphasizes this broad view.

Let us carefully examine each of the seven clinical areas. First, an understanding of the normal aging process forms the foundation of clinical geriatrics. Aging is a continuous yet variable process. It occurs at every level, ranging from individual cells to organ systems. We do not begin to age at some arbitrary point in time and then continue in a stepwise fashion, with the steps marked by years or decades. Although aging is continuous, the rate varies from organ to organ within and among individuals and species.

Why aging occurs is not fully understood. Theories relate aging to wear and tear of organs and tissues, endocrine changes, free radicals and their effects on tissue, and nutrition. Consideration of this fundamental question is stimulating for all but falls more within the daily work of gerontologists than of geriatricians. It is the appreciation of the aging process that forms the base of geriatricians' clinical knowledge, just as an appreciation of human embryology provides the base of knowledge for perinatologists and neonatologists. Often, the challenge is in separating the consequences of normal aging from disease states and in correctly integrating knowledge about the aging process into the understanding of diseases and their management modalities. For example, most people experience some loss of memory with aging, but only a few suffer from dementia. Geriatricians must be able to differentiate benign senile forgetfulness from early-onset dementia. Most importantly, the geriatrician is charged with ensuring that their patients age successfully.[2] The concept of successful aging, introduced by Rowe and Kahn, describes the acquisition of years without the acquisition of disabilities.

Second, clinical geriatricians have a special interest in the group of diseases that are seen almost exclusively, or much more commonly, in the elderly. While the list is limited in number, its scope is extremely broad. Geriatricians move from acute-care medicine as they treat patients with hyperosmolar nonketotic coma, to long-term care as they attend to patients with dementia, to prevention as they screen for breast and colon cancer. As with any generalist, geriatricians claim no organ system. They must be as knowledgeable about cardiology as gastroenterology, neurology, dermatology, or any number of areas all physicians have been studying since their first internal medicine clerkship. Because many frail, chronically ill elderly have limited access to other specialties, geriatricians are probably called on to evaluate psychiatric, gynecologic and urologic questions more often than other generalists. This is not to say that geriatricians manage problems in all these areas without help; however, geriatricians are, for example, as comfortable coordinating the diagnosis and management of colonic angiodysplasia as they are managing giant-cell arteritis, and they are always cognizant of the limitations of their knowledge.

A third area is represented by common problems that present atypically in the elderly. Classic signs and symptoms that physicians rely on to make diagnoses may be absent or altered in the elderly. An appreciation of these atypical presentations is essential to the care of acute illnesses in the elderly. For example, an 85-year-old woman with congestive heart failure and atrial fibrillation of recent onset was brought to our geriatric evaluation program. The patient's family was concerned about her increasing lethargy, weakness and anorexia and wondered whether these signs and symptoms were problems of old age. She did prove to have a problem of old age, apathetic hyperthyroidism, with a thyroid hormone level of 21 mg/dL. Diagnosing and managing this atypical presentation of hyperthyroidism relieved all the patient's signs and symptoms, certainly improved her independence and may have helped her avoid premature death. It is the variations from the classic cases that, in part, make medicine intellectually rewarding for clinicians. The description and general recognition of the atypical presentations of disease in the elderly, such as infection without fever or leukocytosis or myocardial infarction without pain, have the potential to improve the quality of medical care for acutely ill patients in particular. This area as well as the fourth area need development by clinician-scholars.

The fourth area of clinical geriatrics seeks to provide useful and complete diagnostic approaches to the nonspecific presentations of illness in the elderly. Much of a geriatrician's clinical acumen is manifest when he or she is disentangling such problems as anorexia, syncope, falling, incontinence and weakness. At one major teaching hospital, the house staff have, tongue in cheek, labeled weakness a "fatal disease" because they have observed that death follows a chief complaint of weakness in an extraordinary number of elderly people. Although on a gut level many physicians would agree with this observation, no one can explain it. Indeed, only one or two of the nonspecific problems of the elderly have been investigated in depth, and more questions than answers have emerged. Incontinence is one problem that has been the focus of research; progress has been made toward accurate diagnosis. Indeed, there are now clinical practice guidelines to assist practitioners and patients.[3]

The diagnostic dilemmas posed by care of the elderly are equaled only by the complexity of therapy. Therefore, the fifth area is geriatric pharmacotherapy. Superimposing the aging process on pharmacologic principles and adjusting medications accordingly are fundamental to management of illness in the elderly. Virtually every factor that affects the serum concentration of a drug (pharmacokinetics) and its interaction with the site of action (pharmacodynamics) is potentially affected by the aging process.

For example, not only does gastrointestinal motility change with aging, so do hydroxylation and oxidation by the liver. The proportion of total body water to total body fat decreases with aging. These changes are only a few of the many that affect the concentration of a drug in the body. Not only is the concentration of a drug altered, but frequently the number and type of receptors for the drug are also affected by the aging process. Adjusting even one medication in response to such changes can be complicated. However, only a few elderly people are taking just one medication.

Community-dwelling elderly people take five to eight prescription medications, each of which may have altered the pharmacokinetics or pharmacodynamics of another. The result: frequent drug interactions and adverse reactions. Just as diseases can present atypically in the elderly, so too, can adverse drug reactions. Geriatric pharmacology, however, goes beyond adjusting doses and simplifying treatment regimens to address the issues of compliance, therapeutic response and underreporting of drug-related symptoms. Preventing iatrogenic illness secondary to adverse drug reactions is one way geriatricians make an immediate and often profound effect on an elderly person's quality of life.

The sixth area of clinical geriatrics, the multidimensional assessment, developed in response to the complex interplay of physical, psychologic and social variables that affect the elderly in Western culture. Pioneered by Marjorie Warren during the 1930s in England, this type of assessment attempts to measure physical health, functional ability and psychologic health. Social parameters, such as economic stability, social support systems and family well-being, are then factored into the formulation. This comprehensive data base can be used in community-based assessment or screening. It is the backbone of inpatient geriatric evaluation-management units (GEMs) as well as of outpatient assessment programs because it aids in diagnosis, treatment planning and prognosis. There are literally dozens of instruments for each area of function, and they are being refined continually. Choosing the instrument that suits a patient's and a clinician's needs and that has been validated for the appropriate population, administering the instrument correctly and interpreting the results are skills at which geriatricians are becoming expert. The multidimensional assessment has shaped the role of geriatricians as diagnosticians and, to a large degree, the emphasis of clinical geriatrics.

The last and perhaps most important area of clinical geriatrics is rehabilitation. Rehabilitation is not generally considered to be in the mainstream of clinical medicine, but it is in the mainstream of clinical geriatrics. The principles of rehabilitation—specific control of disease processes, prevention of secondary disabilities, restoration of function and adaptation—augment the purely medical management of illness in geriatric patients to truly maximize independence. Geriatric fellows believe that training in this area is the most useful part of their clinical learning experience. Recommendations of geriatric consulting teams or the plans of geriatric assessment units almost always include the effective use of rehabilitation.

These areas that make up the body of knowledge are given life and meaning through the multifaceted art or approach of geriatrics. The well-being of a patient, particularly an elderly patient, depends on psychologic, social, economic and environmental variables usually not considered within the realm of clinical medicine. Therefore, the geriatric approach is by necessity a holistic one. Knowing a patient's living situation, significant others, social support system and even means of transportation is as important for a geriatrician as is the baseline examination. Geriatricians routinely consider the social support system in deciding whether a problem can be managed at home or whether it necessitates hospitalization or additional home-care services. Similarly, geriatricians often become involved in the difficult process of convincing elderly persons to stop driving or traveling alone. These decisions require a complete knowledge of the elderly and their families.

Contrary to the stereotype of the constantly complaining old person, the elderly underreport symptoms and problems. Unless they are asked about their shortness of breath, arthritic pain, cold house or near misses while driving their car, they will suffer in silence. When a spry 92-year-old woman missed a routine appointment at our office, we called her apartment. A neighbor answered the phone and indicated that our patient was "sick and had gone to her bed." In fact, our patient was in congestive heart failure. Once admitted to the hospital and treated, she regained her "strength" and ability to keep on going a little while longer.

This example demonstrates two important aspects of the holistic approach: first, its necessity and potential for positive outcome and, second, its active (versus passive) nature. It may have taken two or three days for our patient or her neighbor to decide that rest was not sufficient therapy. If we had not called, and had not been able to decide quickly (because of our knowledge of her baseline living situation) that hospitalization was required, the outcome may not have been as good. Geriatrics cannot be practiced in medical isolation; an active holistic approach is essential.

In addition to knowing and caring for a whole person, the geriatric approach encourages a role of advocacy on the part of physicians, nurses, or social workers toward the elderly. Geriatricians are especially cognizant of this role because often their patients are not able to be their own advocates. Most physicians resort to this advocacy role when they have to make decisions concerning life-saving therapy, resuscitation or risky therapy. Frequently, however, geriatricians are called on to uphold an elderly person's status as a person in the minds of busy hospital or nursing-home staff, to arbitrate family squabbles or to testify in competency hearings. In addition, the role of advocacy extends to public advocacy for the elderly. Geriatricians are regularly called on to testify at congressional hearings, sit on task forces, work on various city or state commissions on aging and participate in talk-show interviews. The role of advocate, which is born of a commitment to the holistic approach, is always a part of a geriatrician's activities, particularly as he or she works within the family structure.

The geriatric approach includes the family in all aspects of an elderly person's care. In most cases, the family is the primary provider of care, even for the most disabled elderly. If geriatricians do not involve family members in the formulation of the treatment plan, and then provide the necessary emotional support as they carry it out, there is little hope of success. The daughter of one of our patients with end-stage Alzheimer's disease calls regularly with "progress reports" on her father's care. Such regular reporting does not mean that we are actively involved in changing the care plan. Actually, the care plan has remained the same for almost six months. Yet, these regular calls are essential to maintain the daughter's confidence and coping mechanisms. Frequently in geriatrics, maintaining a family's functioning *is* the treatment plan.

Implied in all that has been said so far is that the approach of geriatrics requires attention to the environment. An elderly person's environment often makes the difference between relative independence and total dependence and can usually be altered to foster independence. A frail octagenarian living in a city apartment equipped with an elevator and within walking distance of transportation and shopping can be much more independent than the same frail elderly person would be living in a multi-level suburban house that is far from transportation and shopping. Similarly, night-lights and handrails improve safety and decrease the risk for falling. Knowledge of the environment also allows for a personalized treatment plan. It would be much easier for anyone to understand an increasing exercise regimen if it is described in terms of "the number of trips down a hall to be attempted in a day" rather than in terms of the number of unassisted feet of ambulation. Attending to the whole patient, the family and the environment requires a team.

Only a well-functioning team can cover all the areas that make up clinical geriatrics. Typically, the team consists of a geriatrician, a geriatric social worker and a geriatric nurse. This core team works closely with a complementary team of psychiatrists, physiatrists, physical therapists, occupational therapists, dentists and podiatrists. This multidisciplinary team must be comfortable working in tandem or as an interdisciplinary team, depending on the situation. A well-functioning multidisciplinary team often performs in the same way that a relay team does. Each person runs a good race, accomplishes the individual goal and passes the baton without missing a step. Each member is needed for winning the race or, in the case of geriatrics, for maximizing an elderly person's well-being. The team must also be able to function in an interdisciplinary manner. In other words, its members must be able to work together, sharing roles and exchanging positions as members of a basketball team would. Geriatrics is a team endeavor.

A Geriatrician's Role

Geriatricians potentially have five roles. Some geriatricians juggle all five; others choose two or three to balance. The roles cover a wide spectrum of clinical practice opportunities. The five roles—primary-care physician, geriatric consultant, geriatric unit director, educator and researcher—are explored in detail.

The content and approach of geriatrics make all geriatricians generalists. As such, geriatricians are ideally suited to provide primary care to elderly people. Providing such care for most elderly patients is no more or less challenging than providing care for other adult patients. For extremely frail patients, providing primary care always involves a team and routinely requires a geriatrician's special skills and approach. The notion of geriatricians providing primary care presents a problem—too few geriatricians.

Currently, people over age 65 comprise approximately 12 percent of the population. As a group, they require 50 to 100 percent more health care than young adults do. This large proportion of elderly people must be contrasted to the 2 percent of physicians currently considering themselves geriatricians.[1] It must be further emphasized that only a few hundred of this 2 percent are actually "trained" geriatricians.[4] Clearly, their numbers alone prohibit geriatricians from providing continuing medical care to the entire population over age 65. The provision of comprehensive primary care to the most frail, most complex, community-dwelling and institutionalized elderly is, however, a goal within the reach of the currently small number of geriatricians. Providing primary care is a role physicians, and particularly geriatricians, use to anchor their other roles.

At the next level, and often linking the primary-care and consultant roles, geriatricians provide secondary and tertiary inpatient care. Increasingly, this kind of care is provided in geriatric units. There are two dominant models for geriatric units. Most units exist as evaluation-management units. They provide comprehensive evaluations and interdisciplinary treatment plans for frail elderly patients who are at risk for substantial functional decline. As is consistent with the approach of geriatrics, such units use the expertise of several specialties and disciplines within an interdisciplinary model. A patient may be admitted to a hospital for a cerebrovascular accident, pneumonia or myocardial infarction. Once stabilized, the patient is transferred to the geriatric evaluation-management unit. Studies[4,5] have shown that such units are effective in improving the functioning of appropriately selected patients. Furthermore, use of such units has been shown to reduce mortality. These resources are scarce and must be rationally allocated. Most units are not intended to treat every elderly patient at risk for placement in a nursing home or for suffering a complicated and prolonged hospital course, even though all might benefit from them.

The other model is more similar to traditional acute care. Elderly patients are admitted to a unit on the basis of age. All patients over age 75 or 85 would go to a geriatric unit. The average length of stay is the same or less than that of other patients with similar diseases. Patients are treated for acute problems in an environment where the nurses, physical therapists and house officers are especially cognizant of the problems of elderly patients.

Although primary-care medicine is at the center of any physician's activities, current geriatricians may spend more time in the role of consultants. Many elderly people have had long and trusting relationships with their physicians. They are reluctant to change physicians solely because of advancing age. Outpatient evaluation programs have sprung up to provide comprehensive, interdisciplinary evaluations that augment but do not jeopardize these highly valued and established doctor-patient relationships. The elderly or their care-givers often "self-refer" to such programs for a second opinion regarding dementia or functional decline. Although it has not been conclusively shown, the evidence indicates that such evaluations lead to improvement in function and quality of life.[6] In addition, geriatricians and geriatric teams provide consultation services similar to those of physicians for hospitalized patients. The consultation services at the University of Pennsylvania are examples of this role.

At the Hospital of the University of Pennsylvania, the Foerderer Geriatric Program is staffed by six geriatricians, two nurse-clinical specialists and a social worker. The team performs physical, functional, mental status, neuropsychologic and laboratory evaluations. This battery of tests requires approximately six hours to complete, but at the end of the evaluation, the team has the information necessary to make comprehensive recommendations. Similarly, the team provides in-patient evaluations to patients on nonmedical services. A severely depressed elderly patient who is admitted to the psychiatric floor is likely to have several medical and social problems and even some functional problems, which the team evaluates and for which it recommends appropriate therapy. To this role of in-patient and out-patient medical consultant is added another consultant role.

Several hospitals have incorporated geriatrician-consultants into their ethics committees. Because the elderly are often faced with physical and mental compromise and because geriatricians work so closely with the elderly, even young geriatricians have considerable practice experience in sorting out ethical problems. Philosophic, spiritual and legal perspectives can be meaningless when a geriatrician is faced with ethical problems if pragmatic considerations are not addressed. A geriatrician works in multidisciplinary settings continually and therefore is effectively able to bring several points of view to a small, well-functioning ethics committee.

The role of a geriatrician-consultant is a difficult one. The nature of the problems are complex, and for many problems there is no right answer. The role is made more difficult because of the expectations that many people have regarding consultants. Consultants are advisors. They must be recognized as experts and empowered because of that specialized knowledge. Usually, the person engaging a consultant is the person who will implement his or her recommendations.

These basic expectations are frequently unmet in the case of geriatric consultants. Often, the person engaging a consultant is a patient or a member of his or her family, yet the person being advised is another physician. Many physicians do not recognize the expertise of geriatricians and therefore may not be willing to accept their recommendations. This situation is, of course, exacerbated by the fact that the advice is unsolicited and may involve areas not usually in the realm of internal medicine. This situation may change as the acceptance of geriatrics increases. Currently, however, a geriatrician-consultant is in a precarious position.

The last two roles of geriatrics—educator and researcher—theoretically can be viewed as optional, yet practically are vital to geriatrics. Given the small number of physicians considering themselves geriatricians and the even smaller number who have received formal training, it is difficult for a "card-carrying" geriatrician to escape teaching at all levels.

Medical schools are responding to the directives of the Association of American Medical Colleges to improve the teaching of geriatrics at the undergraduate level. With the inclusion of specific geriatrics-content questions on the American Board of Internal Medicine and the American Board of Family Practice certification examinations, postgraduate training programs are looking to increase the exposure of residents to the principles of geriatrics.[7] Last, practicing physicians who spend at least 50 to 60 percent of their time treating elderly patients want continuing education opportunities in this area.

As a result, almost every geriatrician does some teaching. Occasionally speaking at a community-hospital grand rounds or supervising a medical student may be at the less active end of the spectrum. A geriatrician who enjoys teaching may be invited to give one or more lectures a month, participate in curriculum-development decisions, supervise students in choosing elective courses and attend on general medical services. Teaching inevitably leads to writing, and the written word must be penned. There has been a dramatic increase in the number of textbooks and review articles on geriatrics topics (see textbooks listed in reference section). Geriatricians are busy teaching on all levels and in all media.

Although participation in research is less universal, it is difficult to practice geriatrics and not be tempted to study one or two of the many questions facing this field. Geriatrics research can be categorized in one of three ways: basic biomedical, clinical or health services research. Basic biomedical research looks at cellular and molecular processes of aging. Researchers in this area explore questions that may contribute to a real understanding of aging. Clinical research is concerned with the interplay between aging and disease and involves both etiologic basis and management of disease. Understanding why the elderly are prone to dehydration, and how to best treat them; defining the etiologic basis of Alzheimer's disease; and understanding the unique features of the inflammatory response in the elderly are examples of clinical-research questions facing geriatrics. Health services research looks at the method of providing care and tackles such questions as: Are geriatrics units effective? How do we best educate geriatricians? What does it truly cost to provide interdisciplinary care? There is plenty of room for basic biomedical, clinical and health services researchers at the geriatrics table.

In summary, geriatricians are in short supply; therefore, they all wear many hats. The roles of consultant, educator and primary-care physician are clearly dominant and are shared by academic and nonacademic geriatricians alike. In more specialized settings, such as regional centers (teaching hospitals or Veterans Affairs Medical Centers), geriatricians provide acute care within geriatric units. Research, whether basic biomedical or clinical investigations, completes the picture (particularly for academic geriatricians). Geriatrics is ideally suited for physicians who thrive on variety. Heterogeneity best characterizes the patients, roles and practice settings encountered in geriatrics.

PRACTICE SETTINGS

Practice settings for geriatricians are superficially similar to those for other physicians. Viewed individually, the settings may even be exactly the same. It is the mixture of settings more than the characteristics that is unique to geriatrics.

Even though geriatrics is mostly an out-patient practice, geriatricians are likely to have a busy hospital practice, too. The majority of medical resources are consumed in the last year of life, and the biggest ticket item is in-patient services. Currently, 30 to 40 percent of patients admitted to medical services are over age 65. The elderly have longer hospital stays, and therefore more in-patient days, than young people.[8] Among the very old, even fairly routine hospitalizations can lead to prolonged hospital stays. In fact, this is the rule rather than the exception. The elderly also undergo many surgical procedures that only a few years ago were considered too metabolically stressful. For example, the mean age of patients receiving coronary artery bypass grafts has risen and is now over 60. All this means active in-patient services for geriatricians. Among a small number of hospitals, acute geriatric medicine is providing a geriatric unit. For most hospitals across the country, geriatric patients are located in traditional hospital settings rather than in such specialized geriatric units.

An academic geriatrician like Dr. Jones may maintain a hospital census of ten to 15 patients. At least half the patients are on nonmedical services. An 85-year-old grandfather is on the urology service because of benign prostatic hypertrophy. A 67-year-old church worker and community activist is on the cardiovascular surgery service for coronary artery bypass grafting. A 74-year-old suburbanite with mild cognitive loss and depression is on the psychiatry service. A 70-year-old former dancer is on the orthopedic surgery service receiving a total-knee replacement. Medical patients have the usual array of cardiovascular, neoplastic and infectious diseases. Inpatient geriatrics is bread-and-butter medicine.

In-patient geriatrics is usually not critical care. Elderly people get myocardial infarctions, go into shock and require intubation. Geriatricians, however, are not called to see such patients. Most geriatricians are comfortable with this tacit triage. Managing critically ill patients requires skills that most physicians do not routinely use. Confidence in such skills can be assured only if they are used regularly. Geriatrics is primary and secondary care, not critical care.

Outside the hospital and in the office, geriatricians have the luxury of choosing the kind of practice they want. The demand for geriatric services exceeds the supply of geriatricians. In these times when most specialties are extending their hours, marketing their services and affiliating with preferred-provider organizations (PPOs), independent-practice associations (IPAs) and health maintenance organizations (HMOs) to make it in the medical marketplace, geriatricians enjoy more business than they can handle (see the Overview). The American Medical Association and some specialty organizations have expressed concern over the doctor glut and have initiated discussions of ways to limit the number of physicians in the future. Whereas some specialties, particularly surgical specialties, are the target of many such discussions, no one is talking about limiting the number of geriatricians or directing the kinds of practice they have. Demand for services is not a consideration in practice decisions—there are others.

Maintaining a balance between the role of a consultant and the role of a primary-care physician is a challenge. Geriatricians could easily fill all their office hours with comprehensive evaluations. Some geriatricians would say this approach is the most appropriate use of the limited number of office hours such physicians have. There are advantages to the geriatrician concentrating on comprehensive evaluations; that is, on their role as consultants. First, a larger portion of elderly patients can be reached. Two percent of the physicians cannot provide continuing care to all the elderly. However, they probably can evaluate the 5 to 10 percent of the elderly who are frail or otherwise at risk for functional decline. Second, the battles over turf may be less intense if geriatricians act primarily as consultants. Understandably, general internists and family practitioners are concerned that as patients are divided up, not only on the basis of organ system but also on the basis of age, they may be left doing physical examinations for insurance companies. If geriatricians reserve their services for the frail and limit them to evaluations, such concerns may seem less founded to other generalists. Last, the potential for disseminating information to nongeriatricians is greater if patients are evaluated and referred back to their primary-care physicians along with educational information and specific recommendations.

The disadvantages of geriatricians limiting their practice to consultation are two-fold. First, following up patients over time provides perspective that sharpens clinical acumen. In geriatrics, as with most of medicine, the difficult task is long-term management, not diagnosis. Every third-year medical student knows the differential diagnosis of dementia and which variants are curable. Most third-year students even have a cookbook approach to evaluation, but once the diagnosis is made, they are often at a loss for developing an ongoing plan of action. A single set of recommendations is analogous to a coach developing a game plan, without a strategy for continuing modification, then turning it over to someone else. Second, the rewards in geriatrics come from observing and being a part of the small changes that effective therapy can bring about. For many geriatricians, this is the disadvantage that outweighs the rational advantages. Therefore, most geriatricians attempt to balance their time, with 60 to 70 percent of it being allocated to evaluation and consultation and the remainder to primary care.

For now, the choice is a geriatrician's. An office practice limited to evaluation/consultation and one limited to longitudinal care are equally viable. It is difficult to project which practice would be busier for physicians or more beneficial for society. Certainly, a balance is most satisfying.

Three long-term-care settings are the other major practice options for geriatricians. Long-term care is provided in continuing care retirement communities (CCRCs), home-care settings and, of course, nursing homes. CCRCs are increasing in number throughout the country. Such communities are living situations that provide a continuum of services, ranging from independent living to skilled nursing-home care. Although the arrangements vary (see Sommers & Forrest, 1992, for a detailed description of the types of CCRCs available), most CCRCs offer cleaning service, meals and such amenities as laundry service and transportation to the elderly who can live independently. Most of them also have back-up emergency medical services, and residents have the option of receiving all care on the premises. Although most residents of such communities have had longstanding relationships with physicians, the move to a CCRC often means relocating to a new geographic area. For this reason, many residents avail themselves of the physicians' services. A well-run CCRC becomes a part of the "team" by assuming the details of caring for the elderly. Residents who attend congregate meals have a balanced diet, as well as a pool of people, staff and other residents to monitor oral intake. Residents who are temporarily unable to go to the dining room do not have to rely on Meals-on-Wheels or their neighbors' good will— meals are simply brought to their rooms. Disease-prevention and health-promotion programs are also a common feature of such communities.

The holistic, interdisciplinary approach flourishes in this environment. Home visits can be made efficiently. The nurse on duty can provide routine care, supervise therapy and be available for emergencies. Mr. Avery experienced worsening of his hypertension and chest pain a few days before Christmas. He was able to be discharged after a short hospitalization *before* Christmas because the nurse at the life-care community was available daily. She checked his blood pressure and called his physician with the readings. The result: Mr. Avery spent Christmas at home with his family. Remaining at home and comfortable despite illness is the goal of CCRCs and home care.

Home care, however, is the least developed of the long-term-care options. Home-care agencies have burgeoned since Medicare began reimbursing their services in the early 1980s.[9] Because of Medicare-reimbursement regulations, the majority of care provided is skilled-level care. This means that the average frail elderly person who merely requires help with bathing and cooking is not eligible for home-care services. For the most part, physicians have not yet become involved in home care. Borrowing from the British system, there are models for home care that use a nurse-physician team to provide care for homebound patients. Physicians who participate in this kind of home-care program describe a change in their practice patterns. When obtaining a chest radiograph requires four people, an ambulance and the better part of a day, much more care and thought are given to the examination of the chest. The stethoscope is restored to its former glory. The special skill and gratification of this type of practice should promote increased involvement by physicians in home care.

For many people, nursing homes are synonymous with long-term care as well as geriatrics. To be sure, there is much work to be done in nursing homes. Many patients have been placed in nursing homes inappropriately; most of them have never received a comprehensive evaluation of the problems that diminish the quality of life, such as incontinence. There may be only two or three professional nurses or other skilled health-care providers in a large nursing home at any given time. Despite the fact that nurses' aides regularly care for the elderly, they are often inadequately informed about the etiologic bases and forms of management of problems common among the elderly.

Until recently, the image of nursing homes as a place for unwanted elderly people has been dominant. The for-profit nature of most nursing homes made them all the more distasteful in the era when "for-profit" was interpreted as poor quality. The teaching nursing-home programs sponsored by the Robert Wood Johnson Foundation and by the National Institute on Aging have brought teaching, research and excitement to nursing homes. Diagnosis-related groups and the pressure to limit hospital days have meant that nursing homes are more like step-down units. People do not always go to nursing homes to die now. They go for nursing care and recuperation. For a nursing home–affiliated physician, this means a wider variety of diseases and problems, more acute medicine and more challenges.

These three settings and five roles are bundled to make three types of jobs. Academic jobs are the most plentiful. They are also the ones with the most number of items in the bundle. Increasingly, however, large group practices are recruiting geriatricians, as are long-term-care facilities.

As universities and hospitals increase the curricular content on geriatrics, the need for geriatrics faculty becomes apparent at once. Because fewer than half the medical schools have established programs, most jobs involve starting a program. A school may have lectures on aging-related subjects scattered throughout the curriculum, a clinical base and even a few faculty members who have an interest, although not a primary interest, in aging. A geriatrician is expected to mold these beginnings into a geriatrics program. Descriptions for those jobs are usually nebulous. The institution probably has an idea as to which component of a geriatrics program is its highest priority—a geriatric evaluation-management unit versus an outpatient clinic versus a home-care program. Some institutions have determined the place of geriatrics in the organizational structure. Other than that, the ball is going to be the geriatrician's to run. For the creative and adventuresome, such jobs are a godsend. However, adventure should be entered with open eyes.

The jobs let you start at the top and build something if two preexisting conditions are met. First, there must be resources. Geriatrics is labor- and resource-intensive. Without hands to help in the delivery of care and dollars to develop the programs, the job is impossible. Not even a "super doc" can continually teach all levels of students, run clinics, provide consultations, plan programs and still generate enough patient revenues to keep the program afloat. Second, there must be a commitment to geriatrics. This is a new area that does not yet have universal support. Without the demonstrated support of deans, department chairs and hospital executive officers, developing a geriatrics program will be painful and probably unsuccessful. If these two conditions are met and one has an entrepreneurial spirit, such jobs offer the most learning and excitement possible.

Not every academic geriatrics position requires starting from scratch. There are 60 to 70 established programs or divisions in the United States and one full-fledged university department. In these settings, being a geriatrician is a cross between being a subspecialist and being a generalist. As with any academic position, teaching and research are the core activities. Clinical activities usually involve work in two or three of the settings described. Responsibilities are usually shared and rotated among the group so that the amount of clinical activity varies from month to month. Overall, it seems that most academic positions require at least 50 percent clinical time.

The amount of time devoted to clinical activities is, of course, much more for geriatricians in group practice. Large group practices have long attempted to incorporate physicians of a wide variety of specialties into the practice, the idea being that referrals could be made internally, creating a sort of PPO. Many such practices, particularly those located in the suburbs or other places beyond commuting distance to established geriatrics programs, are recruiting more geriatricians. Such positions frequently offer the opportunity to continue to practice general medicine. The roles of primary-care physician and consultant are clearly dominant. Other generalizations about the settings must be made cautiously, however. Increasingly, group practices are affiliating with nursing homes and life-care communities. So within a group practice, a geriatrician may spend 50 percent of his or her time in the out-patient setting and the other half in geriatric evaluation units, doing consultations or attending to patients in long-term-care facilities. It is equally probable that a geriatrician could split his or her time between the out-patient and long-term-care settings.

The third type of job geriatricians are recruited for involves CCRCs. Large (more than 800 residents) communities may choose to have geriatricians provide health care. As has already been discussed, in such a situation geriatricians are the primary-care physicians for elderly that range from the well to the severely disabled. Educating staff and residents is a vital part of these kinds of position. However, unless a life-care community is affiliated with a medical school, teaching students and other physicians may not be a part of the job. For a geriatric clinician, this type of job probably offers the most potential for innovative practice and continuity. However, such positions are probably the least common of the three types of job currently available, although this situation may well change in the future.

For now, geriatrics offers the most opportunity for academic positions. Medical schools and teaching programs are eager for geriatricians to educate their students and residents. Such positions involve a mixture of all the roles and practice settings described. More strictly clinical positions can be found in large group practices and life-care communities. Large group practices need primary-care physicians as well as consultants, whereas long-term-care facilities need only primary-care physicians. A would-be geriatrician can, more than any other specialist, choose the practice setting that most suits his or her clinical needs. This is particularly important in an era when the physician's professional autonomy has been steadily eroding.

WHY GERIATRICS?

A genuine enthusiasm for the content and approach of geriatrics is the first and most essential reason for choosing the field. There are also practical and life-style–related issues that should be considered. On the positive side, opportunities abound in geriatrics, it provides a forum for addressing medicine's most difficult problems, and it is second to none in real doctoring. On the negative side, there is still uncertainty about the future of geriatrics, and the field is not a money-maker.

The negative first: money. It cannot be emphasized enough that geriatrics is time-intensive. Unfortunately, only a portion of this time is reimbursable. It may take a total of five or six hours of professional time to perform a comprehensive assessment on a frail elderly person. In many cases, the social workers' and nurses' time is not directly reimbursable. It may take even an experienced geriatrician one and a half hours to complete the medical portion of the evaluation. If one were to fill that same block of time with five or six short visits, the pay would be much better. There are studies in progress that attempt to show that, in the long run, this time is, in fact, cost saving. However, for a practitioner trying to pay the rent, this is of little solace. Because not all elderly patients require a "megaevaluation," the case mixture is as important for an individual geriatrician as it is for hospitals, HMOs and nursing homes.

Analogous to the case mixture is the time mixture. It may not be possible for geriatricians to spend more than a small amount of time on out-patient evaluations unless the costs are charged to the patient or the evaluations are otherwise subsidized. In-patient acute medicine is reimbursed more in accordance with time spent. Therefore, even though the demand for geriatric services is such that a geriatrician should be able to tailor the proportion of time spent in each role and in each practice setting, certain mixtures may not be financially viable.

The ABIM's decision to recognize experts in geriatrics may be one of the most compelling reasons for entering the field. The ABIM and the American Board of Family Practice (ABFP) have indicated that geriatrics has a unique body of knowledge as well as a professional presence but that these aspects must be further developed if the future needs of the elderly are to be met. These organizations therefore have proposed that recognition be given to Board-certified internists and family practitioners and to subspecialists who have received additional training in geriatrics. The aim is to stimulate the growth of a group of geriatricians who can provide leadership and training. So for a pragmatist, geriatrics represents an area slated by the powers-that-be for growth over the next two decades. The nature of that development toward leadership and education is attractive for a physician who wants to have an impact in several spheres. Because geriatricians are being viewed as future educators, researchers and policymakers, it is a field for people who enjoy wearing many hats. In the 1984 Kent Lecture,[10] Knight Steel described a geriatrician as someone who, in addition to clinical responsibilities, was asked to speak to community groups, lecture medical students, sit on task forces and develop curricula. These various functions are exciting to some physicians, yet maddening to others. A more traditional scientist who is fascinated by some aspect of aging and wants to delve into that area without restraint should not be deterred but should be aware of the pressures to do otherwise.

The other reasons for entering geriatrics have to do with satisfaction. Physicians who derive satisfaction from bringing state-of-the-art medical technology to a problem may well be disappointed in geriatrics. A good deal of geriatrics is low technology or involves extending current technologies to include elderly people. Similarly, physicians who derive gratification from curing disease may be better suited for surgery. Geriatrics involves many problems for which there are no cures. Satisfaction must come from meeting that challenge. The processes employed in meeting the challenge of chronic disease are probably as important to the outcome as any other variables. Satisfaction in the way a diagnosis is made is as important as making the diagnosis. Last, recognizing changes in the quality of life and deriving the gratification from improving the quality of life are probably the most essential ingredients in making a competent and happy geriatrician.

TRAINING

Happily, the days of self-declared geriatricians are over. The ABIM and the ABFP have decided to issue a certificate of added qualifications to recognize expertise in geriatrics. Within internal medicine, there are four pathways after certification in internal medicine to achieve this distinction.

First, one can qualify to sit for the examination by completing two years of fellowship training in geriatrics at an accredited program. Second, one can take the examination after a two-year fellowship in general internal medicine that includes one year of geriatric medicine. Third, the examination is open to Board-certified subspecialists in internal medicine who complete an additional year of training in geriatrics associated with an accredited residency program. Diplomates of the internal medicine certification examination who enter residency before 1993 and who have four years of clinical practice with substantial experience in geriatric medicine will also be able to take the examination. These admission requirements will be reevaluated in 1993 and changed to reflect the changes in the growth of geriatric medicine and its knowledge as well as changes in internal medicine and geriatric medicine training programs. The ABFP is developing similar guidelines. The various pathways are intended to unify physicians with different emphasis of training through their common interests in the elderly.

All accredited fellowship programs are not alike. One should not lose sight of the fact that a fellowship must provide the training necessary to be a clinically competent geriatrician. This means that, at a minimum, a program should provide training in three fundamental areas. First, the program should provide an environment that will allow a fellow to learn content areas that make up the body of knowledge of clinical geriatrics. Second, it should provide the opportunity to practice in settings that are unavailable to most physicians in the first three postgraduate years. Such settings, of course, include nursing homes, home-care communities, geriatric units, diagnostic evaluation centers, geriatric consultation services, geropsychiatric units, rehabilitation units and hospices. Although probably no single program offers all these practice settings, most programs currently offer opportunities to practice in a nursing home or other long-term-care facility, and a smaller percentage offer opportunities to practice in one or two of the other settings mentioned. Third, training programs in geriatrics should provide opportunities to work as a member of a multidisciplinary or an interdisciplinary team. Because the team approach is an integral part of geriatrics, this is an essential part of training. Finally, many fellows will want to gain research experience. This will require one or two years of additional training. If an academic career is contemplated, research training is mandatory, not optional. Those interested in geriatric fellowships should contact the American Board of Internal Medicine or the American Board of Family Practice for a list of accredited programs.

THE FUTURE

The forces that will shape the future of geriatrics are the same forces that will act on medicine as a whole. Medicine is becoming a public industry, and the product as well as the producers will be scrutinized with increasing detail. The nature of the consumer or patient is changing and will demand a change in physicians and the delivery of health care. Changes in the practice patterns of physicians and the corporatization of American medicine are already under way and are likely to continue. These trends will have an even greater impact on the elderly in the future. These forces will, for pragmatic reasons, bring geriatrics into the mainstream of adult medicine. The subsequent effect will be that in 15 to 20 years, physicians who specialize in geriatrics will be more consumed with gerontology—the study of aging—and less with the practice of geriatrics. Before developing the future scenario, let's look at the forces, beginning with the most important—the consumer. There are two sub-groups of consumers: the elderly and their care givers. What are the dominant trends in these groups? The number of elderly is increasing. The gain in life expectancy from 49 years in 1900 to more than 75 years currently has increased the proportion of elderly people in the population. In 1950, people over age 65 represented approximately 8 percent of the population; they now represent 12 percent of the population[11] and in 2030 will represent more than 18 percent. Among the elderly, the fastest-growing group is those over 85. Demographers estimate that the number of the old-old will continue to increase well into the next century. This phenomenon will take place at a time when the number of people in other age groups may well decline. The age groups with declining numbers are, of course, the care givers. These two demographic trends together comprise the "demographic imperative." Simply stated, the number of elderly who need specialized services and daily care is increasing, creating a need that the "system" in its current form will not be able to meet. This imperative is already 20 years old and has stimulated legislation, such as Medicare, and much of the current interest in geriatrics.

The characteristics of the elderly and their care givers, more than sheer numbers, will shape future directions. Despite dramatic changes in longevity and a decrease in the number of totally disabled elderly, the overall number of disability days has not changed for the elderly over the past 20 years. This means that the number of days that elderly people limit their activities because their joints ache, because they are depressed or because they just do not feel well has not changed over the past 20 years.

This lack of progress in health status is in sharp contrast with other areas. The level of education in this country is increasing. Many of today's elderly ended their formal education at eighth grade. Only 13 percent of people over age 85 have a high-school education. However, of those between ages 65 and 75, 18 percent have a high-school education. These figures reflect a trend toward increased education among the elderly that should persist well into the next century. The mean educational level now for all age groups is 14 years. Although there are certainly subgroups who have not achieved this level of education, by and large people in this country are more educated now than in the past.

With education come several other changes that influence the characteristics of elderly consumers. Income, concern for health and expectations regarding the doctor-patient relationship all increase in parallel with increasing education. Having an adequate income increases access. Elderly people who, over the years, have had a reasonable income enter retirement years with substantial wealth. The vast majority of elderly men who have worked all their lives own their homes, have paid off the mortgages and have retirement benefits. Such assets allow elderly people to pay the copayment associated with Medicare, to further insure themselves with MediGap insurance and, in some instances, to ensure their long-term care needs by moving into a life-care community. It also allows such elderly people to have more choices. They can choose their physician on the basis of criteria other than whether Medicare assignment is taken. They can choose to have preventive and screening measures done that are not covered by third-party payers. They can choose to remain at home with the help of a paid care giver.

Although the increased income associated with higher education provides the means to pay for choices, it is the heightened concern for health that is associated with education that provides the motivation to seek choices. The explosion in health awareness and health-seeking behaviors is greatest among the most educated. Educated people smoke less, exercise more and eat fewer high-fat foods than do their less educated counterparts. In fact, with the exception of beliefs concerning exercise, elderly people may have stronger commitments to health practices than young or middle-aged people. Polls indicate that the U.S. populace, wants more, not fewer, health services. The important word here is health. People want services that are going to help maintain health. For elderly people, this most likely means an approach or group of services that addresses all their problems and has as its foremost goal maintaining quality of life, in other words, the geriatrics model for approaching a patient, not the acute-disease model.

Trends toward more education, income and concern for health affect consumers' expectations for the doctor-patient relationship. Many of today's elderly people grew up in an era when one did not question the doctor. The relationship was paternal—the doctor gave the orders, and the patient was supposed to follow them. Physicians spend less time with elderly patients despite the fact that the elderly have more medical problems. The elderly complain to one another and to researchers that their physicians do not explain medications, do not ask them about side effects caused by their medications and are quick to attribute symptoms to old age. These hurried encounters with physicians are not satisfying for the elderly, but they are what the old have come to expect. Educated young patients, on the other hand, have come to expect something quite different. They view physicians as advisors, not as a parent or a boss. They ask questions, want to be involved in decision making and often spend considerable time learning about their problems. It is difficult to imagine a physician telling a "yuppie" to "just take the medicine." When these educated young people become care givers for their elderly parents or grandparents and bring their own expectations of the doctor-patient relationship to an elderly person's physician, there is often a clash. They cannot accept that mama is senile and there is nothing more to do except wait six months for the next follow-up appointment. The result is that a search for a geriatrician and, more importantly, a geriatrics team, is undertaken.

As one colleague put it, "People come to geriatricians looking for a doctor. There may be a glut of *physicians,* but there is a shortage of *doctors.* When you're sick, you know the difference." The elderly and their care givers want doctors and, in the future, they will expect and demand this from the medical community. Consumers will expect physicians to know how to manage dementia. They will know that treatment involves accurate diagnosis, attention to the environment, involvement of the family, judicious use of medications as well as, hopefully, a whole host of primary treatments. In short, the increased education and income that characterizes more and more of the elderly will heighten concern about health and change the definition of acceptable health care for the elderly.

Consumers know what they want and, for the first time, providers of health-care services are listening. For years, people have been complaining about long waits and unpleasant conditions in emergency rooms. In fact, having to go to an emergency-room physician for a minor problem because there were no other physicians available after 5:30 pm has been a longstanding dissatisfaction. The "problem" was studied, discussed and restudied for more than a decade. Only recently has a solution emerged. The urgicenter, storefront doctor and doc-in-the-box are direct responses to the consumers' need for quick, available care for acute problems. In the same vein, women and couples who desire an alternative to the sterile medical approach to normal birth have supported the growth of an alternative. Birthing suites and rooms are a part of virtually every active maternity service. Even the most traditional and conservative Northeast teaching hospitals have realized that unless they have these alternatives, they are unable to attract the kind of patients they want. Out-of-hospital birthing centers staffed by midwives and backed up by physicians are flourishing in most major cities. Home births, which a few years ago were limited to the poor and royalty, are also increasing in response to consumer demand. These changes in acute medical care and obstetric care have certainly not been accepted by the medical community without controversy. However, the fact that they are now well established indicates medicine is listening to its consumers.

The reason we are listening now and did not before is a subject that is dealt with in much greater detail in other chapters. However, there are two reasons worth highlighting here. First, the physician surplus has made physicians much more willing to listen. Individual and group practices that have not adjusted their hours, hospital affiliations and regular services to accommodate patients' preferences have suffered. One only has to look at the lead articles in *Medical Economics, Private Practice* or any one of the other many magazines devoted to the business of medical practice to know that this is true. Articles on building a practice tell physicians how to use blood-pressure screening and lectures on preventive medicine to attract new patients to the office. They discuss strategies for scheduling patients that will maximize patients' satisfaction and physicians' use of time. The underlying theme of all such articles is know what your patients want and deliver it. Physicians in groups that do not listen either starve or are swallowed up by the corporatization of medicine.

Paul Starr's landmark work, *The Social Transformation of American Medicine*,[12] describes this corporatization. On the microlevel, the solo practitioner is becoming extinct. Most new physicians are joining group practices. Increasingly, such groups are large, multispecialty practices that are part of health-care organizations or networks. Moving into a larger scale, health-care corporations, sometimes called "for-profits," are taking large pieces of the health-care pie for themselves. Such organizations comprise a number of hospitals, nursing homes, physician practices, supply companies and outpatient diagnostic and surgical centers and, of course, span many cities and regions of the country. They run teaching hospitals and have entered the arena of medical research. Hospitals became medical centers in the 1970s and health-services organizations in the 1980s. We can argue about the ethics involved, lament the passing of the first-floor doctor's office, but there is no denying that a change has occurred. Just as the mom and pop stores gave way to chains of convenience stores, individual physician's practices and hospitals are giving way to health-services systems.

Not all such large organizations are for profit. In fact, most of them are still nonprofit organizations. However, the tax status and means of raising capital may be the only real differences between for-profit and not-for-profit organizations. Both types of organization are using sound business principles for management purposes.

A basic principle of finance is that risk can be reduced by investing in a diverse group of businesses. Both for profit and not-for-profit organizations make use of this principle. It is not uncommon to see a nonprofit hospital forming subsidiary corporations that oversee the management of for-profit ventures in laundry service, food service, diagnostic imaging or even the building and management of housing.

Health-care organizations that are sensitive to business principles are not going to ignore a basic tenet of marketing. Rule 1 in marketing is that supply is a function of demand. Understand the demand through gut instinct but more likely through surveys and models, then supply the product or service to meet that demand. In attempting to "define" new markets, marketing specialists would study the characteristics of high users of the product and then seek out populations with those characteristics. In the most general terms, such an analysis leads health-care providers to the elderly. The elderly are high utilizers, and they are also the fastest growing segment of the population. The decision of a national chain of nursing homes to develop Alzheimer's units and teaching nursing homes was probably based on such an analysis. Dementia is probably the most common diagnosis among its nursing-home residents. Alzheimer's disease, of course, is the most common cause of dementia. Sophisticated families recognize that patients with Alzheimer's disease have special needs. They want to be assured that those needs will be met by a nursing home. Similarly, consumers who choose a teaching hospital to get the best acute care would choose a teaching nursing home to get the best long-term care. This corporation understands the demand within certain segments of the population and has formulated a strategy for meeting that demand.

In short, geriatrics is going to become good business for corporate medicine over the next ten to 15 years. Consumers want it. Physicians are already practicing in groups that will facilitate implementation of the team approach. Finally, the holistic approach, which often uses a case-management system, is consistent with the concept of managed care—the backbone of most HMOs.

The final reason that geriatrics will move into the mainstream of health care has to do with quality and the public's unwillingness to compromise on quality in health care. The evidence is mounting that geriatrics improves the quality of care for elderly patients. Geriatric evaluation-management units reduce not only morbidity but also mortality.[13] Geriatric consultation teams are effective in providing recommendations that improve the care that elderly patients receive.[14] Geriatricians in nursing homes are associated with improved outcomes.[15] The kinds of outcome that reflect quality are being scrutinized. The recent publication of the names of hospitals in which mortality was either much higher or much lower than expected indicates the public's interest in quality issues. The commitment to quality care along with corporatization and consumerism will pull geriatrics into the mainstream of health care. How this phenomenon will change the roles, practice settings and job opportunities for geriatricians in the future is not known. However, because we are aware of real trends, it is worthwhile for the purpose of career planning in medicine to look into the crystal ball.

The Next Ten Years: Transition

Over the next ten years, the roles of geriatricians probably will not change substantially. The kinds of job opportunities specific to geriatricians will probably also remain constant until the latter part of the decade. What will change is the number of people seeking geriatrics training and recognition for their skills in geriatrics. This group of trained geriatricians will provide the clinical force necessary to bring geriatrics into the mainstream of health care.

Geriatricians will continue to juggle the roles of primary-care physicians, consultant, teacher and researcher, with the roles of consultant and teacher dominating. The highest priority will be to teach new physicians and medical students to care effectively for the elderly. Academic medical centers will continue to place strong emphasis on the recruitment of geriatricians.

The inadequacies of current postgraduate training, particularly in internal medicine, are being widely appreciated and will mandate change during this transition period. With the changing patterns of disease and hospitalization practices, internal medicine, like family practice and pediatrics, is becoming an out-patient specialty. Graduates of training programs complain that residency training does not provide them with the skills necessary to practice current medicine, much less future medicine. The management of recent-onset diabetes, the evaluation and management of Alzheimer's disease and the management of chronic renal failure are all out-patient problems. Decisions regarding these problems are made in an out-patient setting, not in a hospital. Therefore, young physicians are finding themselves at a loss for managing these problems in any patient, much less an elderly patient. The HMOs, IPAs and corporations that hire young physicians feel that they are paying for the inadequacies of training. Training programs will be restructured, and geriatricians will be an integral part of the process.

Outpatient geriatric evaluation and primary-care programs will become a part of most university-based training programs. Geriatricians will provide the care and teaching within such programs. Long-term care will also become a part of training programs. Affiliations between medical and nursing schools and nursing homes will become commonplace. Developing the curricula, practice sites and evaluations of such programs will consume most of a geriatrician's time and energy over the next half decade. For a person who is interested in a career as a clinician-educator, geriatrics is a good choice.

During the same period, the author believes that consumer demand for geriatric services will stimulate many clinically oriented internists and subspecialists to seek recognition in geriatrics. It is well known that most subspecialists spend as much as 40 to 50 percent of their time providing primary care. Depending on the specialty, a large portion of such primary-care practices will be made up of elderly patients. Consumer demand will make subspecialists with geriatrics training more attractive. A cardiologist/geriatrician or rheumatologist/geriatrician will be sought after by HMOs, multispecialty practices as well as by academic institutions. As more specialists subspecialize in a procedure or technical skill, geriatrics will offer an alternative for physicians who want to remain generalists within their subspecialty.

The latter part of the decade will be characterized by a fairly large base of clinical geriatricians, academic geriatricians who may be ready to move into a different sector and middle-class, elderly enrollees in HMOs. The HMOs and other health-services organizations will be interested in developing clinical services to meet the needs of their elderly clients. Geriatricians will then be called on to develop clinical services that are cost-effective and appropriate for such organizations. Widespread development of geriatric services within HMOs, IPAs and multispecialty groups will herald the arrival of geriatrics in the mainstream of health care.

The Mainstream

In 2007, the elderly will comprise approximately 15 percent of the population. Most of the young-old will be the people known as idealistic demonstrators on college campuses in the 1960s. The old-old will be the more conventional "baby boomers." Physicians who take care of such patients will have grown up in the era of diagnosis-related groups, HMOs, IPAs, PPOs—the era of medical organizations. Special recognition for expertise in geriatrics will have been in existence for almost 20 years, and geriatrics training in medical school and residency will have been widespread and established for about the same length of time. Hopefully at this point, when the average physician says "geriatrics is what I do every day," it will actually have some meaning.

What will full-time geriatricians do at this time? After 2000, geriatricians will be in leadership positions in administration and academia. The states that experience population growth during the latter part of the twentieth century will be faced with trying to meet the needs of their growing elderly populations. CCRCs and HMOs will become more similar with regard to the services provided as their clients age. Such organizations will need creative administrators and program developers to meet the needs of their clients. Geriatricians will, of course, be needed to train other geriatricians and to conduct the research that will carry the field forward. Geriatricians will be able to choose the amount of time spent doing clinical work. In contrast to the situation in the 1990s, the pressures will probably be to perform less rather than more clinical service.

Clinical services will be provided by general internists and family practitioners who learned geriatrics during their residency training. Full-time geriatricians will probably follow one of two paths—administration or academics. Geriatricians who choose administration may work in the private or public sector. In both instances, the job will consist of program planning and development. State and county health agencies, which have grown accustomed to divisions of maternal and child health, will be just as accustomed to divisions of elderly health services by 2010. Geriatricians will run these divisions. In contrast to many state departments of aging of the 1990s, which do not provide direct service and only educational and technical support, agencies of the future will plan and deliver care for the elderly. State-run long-term care in the form of nursing homes and home care will ensure access even for the indigent. A routine, standardized evaluation and certification for long-term care will be available to all potential patients, and the division of elderly services will almost certainly administer that evaluation. Quality improvement of physicians' services—within not only long-term care but all geriatric care—will be the final area within such a geriatric health official's domain. Within the private sector, corporations that specialize or invest in CCRCs, nursing homes or home care will need medical directors and advisors. Health maintenance organizations will have divisions of geriatric services to develop the corporate image and to maintain the bottom line. For geriatricians who choose the administrative path, the field will not be a hands-on specialty.

Geriatricians who choose the academic path will be devoted to pursuing answers to the major problems of the elderly. They will be expected to give clinicians effective management for Alzheimer's disease and similar diseases of the elderly. General descriptive studies that raise more questions than they answer will be a vestige of geriatrics' infancy. Many geriatrics teaching settings that pioneering geriatricians developed will no longer be staffed exclusively by geriatricians. General internists and subspecialists will also teach in nursing homes, evaluation units and home-care communities. Geriatricians will no longer be expected to wear many hats; one will be enough. Academic geriatricians will be gerontologists first and foremost. It will be their charge to carry the field forward.

Geriatrics is a young field built on a body of knowledge and an approach to care of the elderly. Current geriatricians juggle four roles— primary-care physician, consultant, educator and researcher. The roles of consultant and educator are clearly dominant and are likely to remain so over the next ten years—the adolescence of geriatrics. However, as geriatrics and the population mature in the ensuing years, geriatricians will be called on to provide answers to the problems of the elderly, either through development of policies and programs or through gerontology. Young geriatricians and physicians currently thinking about geriatrics as a possible career pathway should look to this future and solidify their administrative or research skills in preparation for the challenges ahead.

REFERENCES

1. Kane R, Solomon B, Beck J, et al: *Geriatrics in the United States: Manpower Projections and Training Considerations*. Santa Monica, Rand Corporation, 1980.
2. Rowe J, Kahn R: Human aging: Usual and successful. *Science* 273:143–149, 1987.
3. *Urinary Incontinence in Adults: Clinical Practice Guideline*. AHCPR Pub No 92-0038. Rockville, MD, Public Health Service, March 1992.
4. Lefton E, Bonstelle E, Dermont F: Success with an inpatient geriatric unit: A controlled study. *J Am Geriatr Soc* 31(3):149, 1983.
5. Rubenstein L, Weiland D, English P, et al: Sepulveda VA geriatric evaluation unit: Data on four year outcomes and predictions of improved patient outcomes. *J Am Geriatr Soc* 32:503, 1984.

6. Martin D, Moryer R, McDowell J, et al: Community based geriatric assessment. *J Am Geriatr Soc* 33:602, 1985.
7. Proposal to American Board of Medical Specialties to issue a certificate of added qualifications in geriatric medicine, 1985.
8. Garnich D, Short T: *Utilization of Hospital Inpatient Services by Elderly Americans.* Hospital Studies Program Hospital Cost and Utilization Project Research Note, DHHS Publication No. (PHS) 85-3351. US Department of Health and Human Services, 1985.
9. Doty P, Liu K, Wiener J: Health Care Financing Administration: An overview of long term care. *Health Care Financ Rev* 6(3):69, Spring 1985.
10. Steel, K: Geriatric medicine is coming of age. *Gerontologist* 2(4):367, 1984.
11. US Census Bureau, 1992.
12. Starr, P: *The Social Transformation of American Medicine.* New York, Basic Books, 1982.
13. Rubinstein L, Josephson K, Weiland D, et al: Effectiveness of a geriatric evaluation unit: A randomized clinical trial. *N Engl J Med* 311:1664–1671, 1984.
14. Campion E: An interdisciplinary geriatric consultation service: A controlled trial. *J Am Geriatr Soc* 31:792, 1983.
15. Jahnigen D, Kramer A, Robbins L, et al: Academic affiliation with a nursing home: Impact on patient outcome. *J Am Geriatr Soc* 33:472–479, 1985.

SELECTED TEXTBOOKS

Rowe J, Besdine R: *Health and Disease in Old Age.* Boston, Little Brown and Co, 1982.
Butter and Bean: *The Aging Process. Therapeutic Implications.* New York, Raven Press, 1985.
Covinglon T, Walker J: *Current Geriatric Therapy.* Philadelphia, WB Saunders, 1984.
Cassel C, Walsh J: *Geriatric Medicine.* Volume II: *Fundamentals of Geriatric Care.* New York, Springer-Verlag, 1984.
Hazzard WR, et al (eds): *Principles of Geriatric Medicine and Gerontology, 2nd edition.* New York, McGraw Hill, 1990.
Lavizzo-Mourey R, et al: *Practicing Prevention.* Philadelphia, Hanley and Belfus, 1990.
Somers A, Forrest N: *Continuing Care Communities.* Philadelphia, Springer Press, 1992.

CHAPTER 6
OCCUPATIONAL MEDICINE
David Gluck

I used to believe that nothing could ever tempt me to write anything more extended than a one-page memo, let alone a chapter in a book. The editor, however, found my Achilles heel. As a physician in occupational medicine (and an internist as well) who has, as of this writing, enjoyed some 30 years of specializing in the field, I cannot resist encouraging others to explore this rewarding profession.

In the pages that follow, I will try to sketch many of the main beams that give occupational medicine its distinct form. I begin by trying to define the specialty; I then provide some specifics on characteristic programs and functions of an occupational-medicine service. I examine some of the special challenges and gratifications that are rather idiosyncratic to the field; I then speculate on what the future (a promising future) may hold. Finally, there are some items of particular interest for readers who may wish to consider joining the growing ranks of physicians who choose a career in this multifaceted and stimulating specialty.

DEFINING OCCUPATIONAL MEDICINE

The necessity of having to define this branch of medicine, a recognized subspecialty within preventive medicine, speaks volumes on the relative neglect shown occupational medicine in most medical school curricula.

Physicians in the field practice in government, academia or industry.

Physicians in occupational medicine, whether through teaching and research or through clinical practice, are invariably concerned with promotion of the health of workers.

In the business setting, reaching for that goal calls for attention to
many areas: to job applicants, elements of the work environment, materials involved on the job, ill and injured workers, worried workers, employees with deteriorating performance and, not least, apparently healthy
workers.

The quality and components of any occupational physician's practice depend on the type of business or industry that he or she may serve.
Physicians who are employed in the petrochemical sector face far different challenges than those who work for banking and insurance firms.
Newspaper and magazine publishers, hospitals, electric utilities, telephone companies, defense and aerospace firms, food processors and
computer-chip manufacturers, to cite just a few examples, have all realized the advantage of acquiring occupational-medicine services.

The smaller the company or organization, the more likely that the
doctor-company relationship will develop on a part-time, fee-for-service
basis, with the physician maintaining a private practice. Many such physicians offer assistance to a roster of small organizations simultaneously.
In addition, a number of companies market occupational-medicine services and retain a staff of physicians.

As a result of the author's experience, the observations presented
are those of an occupational physician employed full time on the staff
of a major corporation, initially with clinical responsibilities alone and,
subsequently, with considerable administrative tasks as well.

SPECIFIC PROGRAMS AND FUNCTIONS

In the usual corporate setting, an occupational physician has an
advisory and service role, fulfilling just one of many staff functions for a
company. The line functions, which combine to produce the company's
products, rely on the medical department to provide support for all
health-related needs.

A wise company strives to let its workers know that "the company
cares." As a rule, most business entities proudly assert that their employees represent their most important asset. From this essential principle
flows much of the conceptual support for occupational-medicine services,
especially important during the annual tug-of-war to allot scarce budget
dollars among a number of company divisions, many of which are more
apparently related to the organization's products and hence to its vital
"bottom line."

Depending on the type of work performed, the federal Occupational
Safety and Health Act (OSHA) of 1970 may also have an important role
in influencing allocation of company resources to support health-care

needs. This key statute has led to the development of comprehensive guidelines for permissible exposures to potential hazards in the work place.

There are detailed steps that an employer must take regarding engineering specifications, environmental testing and general safety measures, as well as requirements for specific medical examinations for workers with particular exposures. Depending on the industry, monitoring those exposures and performing those examinations may represent a substantial responsibility for the occupational-medicine department. A recent example, and one that affects all medical departments directly, is OSHA's 1992 standard concerning bloodborne pathogens. It mandates training, protective procedures and the opportunity for hepatitis B virus vaccinations for any employee whose assignment may involve exposure to blood or other potentially infectious materials.

All 50 states have promulgated workers' compensation statutes, through which employees are granted prompt attention and support for the care of injuries or illnesses that are occupationally related. Helping provide for such medical attention is a legal requirement placed on an employer; such a requirement thus naturally forms a basic responsibility of the employer's occupational-medicine department.

An ill or injured worker is a central concern for an occupational physician; indeed, mobilizing a skilled and instantaneous response to emergency medical situations is among the highest priorities. Of course, the vast majority of employees helped by a clinic will not present with urgent problems, but the ready attention of an occupational physician serves to complement the role of a private physician and often can permit an ill or injured employee to remain at work by managing disease or injury at an early stage. Because an occupational-medicine clinic is most often a free service and conveniently located on site, hurdles that can interfere with visiting a private physician are removed, and the clinic receives a large number of patients whose symptoms or concerns are at an early, more manageable stage. In addition, company physicians are the knowledgeable, professional ombudsmen who, with a dog-eared directory of medical specialists, can help guide anxious fellow employees through the maze of health-care choices in a truly disinterested fashion.

A company's staff physicians also have the special advantage of close-at-hand knowledge of the work setting. This knowledge adds an invaluable dimension to every aspect of the doctor-patient relationship. Take, for example, the single issue of rehabilitation. Who better than an occupational physician is in a position to judge the physical fitness of a worker in relation to his or her work? In regard to diagnosis, physicians who are keenly aware of an employee's daily work environment and the special stresses brought to bear there are in a far better position to look past the presenting complaint to obtain a more complete picture.

Periodic preventive-health evaluations have generally held pride of place in the array of programs offered by modern occupational-medicine departments. Screening examinations for apparently healthy employees are rightly recognized as a special benefit for the employees as well as for their employer. In recent years, such programs have tended to evolve from an annual overloaded examination for privileged executives to a more general offering whose periodicity and contents are keyed to the age, sex and specific risks of an examinee. More and more, the elements of periodic medical examinations must measure up to a scrutiny of their costs and benefits. Nonetheless, at the core of the process stands a concerned physician whose expression of interest in the ability of a person to control identifiable risk factors exerts a powerful and beneficial impact.

The public-health lessons embodied in the dramatic decreases in mortality from coronary-artery disease and stroke over the past 25 years have not been lost on alert business executives. The appalling upward trend in death from lung cancer among women is equally impressive. Such examples vindicate decades of exhortations by preventive-medicine specialists. For the most part, we do have our lives in our own hands. What we once viewed as innocent life-style choices—diet, tobacco, alcohol—have proved to be decisive risk factors, influencing virtually every category in the top-ten list of major causes of death. In the one-on-one setting of a periodic medical examination and review, an occupational physician has the luxury of being able to take the time to help focus his or her patient's attention and understanding on such remediable problems as smoking, high cholesterol levels, sedentariness and hypertension. Importantly, there is usually a ready opportunity for close and regular follow-up examinations at the work site, thus facilitating compliance. Periodic evaluations are an example of primary and secondary prevention at its best. Physicians who are capable of long-range goals can take real satisfaction in the preventive-health programs of the occupational setting. Physicians who must be involved with the regular removal of "hot" appendixes should look elsewhere. Few workers will awaken ten or 15 years hence and call to thank you when they fail to have a heart attack that day because of your past efforts; the satisfaction is "self-feeding."

Because so many firms are either multinational in scope or involved in considerable international activity, an occupational-medicine department is often expected to provide assistance for the business traveler as well. Efforts must be mounted to stay abreast of the latest information from the Centers for Disease Control on immunization guidelines, with special attention to locations of new disease outbreaks. When feasible, inoculations are administered, and a traveling employee is often armed with a special kit that contains prophylactic medications as needed (e.g., antimalarial agents) along with literature concerning appropriate health-related travel information.

Naturally, immunization needs exist for nontraveling employees as well, and the company dispensary can be relied on to publicize a late-fall campaign for selective influenza inoculations, as well as to keep an eye on the need for regular tetanus/diphtheria updates. Unfortunately, as of this writing, the quandary posed by the risk of liability exposure that clouds plans for an otherwise desirable rubella immunization drive has yet to be resolved.

Each clinic visit has the potential for opening the door to a counseling session. It is now commonplace to recognize that the lion's share of presenting complaints have no organic source but, indeed, are psychologically based. Modern occupational-medicine departments often add certified counselors to their staff to augment the response in this key area. Professional counselors are expected to administer the company's employee assistance program (EAP) and to ensure absolute confidentiality. An EAP can help guide preoccupied employees to a constructive approach in a variety of problem areas: marital and family discord, financial strain, drug and alcohol dependencies and frank psychiatric syndromes as well. In most corporate settings, such counseling is confined to several sessions; thereafter, referral is made to appropriate community resources according to need. Many such programs extend such counseling services to family members as well.

An occupational physician has a potential contribution to make toward maintenance of a safe work place, well beyond the obligations imposed by governmental regulations. For example, before a company fills assignments that have special physical requirements, preplacement examinations that are discretely targeted to assess an employee's capabilities are in order. Keeping in mind the important requirements of the Americans With Disabilities Act, every attempt should be made to achieve a safe fit between a disabled employee and his or her work assignment. To preserve the health and safety of an affected employee or co-workers, temporary or even permanent work restrictions may be needed. Because every employee who suffers a work-related injury or illness must report to the medical clinic, there should be every opportunity to work with other members of the company's "safety team" to focus on trouble spots. Depending on a given situation, an occupational physician's in-depth understanding of toxicology, epidemiology and disease processes may make an invaluable contribution to uncovering and relieving real or potential hazards in the work place.

Naturally, the specific form of occupational-medicine programs varies greatly from company to company. Such differences reflect not only the general type and profitability of the business or industry at hand, but also its corporate culture, in which such services can either limp along or flourish.

The role of an occupational physician often extends beyond the specific programs described. In an administrative or advisory role, a company physician's opinion may be sought by a wide variety of departments: executive, legal, risk management, personnel, benefits planning and administration, operations and even marketing and merchandising. If an occupational physician chooses an interesting and supportive company, he or she can be assured of a challenging and fascinating career.

PERSONAL CHALLENGES AND GRATIFICATIONS

The year before I passed my Board-certification examination in internal medicine, I had just come out of a two-year stint as an Army Medical Corps captain at First Army Headquarters Base Hospital. With a young family, the idea of joining a group practice was appealing, but there were very, very few such practices in the New York metropolitan area at the time. Imagine with what happy anticipation I went to interview an internist in one such rare and prestigious group who, luckily enough, was a friend who had been just a year ahead of me throughout my medical residency. A good, sincere fellow, too; a thinker . . . smoked a pipe. He got to the point quickly. "David, after all the years of training for ITP and SLE, do you know what I do? I'm seeing sore throats. Sore throats . . . all day long!" I had not seen anyone look so gray in a long time. If I had any apprehensions about private practice (and I had), this experience clinched it.

Within weeks I accepted a position as a staff physician at Western Electric headquarters. Although I have had to explain occupational medicine to family, friends and new acquaintances ever since, it was a wonderful decision.

The initial transition, however, may not be easy for a young physician entering the field. I would nominate the adjustment to "employee" status as a major challenge. This new role may well require a reshaping of one's previous daydreams. Generalizations are, by nature, inexact, but to suggest that most physicians are extensively trained to think and act independently is probably not far from the mark. How, then, does such a professional enroll as an "employee"—just one of thousands of employees—and sign on for fixed hours, designated holidays, rationed vacation days and voluminous company rules and procedures and, of all things, report to a "boss" as well? It may help to remember that, even outside occupational medicine, most physicians are no longer in independent practice, no longer their own bosses. All such physicians, including occupational physicians, defend unswervingly their right to practice according to high professional standards, but all of them must become team members as well, learning to plan their activities in a responsive way to achieve the most effective results for the group as a whole. Reconcile yourself to the thought that repeated lateness, for example, may outweigh diagnostic acumen by lending itself more readily to review and appraisal. Or, were you not counting on getting a raise?

It is essential, on joining a company, that an occupational physician not view himself or herself and the medical clinic as some uniquely transplanted professional appendage grafted onto the outside of the organization. Much of an occupational physician's success will surely depend on the warmth of the welcome that he or she offers fellow employees. And the sooner they come to see the physician as a real part of the company, a trusted co-worker who understands the company's philosophy and shares a belief in its future, the better. A physician who chooses to remain aloof from such involvement is not choosing wisely.

A paramount issue for an occupational physician is, of course, the nature of the doctor-patient relationship in such a setting. Can a physician employed by a company retain a confidential relationship when caring for co-workers? Nothing is more important. Without a clear policy of confidentiality that is respected to the nth degree, the medical clinic may as well close down. The worth of a physician's services to a company hinges on the faith and trust of its employees. The Code of Ethical Conduct for Physicians Providing Occupational Medical Services, which was articulated in the 1970s by the American Occupational Medical Association, among other principles, states:

> Physicians should treat as confidential whatever is learned about individuals served, releasing information only when required by law or by overriding public health considerations, or to other physicians at the request of the individual according to traditional medical ethical practice; and should recognize that employers are entitled to counsel about the medical fitness of the individual in relation to work, but are not entitled to diagnoses or details of a specific nature.

It follows, then, that when Jane Z. visits the dispensary and is not permitted to return to work, her supervisor or manager must be apprised only that she was found medically unable to work, along with some estimate as to the length of her anticipated absence. Inquiry by management concerning the underlying health problem is politely but firmly turned aside. There is no compromise possible on this principle, in much the same way that one must be committed to communicate information concerning health hazards to persons who may be affected. Any organization worth affiliating with will respect a physician's professional obligations and will understand that what best serves the health of the employees best serves the company as well. If not, it is time to leave.

Although amassing great wealth is not among them, the gratifications in an occupational practice are many and various. Because an on-site medical clinic offers a service provided by the company, no fees are charged. This is one potentially negative aspect of the doctor-patient relationship that need never intervene. And, of course, with the facility maintained at the expense of the company, an occupational physician has no overhead. Naturally, as a manager, staying within a budget is a necessary concern, but the company should provide ample administrative assistance. Generally, evenings and weekends are free time for the physician to enjoy as well. In addition, many companies have realized the worth of a continuing relationship between occupational physicians and local medical centers and encourage them to take half a day each week, under the company's aegis, to contribute their skills at a clinic of interest. Continuing medical education meetings and courses are supported as well.

However, the real joy of an occupational-medicine practice is found in the solid core of the hands-on preventive medicine with which such physicians are involved. Some clinics insist on a system of visits by appointment only, whereas others have an open-door, drop-in-any-time approach. Whichever approach works best, and depending on a physician's standing orders for the nurses or, possibly, the assistants who may be on his or her staff, the physician should be seeing most patients who arrive with medical problems of more than a minor degree. Because the physician has been smart enough to inspect every work area for which he or she is responsible, he or she is in a good position to establish a knowledgeable rapport with patients from the outset. Because the primary goal is service, and with the comforting thought that the rent is already paid (as is the company's general-liability policy, which incorporates malpractice coverage), the physician has the luxury of taking whatever time is needed to explore important issues and of scheduling freely whatever revisits are necessary. Because an occupational physician is not an employee's private physician, he or she expects to complement the latter physician's services in the work setting, and attempts should be made to effect timely communications between the two physicians. When referrals to outside specialists are appropriate, the occupational physician will be in a position to provide authoritative and disinterested recommendations. When patients express their earnest appreciation for such efforts, and they will, the experience will assure the occupational physician of the wisdom of his or her choice of practice.

The types of patients are drawn from a special subset of the population. Virtually all of them are alert, mature men and women who are concerned with earning a living. For the most part, they are committed to their careers in a deep sense. They were selected for their skills. They take pride in their achievements. Just as occupational physicians do, accountants, architects, attorneys, clerks, engineers, keypunchers, packers, photographers, printers, psychologists, secretaries and truckers draw much of their central identities from their labors. The physician's role can be a critical one in helping protect their health and, as disabilities arise, in helping preserve their careers by seeking appropriate job accommodations and rehabilitation.

Occupational physicians are uniquely situated to be able to have an impressively broad impact. In contrast to psychoanalysts, who may deal with only a score of patients over a long period, it is not unusual for occupational physicians to touch the lives of hundreds of thousands of employees and family members. And because of the profound importance that employees attach to preserving their careers, occupational medicine is uniquely situated to address some of the major public-health issues in society today.

A prime example, of course, is the approach of occupational medicine to alcoholism. Alcohol dependency has been shown to afflict 5 to 10 percent of the working population; it is the underlying cause for as much as 25 percent of the occupancy of all acute-care general-hospital beds. It is also the basis for one third of all emergency-room visits. Yet, alcoholism has been left generally ignored, as in a conspiracy of silence, by patients and their families, by many physicians and by most hospitals. A patient denies the addiction, the family avoids the "stigma," and the personal physician, who has no training in a ready therapeutic approach for such a refractory problem, complies through silence and by secondary diagnoses that deflect attention from the primary problem.

For occupational physicians, however, here is a challenging problem that cries out for action. A not inconsiderable percentage of any company's work force is doubtless afflicted with this progressive illness, which by its very nature blocks victims from initiating remedial steps.

Alcoholism saps productivity, erodes physical and mental health and contributes enormously to the mortality tables not only in relation to cirrhosis and a number of cancers but through accidents, homicides and suicides as well. If uninterrupted in its progress, marriages and careers are lost—lives are lost. Happily, within industry, the "magic bullet" for alcoholism exists.

Occupational physicians who acquire in-depth knowledge of alcoholism will discover that, if the victims can garner sufficient motivation, diseases of dependency can be overcome. With this knowledge, such physicians can guide companies to an effective approach based on a challenge to perceived chronic inadequacies in job performance. No prior diagnosis on the part of management is called for. An employee is given a choice by concerned management: your career is at risk—either agree to cooperate with a professional assessment of whatever it is that may have caused this persistent decline in performance, and cooperate with recommended treatment, or face dismissal. In the author's experience, 98 percent of employees who are given this choice agree to cooperate. Of those who are found to suffer from alcoholism, invariably a majority of such supervisory referrals, at least 70 percent can be counted on to participate for an extended period in the recovery process and return to satisfactory, or better, performance levels. A remarkable batting average for this tenacious disease! Victims can let everything slip away while clinging to the bottle—wives, children, bank accounts, families and friends; nothing and no one persuades addicts to loosen their grip on the supply of alcohol—until their careers are put at risk. This approach does not always work but, then, neither does penicillin.

Naturally, a company is not limited to focusing on employees whose performance has reached an advanced state of decline. Its EAP can reach out to all employees and their family members, offering voluntary confidential counseling for a variety of problems, including alcohol or drug dependency.

Cigarette smoking is another good example of a dangerous addiction that both challenges the creativity of occupational physicians and provides an opportunity for some rewarding preventive steps. With 1,000 premature deaths per day ascribed to smoking, it is clear that everyone in society has an obligation to help change the situation. A company's occupational-medicine service can not only approach employees in the clinic setting, it can also be the driving force behind a number of company-wide approaches ranging from participating in national smoke-out days to conducting courses on how to quit smoking throughout the year. Occupational physicians may bring companies a major step forward by providing leadership in the establishment of policies that either restrict or abolish smoking at the work place. This approach can help a number of smokers in shedding their habits while improving the quality of air for their co-workers to breathe.

Certainly, hypertension is a critical risk factor that is ideally suited for handling in the work setting. Because most people with high blood pressure are asymptomatic, they neither visit their private physicians because of the problem nor, once started on medication, show compliance with regard to drug therapy. Enter the occupational-medicine department, whose efforts in regard to blood-pressure regulation can range from periodic examinations, to efforts at mass screening (including bringing the sphygmomanometer to the employees) and follow-ups with private physicians, to more elaborate attempts to take on the entire issue: from initial diagnosis and prescription, to long-term care at company clinics. Because the staff of the occupational-medicine department focuses on prevention, a system of follow-up reminders to employees with hypertension is taken seriously. Because of the relative ease of making a visit to the company clinic, such employees find compliance less of a hardship.

Interested occupational physicians can have a beneficial impact in a variety of ways that extend well beyond the roles described. For instance, cafeteria services are often pleased to cooperate in planning and publicizing their food offerings to comply with desirable nutritional goals. As an example, calling attention to special entrées that help control cholesterol levels on the menu boards each day not only makes an immediate contribution in reducing intake of saturated fats and cholesterol but serves a heuristic function as well. There are a number of other modifications that may be useful and feasible.

In most companies, the risk-management department and the safety manager consult closely with occupational-medicine specialists as issues of potential toxic exposures and safety arise. Even in the absence of any hazard intrinsic to the raw materials or products of a company, occupational physicians must be prepared to deal with unusual or unexpected environmental challenges, such as asbestos, polychlorinated biphenyls and radon. A physician's clinical judgment on such matters can often contribute to a balanced, appropriate response on the part of the company that assures no delay in safeguarding the health of employees.

Many private industries and businesses produce or sell health-related products. Although courses on this subject are not offered in medical schools, an occupational physician's judgment may be sought concerning such products. Are the printed package claims and instructions accurate? Does the product represent an ethically appropriate offering or does it smack of quackery? Does the research behind the product appear authentic or is further review required? A timely opinion may spare consumers unnecessary expense and discomfort and spare the company considerable embarrassment, financial and otherwise.

In the past few years, the broad area of benefits design has emerged as a special challenge to business organizations as they watch their health-benefits expenditures go off the charts. Expenditures for health insurance, which had once been viewed as part of a package of "fringe benefits" along with vacations and holidays, are now adding up to an enormous drain on company resources. This situation has ushered in a fresh look at every aspect of physician- and hospital-payment benefits, and a new set of ground rules is emerging. Many companies have included their occupational-medicine specialists in this planning process for the first time. Whether a company is self-insured for such benefits and uses an insurance company for administrative services only, company management may well benefit from the counsel of one of its own staff who has special expertise in health-related matters.

For example, here are some questions that might arise over just one facet of proposed health-insurance modifications: Are provisions that necessitate second surgical opinions likely to be worthwhile? If so, what surgical procedures should be listed? What credentials should physicians who render second opinions have? Might there be an advantage in permitting reviews by nonsurgical specialists? If Board-certified specialists are required for second opinions, how can employees best be guided to such physicians? If a surgeon has a pathology report that confirms cancer of the uterus, is a second opinion regarding hysterectomy necessary? If, in the end, an occupational physician is able to influence the shape and communication of employee-benefits plans, he or she can be confident in having made a singular contribution to the welfare of all the company's employees and their families. The challenge of benefits design is an especially good example of the sort of unexpected creative opportunity that may await occupational physicians.

As their administrative responsibilities grow, occupational physicians will be increasingly called on to represent their companies on the boards of community and national organizations. There are many voluntary, nonprofit groups that rely on contributions of time and effort by responsible corporate citizens. Such participation provides an excellent opportunity to learn, and also gives a boost to communities in general. One area of particular interest for occupational physicians are the activities of local business-health coalitions. Such coalitions usually draw representatives from organizations throughout the immediate geographic area that join out of a shared concern for the cost, accessibility and quality of health-care services in communities. Health-care professionals can have an important role in the success of such groups.

FUTURE TRENDS

This section was written during a period of unprecedented upheaval in the traditional relationships among patients, physicians and hospitals. The author has already noted the increased attention being given to health-care costs by the business sector of the economy. In general, there has been a trend toward shifting some of the financial burden back to employees to stimulate cost consciousness and an alert consumer attitude. At the same time, federal and state governments are generally ratcheting down on once-generous health-care plans for their employees. These major consumers are on the lookout for competitive provider offerings that promise a restraint on rising costs. Less hospitalization, less complicated care. Prepaid health plans—health maintenance organizations (HMOs) in a variety of formats—and preferred-provider organizations (PPOs) have mushroomed in this fertile soil, against a background of a surplus of physicians and hospital beds and overwhelmingly burdensome malpractice-insurance premiums for practitioners. Proprietary hospital conglomerates arise, complete with stockholders; health care becomes a "product"; patients are now "consumers." Physicians in this highly competitive new world now sign up on panels of HMOs, in which their annual income hinges on ordering fewer tests and making fewer referrals to specialists. A haze of doubt intervenes in the private doctor-patient relationship.

By sheer contrast, it is likely that occupational-medicine clinics, serving as concerned and helpful ombudsmen, will continue to gain in reputation with their potential clientele. Average citizens will no longer have a comforting sense of easy access to the reliable private practitioners of yore; increasingly, anxious patients will sense that they are "subscriber number X," as their HMO's switchboard tries to find open slots for them (and their aching backs) with "primary doctor Y," who will be rotating on to a duty assignment with "clinic Z" the following day. The convenience, the warmth of welcome, the lack of being herded or shuttled in and out, the understanding and recognition of a patient as a known personality with a respected role in the organization, the sense of disinterestedness shown in looking for the right solutions and best referrals, the time taken to reach out and help with beneficial changes in life-style—all these facets of occupational-medicine clinics should combine to help fill the crucially important private-physician void.

The gatekeeper function will likely be a growing trend as occupational physicians join in efforts to achieve economies in health care while preserving its quality. Here, a physician goes beyond the role of advisor and guide in the selection of special health-care services. The gatekeeper, or case manager, approves or disapproves further services based on an appraisal of the given situation. Under the terms of a patient's medical policy, services may be limited to selections indicated by the gatekeeper physician.[1] One can already point to some circumscribed examples of case management by occupational physicians in a few concerned companies. For instance, one national company that distributes goods and services already pays a portion of the charges for in-patient alcoholism rehabilitation when obtained at an approved facility; however, it will pay 100 percent if the patient agrees to admission at one of the small number of freestanding rehabilitation centers that have been chosen by its occupational-medicine department for high quality of care combined with impressively modest fees.

Case managership is an important example of the potential for occupational medicine to move beyond the traditional role of complementing the services of private physicians. Certainly, with regard to employees who are economically disadvantaged, company clinics have long attempted to amplify their services. With the future promising fewer community clinic supports for those in marginal financial circumstances, the coming years should see increased attention to an enlarged offering of comprehensive health-care services in the work place.

At the very time that the roles of occupational physicians are expanding, the choices open to private practitioners are becoming increasingly constricted. The HMOs and PPOs plan to enlist a substantial portion of the working community. Their subscribers will be financially constrained to limit their selection of physicians to the chosen panel. Physicians in such organizations will be practicing "managed medicine," supervised by an administrative review apparatus that will have a broad impact on what had once been independent professional decisions. The allure of such a private practice will noticeably dim in some circumstances, and consideration of a career in occupational medicine should become increasingly attractive in contrast.

This shift in the scale should be occurring just as business organizations finally begin to register the impression that, as health-care expenditures as a percentage of resources have risen dramatically, the organizational importance of maintaining coherent occupational-medicine services has grown as well. The erosion of net profits, as perceived by many companies, forces organizations to take remedial action. In the author's judgment, demand for skilled occupational physicians should continue to increase for many years to come. Even as the total number of physicians in the United States continues to expand toward a total of approximately 665,000 in 1995, giving this country a new record of 249 physicians per 100,000 population, occupational medicine will have an undersupply.

BECOMING AN OCCUPATIONAL PHYSICIAN

This chapter previously referred to the serious deficiency in medical school curricula regarding issues that are essential to occupational medicine. A fair estimate is that only approximately four hours in four years are devoted to the subject! Hardly capable of whetting a student's appetite for the field. And doubly unfortunate, too, because any physician, whether general practitioner or specialist, must be said to be handicapped without the ability either to include a meaningful occupational history in a patient's evaluation or to see the possibilities for occupational variables in the differential diagnosis.

Opportunities for graduate education are on a par with the restrictive situation at the medical school level. In 1986, there were 126 residents in occupational medicine programs in the U.S.; by 1991, this number was little changed at 130, distributed among 32 programs.[2] Because approximately 80 percent of the dollar support for graduate education is dependent on patient-care revenues, occupational-medicine residents are already at a disadvantage. Compounding the problem has been the pallid level of governmental support in the form of programs. The National Institute for Occupational Safety and Health has flattened its funding for occupational-medicine training centers for the past several years. In 1991, it distributed just $10 million to a small number of such centers, for example, Cincinnati, Johns Hopkins and University of California for both training and project grants.

Nevertheless, although the American Board of Preventive Medicine has requested formal residency preparation, since 1984, to qualify for the occupational-medicine certification examination, the field remains open to physicians from a variety of disciplines: internal medicine, family practice, general surgery and psychiatry, to name a few.

Such physicians are able to hone their skills in a number of ways in addition to making use of the experiences offered by the position itself. The local component of the American College of Occupational and Environmental Medicine (ACOEM) can usually be relied on to sponsor several educational events during the year; the ACOEM's monthly publication, the *Journal of Occupational Medicine,* has a wealth of pertinent articles; and excellent, comprehensive textbooks in the field have appeared in the past few years. Also, the ACOEM cosponsors (with the American Association of Occupational Health Nurses) an annual American occupational health conference at which postgraduate seminars and scientific papers are presented. In addition, a few medical centers conduct "mini-residencies" in occupational medicine for physicians seeking special training while continuing their careers.

Nor should one overlook the considerable amount of information available from one's fellow professionals in occupational medicine. In the author's experience, there is virtually no sense of competition among occupational physicians; rather, there is a strong impulse to cooperate in offering helpful solutions to the unique problems that often arise in this fascinating discipline. In this regard, there are essentially no walls between corporations. Given the width and breadth of the field, and its sometimes complex organizational relationships, this reliable support by one's colleagues proves invaluable.

While I was a busy Cornell medical student back in the 1950s, there was an elective "moment" during public health when I spent an hour one morning with a handful of classmates visiting the occupational-medicine department of a large oil company headquartered at Rockefeller Center. It was some eight years later, on entering the field myself, when I recalled that brief occasion and realized that, without that earlier experience, I might never have made this happy choice.

As the reader considers all the future practice alternatives and organizational structures detailed in this book, allow the author to suggest that he or she take the opportunity to explore this excellent career path in a similar, tangible fashion. The author has no doubt that the staff of the ACOEM, should the reader speak to them, would be pleased to supply the names of local occupational physicians who would probably be delighted to receive a visit. Tell them the author sent you . . . and good luck!

SUMMARY

Occupational medicine, a subspecialty of preventive medicine, should be a better-recognized practice alternative.

Occupational physicians are primarily concerned with promotion of the health of workers through a variety of in-house programs. Full-time occupational physicians must adjust to the role of management "employee" while preserving doctor-patient confidentiality. It is recognized that employers are entitled to counsel concerning the fitness of employees in relation to their work assignments.

There are a variety of special professional gratifications associated with occupational medicine, not the least of which is the potential for a broad impact by improving preventive-health practices.

In the atmosphere of high employee health-care expenditures, demand for skilled occupational physicians should continue to increase.

REFERENCES

1. Eisenberg JM: The internist as gatekeeper. *Ann Intern Med* 102:537–543, 1985.
2. Appendix II. Graduate medical education. *J Am Med Assoc* 268:1170–1176, 1992.

Note: For detailed information on residency-training programs, write to the director of education of the American College of Occupational and Environmental Medicine, 55 W. Seegers Road, Arlington Heights, IL 60005. The telephone number is (708) 228-6850.

CHAPTER 7

RESEARCH-ORGANIZATION AND MANAGEMENT PHILOSOPHIES:

Their impact on physicians in academia and industry

Seth Allen Rudnick
Alan S. Rosenthal

The tendency toward subspecialty training has been accelerated by the ever-increasing complexity and accuracy of the information available on the pathogenesis of disease. Data[1] suggest that more than 50 percent of the graduates in internal medicine are now eligible for Board certification or are certified in a subspecialty, and the duration of their training has been extended to accommodate this increasing level of sophistication in highly restricted areas of medicine. Therefore, it should come as no surprise that the organizational impetus that has led to subspecialty training has had similar effects on the organization of research endeavors in the pharmaceutical industry.

Analogous changes have occurred with the development of such subspecialties as surgical oncology and pediatric infectious diseases and new specialties, such as geriatrics and emergency medicine. This section reviews the organizational role of physicians in the pharmaceutical industry in relation to the traditional role. It recognizes that the profound changes that have occurred in medical knowledge have, in turn, altered societal expectations of how physicians approach new career challenges in medicine.

ROLES OF PHYSICIANS IN INDUSTRY AND ACADEMIA

One obvious difference exists between the organizational role of an academic physician and that of an industrial physician. In the academic setting, expectations of teaching, research, administration and clinical care have evolved. In this setting, physician-teachers should be competent, should have extensive knowledge of their field and should convey a sense of excitement to their students. At the same time, physician-teachers should maintain active research efforts at the cutting edge of science with full understanding of the field, its competition and its direction. They should maintain clinical skills and serve as role models for interns, residents and fellows. Finally, they should handle administrative tasks with a sense of priority and an understanding of the needs of the employees of the institution. This is obviously an unrealistically broad job description and, yet, one that is theoretically in place at almost every academic institution in the country.

Pharmaceutical companies have fewer and far better-defined roles for physicians. An administrative or research role in the industry carries with it responsibility for directly running laboratory or clinical research and managing resources and priorities appropriately. There is little room in that construct for the traditional role of teacher or clinician. Despite this apparent narrowness in the pharmaceutical industry, choices in one of the classic academic directions are both possible and often encouraged. For example, some pharmaceutical companies run exemplary clinical research units as part of an academic institution that studies novel therapies for specific diseases and conveys them to student and faculty alike. Nevertheless, such units are scarce, and this role for an industrial clinician is limited. However, the role of teacher and the role of sharer of information are increasingly important to physicians in the pharmaceutical industry, just as they are to physicians in academia. Subspecialty-trained physicians with more thorough understanding of disease processes have only recently become available to the industry. Their ability to maintain ties with a collaborative research group, such as the National Institute of Allergy and Infectious Disease, the National Cancer Institute or the National Heart, Lung, and Blood Institute, requires a high degree of scientific credibility. This credibility is earned only by publication and presentation. Indeed, progressive pharmaceutical companies are placing increasing emphasis on publication as a reasonable outcome of corporate-sponsored research.

Training

Preparation for the breadth of responsibilities in academics is, not surprisingly, constrained to a basic-research or a clinical-care pathway. However, preparation for the role of physician-investigator or physician-administrator in industry often requires skills in management not easily acquired in "traditional" academia (see Chapter 9). Training in the academic setting is formalistic, with designations that are clearly rooted in that tradition. Student begets intern begets resident begets fellow begets young faculty member, and so on. During the entire process, increasing levels of responsibility and information are borne by the person so designated.

These increasing responsibilities are rarely accompanied by the acquisition of less scientific skills, such as management skills or teaching skills; rather, such skills are taught ad hoc or by example. Conversely, the training that occurs for physicians in pharmaceutical environments ranges from informal science education, to formal but flexibly structured management training, to rigidly structured data-gathering and presentation skills required for regulatory submissions. The flexible approach with increasing management responsibility still demands postgraduate training. This training is tailored to a person's needs and usually consists of brief courses sponsored by such groups as the Pharmaceutical Manufacturer's Association or the American Management Association. Furthermore, increasing management responsibilities and status are often reflected by changing titles in a pharmaceutical company and, in contrast to academics, not by increasing mastery of scientific information. This dichotomy has, in fact, frequently created problems within the pharmaceutical industry as creative and innovative scientists have demanded an alternative track to increasing management responsibility to receive increasing recognition and remuneration.

Philosophic Model

The reasons for entry of physicians into the pharmaceutical setting have changed during the past decade as the need for increasing scientific sophistication has arisen. Yet, the types of person who will be attracted to this setting will continue to have differing philosophic approaches. Perhaps the major philosophic difference between the research approach of academia and that of industry is defined by the demands of the market. The market-based need for a long-term, competitive, sustainable advantage drives all successful companies, whether or not pharmaceutical. Without a sustainable advantage, any company will eventually succumb to market forces. With it, a company can survive and prosper, bring value to its shareholders and increase stability for its employees. The income that derives from such an advantage is the key to the success of a company. It must therefore be highly quantifiable and relatively predictable. In that sense, research in a corporate setting must ultimately lead to a profit. This is in stark contrast to the strategic goals of an academic medical institution, which are based on the needs of society. Such goals vary, but the general perception is that they are not based on profits. It is worthwhile to remind ourselves that the "physician as scientist" is an outgrowth of the medical institutions that provide degrees and training in the delivery of health care. Before Sputnik aroused public interest in science and, consequently, led to a massive influx of federal funding, medical research was viewed primarily as an activity reflecting personal interest rather than as the force that determines tenure, as it is currently viewed.

Regulation
Despite the perceptions of society to the contrary, the careers of physician-scientists in both academia and industry are highly regulated. Most importantly, governmental regulations dictate an almost uniform response to safety and health requirements in both settings. Physicians and the therapies that they prescribe are heavily regulated in academia as well as in industry. This regulation clearly slows innovation but enhances safety.

Despite the personal frustrations such regulations create for physicians as practitioners of their arts, the authors believe that the trade-off is worthwhile for society. However, for patients with diseases that might become more readily manageable or curable with more rapid innovation, there is clearly inhibition of widespread introduction of new drugs and diagnostic approaches. Surprisingly enough, the regulatory environment surrounding academia is as complex, in a sociologic sense, as the regulatory environment surrounding the pharmaceutical industry. Pharmaceutical companies simply have to show that the data that they present on a new compound are verifiable and demonstrate safety and efficacy and that the manufacturing standards the government requires have been adhered to. Academic centers are not regulated solely by a series of state and federal agencies that oversee and fund their operations. Other professional agencies and specialty-licensing Boards have a self-evident and growing role in the operation and standards of acceptable academic practice. This situation inevitably adds layers of bureaucracy to defend such institutions.

RISK AND INNOVATION
The need to innovate in academic and pharmaceutical settings is of equal theoretic importance. Yet, innovations in basic research have been, and continue to be, driven by academic centers; conversely, academic centers have proved themselves incapable of developing such breakthroughs and have turned (and continue to turn) their ideas over to industry for practical application. Given the previously noted strategic need for innovation in industry, what changes the risk-taking level for physicians and scientists in industry as opposed to academia? Possible explanations for differences in approaches to research and development may be inherent in organizational structures, expected role performances, demonstrations of success (reporting of results) and, ultimately, the manner in which these aspects are controlled.

Differences in Structure

Do the previously mentioned differences in research-and-development results lead to or stem from differences in organizational structure? For industry, the organizational structure is relatively new, and its impact is less clear. The most likely answer for academia is that its organizational model long antedates its current behavior. The organization of an academic institution is inescapably flat but has distinct classes compared with an industrial concern (see Figure 1A). Although students, young and old faculty members, departmental chairmen and deans exist, the very description of such classes and the consistency of this organizational hierarchy from school to school suggests an inherent conservatism combined with a setting in which the most junior member could quickly reach all but the highest level with information or insight. For example, it is not at all unusual for a departmental chairman in a medical school to make rounds and see second- and third-year medical students on the ward or to have a student in his or her laboratory who is preparing for a doctor of philosophy degree.

This situation stands in contrast to the much more rigid hierarchy that most industrial concerns have evolved (see Figure 1B). To a certain extent, the hierarchic arrangement reflects mechanisms for rewarding persons with subtle discriminations in salary and title but little differentiation in responsibilities. An associate director to whom nine employees report in one company is not much different from a director to whom 20 employees report. The subtle differences that exist, however, allow a salary range that reflects past as well as potential contributions to the organization. Despite its use as a mechanism for reward and recognition, this organizational hierarchy often slows the flow of information to the uppermost levels of company management. In recognition of this problem, industrial concerns continually attempt to rearrange their organizational structures to accelerate the flow of information.

A common mechanism for handling this lack of flatness in the pharmaceutical industry is the matrix, or team, approach, whereby junior as well as senior members of a company collaborate as drug projects move forward. The analogous situation is apparently unnecessary in the academic setting because its formal use is infrequent. However, it may be used for an urgent problem in this setting. For example, a collaborative group—search committee—is used under the extraordinary circumstances when a departmental chairman or dean is sought. This democratization of choice is, in fact, yet another difference between academic and industrial settings; the flat organization demands an input from its constituency that the hierarchic organization finds potentially counterproductive. One should recognize that generic statements about academic or industrial organizations are not uniformly accurate. Thus, the most effective industrial hierarchies, such as those at Minnesota Mining &

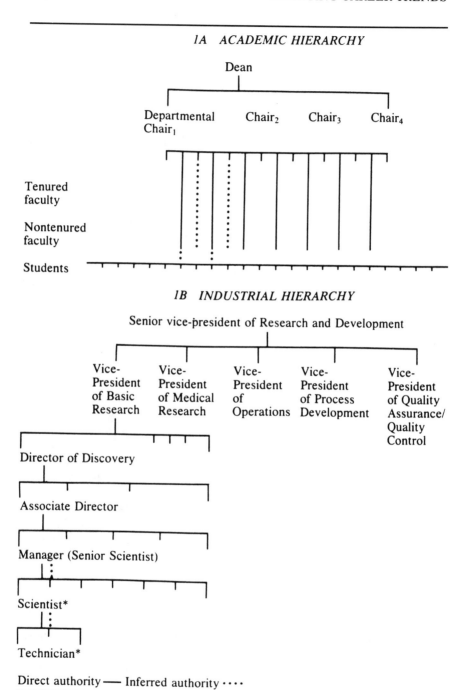

1A   ACADEMIC HIERARCHY

1B   INDUSTRIAL HIERARCHY

Direct authority —— Inferred authority ····

*Only at the level of Senior Scientist or Scientist, and primarily in the area of drug discovery, does an industrial research organization begin to approach the flatness of the academic setting.

Figure 7.1   Comparison of academic and industrial hierarchies.

Manufacturing and Johnson & Johnson, encourage the flow of information from the lowest to the highest levels and innovation by all levels. This ability to innovate and force to adapt is one that marks the most successful industrial concerns.[2] Conversely, academic environments are occasionally beset with rigid hierarchies that preclude the flow of information as well as innovation. Although such rigidities vary from university to university, and even from department to department, they are certainly as common as the flattened, communicating structure of industrial organizations.

At the same time that one looks at the flatness of an organization, one recognizes that with increasing responsibility in the academic setting, risk appears to decrease. Therefore, the willingness to innovate may well increase. Although no studies have examined academic as opposed to industrial innovation on the basis of contract versus tenure, it is clear that organizations that have profit-and-loss statements tend to increase the risk for senior and middle-level managers. Accountability and analysis of failure are hallmarks of a successful and responsible industrial concern. However, the flexibility to respond to failure quickly and without organizational review is often deficient in industry. This situation contrasts strongly with the academic setting, in which a departmental chairman or a dean of a medical school could conceivably act quickly but rarely measures or assesses failure and success on any but a long-term basis.

The increasing "risk with responsibility ratio" of industry with supplemented authority is obviously compensated for by vastly different salary structures. More importantly, a rapid review process and an ability to discriminate between success and failure are far more important in an organization that frequently judges success on the basis of its ability to satisfy market demands than in an organization that judges success on the basis of its ability to meet the needs of society.

Academic Model of Research

The goal of research in academia and the role of a physician in achieving that goal have evolved during the past three decades. The original goal of a physician in an academic environment was to apply the tenets of clinical practice to gain information that could easily be transferred to patient care. This role evolved rapidly during the late 1950s through the early 1970s because of the increasing availability of research grants. Although the imposition of more and more constraints on funding since the early 1970s has increased the competition for such grants, they clearly permitted major discoveries in molecular biology and receptor pharmacology in the 1960s and 1970s. Such discoveries both permitted and forced the performance of extensive basic research by clinicians and doctoral candidates, perhaps lacking doctor of medicine degrees but having doctor of philosophy degrees. Interestingly enough, the academic environment became primarily an entrepreneurial milieu that demanded constant innovation based on current information.[3]

The peer-review grant mechanisms supported novel concepts or well-executed experiments that furthered the understanding of disease processes at levels that were heretofore unknown, such as the molecular biology of the immune system. However, such research also required large laboratory groups with a broad array of discovery tools and a willingness to commit resources to efforts that would show continuing promise, leading to grant renewals and long-term efforts aimed at an understanding of specific disease mechanisms. An example of research that led to an extensive understanding of disease processes is summarized by Tonegawa in an article on the immune system.[4] This complex approach necessitated the education of faculty as well as of students, technicians and postdoctoral fellows to allow them to participate in such broad research probes. Therefore, the institutional review system for grant proposals and the departmental focus on particular and mutually supportive research interests coalesced into what have become academic research departments. Thus, instead of responding to market forces, the current academic model is, in theory, focused on ensuring the scientific and academic reputations of investigators as well as institutions. The management and strategic models that support academic endeavors obviously differ markedly from those that support research in the pharmaceutical industry.

Pharmaceutical Model of Research
In the pharmaceutical industry, development of new molecular compounds is the basic thrust of research. Moreover, such compounds must be marketable, with basic research serving to support the ability to develop new compounds that are effective in the management or cure of disease. The industry's goal is solely the development of effective therapeutic agents, whereas the goals of academia are to serve society at large as well as to conduct research in general.

Before the explosive growth in the understanding of diseases that occurred in the past 30 years, drug companies identified promising compounds by "brute force," often described mirthfully as the "Shakespearean approach," in other words, enough monkeys (biologists) and typewriters (chemists) and you ultimately get King Lear! Relatively simple models of disease were used as targets to screen compounds to look for active agents. As the pathophysiologic basis of disease processes has become better understood, the approach used to identify candidate compounds has become more sophisticated. In fact, the use of enzymes and receptor targets to search for promising compounds has led to increasing automation and, consequently, more "precise" identification of active agents. Examples of receptors that have been used in this manner are H_2 (histamine) antagonists and β_2-adrenergic agonists. Use of such models for studying disease processes has resulted in greater overlap between academic and pharmaceutical research in this field and in the screening of compounds for therapeutic application. It is, therefore, not surprising that the free flow of staff candidates from the academic to the industrial setting and vice versa has been increasing in response to the increasing need for sophistication in pharmaceutical research, which must be built on an academic base.

Reporting of Results

If differences in organizational hierarchies and strategies have led to differentiation of roles and goals for physicians in industry as opposed to academia, one should be aware that the summarization and reporting of information have reinforced differences in approaches as well. In the academic setting, innovative ideas are expected to be communicated publicly as quickly as possible. The data obtained in this setting are not necessarily refined and defensible, being, instead, innovative, creative and often preliminary. Many experiments have not been reproduced, and the source data are rarely published. In fact, the drive for academic success demands repetition of experiments that yield unexpected results and usually encourages second, third and fourth approaches to the same issue.

Conversely, the goal of a report from the pharmaceutical industry is to win regulatory approval. The analysis is often far more detailed, including charts, graphs and source data that would be rejected by any respected journal as being far too complex and cumbersome for public consumption. Such data support the reproducibility of the findings, which have often been obtained from a number of studies during development, toxicology or clinical stages of testing. Source data are always available and often accompany submissions to regulatory agencies. In fact, the major risk for a pharmaceutical company is premature disclosure before patent and development status can be secured.

Decisions to Start, Maintain or Discontinue Research

Why does innovative research remain the domain primarily of academic institutions while rapid development appears to require an industrial approach? The preceding sections have explored research-and-development strategies, organizational hierarchies and the roles and responsibilities of physicians in this regard, but they still may not have addressed the differences in outcome. In theory, one should note that the primary area of interest of a pharmaceutical company is independent of the research interests of its investigators. In practice, this is often not the case, and novel research is carried out at the fringes of this area because of management or investigator interest. However, the area of primary therapeutic interest, which is dictated by return on investment, promotes research in a certain arena. Nonetheless, the discovery of compounds outside that focus may still be encouraged. However, such research is rigorously controlled in the pharmaceutical setting. By contrast, novel research not strictly related to the primary focus of an academic department is not subject to such financial constraints. The resources needed to continue promising research in the pharmaceutical industry are more likely to be forthcoming when the findings are subject to consistent and rigorous review by groups analogous to the decision networks of the National Cancer Institute.[5] Such research is continued or discontinued on the basis of decisions that rely on strict adherence to rigorous criteria. Research for the development of compounds is generally not subject to review by such decision networks; however, failure to develop compounds quickly discourages further research in a particular area.

Having passed decision points to identify promising compounds, the research-and-development department of a pharmaceutical company moves compounds through its pharmacology section, which evaluates the effects of such compounds in specific in vitro and in vivo models. If activity standards have been maintained, such compounds are then subjected to toxicologic screening to define their relative safety and potential starting doses in the management of various diseases. This system for the development of compounds at an accelerated pace is generally without parallel to, but is highly dependent on, the system that exists in the conventional academic setting.

DECISION MAKING FOR PHYSICIANS IN INDUSTRY

Past

The original role of physicians in industry was dramatically altered by the 1962 revision of the Food and Drug Act. After the revision was enacted, the complexity of conducting clinical trials and reporting on safety and efficacy changed the approach to drug testing from one of simply choosing the route of administration to ensure the safety and efficacy of a drug to one of understanding disease processes. The inevitable result over the ensuing 30 years was an increasing influx of physicians trained in specialties, such as internal medicine, surgery and obstetrics and gynecology, and, more recently, in subspecialties, such as oncology, infectious diseases, immunology and rheumatology. Early during this period, the primary career choice was to practice in a setting where house calls, night calls and the demands of running a private practice would not exist. Similar decisions were theoretically made by physicians who opted for other industrial settings, such as the insurance industry or occupational medicine in the corporate world.

Present

More recently, career choices have been dictated largely by the diminishing resources available to the academic sector and the increasing resources available to industry. In the 1989–1991 annual survey report prepared by the Pharmaceutical Manufacturer's Association, which summarizes 1988–1990 expenditures for research and development, the total expenditures by the pharmaceutical industry for human application jumped from $6.341 billion to $7.888 billion.

Ultimately, expenditures by pharmaceutical companies will surpass the funding available to the academic world. Hence, it is interesting to note the reasons that physicians are currently deciding in favor of careers in industry. A group of physicians in the pharmaceutical industry who are known to the authors were selected from such companies as Genentech, Xoma, Bristol Myers and Ortho. An open-ended questionnaire sought reasons for leaving academic or governmental positions to work in the industrial sector. In general, there was a conviction that tools and techniques available for the management of major diseases were being more wisely used within industry than within academia. For example, one clinical researcher noted, "My wish to be part of this development process whether working with recombinant DNA molecules, monoclonal antibodies, or classical new chemical entities was the overriding decision choice." Other comments included, "I have an opportunity to be part of a strong, scientific and clinical research environment in which the integrity of experimental design and the analysis of data is considered always to be of paramount importance."

A senior research administrator sensed the differentiation between industry and academia strongly: "In industry, quality research must be focused on making the critical developmental therapeutic choice. Basic research knowledge is not accumulated for its own sake nor just to add to the base line of information. It is accumulated to pinpoint as rapidly as possible the moment when that knowledge can be utilized to discover and then develop a new therapeutic product. This is an exciting challenge which requires team work and a coordinated approach."

In the academic setting, collaboration and coordination between laboratories is difficult to achieve. When it is attempted, it often must be done with "carrots but no sticks." Another comment from an industrial administrator with experience in a cancer center contrasted the two situations: "In this era of diminished federal funding, the lowered priority for cancer center grant support, outstanding research has become difficult to achieve. In industry, collaboration and coordination are the essential components of success. When the resources are adequate, this can be as exciting a challenge as exists for a research director." These comments drawn from physicians ranging from young investigators in a molecular biology–based research company to more experienced researchers in classical pharmaceutical companies reflect changes in the availability of resources and the expanding excitement and challenges of industry. Surprisingly enough, none of the respondents expressed feelings of hesitation or regret about leaving the academic or government setting.

Future

The evolution of the past 30 years will continue and accelerate during the next decade. The need—more than that, the demand—for skilled scientific judgment will accelerate the migration of subspecialty-trained physicians from academia to influential positions in industry. Their input in decisions to continue or discontinue the development of promising compounds will represent a major influence in the industry as a whole. This responsibility will require expanded training and knowledge of the drug-development process, from discovery to production methodologies, pharmacologic and toxicologic screening and the expanded role of clinical pharmacology. In this regard, an understanding of pharmacokinetics and pharmacodynamics will permit formulation of rational decisions in promoting or halting research on promising compounds. This is an exciting and interesting challenge for physicians and clearly matches the discovery role that will still retain favor in the academic and governmental settings.

What is becoming increasingly clear is that for the foreseeable future, both academia and industry will continue to offer attractive but clearly disparate opportunities for career advancement and personal satisfaction. More importantly, it is becoming evident that personality traits and behavior will dictate satisfaction, not differences in intellectual challenge between academia and industry. Indeed, the complexity of one's intellectual expectations and experiences will be comparable, both clearly offering an opportunity to contribute to the health and welfare of society.

REFERENCES

1. Tarlov AR: Consequences of the rising number of physicians and of the growth or subspecialization in internal medicine, in Bowers JZ, King EE (eds): *Academic Medicine: Present and Future*. North Tarrytown, NY, Rockefeller Archives Center, 1983, 106–121.
2. Peters TJ, Waterman RH: *In Search of Excellence: Lessons from America's Best-Run Companies*. New York, Harper & Row, 1982.
3. Drucker PF: *Management: Tasks, Responsibilities, Practices*. New York, Harper & Row, 1973.
4. Tonegawa S: The molecules of the immune system. *Sci Am* 253:122–131, 1985.
5. Driscoll JS: The preclinical new drug research program of the National Cancer Institute. *Cancer Treat Rep* 68:63–76, 1984.

CHAPTER 8

HEALTH MAINTENANCE ORGANIZATIONS:

A new development or the emperor's old clothes?

Thomas James, III
David B. Nash

Until the past two decades, prepaid medical practices have been regarded as something of a medical anomaly. Although prepaid medicine has been in existence in the United States for more than 60 years, its impact on the overall delivery of care has been minimal until recently. However, since the inception of the Health Maintenance Organization Act of 1973, there has been a virtual explosion in the number and size of such practices. In this era of diagnosis-related groups (DRGs) and Relative Value Resource-Based Scales (RVRBS's), physicians in every phase of practice have felt tightning constraints from utilization control and other measures of fiscal accountability. Currently, nearly every practitioner is, to some extent, involved in prepaid medicine. This chapter will explore the elements of prepaid care with its many stylistic differences.

The claims for successes or failures of health maintenance organizations (HMOs) have been founded largely on the philosophic premises of their advocates and detractors. Initially, prepaid practices were established for economic reasons. They could provide a ready cash flow for a practice group and, at the same time, fix the cost for health care for an employer. With further growth of the movement, the concepts of health maintenance and preventive medicine were introduced into prepaid programs. Expectations were set and marketed for programs that could provide personalized and responsive care. Health maintenance organizations were touted as providing members with acute, chronic and preventive care. Finally, the business community was told that with the development of proprietary HMO chains, one could expect to see true business sense interjected into the delivery of health care. The concept of "managed health care" arose. This concept would allow the business community to hold a provider group accountable for the cost and outcome of its employees' health benefits.

The rapid growth of HMOs has been attributable not only to financial incentives but also to the promise of a panacea for the entire healthcare system.

Physicians have viewed prepaid medicine with both optimism and alarm. Physicians who join a group-model or staff-model HMO may do so for a variety of reasons, including freedom from handling the business elements of practice, guaranteed income and defined work hours and responsibilities. Many physicians in private practice have opted to join independent-practice associations (IPA). They may do so for entirely different reasons, including maintenance of their current patient population, guaranteed cash flow or "getting a leg up" on the competition. On the other hand, many physicians have opted to avoid involvement with HMOs. They have feared the loss of individual control and may feel strongly about loss of "freedom of choice" for patients. Many physicians object to the external control measures imposed by the quality-assurance and utilization-review systems of HMOs.

The promises of a more controlled and managed practice that offers greater benefits and fewer hassles for physicians and patients have been realized by many physicians who participate in HMOs. Other physicians have found that the imposition of organizational structure inhibits rapport and leads to a bureaucratic form of practice.

DEFINITIONS

Richard M. Cooper, past president of Focus Health Care Management Corporation, has defined an HMO as "an organized system which accepts responsibility and risk for both the financing and delivery of comprehensive health care services to a defined, voluntarily enrolled population for a fixed monthly prepaid amount. Thus, HMOs not only insure against the cost of health care, but also assure the actual provision of needed health services".[1] Prepaid systems (HMOs) are legally charged with the responsibility for providing health-care benefits to persons who are enrolled in such programs. An HMO may choose one of a variety of models to serve as the vehicle for the delivery of health-care services.

The traditional format has been a closed-panel plan. In this format, an HMO uses a small body of physicians as the only authorized providers of care. In most cases, the physicians are in the primary-care fields of internal medicine, family medicine and pediatrics. An HMO may or may not contract with physicians in such specialty areas as surgery, psychiatry and obstetrics and gynecology. Many large closed-panel plans have

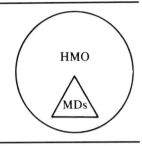

Figure 8.1   Staff Model Health Maintenance Organization. (Reprinted with permission from Health America.)

physicians in medical, pediatric or surgical subspecialties. However, most small HMOs (i.e., fewer than 20,000 members) restrict their closed panel to physicians in the primary-care fields.

In the staff model, physicians are actual employees of an HMO. The physicians may function as a group; however, each physician has a legal contract directly with the HMO (Figure 1). In the group model, an HMO contracts with an organized group of physicians (Figure 2). The group may treat only prepaid patients or may also be engaged in a fee-for-service practice. In the latter case, the HMO contracts with one physician, who serves as the medical director. In most cases, the group also has a president, who may be the same physician as the plan's medical director. Both the group model and the staff model function from defined health centers in which physicians see primarily their patients.

In contrast to the closed panel plans are the open panel HMOs. In an Independent Practice Association (IPA), an HMO contracts with a number of physicians in their own offices (Figure 3). Unlike physicians in the staff or group model, who are generally paid salaries, physicians in an IPA may receive funds on a capitation or on a discounted fee-for-service basis. Physicians in an IPA are placed, in some measure or another, on a "risk" basis for the cost incurred in the provision of care for

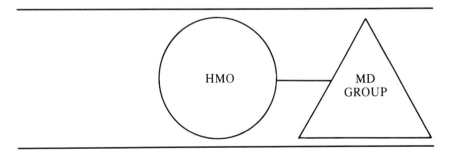

Figure 8.2   Group Model Health Maintenance Organization. (Reprinted with permission from Health America.)

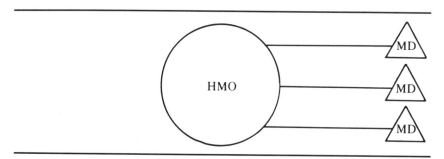

Figure 8.3 Independent Practice Association. (Reprinted with permission from Health America.)

their patients. Physicians in the staff or group model may or may not be placed on any kind of a risk-sharing basis. If such a risk pool is set aside, it is generally for a bonus.

In the network model, a series of groups develop contracts with an HMO for the provision of care. Each group serves in the same fashion as an individual physician does in an IPA. Another variation of the network model is the combination of the staff model or the group model with an IPA. In this variation, the staff or group serves the same role as a large independent office would with an IPA (figure 4).

HMO Look-a-likes: Point of Service, PPO's and Other Animals

A number of insurance carriers, such as Travelers, Prudential, Aetna and Cigna, have developed a series of insured products that look like HMOs. They may be filed through the various state insurance departments rather than the HMO departments, so they are regulated differ-

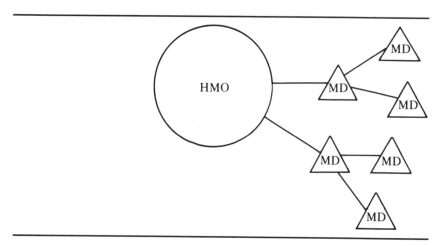

Figure 8.4 Primary Care Network. (Reprinted with permission from Health America.)

Figure 8.5 Point-of-Service Plans. Point of Service plans create incentives to stay with the primary-care physician in network. Having the freedom to choose any doctor may mean the member gets soaked financially.

ently. These entities are more likely to be sold to national companies rather than to local or regional companies, such as many pure HMOs are. The impact of this on a traditional office is that the physician may be participating with one insurance company on an indemnity basis and find that now his or her patients are covered through a managed-care product. The rules may be exactly the same for the physician in the IPA; that is, the patient may need to come through a primary-care physician for authorization before referral to a specialist. Because these companies are national in their scope, they are more likely to use a telephonic referral system than a paper referral system. This may impact the office, in that staff time is required for phone communication more often with the carrier to request approval.

Several companies are now experimenting with "swipe-card" technology that would allow physicians to use the insurance card with a magnetic strip in much the same fashion as a person would at an automated bank machine. That technology, along with a major effort at standardization of electronic data transfer, will help physicians in private practice as the managed-care companies expand.

A variant on the managed-care themes are the Point-of-Service (POS) plans (figure 5). In these plans, patients may elect to go through their primary-care physician for referrals to participating specialists and receive a higher level of benefits. Should the patient decide to ignore the network, he or she will have coverage but at a much reduced rate. Typically, there are deductibles that must be met as well as coverage at a 70- or 80-percent level. This economic lever tends to drive members through their primary-care physician and into the network to receive the higher benefit level.

Preferred-Provider Organizations (PPOs) have an entirely different setup. These organizations are so polymorphic that they virtually defy definition.[2] The underlying basis for PPOs is their marketing aspect. A PPO develops an arrangement with an employer. The PPO indicates that if the employer channels its insurance dollars through the PPO, it will guarantee a certain percentage (e.g., 15 percent) reduction over the employer's expenditure for the previous year. In turn, the PPO contracts with a limited number of physicians and provider institutions. All members of the PPO have free choice among the preferred-provider list. The providers agree to bill the PPO at a percentage discount. By limiting the pool of providers and physicians to a group known for more efficient utilization, the PPO expects to effect a cost savings. Unlike HMOs, utilization-review measures (other than these defined limitations) are not an integral part of PPOs. These organizations may be set up by employers, hospitals, physician groups or insurance companies. By 1990, thirty million people were enrolled in one of 708 established PPOs.

HISTORY OF HEALTH-MAINTENANCE ORGANIZATIONS: HOW DID WE GET WHERE WE ARE?

Surprisingly, prepaid health care is as old as the health-insurance industry. The first prepaid health plan began as a cooperative in Elk City, Oklahoma in 1927. During the 1930s, further prepaid plans developed around such construction projects as the Hoover Dam. Schoolteachers in Texas paid pennies per week during the Great Depression to guarantee them a hospital bed at Baylor Medical Center, should they need it. By World War II, Kaiser Industries felt a need to provide coordinated health care for its employees. Prepaid health care at Kaiser construction sites was the beginning of the Kaiser-Permanente system—the "granddaddy" of prepaid health plans in the United States. During the 1940s and 1950s, other plans, such as the Group Health Cooperative of Puget Sound (Seattle), the Health Insurance Plan of Greater New York (HIP) and the Group Health Association of Washington, D.C., were formed. These plans have grown to become true giants of the industry. However, they were regarded as anomalies of the health-care system by physicians not practicing in those metropolitan areas.

In the early 1970s, under the influence of Senator Edward Kennedy, public sentiment toward the development of a national health-insurance system arose. The Republican response to a form of socialized medicine was to encourage private enterprise to develop prepaid health plans. Paul Ellwood, president of Interstudy, coined the term "health maintenance organization".[3] He formulated many of the initial policy considerations in the development of HMOs. Ellwood's influence was clear in President Nixon's 1972 declarations that his administration would endorse the development of HMOs. This endorsement led to the formation and passage of Public Law (PL) 93–222, the Health Maintenance Organization Act of 1973. This act provided grants for development, and federal loans to subsidize, the inital operating deficits of new HMOs. The unique aspect of this law was section 1310, which provided a "dual-choice mandate." This section, which is currently under fire, requires any employer with 25 or more employees that operates within the service area of a federally qualified HMO to offer a closed and an open federally qualified HMO in addition to any other insurance that company chooses to provide. This section was incorporated in the law to balance the other demands placed on any HMO that became federally qualified. Although an HMO could provide this dual-choice option, it had to meet a minimal benefit level, service commitment and quality-assurance program as mandated through the HMO act. Enforcement of these laws resides with the Office of Health Maintenance Organizations (OHMO), a division of the Department of Health and Human Services.

The impact of PL 93–222 was dramatic. In 1972, there were fewer than 40 HMOs, which had approximately three million members. By 1992, there were 610 HMOs with forty million members.

During the Democratic administration of the late 1970s, federally qualified HMOs, although regulated through the OHMO, received lenient treatment. Because of a dearth of managers well versed in medical economics, many newly formed HMOs were in serious financial trouble. The federal government funded many such plans, not forcing them to repay their loans on schedule.

In 1981, with the Reagan administration coming to Washington, there was a change in the government's posture toward HMOs. Health maintenance organizations that were experiencing financial difficulty were forced to develop plans for corrective action that were more realistic. If plans for better financial management were not developed, the OHMO would begin to recall the loans. Incentives were arranged so that private investors could enter the market. Many struggling HMOs were acquired by such proprietary organizations. An era of social reform was being displaced by economic realities. The not-for-profit HMOs, in turn, began to place greater emphasis on efficiency than they had previously. Economies of scale have allowed Kaiser-Permanente, the Group Health association of Washington, D.C., the HIP and Group Health Cooperative of Puget Sound to form an alliance for purchasing and marketing purposes. The growth of HMOs has so far been concentrated in urban areas, where 71 percent of them are located. Blue Cross and Blue Shield now own or manage 81 HMOs, evidence of their concern about the future of traditional inpatient care.[4-6]

The late 1980s and the 1990s bore witness to a consolidation of HMOs. Although HMO membership has doubled since 1987, the number of plans in existence has dropped by 126. Small operations will be purchased by or merged with large plans. Communities that currently have five to 20 HMOs are finding it impossible for more than two or three of them to continue to operate efficiently. This consolidation may result in a greater number of network models as disparate plans move together.

A Historical and Social Model

A number of conceptual models can be used as a framework to examine the historical development of the changes that are now taking place in American medicine. Western culture has traditionally provided compensation for services rendered. Thus, units of service are handled economically similar to units of production. Time and knowledge are cost centers as much as materials are. Although this model may seem obvious from Western experience, it is not universal. Oriental cultures have traditionally provided rewards for healers until there is illness. At that time, the rewards are discontinued. The prepaid staff model and group model developed during the 1960s are based on a different economic principle. It was assumed that if a physician were provided a comfortable income and adequate benefits he or she would be freed of the fetters limiting his or her ability to practice. It was assumed that if the physician were sufficiently self-motivated, he or she would provide for the needs of HMO patients.

No economic therapy has universal application. Most physicians are not motivated solely by monetary reward. On the other hand, few physicians are not motivated to some extent by financial incentives.

Given these economic realities, there has been a progression over the last century of professional activity. The trend toward organizational medicine has been described by many observers. The social and economic forces clearly point toward an increasing reliance of the population on some form of managed health-care system.

At the turn of the century, there was no such thing as health insurance. The activities of practitioners resulted in some form of direct reward. Typically, the reward was monetary; however, payment in service or produce was not atypical. Physician's expectations regarding income were lower. There were relatively few specialists.

The 1920s and 1930s saw the development of third-party reimbursement plans. Initially devised to prevent catastrophic losses, such plans interjected a third party into the health-care delivery system. The first format provided reimbursement to patients for out-of-pocket expenses.

The intent was to protect the public against catastrophic medical expenses for the treatment of serious illness or injury. It was fully expected that the public would continue to seek routine care at its own expense. The growth of labor unions paralleled the increasing level of benefits afforded through third-party plans. Greater attention was being paid toward first-dollar coverage, which is based on direct payment to a provider rather than to a patient. Still, much of the population had no health insurance. Physicians provided much in the way of free care to patients without insurance, especially the elderly and the indigent. It was an expected aspect of professional life to perform this "charity work."

Passage of the Medicaid and Medicare acts brought third-party reimbursement to huge segments of the population that previously had no health insurance. Simultaneously, physicians had become oriented more toward specialties, shying away from primary-care practice.

By the late 1960s, virtually all segments of the population had some form of third-party coverage. Competition for those insurance dollars ensued. Consumers did not need to shop on the basis of cost because payment came from the third-party payer and not from their own pockets. Physicians and institutional providers competed more on the basis of services and perceived quality of care than on the basis of cost considerations. The subsequent rapid escalation of health-care costs has been blamed on virtually every segment of the health-care delivery system and of the public. In a cost-plus-based delivery system, competition could only drive the charges higher.

During the late 1960s and early 1970s, health economists recognized general trends that were taking place in response to changes in the attitude of the public. Interest in prepaid health care was rekindled. Although prepaid health plans had been in existence for nearly 50 years, they were limited by the number of participating physicians and institutional providers. Because employers were coming to realize that health-care expenditures were rising rapidly, they began to shop for and demand systems that would provide adequate benefits at an acceptable cost. Labor unions, fearful of the loss of benefits, also endorsed the concept of HMOs. During the late 1970s, HMOs were perceived as a panacea that could provide high-quality health care at an acceptable cost. In the 1990s, HMOs have to balance cost, availability of service and choice.

The elements of fee-for-service practice and prepaid systems can be compared by listing them in a tabular format (Table 1). As can be seen, the greater the benefits, the greater the need for third-party control of doctor-patient interactions. This control may be judged as a rational and necessary extension of quality assurance. It may also be perceived as a bureaucratic burden on physicians in the provision of care.

By 1992, approximately 87 percent of Americans had health coverage of one form or another. However, there were estimated to be 35 million citizens who had no insurance protection. This huge gap occurred

TABLE 8.1
COMPARISON OF REIMBURSEMENT MECHANISMS

	Fee for service (direct payment to physicians)	Insurance reimbursement to patient	Insurance payment to physician	Preferred-provider organization	Independent-practice association	Staff/group model health-maintenance organization
Free choice of provider (fluidity)	Full choice of any physician in the area according to ability to pay	Same as above	Probably greater because of greater collection rate by physician	To any of the preferred providers	Free choice among primary-care physicians in plan	Limited to physicians on staff; generally a small number
Access	Free access by patients according to office availability of provider	Same as above	Same as above	To any of the preferred providers	Limited by individual physician's office appointment availability for prepaid patients	Defined health centers may have limited appointment availability
Quality assurance	Only in-hospital care	Same as above	Same as above	Same as above	Formalized quality-assurance program in place; usually involves statistical study of chosen topic	Formalized quality-assurance programs emphasizing chart review, in addition to statistical analysis

Utilization review	Only as mandated by hospital	Same as above	Many third parties require prospective or concurrent review of in-patient and out-patient surgeries	Variable; may be hospital limited or may also include all charge procedures	Utilization-review coordinators in place; usually a physician committee involved in review of in-patient and out-patient costs and out-patient procedures	Formalized process involving in-patient and out-patient procedures
Cost	Variable according to physician; no ability to do cost planning by patient	Less cost to the patient, limited primarily by cash-flow relationships	Less cost to patient having only co-payments and deductibles	Variable total cost; out of pocket to patient little or up to usual and customary reimbursement	Very limited out-of-pocket cost	Very limited out-of-pocket cost
Benefit level	Only to the extent patient can pay	Greater cost, limited by extent of insurance policy and cash-flow relationships	Greater level of benefit than above; usually does not cover out-patient office visit	Greater still; covers outpatient procedures by any of the participating providers; may or may not cover routine office visits	Full HMO benefits in accordance with mandated levels; if hospital sponsored, may include education	Full range of HMO benefits; usually including more formalized health-education programs

while the medical industry consumed more than 13 percent of the gross national product, and provided a major issue for the 1992 presidential campaign.

No physician wants a corporation to dictate how to practice medicine or to force him or her to use shortcuts that would reduce the quality of care. No corporate officer wants to infringe on the turf of physicians. Together, however, physicians and the corporate officers can deliver the "health-care product" efficiently and at a competitive price.

TYPES OF HEALTH MAINTENANCE ORGANIZATION

Closed-Panel Plans

The traditional HMO is a closed panel in which members may see only participating physicians at a limited number of facilities. In the staff model, the participating physicians treat only members of the HMO and are salaried employees of it. In the group model, participating physicians may treat fee-for-service patients or may limit treatment to the HMO's members. However, the group contracts with the HMO on a direct-capitation or risk basis.

Staff Model

The staff model is the traditional format. In this model, participating physicians are employees of an HMO. The physicians practice in a facility with personnel who are also employees of the HMO. Although the physicians function as salaried employees, this format hardly reflects "clinic medicine." The physicians are responsible for providing total care for their patients. Each HMO may develop different mechanisms for coordinating care, but participating physicians should expect to work 50 to 60 hours a week in this setting.

THEORY OF PRACTICE   In the staff model, physicians are freed from the responsibilities of office management, billing and collections. They are therefore able to concentrate on patient care. Typically, they are involved in an administrative capacity only if they so choose. The lack of involvement in such aspects of practice can breed a "clinic mentality" unless the HMO has an incentive system that encourages physicians to participate in the decision-making process and to provide personalized care.

TYPICAL DAY   A physician in a primary-care HMO typically works between 28 and 36 hours a week. Most HMOs expect such physicians to see approximately 100 patients a week on the average. Seeing fewer patients is considered underproductive.

The work schedule may include evening hours and weekend hours. The physician is typically expected to provide care in the hospital setting.

However, unlike a fee-for-service practice, the physician is responsible for patients admitted by specialists as well as those that he or she admits. Physicians in private practice may make only a social call on a patient on the orthopedic service. However, a physician in the staff model is expected to make a daily visit to such a patient and to exert pressure on the orthopedist to discharge the patient as soon as is medically appropriate. Depending on the size of an HMO, a physician may have from one to ten hospitalized patients at any given time. In some HMOs, certain physicians tend to treat more hospitalized patients, whereas others provide more out-patient care.

Because an HMO is responsible for total care for its members, there is a greater reliance on telephone calls to assist in management of that care. Patients frequently call the HMO for advice about many problems. Telephone calls, typically answered by nursing staff, necessitate greater involvement by physicians than might be required in private practice.

An HMO physician typically begins the day with hospital rounds before the health center opens. In most cases, the first patient is scheduled around 9:00 AM. Some HMOs may begin their office hours later but extend them longer into the evenings. Most physicians see between 18 and 30 patients per day at the health center. Although this number of patients is much smaller than the number that fee-for-service physicians would see during the same period, HMO physicians spend much more time handling paperwork (a task normally delegated to the office manager in a private practice). The paperwork in an HMO setting is completely different from that encountered in private practice. In the latter setting, insurance forms make up the bulk of the paperwork, especially because of the plethora of third-party insurers. Private physicians must have managers who are adept at handling all the paperwork. However, in the staff-model HMO, much of the paperwork, such as completing specific ordering forms (e.g., radiograph forms, consultation forms and "encounter forms"), is handled directly by physicians. Most HMOs involve physicians in filling out forms to make them aware that they are actually filling out purchase requests for services! The volume of paperwork helps discourage physicians from making unnecessary referrals and ordering unnecessary laboratory tests and radiographic studies.

Physicians are encouraged to make telephone contact with consultants. Although consultation is requested as needed in fee-for-service practice, the rationale may be different in an HMO setting. In both settings, the primary purpose of a telephone call is to communicate about a patient. However, in the HMO setting, a secondary purpose is to discourage the consultant from overutilization of services by ensuring that patients are returned to the care of their HMO physicians.

Many HMOs schedule center meetings, staff meetings or other activities during lunchtime. In some settings, the physician may be free to leave the facility at that time, but in many others leaving becomes an impossibility. Lunchtime is typically set aside for handling paperwork, returning telephone calls and clearing prescription refills. The same activities may take place at the end of the afternoon. Health maintenance organizations that are strongly influenced by market forces may base much of their marketing strategy on alliances with numerous hospitals in any given community. Physicians who might otherwise practice at one or two hospitals may find themselves on the staffs of three or four hospitals. Maintaining hospital privileges often requires spending time attending hospital functions and committee meetings. Moreover, additional hospital affiliations prolong the time required for making rounds because of the need to travel from institution to institution.

In contrast, HMO physicians do not have to be concerned about costs. There is much greater reliance on the use of laboratory tests and radiographic studies in HMOs than in most general private practices. Many HMOs have facilities immediately available for performing laboratory tests and radiographic studies. Patients may have more complaints and require more time of an HMO physician than of a physician in a fee-for-service practice. In an HMO, then, fewer patients may be seen while the time spent with each patient is greater.

REIMBURSEMENT   Physicians in most staff-model HMOs are paid salary with bonus potential. The remuneration includes reimbursement for in-patient and out-patient care. Many HMOs have developed formulas based on specialty, experience and Board-certification status. In other health plans, a physician may negotiate his or her level of compensation. Some plans have developed incentive systems based on units of productivity, cost sharing or risk pools. Incentive systems are currently widespread.

The standard HMO contract for physicians in a staff model provides a number of benefits, including vacation time, sick time and educational leave. Typically, there are provisions for various types of insurance, including health, dental, malpractice, disability and life. It is worthwhile to examine what these benefits actually provide.

The health insurance usually consists of membership in the HMO. Coverage may be restricted to the physician or may be expanded to include family members as well. Many physicians and their families feel uncomfortable being treated by the physicians' colleagues. A physician who feels this way should inquire whether alternative insurance is available.

An important benefit is malpractice insurance. Most health plans provide for "claims-made" coverage. This form of coverage protects against claims made during the time the policy is in effect. A more expensive but less widely available form of coverage is "occurrence-based." This form protects against claims made at any time if they refer to actions that occurred during the time the policy was in effect. This form of coverage is especially important for obstetricians and pediatricians, for whom the statute of limitation may be as long as 21 years. Occurrence-based coverage is much more valuable than claims-made coverage because it protects physicians for life. Because such coverage generally is not available, physicians must inquire about "tail coverage" from HMOs that offer only claims-made coverage. Tail coverage is purchased at the time a physician leaves an insurance carrier. A single payment protects against claims that arise any time thereafter for actions that occurred during the time when the previous malpractice coverage was active. In effect, tail coverage transforms a claims-made policy into an occurrence-based policy. Whenever a physician leaves a practice with a claims-made policy to enter a new practice, tail coverage must be purchased. If a physician leaves one practice to join an HMO and then leaves that HMO, the physician needs to be sure that a tail policy covers each change in practice.

Physicians must therefore know their responsibilities toward payment for tail coverage, either in entering an HMO practice or in leaving it. Some HMOs provide tail coverage on entering or exiting.

Group Model

In the group model, an incorporated group of physicians contracts with an HMO to provide care for its members. The HMO may have a medical director who is in charge of providing health-care services, but most physician groups have a president to represent them in negotiations with HMOs. The medical director and the president may be the same or different persons. The group may limit its practice to members of the HMO or it may see fee-for-service patients as well.

THEORY OF PRACTICE. Advocates of the group model point to physician cohesiveness as a major advantage over the staff model. However, some staff-model HMOs are as cohesive as their group-model counterparts; conversely, some group-model practices are fragmented. Still, the structure of the group model lends itself to tighter organization than that afforded by the staff format.

In practices in which fee-for-service and prepaid patients are combined, there is the potential for having the best of both worlds. Prepaid patients may receive more personalized care, whereas fee-for-service patients may experience greater efficiency in the delivery of care.

Critics of the group model emphasize its bipolar priorities. Fee-for-service patients bring in more income to the group if they engender numerous internal referrals and increased laboratory and hospital services. Prepaid patients provide more income to the group if the physicians provide fewer services. This dichotomy of financial rewards is problematic for many physicians in group-model HMOs. Such physicians may become resentful of the intrusion on their time by prepaid patients, who are viewed as a drain on income.

TYPICAL DAY   Unlike the staff model, the style of practice in the group model can vary considerably, depending on its proportion of fee-for-service patients. If the practice is devoted solely to members of an HMO, the daily format will completely resemble that of the staff model. If there are relatively few prepaid patients, the practice will assume the characteristics of a fee-for-service group. If the proportions of prepaid and fee-for-service patients are about equal, the physicians may end up spending more time on the prepaid patients than on the fee-for-service patients.

Group-model HMOs tend to have a higher ratio of support staff to physicians than do staff-model HMOs, especially if they see more fee-for-service patients. An increased number of ancillary staff may help reduce the stress on the physicians, although it does increase overhead.

REIMBURSEMENT   Physician groups that contract with HMOs are reimbursed for professional services according to different formulas. Most groups that devote their time exclusively to prepaid patients negotiate salaries and a benefits package; compensation thus is similar to that seen in the staff model. The acquisition of some HMOs by proprietary chains may provide physician groups with stock-option plans, arranged as part of the acquisition, or other joint-venture opportunities.

Many groups are paid a capitation fee for professional services. This fee system may place them at risk for primary care and specialty care. Some risk arrangements include hospital costs. A physician's income is therefore determined by the governing board of the group, based on the capitation arrangements set for the entire group. If the capitation plan covers only primary care, the physician needs to be aware of the risks and penalties or potential profits from utilization occurring among specialists and within the hospital. Generally, risk arrangements have the potential for generating greater income than that afforded by salary plans, but they have the disadvantage of penalties if normative goals are not attained.

Life in an Independent-Practice Association

There is no question that fee-for-service practice has changed radically over the past several years. No longer is a physician in such a practice the "captain of the ship".[7] He or she now has a number of reporting requirements, all dependent on the rules of the payer. The physician may have to call for authorization for hospital admissions or for procedures or referrals. An internist, for example, may have a practice that is made up largely of elderly patients. A family physician, on the other hand, may have a large number of families from one or two companies or from a certain neighborhood. Such a practice thus acquires a certain homogeneity.

Most physicians who join an IPA find major changes in their practice. Initially, few patients sign up to make use of their services. Months or years may pass before the practice comprises several hundred patients. Most of the initial patients are new patients, not previous patients who have merely converted to a different mechanism of payment. This experience surprises many physicians who decide to join IPAs to preserve the size of their existing practices. Many of the new patients are not from the same socioeconomic or educational group as the bulk of the other patients. Also, a small cadre of new patients are high utilizers. They may be new to the HMO concept or may be dissatisfied with their previous HMO physician and looking for a new provider who is more attuned to their perceived needs.

The first several months of involvement with an HMO can be discouraging to physicians who have recently joined IPAs. Physicians who are accustomed to viewing each new patient as an additional source of revenue begin to believe that each new patient from the HMO is a drain on their capitation funds. It becomes extremely difficult for physicians who are used to thinking in terms of dollars accrued for each unit of service to make the transition to viewing the practice of medicine in an actuarial framework. Once there are 300 to 500 new patients, however, the ready cash flow becomes evident. To be successful in IPAs, physicians must recognize their actuarial basis and must understand that for each patient seen in the office, there are several patients in the pool who never darken their door. The nonutilizers help pay the expenses generated by the utilizers. If physicians think only in terms of apparent costs, they will react with resentment each time they see a prepaid patient.

To be happy within an IPA, a physician must be able to transcend this concern for dollar flow and think in terms of his or her role as a case manager. A primary-care physician is once again placed in the role of *the* coordinator of all care for the pool of patients.[8–10] That physician is the practitioner to whom a patient must look for primary and specialty care. This role has not been experienced by family physicians for 30 years. On the other hand, the case manager also must care for patients who he or she may not like, the so called entitled demanders.

In most private practices, physicians who are at odds with certain patients merely tell them that they might be better served by other physicians. In some IPAs, physicians may "fire" patients in the same fashion as patients may discharge their physicians. However, some plans make it difficult for physicians to rid themselves of troublesome patients. In particular, such plans attempt to ensure that physicians do not "dump" patients who are a financial drain on their practices. However, there are times when a doctor-patient relationship is extremely difficult to establish and maintain.

Many problem patients have borderline personality disorders. In private practice, such patients go from one physician to another demanding services. They may become dissatisfied quickly and merely find another physician. They may have shopping bags of medications as a result of this behavior, or they may undergo frequent surgical procedures. In the captive environment of an HMO, such patients become frustrated, boisterous and angry. Physicians who are accustomed to having positive relationships with their patients may become confused and resentful when dealing with such patients. They may worry about malpractice claims even though there is no evidence that prepaid patients file legal suits more often than their fee-for-service counterparts. How can this problem be resolved? Many HMOs have no ready answer. They may have a rudimentary member-services department. However, that department may serve as patient advocate rather than as physician advocate. A physician can gain satisfaction in being the first person to be able to control the excessive behavior of a patient with a borderline personality disorder; such success, however, certainly does take a toll on the physician and his or her staff.

Some HMOs have medical advisory councils to help physicians deal with problem patients. The physician or the patient may present the problem to such a council, which then makes a judgment on medical treatment. This kind of peer review can help physicians as well as become a major mechanism for quality review within IPAs.

Tables 2 and 3 summarize the advantages and disadvantages of participating in an HMO and an IPA.

THE PAPER TIGER

Staff-model and group-model HMOs rely on peer pressure for control of utilization. Peer pressure may not function effectively in this manner in an IPA because the physicians are in their own individual offices and away from each other in most cases. Most IPAs make use of rules, paperwork and a bureaucracy tempered by the clinical judgment of the medical director to set the standards for control of utilization. Some IPAs require minimal paperwork, whereas others have extensive paperwork. Virtually all IPAs require telephone authorization for hospital admissions. Some IPAs require that telephone authorization be granted by the plan before referral to a subspecialist may be made. All IPAs provide feedback to participating physicians with regard to their utilization patterns. In an era of DRGs, such feedback is not an unexpected aspect of practice. Application of the various requirements of IPAs to daily practice presents a real challenge. Physicians who are accustomed to seeing patients at regular 15-minute intervals may find interruptions to make necessary telephone calls disconcerting. Increasingly, physicians are be-

TABLE 8.2
CLOSED-PANEL HEALTH-MAINTENANCE ORGANIZATIONS*
(GROUP OR STAFF MODEL)

Advantages	Disadvantages
1. Guaranteed income with defined patient population and no start-up costs	1. Erosion of autonomy and control over one's destiny
2. Structured work environment with predetermined hours and limited "on-call" schedule	2. Inflexible schedule with heavy patient-demand and corporate-time pressures
3. Few "business-of-practice" headaches	3. Limited input to practice organization—determined by unclear chain of management command
4. Elimination of the direct monetary relationship between physician and patient—no worry about ability to pay for repeat visits	4. Generally lower overall incomes than private practice
5. Excellent fringe benefits packages	5. Emphasis on cost-effective care sometimes felt to be excessive
6. Collegial atmosphere and built-in consultation network	6. Angry, entitled patients who did not choose *you* as their physician

*Reprinted with permission from *Physician's Management*. Adapted from Nash DB: HMO Practice: Advantages and Disadvantages, May 1985

TABLE 8.3
OPEN-PANEL INDEPENDENT-PRACTICE ASSOCIATIONS*

Advantages	Disadvantages
1. Preservation of cash flow—physician contracts with IPA on capitation basis	1. If "fee-for-service" IPA, physician assumes financial risk—a predetermined amount is allocated for covered services
2. Maintenance of traditional doctor-patient relationship; no need for patients to change doctors	2. Mixture of covered and uncovered patients creates possibility of a "two-class" practice
3. Widening of referral base to attract more patients	3. Tangled lines of communication and no real "system" in operation; bureaucracy
4. Preservation of individual style of practice—little peer review	4. No real collegial atmosphere as in true group practice
5. Opportunity to sign preferred-provider agreement with community organizations and large employers	5. Management problems, such as marketing, might become partially physician's responsibility

*Reprinted with permission from *Physician's Management*. Adapted from Nash DB: HMO Practice: Advantages and Disadvantages, May 1985.

ing required to make telephone calls to other payers as well as to their IPA. The net result is a substantial drain on physicians' time.

In addition to making telephone calls to the IPA for authorization, physicians must make calls to consultants. Most physicians are accustomed to calling a limited number of consultants on a regular basis for advice on management and for follow-up of certain patients. When participating in HMOs, a greater number of consultants must be called. Internists may never have talked to obstetricians about routine obstetric care until they find that failure to do so may have an adverse effect on hospitalization and subsequently on their hospital risk pool. In private practice, family physicians asked to recommend a dermatologist may refer their patients with good wishes. By contrast, patients in HMOs who have skin problems are treated frequently by their family physicians instead of being referred to dermatologists.

This situation represents a dilemma for physicians who participate in HMOs: whether to manage certain medical problems themselves or make referrals to specialists. Ideally, all patients should be dealt with in the same manner, regardless of the method of payment. Most physicians do make treatment decisions based on their patients' needs, but they are influenced by the economics of different payment mechanisms. However, as the number of HMO patients in a fee-for-service practice increases, the practice style begins to standardize, in that all patients are dealt with in the same manner.

A physician's staff needs to be involved in the HMO process. In many cases, the office manager makes decisions to join a given IPA. The office manager should also help teach the front office staff the proper method for handling telephone calls from HMO members. Because the attitudes of HMO patients may be different from those of non-HMO patients, the office staff may feel that HMO patients are too demanding. The staff may thus put unnecessary distance between prepaid patients and the physician, and this can consequently create antagonism. A better approach would be for physicians to send letters to all prepaid patients entering their individual practice or to have the staff make telephone calls to them. With this approach, prepaid patients may be given an explanation of office procedures before their first visit so they do not arrive with preconceived expectations. This approach can go a long way in avoiding problems in the doctor-patient relationship.

Participation in an IPA can be frustrating, especially if the IPA is new and has inexperienced managers or if a physician is unaccustomed to dealing with prepaid patients. If both situations exist, the experience can be even more frustrating. Nonetheless, physicians may benefit greatly by participating in an IPA. Prepaid patients provide a ready cash flow, and an IPA improves the marketing of a practice. Such patients also do not have to worry about the cost of treatment and thus are more willing to return when necessary. Lastly, IPAs retain the preeminent status of family physicians in the health-care delivery system (see Chapter 10).

PHYSICIAN REVIEW: LIFE AS PRACTICED IN A FISHBOWL

Peer review is a standard aspect of the practice of medicine. For physicians with hospital practices, peer review may be regarded as a nuisance, with its required committee meetings, greater emphasis on documentation and commitments of time that are considered nonproductive. In the HMO setting, peer review is accompanied by close scrutiny by the health plan's managers.

Physicians who have recently completed training may feel that they have returned to residency—there is always someone looking over one's shoulder. All aspects of practice in the HMO setting are subject to review. A physician's productivity is carefully monitored. Because many physicians who participate in HMOs see fewer patients than do their fee-for-service counterparts, they are coming under pressure to increase their productivity. Internists in closed-panel HMOs are expected to see 18 to 25 patients in a seven-hour period, whereas family physicians and pediatricians are more likely to be expected to see 20 to 30 patients in the same period. Depending on the type of HMO, there are incentives and support systems to promote or discourage adherence to productivity standards.

The practice of an HMO physician is typically reviewed to determine the number of patients seen in a given period as well as to ascertain the "frequency of return." In a fee-for-service practice, seeing patients at frequent intervals may generate small amounts of revenue rapidly because in most cases less time is required for follow-up visits than for initial visits. In the HMO setting, each follow-up visit represents "lost revenue." Return visits require the time of a physician and his or her staff. From the perspective of an HMO, return visits serve only to "satisfy" patients; they should therefore be kept to a minimum so that they do not create a need for additional physicians and staff beyond what the budget permits. No HMO manager would couch the plan's expectations in such bottom line terms; however, the economic forces invite such an analysis.

Although HMOs are concerned about the number of patients seen and the frequency of return, few plans have been able to measure "intensity" of visits. Clearly, physicians who are able to deal with patients without making unnecessary referrals to specialists have greater "value" to HMOs. Care rendered at the lowest level of the professional hierarchy is less expensive, unless the number of visits and associated costs are increased. For example, the total cost of a visit to a cardiologist for evaluation of chest pain may include a $150 consultation fee, the cost of two follow-up visits at $35 each and the cost of an electrocardiogram, an echocardiogram and a thallium stress test or a coronary angiogram. If this diagnostic workup results in a similar outcome for a patient as would a number of visits to an internist, an HMO would prefer that the patient use the services of the internist as long as the cost for treatment by the internist is less than the amount that it would have to pay to the cardiologist. Most HMOs have only a subjective feel for the efficiency of care, or the intensity of visits.

The Health Maintenance Organization Act of 1973 stipulates that all qualified HMOs have an in-house quality-assurance program. Physicians are judged on the basis of quality of care. In reality, quality-assurance programs are extremely variable in their depth of detail. Unfortunately, most HMOs conduct only a cursory review of quality of care. They may look at morbidity or mortality statistics or perform some random chart audits. An in-depth evaluation of quality of care (as opposed to utilization) occurs only in sophisticated plans. The Accreditation Association for Ambulatory Health Care and the National Committee for Quality Assurance (NCQA) evaluate the quality of care provided by out-patient facilities in much the same manner as the Joint Commission for Accreditation of Hospitals evaluates hospital quality of care. The former organizations list only a small number of HMOs in their roster of participating institutions. Although quality assurance is therefore a stated goal for review of physician's practices, most HMOs do not pursue this goal with adequate effort.

Reviews of utilization are the key to containing costs. All HMOs carefully monitor the utilization practices of participating physicians. In IPAs, utilization review is an extremely important consideration. Physicians who participate in IPAs are not in daily contact with their HMOs so they do not give much consideration to utilization. Feedback that has an impact on the utilization behavior of physicians is critical if an HMO is to survive. Health maintenance organizations that have sophisticated management-information systems are much more likely to do better in this regard than those that require manual reports with episodic feedback. Although the offices of HMO physicians do not have the optical-bar devices found in grocery-store checkout lines, it is clear that the greater the degree of knowledge by an HMO of a physician's utilization "inventory," the greater will be the feedback and impact on the physician's behavior. Physicians who are considered high utilizers will receive close scrutiny and "counseling" by their HMO and then reprimands before termination. Physicians who become defensive in response to scrutiny will find that this behavior is not helpful in dealing with an HMO. On the other hand, physicians who keep detailed records of the intensity of visits may be able to demonstrate to an HMO that they have been affected by adverse selection. Physicians who can explain in numeric terms the reason for high utilization may be able to negotiate with an HMO for stop-loss protection.

Physicians in closed-panel models as well as those in IPAs are subject to review of their hours of work. Physicians in IPAs must be able to demonstrate that they can provide "accessible care" for HMO members whose choose to be their patients. Physicians in the staff model must be able to demonstrate that they are working the hours agreed on in the contract. As employees, physicians in closed-panel HMOs are directly accountable for how they spend their work hours.

Health maintenance organizations therefore review virtually all aspects of physicians' practices—number of patients seen, frequency of visits, quality of care, utilization habits and hours of work. For physicians who are accustomed to being independent entrepreneurs, this degree of scrutiny may be extremely difficult to tolerate. Most physicians feel that they are highly productive and that they have a good sense of how care should be rendered. They feel that they are the only ones who can judge how time is best spent in providing that care. It is anathema to such physicians to justify time spent and style of practice to another party, especially to a nonphysician (see Chapter 9).

However, managed-care organizations are adept at portraying their cost-containment capabilities to the business community. They can demonstrate that they function in a business-like manner. Nonetheless, the translation of medical practice into business language can be garbled at times.

Physicians who participate in IPAs frequently find that filling out the necessary detailed reports takes a lot of their expensive time. For physicians who have a small number of patients (fewer than 200 to 300), a great effort must be expended for return visits because of the paperwork involved. Third-party payers require differing degrees of accountability, and most HMOs require a high degree of accountability. Physicians may feel antagonistic toward HMOs, and this antagonism will be heightened whenever bureaucratic delays occur. Delays in billing or errors in accounting can serve only to cause physicians to question their participation.

Nonetheless, the ready cash flow and improved market share may act as strong incentives for physicians to remain as HMO participants, particularly after they have more than 500 HMO patients. The increased revenue gives them greater opportunity to hire additional staff, make improvements in the office, or streamline the flow of paperwork. By the time a practice has acquired more than 500 HMO patients, the time required for paperwork begins to diminish, so that HMO patients can be seen on a regular basis without difficulty. Many physicians in IPAs find that participation permits expansion of their practices. They may participate in a number of HMOs and not have to worry about dissolution of any one plan.

Physicians in staff-model or group-model HMOs understand that their continued participation in such plans depends on involvement in the peer-review system at all levels. Most such physicians do not feel anger and resentment to the same degree as do physicians in IPAs.

These misgivings can be reconciled only with recognition of the needs of an HMO. An HMO that does not monitor quality of care will find that marked variations that exist may have a negative impact in the marketplace.

INTERFACE WITH THE BUSINESS OF MEDICINE

Marketing

"You are what they sell, and they sell what you are." People join HMOs because of their perceptions of quality care and reduced costs. The public's perceptions are determined largely—directly or indirectly—by an HMO's marketing staff. Once people join an HMO, their perceptions face an immediate test of reality. Initial visits to a physician in an IPA or a closed-panel plan are couched in terms of market-driven perceptions. An HMO enrollee may be pleasantly surprised or may see dreams of medical utopia turn into nightmares. The marketing arena is one in which physicians have a legitimate role. Their interactions with an HMO's marketing department are critical if the integrity of the plan is to be maintained. By the same token, physicians are often oblivious to perceptions of their profession by laymen. They may become appalled at the differences between a physician's perception of good health care and the beliefs of the general public. The marketing staff can show statistics that relate patients' satisfaction directly to waiting time as well as to access to subspecialists.

In the private-practice setting, physicians are also accustomed to working with marketing representatives. That interchange has been evolving over the past few years. Physicians have traditionally avoided advertising. Yet, at the same time they desire the benefits of a better market position. To resolve this apparent conflict, physicians have benefited from advertising done by hospitals or professional groups. They have allowed their names to be used in relation to special services at hospitals, such as physician-locater services or specialty-care–oriented units. More recently, physicians have engaged in direct advertising. Such advertising may range from emboldenment of their names in the Yellow Pages to more overt activity, such as television promotionals.

In this environment, therefore, the marketing staffs of HMOs are now encouraging participating physicians to become more involved in marketing efforts. Such efforts may range from placement of pictures of the staff in printed materials to involvement of physicians and staff in health fairs in the community or on the job site. Many HMOs also employ public-relations firms. Such firms arrange for appropriate publicity for activities taking place in HMOs.

Physicians are frequently asked to participate with the marketing department in sales presentations. Such involvement may be discomforting for physicians who are unaccustomed to attending union meetings to give talks on health-related topics. Such speeches are clearly euphemisms for sales pitches. On other occasions, physicians may be asked to accompany the marketing staff to employer meetings to answer questions about the operation of their HMO. Although physicians may not wish to take time from other professional or personal activities for this purpose, the experience can be enlightening. Physicians may encounter pressures identical to those faced by the marketing staff on a daily basis. Attending such meetings can certainly ameliorate the bureaucratic problems that are found within many organizations. Physicians often accuse the marketing staff of promising the sun and the moon to prospective enrollees.

The marketing staff in most HMOs are paid salaries plus commission. Most physicians are paid directly on a salary or capitation basis. These differences in financial incentives have a major impact on the way each professional approaches their tasks. It is important for physicians to recognize that to be successful, marketing representatives must attract members. It is also important for physicians to give feedback to the marketing staff regarding the effectiveness of specific marketing campaigns. Depending on the size of an HMO, its participating physicians may have more or less direct access to the marketing staff. In IPAs or in large closed-panel HMOs, physicians will not have direct contact with marketers. In such cases, physicians must work through the medical manager to ensure that the marketing staff is realistically promoting health-care services. By the same token, there must be feedback to physicians relating the desires of the organization in the delivery of health care.

Finance
In a fee-for-service practice, it is well known that time and services rendered represent potential income. Physicians in this setting must document their use of time and delivery of services to arrange for appropriate billing. In HMOs, the same principles apply. However, in this setting, greater expenditure of time and services translates into greater cost to the organization. In the staff-model HMO, physicians are direct employees. In IPAs, physicians serve as independent contractors. In both settings, it is crucial for physicians to document their use of time and delivery of services. This approach results in a more detailed accounting of physicians' time, productivity and ordering practices. Only in the largest fee-for-service group practices is the accounting system as sophisticated as that found in most HMOs.

Finance administrators in HMOs worry that participating physicians are free from financial liability. Particularly in staff-model HMOs, there is no special risk to physicians by virtue of their style of practice. The only immediate impact may be on the size of a physician's bonus, if this benefit is available. In IPAs, typically there are risk arrangements set in place such that a physician's income is adversely affected by higher utilization of services.

From the perspective of finance administrators, reimbursements to physicians account for 25 to 35 percent of an HMO's budget. They may consider that physicians appear to have a carte blanche billing attitude. For these reasons, most HMOs have elaborate forms for documenting physicians' expenses. Consultations, for example, are arranged on special referral forms that are sent back to the claims department. Physicians use the referral forms to transmit medical information with a request for services or consultation. The finance staff consider the referral forms purchase orders—purchase orders with an open limit.

Physicians who participate in HMOs tend to complain about the excessive amount of paperwork. However, physicians who have practiced in the armed services consider the amount of paperwork required by HMOs relatively trivial. For physicians in private practice, the paperwork seems excessive. What they do not realize, however, is that the paperwork has always been there—it has just been handled by the office staff.

Health maintenance organizations require physicians to do more paperwork so that they are aware of how many resources they are controlling. Indeed, a primary-care physician in an HMO typically controls nearly one million dollars of health-care expenditures each year. Without knowledge as to where claims originate, the finance department is unable to accrue resources to pay these bills. Usually, only a physician knows where his or her patients are receiving care. Thus, most HMOs require physicians to record all authorized services in some manner, whether on paper, via telephone-reporting systems or by direct input through a computer terminal.

The HMOs that do not have good mechanisms for the flow of paperwork are those that report high "incurred but not reported" expenditures known as IBNR. The dollar amount of such expenditures may help determine whether or not a plan is profitable. For physicians who participate in the staff-model HMO, filling out paperwork should take approximately 30 minutes per day, or approximately 5 percent of their time, if the task is handled efficiently.

As with relations with the marketing staff, it is important that physicians have contact with the finance department. The medical staff should be able to assist the finance department in developing a streamlined flow of paperwork for reporting expenditures. In turn, physicians should receive monthly reports concerning the financial status of their HMO, particularly information relating to expenditures. The reports should be presented in terms of total dollars received and disbursed and in terms of monthly capitation.

In some closed-panel HMOs, there is an important fee-for-service aspect. The accounting department is responsible for the management of its fee-for-service income as well as its income from prepaid patients. In such plans, physicians need to have reports on both types of patient services. Some plans "blind" physicians, preventing them from knowing which patients are prepaid and which are fee-for-service. This approach prevents physicians from using a double standard for health care. Other plans find that it is impossible to use this approach, and they entrust physicians to adhere to a single stanard of care.

The finance department of most HMOs is responsible for providing utilization data. Aberrations in utilization data typically crop up as membership advances rapidly. Hospital utilization is reported on the basis of bed days per thousand members per year. As membership increases rapidly, the hospital-utilization rate remains stable. Apparently, as people join an HMO, there is a lag time before they utilize expensive services. The finance department may report one month that the physicians have done an "incredibly good job of controlling costs" only to find out two months later, after a major increase in enrollment, that there has been a large influx of patients into the hospital and that "the doctors are no longer controlling costs." Sophisticated medical managers recognize this phenomenon and plan for it. In new plans, especially those in which medical management is inexperienced, there may be inappropriate judgments because of unawareness of this phenomenon. For this reason, better-managed plans use a "rolling 12-month average" to assess where they stand regarding utilization. Rolling 12-month averages blunt the impact of large membership gains or losses, giving medical managers and physicians a much truer sense of utilization patterns. It is therefore important, from the physicians' perspective, that the financial officers of the HMO are sophisticated in the nuances of the actuarial basis of utilization reporting. In addition, they must be adept at controlling other elements, such as coordinating benefits available from other insurers, keeping plan membership rosters up to date and disbursing checks to providers and capitated physicians on a timely basis. All these functions are critical to the success of an HMO. Physicians must understand the role of the finance department in ensuring the success of the organization. Most physicians are unaware of the methods used by the finance department to affect cash flow.

Although physicians may be responsible for spending the organization's money, the finance department is responsible for investing income. Health maintenance organizations receive their income before they have provided health-care services. This financial arrangement sets them apart from most other service industries, in which payment is received after services have been rendered. Because HMOs receive income before billing has taken place, there is a positive cash flow. For this reason, HMOs can place their funds in short-term investments. Depending on the soundness of its budgetary and accounting systems, an HMO may place a large proportion of its income in long-term investments that provide relatively high yields. The interest from such investments can have a great impact on profitability.

The other revenue that is available to HMOs results from coordination of benefits. According to the standards set forth by the National Association of Insurance Commissioners, there is a uniform system for financial responsibility when several insurers are involved with payment of a claim. The finance department must have a system in place to coordinate such benefits. The finance department may look to physicians for assistance in determining whether members are being treated for injuries covered by workmen's compensation or whether subrogation or other third-party liability applies. The assistance of physicians in providing relevant information in such cases is, in fact, a revenue-producing activity because it spares an HMO unnecessary expense.

PRACTICE IN A HMO?

There are different reasons for participating in the various types of HMOs. It is important for physicians to distinguish among the various types so that they may assess the potential gains.

Many physicians in private practice decide to treat prepaid as well as fee-for-service patients. Such physicians may participate in one or more IPAs. If it is possible to participate in several IPAs, a physician must decide if the potential additional revenues justify the enrollment fees. If an IPA has no enrollment fee, it makes sense for the physician to participate in it; the number of IPAs that a physician joins may be limited only by the ability of the staff to understand the various forms that have to be filled out.

What are the reasons that a physician would want to participate in an IPA? Physicians who have stable practices may begin to see erosion of their patient populations to HMOs. Thus, an important reason to join an HMO is to preserve an existing patient volume. However, physicians who have reached a maximal patient population must indicate to an HMO that there is a limit to the number of new patients that they are willing to accept.

Participation in an HMO can provide ready cash flow. Once a physician has more than 500 HMO patients, the regular capitation payments can be substantial, allowing him or her to take care of many of the fixed costs of the practice. Participation in an IPA establishes a physician as a successful professional with a secure market position.

There are other, less important reasons why a physician may wish to participate in an IPA. The physician may wish to learn something about the changing economics of the practice of medicine. Participation in an IPA is a rewarding learning experience. A physician may choose to participate because of an irrational fear of stiff competition or because of peer pressure. The decision to join an IPA should ideally be made from a positive point of view.

Physicians join staff-model and group-model HMOs for different reasons. For physicians who are just leaving residency, closed-panel HMOs offer an opportunity to start a medical practice virtually without risk. There are no up-front costs as there are when buying into a practice or becoming a junior member of a large practice. Young physicians who join HMOs learn how office practice truly works and what they like and do not like about this type of medical practice without having to make a commitment to it. This arrangement is a real advantage for young physicians. From the standpoint of HMOs, however, this situation represents a liability, in that physicians who join may not be committed and will be more likely to leave.

Most physicians who have just completed their training do not have strong income potential for several years. As the economic climate changes, the time it takes for physicians to make a substantial income will increase. Health maintenance organizations offer new physicians, or those with only a few years of experience, an opportunity to increase their incomes without dealing with the attendant problems of running a business. For pediatricians or family physicians in highly competitive communities, HMOs may offer greater economic rewards than are afforded by private practice.

Some physicians still join HMOs out of a sense of idealism. Physicians in the staff model are freed from concerns about the costs of treatment. Physicians who actively seek out unusual practice situations may also be attracted to the HMO setting.

Although a primary-care physicians in an HMO works on average of 50 to 60 hours per week, work hours are much more regular and predictable than they are in private practice. A regular schedule allows physicians greater opportunity for spending free time with family or friends.

Lastly, some physicians join HMOs because of difficulty establishing practice practices. As HMOs grow and become more successful, they are attracting physicians who are better trained and more oriented toward personalized care than has been the situation in the past (see the Overview).

Physicians who have been practicing for years may join HMOs because participation in such organizations provides freedom from the increasingly competitive field of medical practice. The HMO setting gives such physicians an opportunity to acquire a more uniform style of practice than they may currently have. Thus, both new and experienced physicians may find that participation in HMOs is an attractive proposition.

PREFERRED-PROVIDER ORGANIZATIONS

Preferred-provider organizations are a relatively new concept. It has been said that if you have seen one PPO, you have seen *one* PPO—the format of PPOs varies greatly.[2] A PPO provides a discount arrangement for health care to an employer group. The insuring organization then contracts individually with its preferred providers for discount arrangements. Employees who join a PPO have full access to any of the participating preferred providers. No gatekeeper or case manager is involved. The providers are paid on a fee-for-service basis according to a prearranged discount. If the PPO selects providers who are already known to be low utilizers and extracts a discount from them, that PPO should be able to deliver high-quality health care at lower cost. In this setting, high utilizers are excluded. A PPO offers the advantage of freer access without the restrictions inherent in having a case manager. However, many PPOs are now finding that unless utilization-review measures are instituted, costs may escalate, rendering them noncompetitive with HMOs.

Preferred-provider organizations may be set up by hospitals, physician groups, employers and insurance companies. Generally speaking, a hospital-based PPO serves as a marketing device for the hospital. The medical staff of the hospital are automatically made members of the PPO, subject to any review and/or fees for participation. The hospital may be made the exclusive locus for in-patient care or it may permit treatment elsewhere but attempt to attract the majority of utilization by establishing incentives, such as requiring heavy copayments for members who utilize other hospitals while requiring no copayment for utilization of its own facilities. Participating physicians are free to practice without restriction on the assumption that members will demand that all in-patient care be rendered in the sponsoring hospital rather than elsewhere. If a PPO is successful, physicians in the community will all want to have privileges at the sponsoring hospital so that they may take advantage of this marketing effort.

Initially, hospital-based PPOs were sponsored by local community institutions, but proprietary hospital chains have recently been entering the market. Humana Care Plus entered the arena in 1983.

Physicians may sponsor PPOs. Many physician-sponsored organizations are set up by county medical societies to preserve traditional fee-for-service practice, yet remain competitive with HMOs in the community. To be successful, such PPOs have to develop control mechanisms or methods for excluding high utilizers. Physicians do not have the ability to alter pricing structures sufficiently within the context of a PPO to make it marketable without excluding physicians and forms of care that are expensive. Physicians have a great deal of difficulty with this kind of policing effort.

Corporations also may set up PPOs and often do so based on experience they have had in the local marketplace. Medical directors in most large companies know physicians whose style of practice is in keeping with corporate goals. They may value physicians who are adept at handling alcoholic employees, or physicians who return orthopedic patients to the work place more quickly, or internists and family physicians who are more conservative in their style of practice. By whatever mechanism of selection it employs, a sponsoring company will refer its employees only to providers on its list. Blue Cross and Blue Shield and such insurance companies as Aetna, Travelers, CIGNA, Prudential, Lincoln and Metropolitan have also established PPOs. By offering employers a traditional indemnity product, a PPO and even an IPA or a closed-panel HMO, some companies, for example, Blue Cross and Blue Shield, are unable to provide them with a variety of health-insurance products. This kind of arrangement, known as the triple option, is attractive to many employers that find the array of health-insurance products on the market bewildering and administratively taxing.

The future of PPOs is uncertain. They may well, like self-insured programs, provide employers with a viable alternative until such time as costs begin to mount. For companies with low health-insurance expenditures, a PPO may be a viable alternative, providing lower-cost health insurance while allowing employees the benefits of wider access to care. Employers that have high health costs may find that the PPO alternative is not nearly as beneficial financially as the more restrictive HMOs. The concept of PPOs first burst on the health-care scene in the early 1980s, and it is still too early to assess their long-term viability.

SUMMARY

Health maintenance organizations are not "New Age" medicine. Prepaid group practice has been in existence in this country for more than 50 years, nearly as long as third-party reimbursement. On the other hand, HMOs do not resemble the emperor's old clothes—invisible payment mechanisms donned by a regal old health-care system.

To be successful, HMOs must demand a whole new cultural response from participating physicians. Primary-care physicians become case managers. They assume total responsibility for all health care. They thus must make judgments concerning what constitutes appropriate care for a given patient while managing limited resources. A case manager cannot perform tests or seek consultations simply in response to a patient's requests. The case manager cannot fall prey to fears of litigation. He or she also cannot "buy" patients' respect with "gifts" of prescriptions, tests and referrals. Participating primary-care physicians must practice a new paternalism. Yet, this new paternalistic response must be couched in terms that make patients feel that their doctors are concerned. A successful primary-care physician in this setting is one who meets this challenge by revitalizing the old virtues of compassion, tempered with the ability to say no.

Primary-care physicians who participate in HMOs must be skillful in making clinical decisions. They must make a differential diagnosis, then consider the relative likelihood of each diagnosis and, finally, determine the outcome with treatment or no treatment. In a sense, physicians must decide what treatment option will get "the most bang for the buck."

To be successful participants in HMOs, primary-care physicians must feel secure enough as professionals that they are not threatened by their status as employees. They will be continually scrutinized by peer review, utilization review and the member-services department. Physicians who practice in a cost-effective manner and deliver high-quality care should not be concerned with such scrutiny.

Competition in the medical marketplace today is resulting in new alliances. Independent HMOs have banded together to form group-purchasing arrangements. Small HMOs have come under the wings of large for-profit entities. Many hospitals and physician groups are seeking to increase their market shares by forming HMOs and PPOs. Currently, there is a relative dearth of medical management when one considers the number of organized units today.

The authors believe that the future will see major reductions in the number of HMOs until a half dozen giants dominate the industry. Some will be purely in the HMO field. However, most will be sponsored by insurance companies and hospital chains, both seeking to enter new markets with new products. Health maintenance organizations with strong financial backing and depth of medical leadership will be the successful ones. Small, independent organizations will fall prey to large, better-managed ones. There will probably be a variety of independent HMOs operating in much the same fashion as independent community hospitals. The for-profit companies will set the tone and dominate the scene for HMOs in the future.

Increasingly, HMOs will develop vertical and horizontal integration of services. Hospital companies are currently seeking more patients by developing HMOs as well as by purchasing hospital-supply companies. Existing HMOs are developing other insurance products to bring members into their health centers and to cover their expenses on an indemnification basis. Undoubtedly, large conglomerates that have no previous health-management experience will move into the arena by purchasing existing companies.

The management of a business entity that employs professionals will become the norm of clinical medicine. Private-practice groups may survive only by adaptation, becoming dependent on health-management companies for patient volume and for management services.

This portrayal of medicine in the future is not designed to paint a bleak picture. Rather, the interjection of a logical order with management skills to help guide professionals may give the American public a new and unique system of care. Undoubtedly, health care can be provided in an accountable format, giving greater benefits to a larger number of people than under the previous fee-for-service system. Whereas other societies have moved toward socialized medicine, American society has moved toward a capitalistic, entrepreneurial style of medical practice. One can only hope that these new directions in medicine will improve the health-care system for all.

REFERENCES

1. Cooper RM: *Physician's Guide to Prepaid Group Practice*. Nashville, Tenn, Health Corporation of America, 1983.
2. Barger B: *The PPO Handbook*. Rockville, Md, Aspen Systems, 1985.
3. Ellwood, PM: Health maintenance strategy. *Med Care* 291:250–256, 1971.
4. Iglehart J: The American health care system. *N Engl J Med* 326:962–967, 17, 15–20, 1992.
5. Iglehart J: The American health care system—managed care. *N Engl J Med* 327:742–747, 1992.
6. Relman AS: Reforming the health care system. *N Engl J Med* 323:991–992, 1990.
7. Starr P: *The Social Transformation of American Medicine*. New York, Basic Books, 1982.
8. Eisenberg JM: The internist as gatekeeper, preparing the general internist for a new role. *Ann Intern Med* 102:537–543, 1985.
9. Hillman AL: Health maintenance organizations, financial incentives, and physicians' judgments. *Ann Intern Med* 112:891–893, 1990.
10. Mechanic D: *From Advocacy to Allocation: The Evolving American Health Care System*. New York, Free Press, 1986.

CHAPTER 9

THE PHYSICIAN-EXECUTIVE

Robert H. Hodge, Jr.
David B. Nash

This chapter discusses the development of an emerging new specialist: the physician-executive. In the first section, one of the authors (R.H.H.) describes his career path in medical management. The second section offers a detailed discussion of the history and development of medical management, with emphasis placed on training programs and the current status of the field.

HEALTH-CARE MANAGEMENT:
A PERSONAL PERSPECTIVE

Why should a physician consider becoming a physician-executive? Most students enter medical school with the goal of becoming practicing physicians. Some students later decide to spend most of their time teaching or doing research, but a resident who becomes intent on becoming a health-care manager or a physician-executive is rare. Yet, there is a growing demand for physicians to assume leadership roles in this field, and many of them are finding it a satisfying career. In this section, I will discuss why physicians should consider a career in management and the types of opportunities and training available.

First, I will tell the reader why I became a physician-executive. As the son of a general internist, I entered medical school determined to go into practice with my father. After medical school, I started my internship and residency in internal medicine, looking forward to caring for patients and becoming a "real" doctor. It was during residency that I subconsciously became interested in management. My interest in this aspect of health care was probably related to how I felt about how patients were treated at the medical center where I worked.

Two experiences stand out. First, as a resident, I had to go to an outpatient clinic one afternoon a week. All the residents hated the clinic, and I was no exception. There were many problems, including overbooking of patients, inadequate medical records, poor reporting back of laboratory results and constant interruptions from the inpatient service that was supposed to be covered at the same time. All these problems, combined with a chronic lack of sleep from invariably being on call the night before, made for an unpleasant experience. This was not good patient care! I kept thinking that there must be a better way to run the clinic. Yet, nothing ever seemed to be done about the situation there, either by the attending physicians or by the hospital administrators.

The second experience was my involvement with the house-staff association. I joined and eventually became president. As president, I was invited to sit on the medical-policy committee of the hospital, and I saw firsthand how the physicians tried to manage and interact with hospital administrators. There were constant battles over resources and institutional policy, and it was frustrating to witness the lack of leadership on the part of the physicians. Again, patient care issues suffered.

These experiences made me realize that there were some real organizational problems that needed to be resolved to improve patient care and that physicians could and should have an important role. My participation in administration as president of the house-staff association made me want to explore this field further. I was not ready to go into private practice without first seeing if I could work in an academic institution and help solve the problems I encountered.

Soon after my arrival at the University of Virginia Medical Center, I was appointed medical director of the general medicine clinic. This appointment was no honor because many faculty members had at one time or another occupied this position only to get out of it at the earliest possible convenience. The major problem that I found was a common one: I had plenty of responsibility but little authority to make needed changes. Most importantly, I had no control over the budget and the allocation of resources. Given this challenging situation, I soon began to appreciate my lack of management skills. My medical-school training had not prepared me for negotiating budgets, hiring personnel or handling the many other tasks necessary to make a clinic run smoothly and efficiently. I began to look around to see if there were any opportunities to learn more about management.

I happened to hear about the 1978 National Conference on Health Care Leadership and Management of the American Academy of Medical

Directors (AAMD), now the American College of Physician Executives (ACPE), and decided to go see what the organization was all about. I found that the ACPE was an organization dedicated to teaching the principles of management to physicians and to providing a forum for interaction among physicians. Meeting with fellow physicians who were in management positions in varied settings (e.g., group practices, hospitals, academic centers and corporations) spurred my interest and commitment to stay in this area. I returned to Virginia with a renewed sense of purpose.

Having decided to concentrate on the management aspect of health care, I took several courses over the next several years from the ACPE that I found helpful. They included accounting and finance, negotiation, power and influence, and left brain/right brain creativity. These courses, along with business courses taken elsewhere (including the business school at Virginia), made the management process much more satisfying and worthwhile.

I then moved to management positions of progressively greater responsibility and became the medical director of ambulatory care services at the University of Virginia Medical Center, with responsibility for the direction and coordination of more than 40 outpatient clinics, the emergency service, out-patient registration and other services. I supervised more than 250 people (including five physicians) and had a budget of several million dollars. Since then, I spent three years as a Program Director in Health for the W. K. Kellogg Foundation; currently I am vice president of a unique managed-care benefit plan supporting the role of primary care.

To date, I am satisfied with the decision I made to enter the field of health-care management. Learning and applying management skills to my administrative tasks has been fun and rewarding. It has allowed me to have an impact on a large segment of the health-care delivery system. I would gladly do it all over again, but I believe that it is possible today to plan more for this type of career and have more choice in positions.

Opportunities and Responsibilities

What are some management opportunities in the health-care field today? In 1983, the ACPE surveyed its membership to determine the management positions held by members as well as the duties and responsibilities of the positions. The results of this survey were published in three monographs: *The Physician Manager in Group Practices, The Physician Manager in Hospitals* and *The Physician Manager in HMOs/Prepaid Health Plans*. In these monographs, the roles, responsibilities and compensation of physician-executives were specified according to practice setting (group practice, hospital or health maintenance organization/ prepaid health plan), and each setting was then divided according to size.

For example, group practices were divided according to the number of physicians in the group.

The most common titles of physician-executives included the following:

Chief executive officer
medical director
director of medical affairs
vice-president of medical affairs
chief of staff
director of medical education
departmental chairman

A job description for each title would normally include activities within the following categories:

general duties inside the organization
general duties outside the organization
quality assurance
educational activities
data management
financial management
risk management
resource management
general management

Each category includes different responsibilities that, in part, depend on the nature and size of the organization. To give an idea of what a physician-executive might do, I will take each category and briefly describe some responsibilities involved. I will use the positions of medical director of a group practice as an example.

General Duties Inside the Organization

This category is the most important for a medical director because it involves direct management of an organization. If a medical director holds the top position of a group practice, the most important task will be to determine the goals and objectives of the practice to establish its direction for the future. For example, the medical director may decide that one goal is to expand the patient population and that one related objective would be to form or join a health maintenance organization to attract new patients. Other goals and objectives, such as providing quality care and being financially solvent, are also important. Of course, the medical director will determine goals and objectives with input from other members of the group, but in the end, it will be his or her responsibility to formulate the final plan. Also, the medical director must give consideration to how to monitor the success or failure of efforts undertaken to achieve goals and objectives. Success depends on being able to work at all levels of the group to ensure that all members of the practice know what is expected of them and that all progress (or lack thereof) is duly communicated.

Many group practices are governed by a board, and the medical director is the key link between this body and the rest of the physicians. In this setting, the medical director must communicate the concerns of the physicians, for example, to the board and vice versa. Communication of such concerns requires attendance at board meetings as well as active participation on key committees, such as the finance and patient-care committees. The medical director, in a sense, represents both sides, necessitating diplomacy of the highest order. The medical director often must decide what is best for the practice and work with both sides to achieve a reasonable compromise.

The medical director frequently has to deal with personnel, both physicians and nonphysicians. For this purpose, the responsibilities and privileges of each person in the practice must be specified in writing. The medical director must determine the type of physicians needed for the practice and often works with departmental chairmen to select appropriate personnel. Salaries must be negotiated, and a satisfactory bonus or incentive plan must be devised. Firing personnel may be the most difficult task, but the medical director must be able to fire or terminate a person without causing undue harm to the person or to the practice.

Patient care is a common responsibility, and the medical director must handle such issues as developing care standards, deciding on equipment needs and determining the fees for various services. Care standards are often developed in conjunction with the quality-assurance committee, of which the medical director is usually the chairman. Equipment needs often create problems because the demands of the medical staff may exceed the budget allocated for this capital expenditure. Unlike an administrator, the medical director has the advantage of a medical background to aid him or her in the decision-making process. However, satisfying needs is a difficult task because it is impossible to please everybody.

The medical director usually serves on many committees, including finance, quality assurance, planning, patient care and credentials. The medical director serves as the liaison between these groups and is often the only person who has the "big picture," or an organizational perspective, in mind. A lot of time is spent in committee meetings, and the medical director must be able to work with the various committees to accomplish the goals set for the practice.

Many group practices engage in research, and the medical director may be the person who determines the appropriateness of such activity, particularly how well it will fit into the structure of the practice.

General Duties Outside the Organization

The medical director is a key link to the external forces that affect a group practice. For example, he or she is often responsible for representing the practice not only to its patients but also to such outside entities as hospitals, third-party payers, regulatory agencies and other health-care organizations. Keeping a hand on the pulse of outside trends will enable the medical director to plan effective strategies for success. A combination of negotiating skills and political acumen is frequently needed to obtain the most beneficial contract or policy for the practice.

The medical director is often in charge of promoting the practice, a function that requires a knowledge of marketing (as opposed to advertising). For example, by promoting health seminars for the public or working with the local cancer society for preventive practices, the practice can build a solid public image without giving the impression of solicitation. With the marked increase in the number of physicians in the past few years, competition is increasing, necessitating an effective marketing strategy on the part of the medical director.

The medical director represents the practice in national associations that can provide assistance. For example, the American Group Practice Association (AGPA) deals with issues relating to group practices of all sizes and can provide invaluable assistance in such areas as marketing, legislative issues that affect group practices and financial managment.

Quality Assurance

As was mentioned previously, the medical director may be responsible for ensuring that care is of a high standard. He or she is often the chairman of the quality-assurance and the credentials committees. In addition to making sure that necessary accreditation has been obtained, the quality-assurance committee may perform audits to ensure that the practice adheres to its written policies and to the rules and regulations of the profession. The credentials committee screens new physicians and makes sure that all practitioners have current licenses. Another responsibility of the medical director is the development of competency evaluations and programs that compare the performance of the professional with established practice standards.

Educational Activities

Education is a time-honored responsibility of a medical director because directors of medical education are employed by many hospitals. In a group practice, the medical director may not only design continuing education programs for physicians but also teach the courses. Nonphysicians may need to take similar programs. Continuing education courses must be certified by an appropriate organization, such as the American Medical Association, and the medical director has to obtain the proper certification. In addition, the medical director is often involved in developing evaluation tools to determine the effectiveness of such courses.

Data Management

Health-care data are an integral component of the practice of medicine, as evidenced by the central role of medical records. The medical director is often responsible for ensuring that care data are used correctly and that confidentiality is maintained. Group practices often also have computerized data systems that store patient demographics and insurance information. The medical director must ensure that such data are used correctly, particularly in relation to critical management decisions. For example, in a group practice, the specific mixture of third-party payers can influence changes in fees that the practice might consider each year.

Financial Management

Many medical directors have the assistance of a financial specialist who keeps track of accounts and advises on the financial status of the practice. However, developing and adhering to a budget are the responsibilities of the medical director and cannot be delegated to the finance officer. The medical director must develop the budget by taking into consideration the overall plan for the practice. Projected expenses must be covered by expected revenues, and capital expenditures must be taken into account, most importantly equipment purchases. The medical director must monitor the budget throughout the fiscal year, and near the end of the fiscal year must review the financial performance of the practice so that a budget for the next fiscal year can be projected.

Risk Management

Risk management is concerned with reducing the liability of a practice whether it be malpractice or general injury due to unsafe conditions. The medical director is responsible for working with the insurance carriers to ensure that all possible precautions are being taken to minimize the risk of a lawsuit. In the malpractice area, this means making sure that the physicians follow an acceptable standard of practice with good documentation of patient care. High risk areas such as obstetrics and orthopedics need to be monitored closely. Educational programs for physicians and other health-care providers are often developed and put on by the medical director in cooperation with the insurer. A good communication system is also necessary so that the medical director can learn of problems early and act on them immediately. This area is closely aligned with quality assurance to minimize problems within the practice.

Resource Management

As mentioned previously, many medical directors are responsible for hiring and firing personnel. Other duties include advising physicians concerning personal issues and mediating conflicts between physicians (which take place all too often!). Handling conflicts between physicians and other staff members is another common responsibility. Issues relating to productivity are also of concern to the medical director. To obtain optimal output (e.g., number of patients seen), the medical director may have to develop an incentive plan that will reward preferred behaviors, yet not adversely affect quality of care.

Physician contracts is another area of responsibility for the medical director. Such documents define wage scales and incentive plans. Breaches of contract often involve grievance procedures that are likely to come to the attention of the medical director first. Similar responsibilities may exist for the medical director in relation to nonphysician employees.

General Management

Of course, anything that does not fit into one of the preceding categories can be considered general management. In a group practice, such management responsibilities might include deciding on the need for consulting services and supervising renovation or capital construction projects. Long-range planning is another important activity that is global in nature. Last, handling emergencies, such as layoffs or other personnel problems, is frequently the responsibility of the medical director.

As can be seen, the medical director has a wide range of duties. Although the various responsibilities may seem overwhelming at first, they offer the medical director an opportunity to lead a group practice effectively and make it successful, efficient and productive.

Why Go into Management?

What are some of the reasons that one might want to become a physician-executive? I feel that the strongest motivation for someone to want a leadership role in this field is a commitment to improving health care. There is a real challenge in stepping forward and providing the leadership to make positive changes. One such leadership position is that of the chief resident. These physicians are committed to the house-staff training program and want to make it a better experience for those who follow. Physician-executvies are interested in achieving the same goal of improving health care, but on a larger scale.

Another motivator is the power that comes with a higher managerial position. Physician-executives suddenly realize that they have people working for them and resources to allocate. Most people will not openly admit that they like power, but that does not mean that it is not desirable. The power to control resources is the power to influence and, used wisely, the power to ensure that goals are achieved.

As a career, medical management has a bright future because of the way the health-care system is becoming more competitive. In part, this competition is due to the surplus of physicians. As a result, I predict that there will be more demand for physician-executives and that incomes will remain attractive. By contrast, the incomes of physicians in private practice on average, have plateaued and are not keeping pace with inflation.

Why Obtain a Doctor of Medicine Degree?

If one decides to go into health-care management, one might ask about the benefit of having a doctor of medicine degree. How do physician-executives and nonphysician administrators differ? There are several advantages and disadvantages to having such a degree.

First the disadvantages. A doctor of medicine degree takes time to acquire, so nonphysician administrators can get started in the field more quickly. Thus, while a physician is finishing his or her training, an administrator is gaining important experience and most likely specializing in a specific area, such as finance, operations or marketing. However, a physician-executive usually does not compete in these areas. I believe that physician-executives are best suited for a general leadership role and that the choice of a physician or a nonphysician as a health-care manager depends more on leadership qualities than on the type of basic professional training.

The second disadvantage is the limit that the management role places on a physician's ability to practice his or her specialty. There is continual debate about whether a physician should continue to practice medicine while having a position in management. The advantages of continuing to practice medicine include a welcome respite from administrative duties and a sense of variety in the work setting. Also, a physician can gain a more direct and different sense of satisfaction from patient care. One-on-one patient contact usually provides more immediate rewards than do the relatively long-term activities that take place in the managerial setting. Moreover, seeing patients allows a physician to get useful feedback on how his or her patients perceive the physician's practice. For example, when I used to see my patients, I quickly learned how bad the parking situation was and how troublesome the billing process was for them. Hospital administrators have a more difficult time getting the same information.

On the other hand, maintaining a practice can be time-consuming. For a physician to maintain his or her skills, a minimum amount of time must be devoted to the practice of medicine. For example, as a general internist, I saw patients half a day each week, attended in out patient clinics and on the in-patient service and took regular rotations for 24-hour call. This schedule comprises the minimum time I feel is necessary to continue to provide quality health care. It is difficult, moreover, to place limits on time. Patients did not always get sick during the time that I was in the clinic, and I was occasionally interrupted from administrative meetings to talk to patients on the telephone or to see them in the clinic. Fortunately, I had excellent backup from other physicians and nurse-practitioners, so I was usually called only for true emergencies.

The time spent practicing and the time spent managing often constitute a balancing act that requires planning. I would encourage physician-executives to practice when possible, but as one moves higher in an organization, practicing medicine may become impractical. However, there is no substitute for finding out what goes on by seeing patients directly.

The third disadvantage is that physicians are trained in what I call the 1:1 mold. They see patients one at a time and deal with their problems individually. This situation is in marked contrast to that which character- izes management, in which one often deals with groups or teams. For example, there may be a problem in the nursing service that necessitates decisions that will affect several hundred or several thousand employees. A physician-executive obviously does not have time to meet with each nurse; rather, a meeting must be arranged by supervisory personnel. Be- ing somewhat removed from the "action" can make a physician feel alienated. A good example of the alienation that develops in house-staff training is when an intern suddenly finds that he or she is a second-year resident and must be a supervisor rather than a first-line provider of care. It is tempting to take care of a patient directly rather than stand back and let the intern do so. To be effective, a physician-executive must learn to delegate and to be a leader rather than a doer.

The fourth disadvantage is that physicians are not educated in man- agement skills. Perhaps medical school curricula will someday have abun- dant courses on management; current curricula have a paucity of such courses (see Chapter 3). Even if the needed courses were offered, how- ever, many students would not take them because most students are intent on becoming practicing physicians. Even at the house-staff level, there is little interest. One year I tried teaching a course on what the house-staff officers needed to know to go into private practice. I found out that house-staff officers became interested in management the day *after* they opened their offices.

Management skills should be taught in medical schools because resi- dents need to know how to be effective leaders of a team. On a medical ward, care could be much more efficient if second- and third-year resi- dents would concentrate on their roles as supervisors and leaders rather than on their role as providers of care. For example, most residents do a complete workup on each inpatient when they should be concentrating on what interns are doing; they should be checking orders, pursuing old records and putting patients' illnesses in perspective. Residents could also motivate nurses to feel that they are part of a team so that an ap- proach to total care can be realized. All too often, however, residents spend their time doing workups that are redundant. In other words, resi- dents are often afraid to delegate anything other than menial work.

Other leadership skills that residents could use effectively include motivation, counseling, planning and management of stress and time. Motivation involves keeping the ward team (including the nurses) con- stantly aware of important roles and goals. Occasional slumps occur, for example, when admissions are high or when discharges are few. By being continually attuned to the situation, residents can help other members of the team achieve their goals. Residents often need to make use of any counseling skills to help interns feel their way through the first year. Many interns are left to sink or swim. Planning skills help residents deal with problems that may arise, such as having to transfer patients to nursing homes or the rescheduling that may become necessary because of breakdown of diagnostic equipment. Management of stress and time helps residents assist other staff members in difficulty and also is essential to their own well-being. The mere recognition of a problem in these areas is an important first step.

The fifth disadvantage is that physicians in managerial positions often have a different peer relationship with other physicians. Once physicians enter management, they notice that they are treated differently by practicing physicians. The change in this relationship stems largely from the responsibility that physician-exeuctives have for controlling health-care resources. Practicing physicians in need of additional personnel or new equipment, for example, approach physician-executives to get their needs satisfied in many ways; some physicians even resort to throwing tantrums. Physician-executives cannot make the right decision for the group practice and remain friends with all its members, just as a practicing physician cannot please every patient. The altered peer relationship may be the toughest obstacle for most physician-executives because it is easy to confuse friendship with respect.

Now the advantages. First, physician-executives know the field of medicine and can be effective patient advocates. Unlike nonphysician administrators, physicians spend a mininmum of five years (two in medical school and three in residency) in health-care facilities learning how to practice medicine. Unlike the administrator, they become intimately involved with the health-care system as a participant, not an observer.

Physician-executives know the needs of patients. As managers, they have an excellent sense of what constitutes quality care and good service. By contrast, nonphysician administrators are more likely to focus on the cost of services and the overall efficiency of the group practice. Physician-executives are better able to balance quality and cost issues than are their nonphysician counterparts.

Second, although I mentioned that dealing with peers is sometimes difficult for physician-executives, they have a built-in advantage in this relationship that their nonphysician counterparts lack. Managing professionals (especially physicians) is a challenge, but it is easier when one is a peer. Most physicians relate better to fellow physicians, even if they are executives, than to nonphysicians. There is always the feeling that peers are better able to understand a problem, particularly if it involves quality versus cost. Many physicians also harbor strong feelings about having to work for nonphysicians.

A doctorate in medicine is no guarantee of success as a manager. It merely adds perspective from the standpoint of medical practice in management decisions. A background in medicine needs to be supplemented by certain skills for the successful pursuit of a career in management.

Obtaining Skills

Perhaps the most common way physicians acquire management skills is through on-the-job traiing. Physicians who are thrust into a managerial position, such as a departmental chairmanship, either sink or swim. For many physicians, this situation does not produce a learning experience. Physicians with no formal training in management skills must rely on whatever natural abilities they have.

A master of business administration (MBA) degree provides the most rigorous training in management skills. Like a doctor of medicine degree, it confers upon graduates definite creditentials, but obtaining this degree has its drawbacks. First, the commitment of time needed to acquire such a degree is too great for the average physician. The two years or longer that this degree takes to obtain means a loss of income for that period as well as a gap in practice experience. It is possible to acquire this degree by going to school at night and on weekends, but attending classes only during these times would stretch out the required time to several years. Some physicians question whether courses in business administration prepare graduates for careers in the health-care field. Most schools that offer such degrees are oriented toward other business settings, such as banking, manufacturing and service industries. It is also unknown whether an MBA after one's name is an advantaghe for pursuing a career in this field. I do not recommend studying to get a master in business (or health) administration degree unless a physician has a total commitment to pursue a full-time career in health-care management, giving up the actual practice of medicine.

As mentioned earlier, I began my training in management skills by reading and taking short courses sponsored by the ACPE and business schools. One advantage of short courses is that they offer limited exposure to a variety of topics so that one can decide relatively quickly whether to pursue such training. Another advantage is that they allow one to put the knowledge that has been gained into practice on the job relatively quickly. For example, after taking a short course on negotiation, I was able to use my newly acquired negotiating skills on the job when handling contracts with various departments. The disadvantages of short courses are their cost (usually more expensive than full-term courses), their lack of medically oriented learning examples and the relatively few opportunities they provide to interact with other persons in the health-care field.

The ACPE also offers a number of other educational offerings. An annual meeting, the National Conference, offers a wide range of general sessions and workshops that expose participants to the latest trends and thinking in medical management and leadership. This annual event is an excellent opportunity to meet and interact with other physician-executives from all over the United States and other countries such as Great Britain and Australia. Members participate in Societies and Forums of the College, which focus on common organizational affiliations and topical issues. Additional short courses are offered at the National Institute in November and at the annual Executive Symposium in August of each year. The courses run from one to four days and give attendees a more in-depth look in certain areas such as the management of professionals in organizations, mastering the art of negotiation and mediation, techniques of financial decision making and managing diversity in the workplace.

The ACPE has also forged agreements with academic institutions such as the University of Wisconsin for degrees such as a Masters in Medical Administration. The Wisconsin program is particularly attractive to those phsycians who wish to study at home. There are limited attendance requirements at the Madison, Wisconsin campus. The ACPE also is sponsoring a certificate program in medical management to recognize those who have taken a number of the ACPE sponsored short courses over time.

As important as education and training in management are to the long-term success of physician-executives, recognition within the medical profession for the management option is equally crucial. Important steps have been taken in this direction by the ACPE. The American Board of Medical Management (ABMM) offers a rigorous Board examination in medical management. The successful applicant is named a Diplomate in Medical Management and is eligible for Fellowship status within the College. A College Fellow must have demonstrated management experience as a physician-executive in addition to successful passing the Board examination. Distinguished Fellow status is granted for those who have made significant and noteworthy contributions to the field.

Educational programs, advanced degrees and specialty status will all lead to the same outcome—a major role for physician-executives in the management of this country's health-care delivery system. The ACPE has directed its efforts toward providing educational opportunities that can be realized without prolonged absence from the work place. A greater effort will be necessary in this regard. Nonetheless, physicians who aspire to the highest levels of health-care management may have to contemplate taking a leave of absence to acquire the necessary educational credentials. The decision to pursue a career in management has to include consideration of this possibility.

Getting Started

Now that I have described the opportunities for physician-executives, how does one get started? I would recommend that a physician first make a conscious decision to explore the field and be open to opportunities that might arise. For example, the physician might volunteer for assignments that involve administrative or leadership expertise, such as chairing committees on finance, planning or allocating resources. By successfully exhibiting leadership at this level, a physician will become noticed and probably will receive offers of new responsibilities in the future. The secret is to get out there, participate and experience the satisfaction of accomplishing specific objectives.

Beginning a career in management is a relatively safe decision for physicians because they can always fall back on their medical skills to earn a living if management is not right for them. It is also not necessary to devote full time to obtain a degree to acquire the skills needed to be good managers. Therefore, I would advise physicians to start small, explore the field and take a few courses to see if the management field has any attraction for them.

I believe that physicians-executives have a bright future because the health-care field is constantly changing because of pressures from cost-containment, new technology and alternative methods of delivery. Physicians should be leaders in the field because they have the necessary background and perspective to strike a balance between quality care and cost as well as other forces affecting the field. As an alternative to the practice of medicine, I wholeheartedly recommend the management field for physicians who would like to be future leaders in the health-care arena.

MEDICAL MANAGEMENT: HISTORY AND DEVELOPMENT

The delivery of health care has become this nation's largest industry, accounting for almost 13 percent of the gross national product. The health-care sector of the economy employs almost five million people and generates $400 billion in annual expenditures.[1] In 1984, corporations alone paid about $90 billion in health-insurance premiums, or about 38 percent of their total pretax profits.[2] This sum was more than corporations paid all their shareholders in dividends during the same period. Some observers have labeled this phenomenon as the development of a new "medical-industrial complex" with the attendant problems of overuse, fragmentation of services, overemphasis on technology and widespread conflicts of interest on the part of physicians.[3]

The first part of this section explores dynamic forces that are shaping the delivery of health care and discusses why the same forces have led to the emergence of a new medical specialist: the physician-executive. The second part outlines the ideal curriculum that must be mastered by physician-executives and describes available training programs. The third part is a report of the current status of the profession. This section concludes with informed speculation about the future roles and challenges of physician-executives.

Until recently, health care was viewed as a social problem and access to services occupied the minds of policymakers in Washington,

D.C., and the private sector.[4] As expenditures by corporations for health care increased and the federal budget deficit worsened, the delivery of health care came to be viewed strictly as an economic problem.

Goldsmith[5] has pointed out that there has been a dramatic shift (as a result of this realization of the economic source of the"problem") in interest away from the providers of health care to the payers of such care. He contends that Congress has now attained major economic purchasing power in the system because Medicare accounts for more than 40 percent of the total hospital product. With passage of the Tax Equity and Fiscal Responsibility Act (TEFRA) in 1982, and with it the implementation of prospective payment for hospital services based on 467 diagnosis-related groups (DRGs), Congress has placed hospitals at an economic risk for decision making by physicians.

For the first time, DRGs tie physicians and hospitals in a tight economic knot with indirect incentives for physicians to control their utilization of resources. Survival of hospitals now depends on a collaborative effort between administrators and physicians; in the past, administrators traditionally acted solely as caretakers of the institutions. With the demise of cost-based reimbursement, according to which hospitals simply passed on their costs to third-party payers, administrators must now husband their resources and involve physicians in all aspects of tactical and strategic planning.

Most physicians are ill-prepared to meet this challenge and view economic forces as being partly the cause of the erosion of their professional autonomy.[6] In the past, physicians were virtually able to set a target income and adjust their fees and work loads accordingly. Prepaid capitation and diagnosis-related groups have combined to erode their financial base. As a group, physicians "can no longer conduct their professional affairs independent of the well-being of their communities".[5]

In addition to this erosion of professional autonomy as a result of economic forces, other factors are operating in the system to squeeze physicians. From 1965 to 1985, the number of physicians graduating from U.S. medical schools more than doubled.[7] This marked increase in the supply of physicians was accomplished without any long-range planning within the health-care system. Policymakers are now faced with the consequences of a physician surplus, including greater competition among physicians for patients, a trend among physicians to accept salaried positions in an increasingly competitive marketplace, a willingness of physicians to sacrifice additional autonomy for their collective interests and the inevitable proliferation of doctors' unions.

The physician surplus has a direct impact on another dynamic force: the corporatization of health care. For-profit medical enterprises have

> . . . been able to make rapid headway during the past decade and a half—buying up existing hospitals; raising capital on the equity markets to build new hospitals in preferred locations where there is little

risk of bad debt; and managing hospitals in middle-income and upper incomes areas where patients, most of them heavily insured, will
not object to paying a little more for comfort and service, even if
they get no more and often a little less in the quality of professional
care. [8]

For-profit health-care companies are in a buyer's market when it comes
to purchasing physicians' services.

Academic health centers are also threatened by these dynamic
forces. They face an uncertain future due to cutbacks in federal resources
allocated to the research community, rising health-care costs, competition from community hospitals and aging physical plants.[9,10] Astute observers have labeled such institutions as "sick citadels," incapable of
meeting the management challenges ahead of them.[11]

Some academic health centers have reorganized along "product
lines" and decentralized decision making by their management.[12] Physicians have been given special training for their increased responsibility
as managers of resources and thus far have gained kudos for their performance in this new role.

However, on a system-wide basis, such forces as prospective payment, the physician surplus, the corporatization of health care and the
uncertain future facing academic health centers have created the need for
a new type of rational health-care manager.

The author's contention is that the physician-executive, an appropriately trained clinician, able to act as liaison between administrators
and other physicians, has rapidly evolved during this crisis period. Perhaps such management-oriented clinicians will be able to chart the course
of the health-care locomotive before the controls are wrested away alto-
gether by politicians, attorneys and businessmen.

The Ideal Curriculum

The dynamic forces within the health-care sector of the economy
have already been described. The evolution of the physician-executive
as an integral part of this industry is by now apparent. Now we will
address two key questions: What is the ideal curriculum to which a physician-executive should be exposed? What teaching and continuing-
education programs are available to help train this new cadre of physicians?

Recently, articles in leading medical journals have decried the
growth of the administrative sector of the medical-industrial complex.
Alper,[13] writing in the *New England Journal of Medicine,* contends that
administrators (the author did not specify whether he meant lay administrators, physicians or both) deliberately use business "jargon" to obfus-
cate the issues and confuse physicians.

> With the hospital divided into profit centers and with physicians viewed as moneymakers (and possibly money losers), I am also forced to wonder to what degree the balance of influence will shift within the institution. Will there be favored specialties, procedures, physicians, and employees and a distortion in patterns of care based primarily on profits?[13]

Himmelstein and Woolhandler,[14] writing in the same journal, contend that "each new reform in the health care system deposits yet another layer of administrators who have the power to say 'no' but not 'yes.'" They believe that administrators, whether or not physicians, have been "transmogrified" from the servant of medicine to its master.

These views are not, surprisingly, popular among physicians. The average clinician has not been trained to read a balance sheet, evaluate a strategic plan or decipher an annual hospital report. The author's contention is that there exists a certain core "fund of knowledge," to borrow an oft-used medical phrase, to which physician-executives must be exposed. One could view this fund as a kind of ideal curriculum to which management-training programs should aspire. After completing this curriculum, physician-executives will be prepared to participate as coequals in the management decision-making hierarchy.

The ideal curriculum closely parallels the core of the Wharton School's master of business administration program, with certain adaptations to the health-care industry. The curriculum is focused on eight themes that, of course, can be tailored to the skills and research interests of program faculty members. These eight themes will now be discussed, not necessarily in order of relative importance.[15]

1. *Marketing* is not advertising; rather, it involves determining and satisfying the demands of health-care consumers. Marketing enables policy makers to attach an appropriate focus to specific tertiary services. Satisfying derived demand, that is, services that are thought to be needed by a community, is not marketing. Educating consumers of health care about preventive-health programs and wellness behavior can also be included under the marketing umbrella.

Competition in the marketplace has made marketing skills an important new tool as it becomes necessary for hospitals to establish brand-name recognition. For instance, the Mayo Clinic, based in Rochester Minnesota, has now expanded by building satellite referral facilities in Arizona and Florida. The for-profit chains, such as Humana, have achieved excellent product recognition in diverse markets across the country.

2. *Finance* helps physician-executives track the flow of funds through an organiztion. A capital-budgeting decision for new construction, for example, becomes increasingly important as reimbursement for capital costs fall under the prospective-payment umbrella.[16]

With the growth of hospital-physician joint ventures, the financial analysis of competing proposals is a key step before implementation of any cooperative program. Medical directors will be participating more frequently in important reimbursement negotiations with insurance companies and other third-party payers, such as Blue Cross. As Medicare prospective-payment systems evolve, physician-executives will have a critical role in the financing decisions that must be made.

3. *Accounting* means accountability. Learning to distinguish true costs from assessed charges enables physician-executives to make more efficient decisions with regard to scarce resources.[17] The growing importance of management-information systems and the abiity to track true costs, especially under prospective-payment systems, is axiomatic.

Hospitals are spending large sums to track these resource-consumption patterns. Most medical directors do not know the true costs of taking care of individual diagnoses—What does it "cost" when a nurse walks into a room, sets up an intravenous line and delivers an antibiotic to a patient? Currently, funding for interns and residents accounts for about $3 billion annually,[18] but the true cost of this training, to the institutions involved, is elusive.

4. *Macroeconomics* clarifies the impact of governmental policies (both fiscal and monetary) on the economic environment of health-care institutions. Community hospitals, health maintenance organizations (HMOs) and large medical centers are all affected by inflation and shifting values of the dollar. There is no insulation in such an interdependent world.

Large groups of hospitals and other providers are represented in Washington, D.C. by important lobbying groups, such as the Association of American Medical Colleges (AAMC), which takes an active role in helping influence economic policies on Capitol Hill. Leading physician-executives are called on to testify before Congress to aid in evaluating the economic impact of competing legislative proposals.

5. *Microeconomics* helps model rationing decisions so that the effectiveness of various proposals can be compared. A comparison of marginal costs and marginal benefits also conserves limited resources. The marginal cost of additional hospital beds may be surprisingly high when compared to the marginal benefit, for example.

Also, as health-care delivery systems become further constrained by capitation plans, physician-executives will be called on to limit medication purchases, supplies, diagnostic services and the like. Cost-effectiveness analyses and cost-benefit analyses are both important microeconomic tools that physician-executives must be adept at using (see Chapter 13).

6. *Strategic planning* enables policymakers to replace fragmented crisis management with well thought out contingency plans. Rather than mount a haphazard response, health-care managers can develop new efficiencies.

The current physician surplus is a good example of the lack of strategic planning within the system. Strategic planning will enable some providers to survive in an increasingly competitive environment—this is especially true for developing HMOs.

7. *The decision sciences,* coupled with advanced applications of probability theory, have been modified from the industrial engineering setting. Emergency triage and complex clinical decision making already take advantage of this burgeoning knowledge base.

Third-party payers (such as Blue Cross) currently sponsor research in this field,[19] which helps assign probability values to the yield of certain diagnostic tests. The intention here is to rationalize clinical decision making and test ordering. Institutions will turn to physician-executives to help implement and enforce clinical treatment protocols shown to have high probabilities of success.

8. *Management* is a broad term, but to physician-executives it involves influencing norms and behaviors—transferring or conveying a set of values. With the growth of multi-institutional systems and decentralized decision making in hospitals,[12] the conveyance of certain values become critical.

Physician-executives must be taught leadership skills as well. Managers, according to Shortell and Kaluzny,[20] are retrospective and are involved in routine decision making that attempts to reduce uncertainty in the environment. Leaders, on the other hand, make strategic decisions, set the goals and objectives of organizations and relate to people in more intuitive and empathetic ways than do managers. Management skills are probably the key ingredient in training the successful physician-executives of the future.

Current Training Programs

Historically, physician-executives held departmental chairs and obtained managerial responsibilities by virtue of their positions within medical schools. Today, however, with the increasing corporatization of health care in both the for-profit and the nonprofit sectors, formal management training and certification are becoming de rigueur for career

advancement. Aspiring physician-executives can obtain this formal training in a variety of settings, in addition to the traditional pathway available
in established master of business administration programs.

For example, the Robert Wood Johnson Foundation, with headquarters in Princeton, New Jersey, has provided funding for the clinical
Scholars Program since 1873. Begun in 1969 by the Carnegie Corporation
and the Commonwealth Fund, the clinical scholars program was born
"because of increasing concerns about unmet needs in medical care and
socioeconomic issues affecting medicine".[21] The goals of the program is
to bring the perspective of physicians who are committed to clinical medicine to bear on the "economic, management, social and other nonbiologi-
cal aspects of medical care." One part of the nationwide program based
at the University of Pennsylvania was, in its formative stages, aligned
with the Wharton School and the Leonard Davis Institute of Health Economics. As a result of this unique emphasis, fully 20 of the 40 scholar
alumni over a ten-year period have received master of business administration degrees.[22] Nineteen of the alumni are in positions of leadership in
academic medicine and/or heading up some health-care delivery programs. On a national level, much of the research presented at the Clinical
Scholars Annual Meeting centers around health policy, economics and
health-care research. Clinical scholars are prolific contributors to the current medical management literature as well.

Similar training programs at the University of Pennsylvania, for
example, include the combined doctor of medicine/master of business
administration track available to qualified medical students as well as a
research-based doctor of philosophy program in health economics. Pen-
sylvania is helping train future teachers of physician-executives through
the National Health Care Management Center based at the Leonard
Davis Institute. In addition, current health-care managers can upgrade
their skills through "WEMBA," the Wharton executive master of business administration program. An entire spectrum of physicians with diverse backgrounds, and at different career levels, are being trained at the
University of Pennsylvania to meet the future demand for health-care
managers.

An administrative medicine program for physician-executives based
at the Center for Health Sciences at the University of Wisconsin-Madison
has been operational since 1975.[23] A 19-credit curriculum, featuring such
courses as "group practice: structure and operation," is the nucleus of
other, flexible programs similar in design to WEMBA. Busy clinicians
who cannot make a full-time, midcareer commitment can pursue this
curriculum in much the same way that corporate executives take Harvard
Business School executive seminars. The core curriculum at Wisconsin
includes current health systems; health-care management, planning and
evaluation; information sciences; values; and clinical preventive medicine. In addition, Wisconsin offers a three-week summer institute in ad-

ministrative medicine as a continuing-education program for physicians with managerial responsibilities.

The University of Colorado at Denver serves as the degree-granting institution for the Western Network for Education in Health Administration.[24] Faculty members from six cosponsoring university business schools participate in the program called the Executive Program in Health Administration. Experienced physician-executives may continue with their current responsibilities while pursuing course work through "computer conferencing and electronic case analyses." The current program involves 25 months of study with a minimum of 48 semester hours of credit. Like the Wisconsin program, the western network also sponsors a nine-day summer institute for all "health-care executives" as a continuing management education program.

Another developing program includes a new master of science in management from the Graduate School of Public Administration at New York University. Specifically geared toward physicians, this eight-course program highlights such topics as policymaking and human-resources management. This program recently received a $465,000 grant from the W.K. Kellogg Foundation to expand its course offerings.[25]

Last, as a harbinger of future efforts on the part of the for-profit sector, Family Health Plans announced a new physician fellowship program. This company is a 25-year-old California-based HMO with health plans in California and Utah and on the island of Guam. It provides services for 200,000 medical-plan members and 100,000 dental enrollees, which certainly does not rank it in the top few HMOs.[26] Nevertheless, to increase their in-house supply of medical directors and to help manage their growing number of plans, Family Health Plans started a six-month fellowship for physicians.

> The Fellowship consists of a reasonable stipend for expenses during the six months of the program and all tuition, materials and books. It is awarded on the basis of: (1) professional and academic performance, and (2) interest in and inclination toward a career in health care management. Application for the program requires a minimum of eight years of private practice experience, board certification and current medical licensure.[26]

As the HMO sector of the industry continues to grow, more companies will no doubt train their own managerial talent in much the same way as Ford or Manufacturer's Hanover does. The degree programs and continuing education seminars described here do not comprise an exhaustive listing of all training programs available for physicians seeking to become managers in the medical-industrial complex. Certainly, there are likely to be dozens of physicians pursuing graduate management degrees through traditional master of business administration and master of health administration pathways. Although the Association of University Programs in Health Admnistration (AUPHA) is responsible for overseeing and approving the academic content of these programs, a central registry detailing all the physician enrollees does not yet exist.[15]

Organization and Certification

The growth of professional societies and special recognition of their unique skills have paralleled the swelling ranks of physician-executives. Some leading professional societies that represent these physician-executives will now be described; emphasis will be placed on the development of the ACPE, mentioned earlier in this chapter. Recent survey data describing this population will also be presented. The author's contention is that such organizations mirror the development of a corporate culture for physician-executives.

The American Group Practice Assocation (AGPA) is the lobbying arm for large group practices and HMOs in Washington, D.C. In 1973, the ACPE was established so that physician-executives who were members of the AGPA could conduct their own educational programs and obtain recognition for their profession as a new medical specialty. In 1976, the Robert Wood Johnson Foundation gave ACPE a three-year, $495,000 grant to develop a curriculum to help formalize educational programs for its members.[27] As a result of this grant, the ACPE creates a standardized educational "package" called the physician-in-management seminars, or PIMS. The PIMS was subsequently divided into two sections and has been held on a yearly basis, for two weeks at a time, since 1976. New York University's graduate program in administration now grants course credit toward their master's degree for attendance at the PIMS sessions.

In addition to offering these formal programs, the ACPE continues to attract new members. This impressive membership growth, from 64 in 1975 to almost 2000 ten years later,[27] is representative of the corporatization of health care that was discussed earlier. By 1992, ACPE had 7500 members!

As the ACPE membership expanded, the organizations' educational forums became increasingly popular and better attended. The American Medical Association (AMA) officially recognized the content of the PIMS and granted the ACPE accreditation to award category 1 continuing medical education credits. This was a crucial point for the ACPE because the category 1 credits served to legitimize the role of the ACPE in the eyes of the greater medical community represented by the AMA.

By 1980, the ACPE had reached a watershed in its young history. Physician-executives had their own growing professional organization, and annual meetings were becoming important networking opportunities. The large for-profit health-care companies were actively recruiting members at these meetings because no other readily identifiable physician group was directly involved in health-care management.

By 1983, the ACPE had relocated from Falls Church, Virginia, to their present headquarters in Tampa, Florida. Requests from the private sector for on-site consultations and assistance in recruiting physician-executives led to continued growth.

Finally, in 1984, the ACPE was awarded a seat in the house of delegates of the AMA. This was another crucial step toward formal recognition of medical management as a certifiable specialty. The ACPE currently sends a representative to sit as a voting member on the Council of Medical Subspecialties (CMSS), a federation representing all fields within medicine. Clearly, the ACPE has made substantial progress toward the goal of establishing medical management as a legitimate new specialty. Perhaps the most telling aspect of this endeavor is the development of an examination, sponsored by the ACPE, that prospective members must pass before they can be regarded as "Fellows" of the ACPE. The examination, the first of its kind in this field, was part of a cooperative pilot effort between the ACPE and the National Board of Medical Examiners based in Philadelphia.

Other organizations have a part, albeit less actively, in promoting recognition and certification of physician-executives. The Medical Group Management Association (MGMA), based in Denver, has 150 physicians among its 5500 members.[28] The MGMA also offers continuing education programs in group management about 40 times each year. The association serves as the headquarters of the Center for Research in Ambulatory Health Care Administration, a center devoted to studying the structure, organization and financing of out-patient health care. The center supports an extensive library of original monographs, videotapes and primary survey data on ambulatory care. A subset of the MGMA, the Society for Physicians in Administration, helps coordinate legislative affairs and other governmental actions and reports on the developments to its membership.

The American College of Healthcare Executives (formerly the American College of Hospital Administrators), headquartered in Chicago, is allied closely with the American Hospital Association and the AUPHA. The AUPHA, mentioned briefly earlier, is the academic body responsible for overseeing the content of all health-administration-education programs (master of business administration, master of health administration) nationwide. According to Peter Weil, director of research and development at the ACHE, the organization has more than 15,000 "active associate" members; only 93 of them are listed as physicians in the organization's master membership file.[29]

The American Academy of Medical Administrators (AAMA), based in Southfield, Michigan, is another organization that sponsors continuing education programs and offers recognition of physician-executives. The AAMA, founded by a physician in 1957, bestows "fellowship" on members as they advance in their careers, but a formal verification and examination process does not yet exist. The AAMA counts 300 physicians among its 1,700 members.[30]

All these aforementioned groups, the ACPE, MGMA, ACHE and AAMA, probably share common goals and objectives as well as physician members. Currently, because the ACPE is composed exclusively of physicians, it has primacy over the other organizations. It will be fascinating to continue to monitor these groups as the number of physician-executives increases. Perhaps these groups will eventually form a federated council in much the same way as the medical subspecialists have formed the CMSS.

Current Status

Four nationwide surveys of physicians in administrative positions have been conducted during the past two years. Arthur Young and Company, in cooperation with the AMA, conducted one, while Witt Associates, an Oak Brook, Illinois, consulting firm, conducted another. In addition, two academically based reseachers have completed independent studies, one having exclusive access to the ACPE's master membership file. The author will discuss all of these surveys, to some extent, to depict as accurately as possible an image of the current status of physician-executives.

According to Thomas Phillips in Arthur Young's headquarters in New York City, they surveyed 250 physician-administrators exclusively in hospitals who were, by August 1984, chief executive officers (or in equivalent major managerial positions, such as vice-president of medical affairs). Their survey of physician hospital administrators revealed that between 1982 and 1983, there was a 27 percent increase in physicians assuming major administrative positions in hospitals.[31] According to the news release, available when the survey was made public:

> Physicians are pursuing administrative roles for a variety of reasons. Nearly 34% said they assumed administrative responsibility as part of their overall career enhancement. Still others indicated that administration provided them an "opportunity to be a policymaker, to provide top management support for medical practitioners, and because of the emerging importance of professional roles in managing the technical complexity of federal Medicare cost containment programs." Dr. Paul Torrens, chairman of Arthur Young's six member Medical Advisory Board, and Professor of Health Services Administration at the University of California, Los Angeles' School of Public Health, attributed the shifting of physicians to administrative positions, in part, to hospital cost pressures. Recently enacted government regulations limiting hospital cost reimbursement for treatment

of Medicare patients is forcing hospitals to implement cost cutting efficiencies in medical care delivery and is placing a demand on physicians to curb unnecessary procedures.[31]

In addition, the Arthur Young survey found that 80.7 percent of the physicians reported directly to the board of trustees. More than 70 percent reported that the board "felt more comfortable" with a physician-administrator than with a lay director.

Witt Associates conducted their market survey by comparing hospital-based medical directors with HMO medical directors. Using their own placement files, they surveyed 90 physicians in early 1986. The profile of the average hospital medical director, according to Witt, is that of a 55-year-old Board-certified (82 percent) internist (37 percent) with only a doctor of medicine degree (95 percent) who attends meetings of the board of trustees but does not actually have a vote (53 percent).[32]

The average HMO medical director has a similar profile in that the compensation package is in excess of $105,000, but the average HMO medical director is younger, and fully 10 percent of them have an advanced degree, such as a master of business administration, health administration or public health. As the size of the institutions increased, so did their likelihood of having an appointed, full-time medical director.

David Kindig, the director of the previously described Wisconsin program in administrative medicine, reported the results of his survey at the 1986 annual national meeting of the ACPE in Monterey, California. Kindig used the AMA's master membership file and culled 13,000 physicians who stated, on earlier job surveys, that they spend more than 50 percent of their time doing major administrative tasks. He interviewed a sample of 878 of these physicians by telephone in late 1985. Fully 13 percent of this sample were members of the ACPE, a finding that supports the argument for the primacy of this group in comparison to other organizations. On the basis of almost 900 interviews, Kindig reported that 30 percent of the physicians are hospital directors, 24 percent direct "educational institutions," 23 percent direct governmental (Veterans Administration) and military organizations, 1 percent run HMOs and the remainder are scattered throughout group practices, clinics and the like.[33]

Kathleen Montgomery, at the time a sociology doctoral candidate at New York University, conducted probably the most thorough survey of physician-executives because she was given exclusive access to the ACPE's master membership file. She surveyed all members of the ACPE in September 1984 and obtained an impressive 80 percent response rate for a total study population of 1029. She then compared her population with the AMA's managers from Kindig's work.[34]

She found that the ACPE membership was, on average, younger than the physicians in Kindig's survey. More than 50 percent of the ACPE's membership were spending more than 67 percent of their time solely on management-related issues, as compared to only 31 percent of their time just five years earlier.

Montgomery found the organizational distribution of the respondents to be of interest because 33 percent were in multispecialty medical groups. These two settings, together with military installations, accounted for almost 60 percent of the ACPE's total membership distribution.

Montgomery's survey confirmed the compensation prackages described in the work from Witt Associates. Last, the leading current job titles for the ACPE's members were categorized as medical director (27 percent), vice-president of medical affairs (15 percent) and medical directors of a department (12 percent). These job descriptions are important because they often accurately reflect the true level of managerial responsibility within an organization.

Physician-executives have many outlets for officially organizing, certifying and maintaning their management skills. The results of the surveys desribed here depict a vibrant and eclectic group of professionals. The surveys are, however, a snapshot in time, and the developing picture is not yet clearly focused. The remainder of the chapter will speculate about the future roles of physician-executives to help focus the final image.

The Future Challenge

We have reviewed some of the major forces that are shaping the current health-care industry, such as corporatization and competition. The emergence of a new specialist—the physician-executive—has been documented. The educational needs of these new managers, and the programs available for fulfilling those needs, have been described. What part will physician-executives play in the future of the health-care industry? What are the major challenges that these new specialists will face as they seek to legitimize their role in the medical hierarchy?

According to one major future-oriented study of the health-care industry (1) physicians will experience slower growth in income and more standardization of their practice behavior; (2) more physicians will practice in organized, salaried settings; (3) physicians who continue in private practice will do so in well-managed groups; and (4) the trend toward managed health care—integration of hospitals *and* physicians into larger, more powerful and more business-oriented units—will continue strongly.[35]

It appears that many of these predictions are already becoming reality. The AMA estimates that almost 40 percent of all practicing physicians under 36 years of age are in salaried positions, and the movement of such physicians toward employment in large organizations made front-page news in the *Wall Street Journal*.[36]

As the delivery of health care becomes more bureaucratized, there will be an acute need for physician-executives to manage the practices of other, employed physicians. In a survey conducted by the American Hospital Administration (AHA), the average nonfederal, short-term, general acute-care hospital employed 3.9 physicians in full time or part-time paid administrative positions as of January 1, 1984.[37] This finding represents a dramatic shift because in 1973, only 4 percent of hospitals reported compensating any physicians for administrative activities.

To meet these managerial challenges, some observers believe that three levels of physician-executives will evolve.[38] "Top physician-executives" will make decisions that directly affect hospitals or their medical staff. They will be responsible for the clinical and managerial activities performed by all subordinate physicians in the hospital. "Middle physician-executives" will make decisions that directly affect activities at departmental levels. "First-line physician-executives" will make decisions that directly affect programs or managerial activities within departments. The roles of all three levels may be stressful because "although not viewed as 'full' clinicians, [they] are expected to perform not only interpersonal roles but also informational roles such as spokesman and disseminator, and the role of negotiator on behalf of their colleagues."[38]

Another important challenge to physician-executives will be to improve on strategic decision-making by hospitals. As Kovner and Chin have demonstrated, strategic orientation of physician-leaders was low in the hospitals that they studied.

> Physician leaders in these hospitals were primarily concerned with their private practices and did not identify with the strategic concerns of hospital officials . . . they tended to see the interests of the hospital from the viewpoint of independent practitioners rather than as hospital clinical managers.[39]

Physician-executives must act as a liaison; they must speak both the language of management and the language of clinical medicine.

Nowhere is this "liaison" role more important than in the developing partnerships between academic medical centers and for-profit health-care companies. Traditionally, the leadership of academic health centers has consisted of "the four horsemen of the apocalypse," including departmental chairmen, the dean of the medical school, the vice-president for health affairs and the teaching-hospital director.[40] The management skills of these physician-executives will be tested as their institutions merge with large for-profit chains.

In a recent conference titled "The Investor-Related Academic Health Center and Medical Education—An Uncertain Courtship," representatives from medical schools, voluntary hospitals and for-profit firms gathered to discuss methods by which they may structure future relationships.[41] Teaching hospitals need huge capital influxes to remodel their aging physcial plants, while for-profit companies seek to develop centers of excellence and to continue to foster vertical integration of services. Recently, the directors of for-profit teaching hospitals were accepted as voting members into the Council of Teaching Hospitals (COTH), an important policymaking body of the AAMC.[42]

As prospective reimbursement for all hospital services becomes more widespread, the merging of clinical and financial data will become increasingly important. Physician-executives will be called on, by virtue of their special skills, to help forge this amalgam of disparate information systems. Evidence is already accumulating that greater participation by physicians in managerial decision making may be associated with lower costs and higher quality of care.[43] Researchers have begun to focus on the internal organization of hospitals as important components of the overall cost equation.[44]

In conclusion, the traditional hospital arrangement with total separation of administration and clinical matters is becoming rapidly obsolete.[45] Physician-executives will emerge with legitimately defined organizational roles, recognition as certifiable specialists[15,46] and the necessary expertise to bring a new managerial rationality to the nation's largest industry, the health-care enterprise.

REFERENCES

1. Levey S, Hesse DD: Bottom-line health care? *N Engl J Med* 312(10):644–647, 1985.
2. Califano JA: A corporate Rx for America—Managing runaway health costs. *Issues Sci Technol,* Spring 1986, p 81–90.
3. Relman AS: The medical-industrial complex. *N Engl J Med* 303(17):963–970, 1980.
4. Thurow LC: Medicine versus economics. *N Engl J Med* 313(10):611–614, 1985.
5. Goldsmith J: Death of a paradigm: The challenge of competition. *Health Affairs,* Fall 1984, p 6–19.
6. Starr P: *The Social Transformation of American Medicine.* New York, Basic Books, 1982.
7. Tarlov A: Shattuck lecture—The increasing supply of physicians, the changing structure of the health-services system, and the future practice of medicine. *N Engl M Jed* 308(20):1235–1244, 1983.
8. Ginzberg E: The monetarization of medical care. *N Engl J Med* 310(18):1162–1165, 1984.
9. Ebert RH, Brown SS: Academic health centers. *N Engl J Med* 308(20):1200–1208, 1983.
10. Rogers DE, Blendon RJ: The academic medical center today. *Ann Intern Med* 100(5):751–754, 1984.
11. Sheps CG: Implementing change with the academic/medical center. *Bull NY Acad Med* 61(2):175–183, 1985.
12. Heyssel RM, Gaintner JR, Kues IW, et al: Decentralized management in a teaching hospital. *N Engl J Med* 310(22):1477–1480, 1984.

13. Alper PR: The new language of hospital management. *N Engl J Med* 311(19):1249–1251, 1984.

14. Himmelstein DU, Woolhandler S: Cost without benefit—Administrative waste in U.S. health care. *N Engl J Med* 314(7):441–445, 1986.

15. Hillman AL, Nash DB, Kissick WL, Martin SP: Managing the medical-industrial complex. *N Engl J Med* 315(8):511–513, 1986.

16. Nash DB, Haught JH, Hopkins A: Capital payment under PPS: Can hospitals still bloom? *Healthcare Finan Manage,* 40(40):29–37, April 1986.

17. Finkler SA: The distinction between costs and charges. *Ann Intern Med* 96(1):102–109, 1982.

18. Cameron JM: The indirect costs of graduate medical education. *N Engl J Med* 312(19):1233—21238, 1985.

19. Clinical Efficacy Assessment Program (CEAP). Philadelphia, American College of Physicians.

20. Shortell SM, Kaluzny AD: *Health Care Management—A Text in Organization Theory and Behavior.* New York, John Wiley & Sons, 1983.

21. Shuster AL, Cluff LE, Haynes MA, et al: An innovation in physician training: The clinical scholars program. *J Med Educ* 58:101–111, 1983.

22. Interim Report to Princeton. Director, Robert Wood Johnson Clinical Scholars Program, University of Pennsylvania, 1985.

23. Detmer D, Noren J: An administrative medicine program for clinician-executives. *J Med Educ* 56:640–645, 1981.

24. The Executive Program in Health Administration. Berkeley, Calif, Western Network for Education in Heath Administration.

25. Untitled. *AMA News,* April 4, 1986.

26. News release (undated). FHP, Fountain Valley, Calif.

27. AAMD celebrates 10 years of growth and achievement. *Med Direct* 11(3): 17–21, 1985.

28. Robischon T: Physicians as managers: A look at the issues. *Medicenter Manage,* September 1985, p 51–55.

29. Weil P: Personal communication, March 18, 1986.

30. O'Donovan T: Personal communication, March 7, 1986.

31. Young A: Trend towards doctor administrators fueled by hospital cost pressures, New release, December 19, 1984, Arthur Young Press Information, New York, NY.

32. Lloyd J: Remarks at the annual National Meeting of the American Academy of Medical Directors, Monterey, Calif, May 15, 1986.

33. Friedman E: Physician-administrators making a comeback. *Med World News* 27(12):34–43, 1986.

34. Montgomery K: Remarks at the annual National Meeting of the American Academy of Medical Directors, Monterey, Calif, May 15, 1986.

35. The health care system in the mid-1990s. A study conducted for the Health Insurance Association of America by Arthur D. Little, January 1985.

36. Wessel D: More young doctors shun private practice, work as employees. *The Wall Street Journal,* January 13, 1986, p 1.

37. Morrisey MA, Brooks DC: Physician influence in hospitals: An update. *Hospitals,* September 1, 1985. p 86–89.

38. Ruelas E, Leatt P: The roles of physician-executives in hospitals: A framework for management education. *J Health Admin Educ* 3(2), part 1: Spring 1985, p 151–169.

39. Kovner AR, Chin MJ: Physician leadership in hospital strategic decision making. *Hosp Health Serv Admin,* November/December 1985, p 64–79.

40. Wilson MP, McLaughlin CP: *Leadership and Management in Academic Medicine.* San Francisco, Jossey-Bass, 1984.

41. Teaching hospitals a target for chains. *AMA News,* March 8, 1985, p 1.
42. For-profit hospitals allowed in AAMC council. *AMA News,* November 15, 1985, p 17.
43. Shortell SM, Evashwick C: The structural configuration of U.S. hospital medical staffs. *Med Care* 19(4):419–430, 1981.
44. Sloan FA, Becker ER: Internal organization of hospitals and hospital costs. *Inquiry* 18:224–239, 1981.
45. Shortell SM: The medical staff of the future: Replanting the garden. *Frontiers Health Serv Manage,* 1(3):3–28, 1985.
46. Health Care Management Review interviews physician administrator leaders. *HCMR,* Fall 1984, p 81–91.

CHAPTER 10

THE FUTURE OF PRIMARY CARE AND FAMILY PRACTICE

Robert B. Taylor

If we have learned anything from history, it is that we must use our resources wisely. We currently struggle to clear pollution from rivers and lakes we once assumed would be clean forever; the oil shortages a few years ago taught us to conserve our fossil fuels; and we are learning the painful lesson that, whether we like it or not, future health care will be rationed in various ways, only one of which is according to the ability to pay for services.

Physicians who have been in practice for two decades or more have seen the time when annual chest radiographs were considered part of good health maintenance, when repair of a simple inguinal hernia necessitated a week-long stay in the hospital, and when a patient with indigestion could self-refer to a gastroenterologist. Those days are over, not only because of new scientific data, but because of profound modifications in how health care is paid for. What is behind these changes? One important factor is government, with its current emphasis on cost-containment and deficit reduction. Another factor influencing change is the intrusion of corporations into the health-care delivery system. As Starr[1] wrote: "By making health care lucrative for providers, public financing made it exceedingly attractive to investors and set in motion the formation of large scale corporate enterprises." Attorneys, judges, plaintiffs and courts have forced physicians into defensive postures and contributed in a major way to the cost of caring for patients with even the most simple illnesses. Hospitals have also exerted an influence as they compete fiercely for the pool of available patients to fill empty beds. Other players include insurance companies, drug manufacturers and, of course, physicians and patients.

The course of these changes already set in motion, as will be traced throughout this chapter, appears to be an incipient reversal of resources in which, for largely economic reasons, control of the health-care system will move from specialists with limited expertise to providers with the broadest skills—primary-care physicians.

WHAT IS PRIMARY CARE?

The term *primary care* means different things to different people. Most would agree with the description proposed by Alpert,[2] which represents an amalgamation of previous definitions:[3-7]

> Primary care can be defined as being within the personal rather than the public health system, and is therefore focused on the health needs of individuals and families—it is family-oriented. Primary care is "first-contact" care, and thus should be separated from secondary care and tertiary care, which are based on referral rather than initial contact. Primary care assumes longitudinal responsibility for the patient regardless of the presence or absence of disease. The primary care physician holds the contract for providing personal health services over a period of time. Specifically, primary care is neither limited to the course of a single episode of illness nor confined to the ambulatory setting. It serves as the "integrationist" for the patient. When other health resources are involved, the primary care physician retains the coordinating role. He or she cares for as many of the patient's problems as possible, and, where referral is indicated, fulfills his longitudinal responsibility as the integrationist.

Petersdorf[8] incorporated Alpert's basic principles by defining primary care as that provided by "a physician of first contact, who provides continuing comprehensive care, employing referrals to other physicians when appropriate and who orchestrates the health care team and often acts as the patient's personal advisor."

In 1977, the Institute of Medicine of the National Academy of Sciences proposed a checklist for primary care that included five elements: accessibility, comprehensiveness, coordination, continuity and accountability.[9]

Thus, according to this constellation of definitions, a patient with epigastric distress would make their first contact with a primary-care provider who, in most instances, would be able to employ the full spectrum of evaluation and management of the complaint. However, if the complaint were beyond the scope of primary care, it would be the responsibility of the "integrationist" primary-care physician to secure consultation or referral—perhaps a gastroenterologist or a surgeon—while keeping in contact with the patient, and perhaps the family, to ensure that optimal care is provided at every step through the health-care system and that such care is provided in a humane, ethical and cost-effective manner.

Who Practices Primary Care?

Weiner and Starfield[10] reviewed care provided to 16,000 patients by more than 90 percent of the licensed physicians in the city of Baltimore and distinguished among four types of visits: first contact visit, referral visit, specialized-care visit and principal-care visit. They concluded that "as a group, primary care physicians included general and family physicians, pediatricians, and general internists. General surgeons and obstetrician/gynecologists have characteristics of both primary care and specialist care. All other physician groups have characteristics of specialists." Thus, for the purposes of this chapter, physicians providing primary care are considered to be practitioners in family practice, general pediatrics and general internal medicine.

It is important to recognize that each of these disciplines is a specialty in its own right; each requires a minimum of three years of residency and has an independent certification Board. Table 1 shows the characteristics of these primary-care specialties, including current numbers of practitioners and manpower projections for the year 2000, according to the American Medical Association (AMA) Center for Health Policy Research.[11]

The term *specialist* is problematic because there is, to say the least, ambiguity concerning its use. Certainly, family physicians, general internists and general pediatricians are generalists in the broad sense of the word. Yet when it comes to talking about medical specialties, they are "specialists" in their various "specialties." A useful distinction is as follows: Family practice, general internal medicine and general pediatrics

TABLE 10.1
CHARACTERISTICS OF PRIMARY-CARE SPECIALTIES

Characteristics	Family practice	Internal medicine	Pediatrics
Number of residency years	3	3	3
Projected change in physician supply by the year 2000*	+3.1% (GP/FP)	−2.4% (Gen IM)	−31.8% (All pediatrics)
Current number of practitioners†	68,275	93,920	39,786

*From Reference 11.
†According to AMA data, 1991.

are specialties *in breadth,* just as ophthalmology and neurosurgery are specialties *in depth.*

To encourage precision in the use of words, all physicians practicing specialties for which certifying Boards exist will be considered "specialists," whether they function as generalists or whether they pursue more narrow fields of medical endeavor.

Is it appropriate to define family practice, general pediatrics and general internal medicine as specialties? Or, for instance, is family practice simply a little bit of this and that, and general pediatrics simply family practice limited to one age group? Does limiting one's expertise to the "bread-and-butter" aspects of a broad spectrum of generally common health problems constitute a specialty? General pediatrics has the greatest comfort in answering yes, standing on its claim of treating only infants and children (despite recent efforts to expand its horizons to include teenagers and "families"). General internal medicine, now broadening the scope of its primary-care training to include aspects of dermatology, gynecology and psychiatry, would seem to have a less secure claim on specialty status. Since its designation as a formal discipline in 1969, family practice has wrestled with defining a specific body of knowledge unique to the specialty.

If primary-care physicians are "specialists," what shall nonprimary-care physicians be called? The term *limited specialist* is descriptive and accurately delineates that such physicians have chosen to limit their scope of expertise; the disadvantage is that this designation requires the use of two words when one might do. The author prefers and will use the term *subspecialist,* which has the advantage of being a single word that connotes that practitioners limit their expertise to a subset of medical knowledge.

In day-by-day medical practice, there can be no doubt that there are "usual and customary" divisions of problems managed by primary-care physicians and by subspecialists. For example, a busy ophthalmologist is not the physician of choice for managing uncomplicated conjunctivitis; a five-year-old child with acute otitis media is probably best treated by a family physician or a general pediatrician; and most cases of peptic ulcer disease are most appropriately managed by general internists or family physicians (only recalcitrant or complicated cases should be referred to subspecialists).

The semantic problems of defining primary-care specialists probably arise from attempts to squeeze general medical disciplines into traditional specialty definitions, which are usually limited to a body organ (e.g., nephrology), a disease process (e.g., oncology), an age group (e.g., pediatrics) or a new technology (e.g., radiology). Instead, primary-care physicians are specialists in their respective fields by virtue of their *process* of patient care, which involves accessibility, comprehensiveness, coordination, continuity and accountability. When we in medicine learn to be comfortable with definitions of specialty status on the basis of the process of care involved, the debates regarding what is and is not a specialty will have been laid to rest.

Who Chooses Primary Care As a Specialty?

Taylor[12] presented comments from primary-care physicians and subspecialists that give insight into the types of physician who choose various specialties. Primary-care physicians report that they enjoy "working with people," like variety in their work activities and have a high tolerance for undiagnosed problems and multiple symptoms. Subspecialists tend to enjoy "taking care of people" (which is quite different from *working with* people), prefer a narrow scope of professional expertise and are most satisfied with action-oriented curative activities. Primary-care physicians indicate more interest in being involved in their patients' lives on a continuing basis than do subspecialists.

Students who choose residencies in primary-care fields are often from rural areas and enter medical school intending to practice in rural and underserved areas.[13] Decisions to enter primary-care specialties are also influenced by experiences in physician offices, role models and the content of medical school curricula. Some students feel obligated by scholarship commitments to choose primary-care service. In graduate medical education, important considerations are the content of residency training programs and the numbers and types of positions available. Factors relating to practice or the health-care system that tend to encourage physicians to enter the primary-care field include the organized support of professional organizations, such as the American Academy of Family Physicians; and the prospect of a position being available on completion of training in a market in which there is an increasing need for primary-care physicians.

What Are the Settings for Primary Care?

Most physicians would agree on what constitutes tertiary care—the technologically complex services chiefly available at medical centers. There is less unanimity of opinion regarding what is involved in secondary care; thus, the term is seldom used. A definition might be derived from Andreopoulos:[14] secondary care involves outpatient services of a subspecialist nature and inpatient services provided in a community hospital or a similar facility. Thus, a 22-year-old man with right lower-quadrant pain who is referred to a surgeon and receives an appendectomy at his community hospital has received secondary care.

Primary care, as defined by Andreopoulos,[14] is "where the health care is entered and basic services received and where all health services are mobilized and coordinated." In contrast to secondary and tertiary care, primary care is generally delivered to a smaller population, is physically closer to the community and its people and is easily identifiable and quickly responsive.

The primary-care system and its practitioners manage most illnesses in most patients. Figure 1 shows a health-status continuum that ranges from no disease to terminal disease leading to death. Throughout this continuum, primary care is the *usual* level of management required, although, from time to time, patients and primary-care providers make use of secondary-care or tertiary-care services to meet specific needs. For example, a middle-aged man with symptoms suggestive of a brain tumor may require tertiary-care services, such as neurosurgical consultation. On obtaining a favorable consultation report, the primary-care provider will continue independent management of the patient's symptoms.

The primary/secondary/tertiary health-care model is far from perfect. I practice in a family medicine center that is part of an academic medical center. I receive regular referrals from colleagues in neurosurgery and vascular surgery, and hence a disproportionate number of my patients have brain tumors and advanced arteriosclerotic vascular disease. Am I really practicing primary care? Certainly the demography of my practice is profoundly influenced by my working in a "medical center" setting. I believe that I am providing a tertiary level of primary care. In contrast, Fletcher and associates[15] reviewed the records of patients treated at a medical polyclinic where generalists and subspecialists of internal medicine practiced together and found that the prevalence of disease in their patients was much higher than in patients who received office-based primary care. They concluded that "although the data indicate these patients' need for accessibility, comprehensiveness, coordination, and continuity is at least as great as patients receiving primary care, this clinic is most appropriately described as a secondary care facility."[15]

Primary care is rendered not only in physicians' offices and hospitals, but also in schools, health departments, community-health and migrant-health centers, dental-health centers, work-site clinics, school health clinics, nursing homes and at homes. In addition to physicians and physician-extenders, primary-care providers include community-health nurses, nurse-midwives, nutritionists, pharmacists, podiatrists, health educators, optometrists and family members.[16] Thus, according to Table 2, patients receive primary care as long as care is provided by themselves, family members or primary-care providers, and they enter the secondary or tertiary health-care system only on admission to a hospital or on referral to subspecialists.

CURRENT HEALTH ISSUES

A number of issues are currently evolving that promise to have profound impact on primary care of the future, including the continuing surplus of subspecialist physicians, a constellation of economic charges and the entry of corporation into the health-care delivery system.

Optimal health / No disease	Disease exposure	Subclinical disease	Disease symptoms	Symptoms and signs	Morbidity/ disability	Terminal disease
NATURAL HISTORY OF DISEASE						
Primary care			TYPE OF CARE			Secondary and tertiary care
Least costly care			COST OF CARE			Most costly care
Health promotion	Disease prevention and anticipatory guidance	Health screening	Disease diagnosis and management	Chronic care	Critical care	Terminal care
HEALTH CARE INTERVENTIONS						

Figure 10.1 Continuum of health and health care.

TABLE 10.2
CHARACTERISTICS OF TYPES OF CARE

Characteristic	Type of care		
	Primary	Secondary	Tertiary
1. Focus of care	Broad	Intermediate	Narrow
2. Population served	Small	Intermediate	Large
3. Types of problems	Common	Uncommon	Complex/rare
4. Type of care	Continuous	Episodic	Discontinuous
5. Dominant practice base	Community	Hospital	Medical center
6. Technology	Basic	Complex	Innovative
7. Approach	Integrationist	Consultant	Referral

Physician Supply

Table 1 showed projected specialty growth of primary-care physicians by the year 2000. There is a growing consensus that the United States health-care system should, like that of Canada and the United Kingdom, be built (or rebuilt) on a strong primary-care base. To achieve this aim, a goal of 50 percent of United States medical school graduates entering primary-care has been endorsed by the Council on Graduate Medical Education, the Bureau of Health Professions, the Federated Council for Internal Medicine and the American Academy of Family Physicians (AAFP).[17] Advocates are hopeful that the 50-percent goal can be met through changes in medical school curricular emphasis, bonuses for those who enter primary care and increased income to primary-care specialists owing to physician payment reform.

The 50 percent primary care goal must be tempered by the realities of graduate medical education. A large number of first-year residents in medicine and pediatric residencies will, eight to 10 years later, be subspecialists in renal disease or rheumatology. For this reason, the AAFP advocates that half the 50 percent be family physicians; virtually all graduates of family practice residencies go on to provide primary care family practice.

Health-Care Cost Containment

Health-care costs now consume 12 percent of the U.S. gross national product. For American businesses, health benefits constitute 8.3 percent of wages and salaries, and 56.4 percent of pretax corporate profits.[18] When the control of health-care dollars was largely in the hands of physicians, patients and insurance companies, there were restrained efforts to control health-care costs. However, the high costs of medical procedures would only be passed from physician to insurance company to subscriber, with greater profits for the former two. Currently, as a result of increased federal emphasis on cost-containment and the growing involvement of corporations in health-care delivery, forceful efforts are being made to contain health-care costs. One reason is greater competition for health-care dollars. Currently, the ratio of physicians to the general population is 1:500. Furthermore, the physician census is increasing three times faster than the number of potential patients (i.e., the U.S. population).[19] Thus, to maintain physician incomes at historic levels would require substantial growth in personal income, a shift of expenditures from other goods and services to health care or a shift of the "health-care dollar" from hospitals and other providers to physicians. The current economic and political climate—slow economic growth and growing opposition to higher medical expenditures—makes it difficult to envision either of the first two taking place; nor do I believe the third option likely to occur.

The federal government continues to influence health-care funding in a number of ways. Medicare reimbursement reform is now underway and includes the goals of making physician payments to various specialists more equitable, controlling costs, improving access to services and assuring quality care.[20] Although primary-care physicians appear to be winners rather than losers in the process, conversion-factor reductions and the realities of the ultimate regulations have led many to conclude that generalists gained, at best, a limited victory.

A system of health-care cost containment is quietly evolving (but is potentially threatening) through the use of clinical practice guidelines. The Agency for Health Care Policy and Research (AHCPR), created by the Omnibus Budget Reconciliation Act of 1989, is charged to develop, disseminate and evaluate clinical practice guidelines under the sponsorship of the agency's Forum for Quality and Effectiveness in Health Care. From this agency has come a committee report that describes and advocates practice guidelines for health-care providers (e.g., the appropriate therapy for pharyngitis or cholecystitis).[21] The current interest in practice guidelines springs from increasing health-care costs and apparent geographic differences in how various problems are managed. Jackson and Nutting[22] report that, "The emphasis on development of practice guidelines has . . . created an environment of concern among physicians, who fear loss of control over their clinical decisions, and high expectations among health policy makers and third party payers, who anticipate a panacea for the crisis of spiraling costs."

Corporate Medicine
Currently, half of all practicing physicians conduct at least part of their professional activities through a health maintenance organization (HMO).[23] Projections that by 2000 more than half the health-care system will be controlled by some 10 to 20 conglomerates may not be far off target. There will, of course, be regional HMOs, and there will always be the hardy phalanx of independent practitioners and small partnerships,

especially in rural areas. However, a growing number of for-profit corporations have been attracted to the health-care field by its potential for high earnings, and such corporate giants are becoming brokers of health-care services. They, figuratively, may begin with little more than an office. They solicit physicians who agree to provide services to their clients at reduced fees, with the implicit threat that physicians who do not participate will see their patients switch to physicians who do participate. Corporate brokers then go to other corporations and sell the services of participating physicians on a capitated basis and at a presumably substantial profit for themselves. In an effort to help assure a profit, the managed care brokers provide incentives for participating physicians—incentives that encourage them to render less care, not more. Of course, such physicians are placed in the delicate ethical dilemma of having a vested interest when determining whether expensive tests are needed. Also, there seems to be little concern that the brokerage system generally excludes indigent patients, who are forced to seek care at "charity" hospitals, which are increasingly competing for funds with HMOs and other conglomerates for their own survival.

Despite the aspects of such delivery systems that physicians may find abhorrent—corporate decision making, rationing of care and systematic exclusion of indigent persons from the health-care system—the "coming of the corporation" is likely to be the force that catapults primary-care physicians into a position of control in the delivery of health care, as will be discussed later.

FORCES SHAPING PRIMARY CARE

In addition to the physician surplus, economic issues and corporate medicine, other forces promise to shape primary care of the future.

Government

The federal government has actively encouraged training and placement of primary-care physicians. Training grants are available to primary care residency programs, and the National Health Service Corp has attempted to place physicians whom it has sponsored in areas of need. It seems likely that state and federal governments will continue to provide support, because there is broad-based public support for primary care.

One aspect of federal financing seems to work against primary care, however. With the current decrease in federal funding of all domestic programs, primary-care training will need financial support from other sources to maintain its programs. An important source of funding is research, and the chief source of health-research dollars is the National Institutes of Health. There is no institute for primary care, and research expenditures through the National Institutes of Health are generally disease-oriented; token amounts are given to the types of research generally done in primary care: health promotion, disease prevention, epidemiology and health outcomes of ambulatory-care decisions. Thus, continuing federal support of primary-care training programs may mandate a shift in research support to favor these aspects of health care.

Legal System: Attorneys, Judges, Plaintiffs and Courts

The legal system in general and professional liability awards in particular are shaping all aspects of medicine. Common causes of litigation include improper treatment related to birth, failure to diagnose cancer, failure to diagnose fracture or dislocation, improper treatment and drug side effects, failure to diagnose pregnancy problems and failure to diagnose infection. These problems are not related to open heart surgery; rather, they can arise in day-to-day office practice. A continuing controversy in family practice involves the unconscionably high malpractice-insurance premiums charged to perform obstetrics. Many family physicians trained to provide obstetric services to their patients are being forced, for economic reasons, to give up that aspect of their practices. Similar problems arise with regard to providing care of fractures, treating patients in coronary care units and performing or assisting in surgery. There are state and federal efforts underway to provide legislative reform. Weiler[24] reports that "although a variety of new statutory rules have reduced the formal legal rights of patient-victims, the legislative effort has thus far produced only modest relief for physicians."

A current tactic of the legal community seems to be to convince the public that attorneys provide protection against the many malpracticing physicians now treating patients. Furthermore, our hopes for legislative reform must be realistic in view of the fact that most legislators are attorneys, and, when their legislative days are over, they will make their living practicing law.

Hospitals

Because cost-containment efforts by the federal government and corporate medicine are aimed at moving patients out of expensive hospital beds, most hospitals are now making retrenchments. Entire floors are being closed, nurses and other ancillary personnel are being laid off and even some hospital administrators are finding that their jobs are in jeopardy. In an effort to keep their doors open and beds full, hospitals are resorting to an ingenious array of devices, including support groups for everything from anorexics and overeaters and potential child abusers to panic-attack victims. There are free screening examinations, tours of new facilities and booths at health fairs. What is even more pertinent for primary care is that hospitals are opening their own ambulatory-care units and extending their primary-care services into the community. In an effort to ensure a continuing flow of referrals, many hospitals are "buying" existing primary-care practices. On one hand, this approach represents direct competition with established primary-care physicians. On the other hand, it offers opportunities for practice in primary care. However one views the expanded role of hospitals in primary care, it must be seen as important—that is, hospitals have recognized that each needs its own loyal group of primary-care physicians to help fill beds and to support technologic services. This can only be seen as a favorable influence on primary care.

Ambivalence of the Public Toward Science and Technology

Our university hospital performed its first liver transplant a few years ago. Coincidence or not, that well-publicized event was followed by a spurt in the number of primary-care clinic visits and hospital admissions. Americans are intrigued by the new technology that seems to reinforce the belief that there is help for the most desperate situation if only the right expert can be found and enough money is available. Nonetheless, patients and physicians alike know that the funds that support a single heart transplant would do infinitely more good for more people if they were spent on immunizations or antismoking education. The cost of keeping one artificial heart recipient alive for several months could feed whole villages in Africa for months. In addition, there is a paradoxic distrust of technology and technologists, and patients are looking for a friend, or an advocate, to help guide them through the system.

As Graner[25] pointed out: "American medicine has from its inception chosen the abstract concept of 'science' as a means of obtaining social recognition. . . . Since the late 19th century, science has continued to enjoy unquestioned legitimacy, but social opinion seems recently to have taken a new, less amiable turn. Although most still realize the benefits of medical research, humanistic access to those benefits is perceived as being difficult, if not impossible, to achieve."

This ambivalence toward science and technology represents an opportunity for primary-care physicians to attain fully the integrationist role described by Alpert.[2]

Patients

When considering influences on primary care, we must never lose sight of the fact that most people seem to want a single physician who will be their friend, advocate and key provider of health-care services. They are looking for a physician who can be a liaison with subspecialists, but who will provide the longitudinal care that can ensure that all important bases are touched. In short, most people, consciously or unconsciously, search for a generic "family doctor."

Our family medicine center has an urgent-care wing, which was opened to allow patients and employees at the medical center to seek prompt, affordable care for common problems. The urgent-care unit has been very successful in providing care to patients who, at least temporarily, need convenient access without asking "Who's on duty?" It has also been a useful device for recruiting patients into the family medicine center because, after a few visits, a doctor-patient bond forms and patients become "regulars" and seek their own physician by appointment when possible.

The primary-care movement arose in the late 1960s in reaction to the perceived fragmentation of health-care services. There is strong public sentiment supporting primary care (despite the paradox that greater prestige and income are currently accorded subspecialists), and this continuing public support will be a favorable influence in times of increased competition during the coming years.

TRENDS IN PRIMARY CARE

Three current trends promise to shape primary care over the next decade. There is a growing tendency to provide more and more care in the office and at home. Primary-care physicians will be competing not only with subspecialists, but also with other types of practitioners in efforts to solidify their patient base. Also, the shift to ambulatory care and the greater competition for patients will take place in a setting of capitated care, with primary-care physicians as the case managers.

Ambulatory Care

Although primary care is not synonymous with ambulatory care (e.g., many hospitalized patients receive care from their primary-care physicians), most primary care is rendered in an out-patient setting. As cost-containment efforts and diagnosis-related groups move more patients from hospitals to ambulatory-care settings, primary care will become even more office-based. There will be an increased tendency to move technology from hospitals to physicians' offices, and one example will be the use of radiologic services. Problems for which yesterday's primary-care physician might have referred patients to hospital radiology departments will be diagnosed by radiologic procedures in an office "down the hall."

Thus, family physicians who have long performed obstetrics, circumcision and sigmoidoscopy are now also undertaking colposcopy, obstetric ultrasound, flexible sigmoidoscopy and fiberoptic nasopharyngoscopy.[26,27] Some family physicians are performing cesarean sections, colonoscopy and upper gastrointestinal endoscopy.

Competition

Although there is a shortage of primary-care physicians in most areas of the U.S., there is no lack of subspecialists. The oversupply of subspecialists has been eloquently described by Petersdorf:[28]

In the communities with which I am familiar, there are few electrocardiograms in search of cardiologists to read them, there is only a rare belch wanting a gastroenterologist, and there is not a single, even slightly plugged coronary that does not have three surgeons waiting in the wings. Moreover, the specialists are young, since specialty training programs are, for the most part, a creation of the 1960s and 70s, and most of them will be in practice a long time.

General and family physicians see 29.8 percent of all ambulatory visits; general internal medicine 11.4 percent and pediatricians 12.6 percent[29] (Table 3). Subspecialists eye these numbers covetously and, as will be discussed, there is a dangerous tendency for subspecialists to dabble in primary care.

Competition will come from other sources as well, including middle-level practitioners such as physicians' assistants and nurse-practitioners. According to the AMA,[30] "The assistant to the primary care physician is a person qualified by academic and clinical training to provide patient care services under the supervision of a licensed physician in a wide variety of medical care settings which are involved in the delivery of primary health care." There seems to be little disagreement that physicians' assistants provide good-quality care and that they are well accepted by physicians and patients. The key phrase is "under the supervision of a licensed physician," thus indicating that physicians' assistants will continue to be part of the physician-directed segment of our health-care system and will continue to be an extension of physicians' services, rather than a competing force.

Physicians' relationships with nurses may become more competitive. Nurses envision a "joint relationship with the physician":[31]

TABLE 10.3
NUMBER OF OFFICE VISITS (IN THOUSANDS) TO ALL PHYSICIANS AND PRIMARY-CARE PHYSICIANS BY REFERRAL STATUS AND PRIOR VISIT STATUS, 1989

Visit characteristics	All specialties	G/FP	PD	IM
Total	692,702	206,301	87,411	78,816
Referral status				
Referred by another physician	37,643	3,712	1,335	2,706
Not referred by another physician	655,059	202,589	86,076	76,110
Prior visit status				
New patient	114,855	29,881	9,942	12,336
Old patient	577,847	176,420	77,468	66,480
New problem	155,640	62,081	38,503	19,700
Old problem	422,207	114,339	38,965	46,916

From Reference 29.

> Neither the nurse *nor the physician alone* (italics added) is prepared to address adequately the broad range of health, medical and nursing concerns of patients encountered in a primary care setting: each professional has a clear identity, each is licensed in his or her own right, and each is in command of a separate body of knowledge, although there is a shared scientific base of preparation and considerable overlap in many functions. Thus, each professional brings a different approach and additional information and expertise to the setting that the other professional recognizes, values and is unable to provide alone.

Nurses view themselves as working with, but not for, primary-care physicians, and the potential for competition in the years to come is great.

Capitation and the Role of Case Managers

The impact of corporate practice on the long-term role of primary-care providers was alluded to earlier. Health-care corporations have long recognized that health care delivered through coordination at the primary-care level is more cost-effective than providing patients with direct access to subspecialists and hence to higher-priced technology.[32] From this awareness has emerged the role of case managers. The concept of a case manager—coordinating care, including the cost of care, of all patients in their charge—melds well with the emerging concept of paying for care on the basis of capitation, according providers a flat fee per patient rather than a per-service fee.

Thus, in the capitation case manager model, a corporation acts as a broker of health-care services, selling a comprehensive package through an employer to patient X and his or her family. The care of patient X is then entrusted to primary-care provider Y, who may receive, for example, $35 each month for assuming the care of patient X regardless of whether he or she requires care in any particular month. If patient X gets the flu and is treated in provider Y's office, there is no additional payment. But, if a consultation or, for example, a chest radiograph is needed, the cost of the procedure comes out of provider Y's monthly $35 fee. That is, the cost of the extra service is borne by the primary-care provider rather than the patient or the insurer. This approach incorporates a strong motivation to hold down health-care costs, although, in fact, appropriate use of health-care dollars has always been the ethic of primary-care providers.

What becomes important in this scenario is the relationship between primary-care providers and the subspecialists.[33] Remember that in the future, there will be even more subspecialists per patient than there are today. If patient X requires a cholecystectomy, the cost of doing the procedure will still come from provider Y's $35 monthly fee. Thus, provider Y will shop carefully and will perhaps do some hard bargaining to obtain their patient's cholecystectomy at the lowest cost. Hence, the system is likely to drive down the income of procedure-based subspecialists, the very subspecialists who profited so luxuriously under the fee-for-service system. In the long run, it seems likely that there will be much closer concordance between the incomes of primary-care physicians and those of subspecialists.

FAMILY PRACTICE AS A PROTOTYPE OF PRIMARY CARE

Of all the practitioners who specialize, dabble or aspire to provide primary-care services, family physicians are the prototype providers who come closest to fulfilling all of the criteria described earlier by Alpert, Petersdorf, and other authors (Table 4). Family practice is the only specialty in which all practitioners are committed throughout their careers to provide primary care. Some general pediatricians and many general internists will go on to subspecialize. Not so family physicians, who are committed to a career in primary medical care.

Current family practice is a legacy from the general medical practice in the days of the horse and buggy and later the Model T Ford. World War II changed the practice of medicine and gave an important impetus to subspecialization, which, by the 1960s, became recognized as a serious fragmentation of health care.

In the mid-1960s, two reports set the stage for a renaissance in general medical practice. The Citizens' Commission on Graduate Medical Education, chaired by John S. Millis, called for the training of "primary physicians" who could offer broad-based health-care services.[3] Concurrently, the Ad Hoc Committee for Education for Family Practice of the Council on Medical Education of the AMA, chaired by William R. Wil-

TABLE 10.4
PRIMARY CARE ROLES OF OFFICE-BASED PHYSICIANS

Primary-care roles	Specialty		
	Family practice	Internal medicine	Pediatrics
First contact	X	X	X
Longitudinal/continuous care	X	X	X
Coordination/integration of care	X	X	X
Care for all family members (all ages, both sexes)	X		
Care for full spectrum of health care problems (medical, surgical, gynecologic, obstetric, behavioral/psychiatric)	X		

lard, called for the training of a new type of specialist—the "family physician."[34] In 1969, family practice became a specialty based on recognition of the American Board of Family Practice (ABFP) as a certifying body. The original 15 three-year family practice residency programs have now grown to 400 such programs that offer 2,500 first-year training positions to medical school graduates. Currently, family physicians are likely to see approximately 107 patients during an average work week of 47.8 hours.[35]

Family physicians provide definitive care in approximately 90 percent of instances (i.e., they provide care without resorting to consultation or referral, making use only of the resources of patients' families, the community and their own staffs). For approximately 7 percent of problems, care requires consultation with another specialist; in 3 percent of instances, referral to another specialist is necessary, and the family physician retains a supportive role for the patient and family.[36]

Numerous articles have described "core concepts" in family medicine. One was written by Chao,[37] who draws on his experience to define seven essential family practice concepts:

1. First contact and utilization
2. Continuity of care
3. Family utilization
4. Patient assessment and treatment—quality of care
5. Family assessment and therapy
6. Preventive medicine
7. Referral and consultation

These concepts adhere closely to the concepts used earlier to describe primary care, with the notable addition of family involvement.[38]

Family Physicians and Current Trends in Primary Care

Family physicians appear to be adapting very well to the current trends in health-care delivery and primary care. An analysis of 2,000 patients age 18 or older who visited 349 providers' offices during a nine-day period revealed that family physicians had somewhat lower resource utilization rates than general internists.[39] In another study that compared primary care physicians with HMOs on the basis of projections made by the Graduate Medical Education National Advisory Committee, Steinwachs and co-workers[40] looked at staffing patterns in three large HMOs that differed in their use of nonphysician providers, family physicians and internists. They found that "the division of general adult care between internists and family practitioners at HMOs also has an impact principally because family practitioners have higher productivity levels than internists. In general, the higher the proportion of adult care provided by family practitioners, the lower the total requirements." Thus, family physicians appear to be proving that they are efficient, cost-effective providers of primary health care, and they appear to be well adapted for survival in the years ahead.

EMERGING CONTROVERSIES AMONG SPECIALTIES

The turbulence of the years to come is likely to bring some battles among the specialties, as groups of physicians not only attempt to protect their own turf but also seek to invade areas claimed by other physicians.

One battleground will be hospital privileges. Subspecialists have traditionally sought to protect their perceived turf by moving to exclude primary-care physicians. General internists and family physicians have fought battles for access to coronary care units and intensive care units, and, in many geographic areas, qualified family physicians are challenging hospitals in their quest for specific procedure privileges, notably cesarean sections. Subspecialists will attempt to draw battle lines according to specialty certification, whereas primary-care physicians will seek to have hospital privileges awarded on the basis of documented experience and demonstrated competence. The author would like to be more optimistic but foresees nothing in the decade ahead but continuing turmoil in this area as subspecialists with shrinking incomes attempt to repel "interlopers" by any means available.

Another area of controversy is direct access by patients to sub-specialists. For example, the American Academy of Dermatology has published a brochure titled "The Case for Direct Access to Dermatologic Care."[41] The brochure praises the usefulness of controlled patient flow and the need to cap medical costs but takes the position that allowing patients direct access to skin specialists could serve both goals. Is the issue one of economic importance? It certainly is to dermatologists, because patients with acne make up half or more of many dermatology practices and because circumventing case managers in the manner proposed would open the door to similar pleas from other subspecialties.

There are a number of subspecialists who, largely for economic reasons, aspire to provide primary care for their patients. AMA Executive Vice-President James S. Todd, M.D., believes that subspecialists can provide primary care. According to Todd, a surgeon might ask the patient if he has had inoculations[17] (of course, I am not sure that surgical offices are prepared to stock vaccines, keep up with changing recommendations, treat side effects or maintain longitudinal immunization records for patients). This situation would put surgeons lacking referrals in the position of counseling patients with family stress, underutilized cardiologists excising skin lesions and dermatologists treating patients with hypertension on days when the schedule is not full. If surgery, cardiology or dermatology are specialties, so are general internal medicine, family practice and general pediatrics. A critical issue in this emerging controversy is whether the primary-care specialties are really "specialties" with specific knowledge and expertise that should be protected from incursions by other specialties, just as surgery protects its turf from nonsurgical disciplines. Certainly, the knowledge base has expanded greatly; therefore, no one who does not keep up with the generalist literature should attempt to practice primary care.

GROWTH AREAS IN PRIMARY CARE

In 1979, Pelligrino[42] issued a triad of challenges to family medicine. "To secure its academic future, family medicine must respond to a triad of essentially academic challenges: Does it have a method and intellectual content not central to any other clinical discipline? Can it make a special and needed contribution to patient care? Can it take a mature stance in relationship to the fields most contiguous to it?"

The challenges can be extended to all primary-care specialties. Can primary care assert itself in regard to method and intellectual content, contribution to patient care and mature stance in relationship to other specialties? The answer to this question lies in two broad areas. The first is bringing excellence to the fulfillment of its mission: providing comprehensive longitudinal care beginning with first contact and fulfilling an integrationist role. The second is the development of its own turf area. Primary care and family medicine must eventually answer the question: What are we doing, teaching, and researching that is not done, and done better, by some other field of medicine? I propose that primary care can excel in the following areas.

Disease Prevention and Health Promotion

Disease prevention and health promotion have sparked little interest in most subspecialists. There are good reasons for this lack of advocacy for prevention and wellness: the rewards are not promptly forthcoming, and it takes a long time to see tangible benefits from persuading a person to stop smoking; disease prevention and health promotion are not procedure-oriented and hence are unlikely to be covered by health insurance; and many physicians are not sure that preventing disease and promoting health are truly "what real doctors do."

These reasons notwithstanding, disease prevention and health promotion represent an ideal growth area for primary care. First, patients want guidance in these areas and are looking for physicians who can meet this need (e.g., "What exercise should I do? How often? For how long?"). Second, disease prevention and health promotion are likely to enjoy support when and if national health care becomes a reality. Industry is already learning that disease prevention and health promotion programs can improve employee health and thereby augment productivity and decrease absenteeism; for this reason, employers are putting money into "wellness" programs. HMOs and preferred-provider organizations (PPOs) are also including wellness services as part of their benefits packages. Certainly, disease prevention and health promotion are logical areas of expertise for primary-care providers and ones that are likely to see increased growth in the future.

Geriatrics

ABFP and the American Board of Internal Medicine jointly sponsor a Certificates of Added Qualifications in Geriatric Medicine, which has put geriatrics well on its way to becoming a recognized subspecialty (and probably a battleground for everyone except pediatricians). For years, elderly patients were subjected to subtle discrimination in the health-care system: they had chronic and therefore unexciting problems; they asked many questions; and they took a long time to dress and undress. In short, they consumed a lot of time and were not challenging medically.

However, times have changed, physicians' schedules are not as full as they were, and virtually all elderly patients are covered by Medicare. Thus, the elderly are now favored patients.

Primary-care physicians were the "geriatricians-in-fact" before geriatrics was discovered by the rest of the medical community. Primary-care providers should hold fast to their claim on geriatric care and should emphasize care of the elderly in education and research.

Occupational Medicine

Occupational medicine represents a logical area of opportunity for primary-care providers, especially family physicians and general internists. As a subspecialty in breadth, occupational medicine includes problems relating to multiple organs and systems and involves epidemiology, health promotion and disease prevention. It seems likely that the future will bring more, not fewer, opportunities in occupational medicine as more companies strive to reduce health-care and production costs by providing more direct services for employees.

Sports Medicine

The American Boards of Emergency Medicine, Family Practice, Internal Medicine and Pediatrics conjointly offer a Certificate of Added Qualifications in Sports Medicine with the first certifying examination offered in 1993.

Sports medicine involves nutrition, training, behavioral science and health care for athletes. In short, it is an important area of primary care. After all, family physicians, pediatricians and general internists were the attending physicians for high school football teams long before every third medical student wanted to be a sports medicine physician.

For the foreseeable future, many more athletes will compete at the secondary-school level than in colleges, and the number of college athletes will far outstrip the number of professional athletes needing arthroscopic knee surgery. In fact, probably the largest patient pool extant is composed of recreational athletes, most of whom seek care for their injuries from primary-care physicians.

School Health

School physicians have multiple roles. Of course, there is the direct care of young patients, and an increasing number of schools are setting up their own adolescent health-care clinics. There may be a sports medicine physician. In addition, school physicians can assist schools in developing health-care policies, "(1) creating new programs (for example, a streptoccocal pharyngitis or even STD [sexually transmitted disease] control program); (2) setting up protocols for school physical examinations, pre-participation sports evaluations, or treatment of sports injuries; or (3) developing infectious disease policies (for example, to govern when students with chicken pox can return to school)."[43]

Adolescent Medicine

A Certificate of Added Qualifications in Adolescent Medicine will be offered by pediatrics and internal medicine starting in 1994. Primary-care providers, including family physicians, should assert their continuing role in adolescent medical care, especially because the problems of adolescence—common infectious diseases, traumatic injuries and behavioral and emotional problems—are the areas of expertise of primary care.

Community-Oriented Primary Care

According to Rogers,[44] "No one in modern society can believe that a physician working in isolation, and simply treating those who come to him on a one to one basis can produce a healthy society." Community-oriented primary care involves integration of direct health care with prevention, rehabilitation and other services on a community-wide basis. The parents of community-oriented primary care are the primary-care specialties, on one hand, and public health and preventive medicine, on the other. As we become more interdependent in the decades to come, it seems likely that community-oriented primary care, now a neglected stepchild, may mature to have an important role in our health-care system.

Administrative Medicine

Administrative medicine will appeal to some family physicians because of its generalist and management orientation. Administrative medicine physicians have important liaison roles, and the growth of managed care will increase the need for skilled physician administrators. These physicians must provide leadership in contract negotiations, quality assurance and community relations.

PRACTICE OPPORTUNITIES IN PRIMARY CARE

Primary-care physicians in 2000 will probably be distributed among the various practice options that currently exist, including private practice, salaried practice, governmental service and academic careers. By then, there are likely to be many fewer private, fee-for-service practitioners than currently exist. The pressures are just too great. New physicians leaving residency lack the resources to open their own offices, and thus most join established groups that can offer a ready patient population and facilities. Small groups, in turn, are being bought out by hospitals or conglomerates. Furthermore, as pointed out by Starr,[1] "Young doctors may be more interested in freedom *from* the job than freedom *in* the job and organizations that provide more regular hours can screen out the invasions of private life that come with independent professional practice."

Somewhere between fee-for-service practices and salaried practices are PPOs (Table 5). A PPO contracts with physicians to provide comprehensive health care to subscribers based on a negotiated fee schedule, usually at discount rates. Participating patients are able to retain their personal physicians, and care rendered through a PPO is brokered by an insurance or other company.

Physicians may be employed by hospitals, HMOs, large groups, industries, schools or other entities. Throughout the rest of the century, the largest single employer of physicians is likely to be HMOs. By 2000, many physicians now in fee-for-service practices will find it economically advantageous to become salaried employees of closed-panel HMOs, as

TABLE 10.5
CHARACTERISTICS OF HEALTH-CARE DELIVERY SYSTEMS

	System		
Characteristic	Fee-for-service practice	Preferred provider organization	Health maintenance organization
Payment system	Service-based	Service- or capitation-based	Capitation-based
Services generally provided	Physician care	Physician ± hospital care	Comprehensive care
Patient choice of provider	Free choice of provider	Provider panel	HMO provider panel
Claims/payment	Personal or third party	Third party	Internal decisions
Risk shared by provider	None	Varies	Yes
Incentive for patient	Personal relationship with physician	Personal physician; increased coverage of services	Broad scope/ coverage of services

their patient bases dwindle owing to competition from HMOs and as the cost of maintaining professional liability insurance increases.

There will continue to be attractive opportunities for service in various areas of the federal government, including Veterans Administration hospitals, the armed forces and the Public Health Service. In addition, many primary-care physicians will be employed full or part time by state or county health offices or by prisons or other state or federal agencies.

The growth of primary care will continue to offer attractive opportunities in academics. As of this writing, faculty positions are available in many of the 400 family practice residency training programs in the United States. As more primary care internal medicine residency positions become available, there will be faculty opportunities in those programs also.

SUCCESS SKILLS FOR PRIMARY-CARE PHYSICIANS

Despite the author's optimistic predictions, the continued growth and well-being of primary care are not assured. General internists, general pediatricians and family physicians need to develop thick skin to withstand the barbs hurled by academic subspecialists at the local medical doctors—the same doctors who constitute their chief referral base. They will need tenacity to hold on to patients despite the incursions of subspecialists into primary care, and they will need to become economically astute so as not to lose the advantage that managed care now offers their practices.

Success Skill Number 1: Learn to Respond to a Patient's Needs

As White and associates[45] deduced, "The patient is a more relevant unit of observation than the disease, the visit, or the admission." We must never lose sight of the fact that the key players in the entire drama of health-care delivery are not physicians, nurses, administrators or corporate presidents but patients. In the competitive arena, it is from patients that the physician derives power, and as long as primary-care physicians are attentive to their patients' needs, they will be the key providers in the system.

Success Skill Number 2: Be Alert to Opportunities

The author previously discussed growth areas in primary care: disease prevention and health promotion, geriatrics, occupational medicine, sports medicine, school health, adolescent medicine, community-oriented primary care and administrative medicine. Opportunities in other areas will emerge, and primary-care physicians must be alert to grasp them when the chance arises. There will be roles for primary-care physicians in home and urgent care. Opportunities will also emerge in technology, and primary-care physicians must be careful that new techniques (e.g., fiberoptic laryngoscopy) or new medications (e.g., newly introduced parenteral antibiotics) do not become the exclusive province of sub-specialists.

Success Skill Number 3: Learn to Collaborate with Other Health-Care Providers

Opportunities in the next two decades are likely to be provided by collaborative ventures. At medical centers across the country, innovative physicians are developing geropsychiatric units, travel-medicine clinics and adolescent-care centers, often based on collaboration among two or more traditional specialties.

Success Skill Number 4: Promote the Well-Being of Primary Care At Every Opportunity

Although physicians have broad-based public support, they cannot assume that such support will last indefinitely. A medical school dean once asked me: "Has family medicine thought what the specialty will do when federal support and public favor turn to another specialty, such as emergency medicine?" Primary-care physicians must use every opportunity to let the public know that, for instance, in an adult population of 1,000 people at risk, only one person will be referred to a university medical center per month, only five will require consultation with sub-specialists, and the rest of the health care of these 1,000 people will be handled chiefly by primary-care physicians, families and patients.[45] Primary-care physicians need to let the public know that coordination of health care by them costs less, that they can provide care for 90 percent of all health care problems and that they are the public's advocates within the health-care system.

Success Skill Number 5: Become Politically Involved

Some people would say that the future of medicine is already out of the hands of physicians, but that need not necessarily be true. Certainly, our economic destiny will be increasingly shaped by nonphysicians, but the corporate managers must still deal with us as physicians, as must our legislators in state capitals and in Washington, D.C.

Primary-care physicians must be sure their voices are heard. To do so, they must become involved in political organizations, and some of the most eloquent must be active in both medical politics and in state and national politics. Without effective representation, they are at the mercy of legislators, managers and subspecialists.

WHAT IS AHEAD IN MEDICINE?

What is happening in medicine that will affect primary care in 2000? First, there will be *rationing of care* on all levels. Rationing is now occurring for economic reasons, and more than 35 million people currently lack health insurance; this figure represents an increase of 10 million, or

25 percent, since 1977. We are entering an era of increasing parsimony at all levels because the cost of care will increasingly be borne by pooled resources.[46] Rationing is already an explicit fact of life in the United Kingdom, where few individuals over age 55 are afforded renal dialysis. Of course, they are not refused because of age, but become "unsuitable" owing to the health problems of aging such as heart disease and diabetes.

As we face the problem of who shall get care when there is not enough care to go around, there will be a *decrease in physicians' autonomy*. Until recently, physicians could call a hospital admitting office and send a patient to the floor. No more. Authorization before admission is becoming the rule, and primary-care physicians and subspecialists alike must call clerks to obtain approval for surgical procedures, hospital admissions, referrals and even certain tests. If physicians fail to obtain the necessary approval, they may bear part of the cost.

The *barriers to access* become particularly onerous with the increasing expectations of the public with regard to health-care services. There have been proposals for health care access reform in the past, but now seems to be the first time in which there are politically realistic initiatives being advocated by the medical community. Plans have been advanced by the AMA ("Health Access America") and the American Academy of Family Physicians ("Rx for Health, the Family Physicians' Access Plan"). The possibility of significant change seems high, and it will be important for physicians to be involved in planning and implementation, because the changes will surely affect the practice of primary-care medicine.

Physicians are being held to *higher standards of accountability* than ever before. The ordering of laboratory tests and radiologic studies must be justified. Hospital admissions are scrutinized by utilization review committees often before a patient reaches the floor. Computerized ordering systems in hospitals now allow administrators to draw cost profiles for each physician on the staff, and, increasingly, subtle pressure from hospital administrators and medical group chiefs will be augmented by the risk of sanctions.

Finally, physicians will see *challenges to their beliefs*. They may have to choose between exploring psychosocial issues with patients and maintaining a negotiated patient volume. They will continue to encounter patients who value convenience over continuity, who will forsake the doctor-patient relationship for the cost advantages of HMO care. Physicians also face the ethical dilemma of having a financial interest in providing "less care" for their patients.[47]

PRIMARY CARE PRACTICE IN THE YEAR 2000

What do I tell a medical student or a resident who is contemplating a career in primary care—family practice, general internal medicine or general pediatrics? What shall practice be like a decade after he or she finishes training? What will he or she be doing in practice? In fact, will there be a job available? What will be this young physician's status in the medical community and in the community at large? Will he or she be able to live well or support a family on the income of a primary-care physician? What will his or her personal family life be like? All these questions and more are asked by medical students and residents as they make their career choices. Some reasonable speculations, based on the issues, forces, trends and controversies presented in the preceding sections, follow.

Practice Style

Young primary-care physicians in 2000 are likely to be in group practice, and many will belong to multispecialty groups. Not all will be working in closed-panel HMOs, because HMOs in 2000 are projected by Ellwood[48] to have approximately 150 million members; thus, only approximately 132,000 physicians would need to be employed by HMOs. (Remember that HMOs require fewer physicians per patient than fee-for-service practices.) Therefore, the remaining physicians, numbering at least 500,000, will not be employed by HMOs; instead, they will be working in some other setting, such as in private group practices, or as employees of hospitals, corporations, schools, government or academic medical centers.

In 2000, physicians are likely to be doing less hospital work than is currently done. I do not believe that this change will occur because physicians will have lost battles for hospital privileges; the force of their political organizations, such as the American Academy of Family Physicians, will effectively combat these challenges. Instead, physicians will find that many hospitals have become large intensive care units, and their temperament and training will lead them out of hospitals into different practice settings.

Physicians will be doing their work more in large ambulatory-care centers, with their special-purpose endoscopy and imaging areas, urgent-care units, gerontology units and pharmacies. Ambulatory-care centers will be affiliated with nursing homes, and physicians will have a great deal of responsibility for patient care in such centers.

Ambulatory-care centers will also have outreach clinics in shopping centers and senior citizen housing units, and a transportation network of vans will bring patients to and from the office setting for their appointments.

Physicians may take their turns each month on their group's mobile medical unit, providing home care to shut-ins and to the handicapped, for whom a visit to the office would be difficult. They also will work closely with the home health care nursing team.

A decade after physicians have finished training, they will be doing more procedures than are currently performed. There will be a steady flow of new technology, which will necessitate taking frequent refresher courses to learn about new procedures. Physicians will find, perhaps, that laser therapy has become part of general office practice the way that flexible sigmoidoscopy did in the 1980s.

At the other end of the spectrum, physicians will be doing much more disease-prevention and health-promotion work than is currently done. Not only will this work be covered by HMO contracts or PPO insurance, but disease prevention and health promotion will also have become accepted by the medical community as the foundation of sound health care. Its research base will have become well accepted, and physicians will have been taught specific skills during medical school and residency.

Physicians will probably see about as many patients as are currently seen—approximately 20 to 25 in an eight-hour day. Diagnosis and sorting the physical from the emotional problems will continue to be the biggest challenges. Physicians will be using computer-based diagnosis, despite its lack of perfection; however, most difficult diagnoses will still be made based on our own fund of knowledge. In contrast, physicians will have a computer terminal in each examination room and will make extensive use of its data base to check newly available therapy, medication dosages and drug interactions. On-the-spot medical literature searches will be commonplace. The computer data base will also contain guidelines for referrals that have been negotiated by a physician's group, HMO or PPO and will allow prompt connections with approved consultants.

The patient-recall system will be fully computer-based, and there will be clinical practice guidelines for the ongoing management of all chronic diseases, such as hypertension, diabetes mellitus, congestive heart failure and peptic ulcer disease.

Physicians will hardly need to carry a pen because all chart notes will be dictated into a word processor, which will transcribe directly from dictation without the intervention of a typist. Likewise, prescriptions will be entered on a keyboard for direct transmission to a pharmacy. Even referral notes and appointments with subspecialists will be entered directly on the keyboard. The computer will also remind if a patient requires a medication refill or an immunization.

Physicians' Income

Within the HMO and PPO settings, negotiated payments will have become a way of life, and this fee schedule is likely to spread to all aspects of primary and subspecialist health care. Furthermore, primary-care groups will have subcapitated payments to consultants.

In addition, physicians' incomes are likely to be more stable than those of current independent practitioners because they will probably receive a paycheck each month. This system has definite advantages, because physicians' employers will also provide fringe benefits, and early retirement will become an option.

Physician incomes will be increasingly affected by physician payment reform, as defined by the Omnibus Reconciliation Act of 1989.[49] Implementation of a new Resourced-Based Relative Value Scale (RBRVS) began in January 1992, but only after "lengthy review of the proposed regulations, including simulations to analyze their likely effect and prolonged dialogue among the Health Care Financing Administration, the Physician Payment Review Commission, and major professional groups."[20] Although primary-care physicians are more likely than other physicians to be benefactors, special exceptions and changes may occur and many remain skeptical.

Readers may ask what their income will be. After adjustments for inflation, physicians' pay probably will parallel that of current primary-care physicians. What will differ will be the incomes of subspecialists, which will have stabilized at an approximately equal level. Why the change? Because primary-care physicians, as the case managers and those responsible for the pool of health-care dollars, will have negotiated with subspecialists to obtain the lowest prices for their patients and their primary-care groups.

Professional Relationships

By 2000, primary-care providers will have shed their second-class image. After World War II, subspecialization commanded the interest of medical schools and teaching hospitals. Local medical doctors lost self-respect and the power to reproduce. Currently, as teaching centers see the locus of care moving from hospitals to the ambulatory-care setting, there is keen interest in changing the curriculum to reflect what is happening in practice.[50] By moving back into medical schools and again achieving respectability, primary care has regained its power to reproduce and will, by the end of this decade, have overcome the anachronistic stigma of lower status.

Primary care will lose its second-class status for an even more practical reason. As has been discussed, primary-care physicians will control the allocation of health-care dollars.[32] There is an axiom that goes as follows: In any system that is dependent on scarce resources, the person who controls the scarce resources controls the system. In the health-care system of the future, the scarce resources will be patients and where care is provided, and the persons in control will be primary-care physicians.

Thus, in this setting, part of primary-care physicians' relations with subspecialist colleagues will involve ongoing negotiations regarding fees; specifically, the fees that they are willing to pay for their services. And primary-care physicians will be in a favored position because all subspecialty fields will be sufficiently overcrowded so there is likely to be competitive bidding for the dollars under their control.

Personal and Family Life

Primary-care physicians will have more free time to spend with their spouses and families, with fewer interruptions, because they are likely to be salaried, have regular duties and assured vacations and time off to attend professional meetings.

They will probably also have more flexibility in their hours and will have discovered ways to tailor their work to meet the need of their life-styles. They may, for instance, work long shifts for three or four days and then be off duty for the remainder of the week. They may be in part-time practice and be otherwise engaged in writing, teaching or some other medically related activity.

By 2000, as corporate employees, they may also request—or be asked—to serve at one of the corporation's sites in cities around the world. Before they go, of course, they will stop at the corporation's overseas travel clinic for the necessary immunizations and medications.

They will have more time for sports, hobbies, reading and "self-actualization." However, they are likely to find themselves doing more of those activities with their colleagues, as their employers seek to foster a sense of "family" within their medical groups or HMO employees.

The Future

By 2000, young primary-care physicians will still have 20 or 30 years of practice before them. What is the long-term future for primary care? According to Woodward,[51] "The challenge of the 1960s was to create primary care response systems; the challenge of the 1980s . . . to sustain them." I predict that the challenge of the early twenty-first century will be to maintain our link to the people, the patient base on which we will have built people-centered practices. By the twenty-first century, primary-care physicians will be truly the key providers, or at least will have the potential to be. Those who began as a social movement—to repair the fragmentation in medicine and to return health care to the people—will have become the keystone of the health-care system, but with computerization, technology and communication systems far more advanced than those currently available. In short, the American people are progressively entrusting management of our nation's health care resources—approximately 12 percent of our gross national product—to primary-care physicians.

To maintain this trust, primary-care physicians must keep in touch with their roots. As Peabody[52] wrote in 1927: "One of the essential qualities of the clinician is interest in humanity. For the secret of the care of the patient is in caring for the patient." Here is the cornerstone of primary care, and as long as primary-care physicians keep this clearly in mind, the future of primary care and family practice—and the patients we serve—is secure.

REFERENCES

1. Starr P: *The Social Transformation of American Medicine.* New York, Basic Books, 1982, pp 428, 445.
2. Alpert JL: New directions in medical education. In: Purcell EF (ed): *Recent Trends in Medical Education.* New York, Josiah Macy Jr Foundation, 1976, p 166.
3. Report of the Citizens Commission on Graduate Medical Education (Millis Commission). Chicago, American Medical Association, 1966.
4. White KL: Primary medical care for families. *N Engl J Med* 277:847–851, 1967.
5. Pelligrino ED: Planning for comprehensive and continuing care of patients through education. *J Med Educ* 43:751–755, 1968.
6. American Academy of Family Physicians: *Education for Family Practice.* Kansas City, MO, 1969.
7. Magraw R: Medical education and health services—Implications for family medicine. *N Engl J Med* 285:1407–1409, 1971.
8. Petersdorf RG: Internal medicine and family practice: Controversies, conflict, and compromise. *N Engl J Med* 293:326–332, 1975.
9. Institute of Medicine. *Primary Care in Medicine: A Definition.* Washington, D.C.: National Academy of Sciences, 1977, p 8.
10. Weiner JP, Starfield BH: Measurement of the primary care roles of office-based physicians. *Am J Public Health* 33:666–671, 1983.
11. *Percentage Change in Physician Supply and Demand by the Year 2000.* Chicago, AMA Center for Health Policy Research, 1988.
12. Taylor AD: *How To Choose a Medical Specialty, 2nd Ed.* Philadelphia: W.B. Saunders Company, 1993.
13. Rabinowitz HK: Evaluation of a selective medical school admissions policy to increase the number of family physicians in rural and underserved areas. *N Engl J Med* 319:480–486, 1988.
14. Andreopoulos S: *Primary Care: Where Medicine Fails.* New York, John Wiley & Sons, 1974, p 18.
15. Fletcher SW, Fletcher RH, Pappius EM, et al: A teaching hospital medical clinic: Secondary rather than primary care. *J Med Educ* 54:384–391, 1979.
16. Milio N: *Primary Care and the Public's Health: Judging Impacts, Goals and Policies.* Lexington, MA, Lexington Books, 1983, p 21.
17. Page L: Primary care shortage? It's all in eye of beholder. *Am Med News* 35:1, 35, 1992.
18. U.S. Dept of Commerce: 1991 US Industrial Outlook. Washington, D.C.: US Dept of Commerce, International Trade Administration, January 1991:44:144–6.
19. Barnett PG, Midtling JE: Public policy and the supply of primary care physicians. *J Am Med Assoc* 262:2864–2868, 1989.
20. Blumenthal D, Epstein AM: Physician-payment reform—unfinished business. *N Engl J Med* 326:1330–1334, 1992.
21. Field MJ, Lohr KN (eds): *Clinical Practice Guidelines.* Washington, D.C., National Academy Press, 1990.

22. Jackson MN, Nutting PA: Clinical guidelines development: Opportunities for family physicians. *J Fam Pract* 32:129–132, 1991.
23. HMO Fact Sheet. Washington, D.C.: Group Health Association of America, 1992.
24. Weiler PC, Newhouse JP, Hiatt HH: Proposal for medical liability reform. *J Am Med Assoc* 267:2355–2358, 1992.
25. Graner JL: Roots of the present primary care crisis. *J Am Med Assoc* 146:42–43, 1986.
26. Pfenninger JL: Colposcopy in a family practice residency: The first 200 cases. *J Fam Pract* 34:67–72, 1992.
27. Rodney WM, Deutchman ME, Hartman KJ, et al: Obstetric ultrasound by family physicians. *J Fam Pract* 34:186–200, 1992.
28. Petersdorf RG: Is the establishment defensible? *N Engl J Med* 309:1053–1055, 1983.
29. U.S. Department of Health and Human Services, Public Health Service, Center for Disease Control, National Center for Health Statistics, 1989 data.
30. *Educational Programs for the Physician's Assistant.* Chicago, American Medical Association, Department of Allied Medical Professionals and Services, 1984, p 3.
31. *Joint Practice in Primary Care: Definition and Guidelines.* Evanston, IL, National Joint Practice Commission, 1977.
32. Boschert S: Primary care doctors seen as key to group practice success. *Fam Pract News* 22:1, 25, 1992.
33. Franks P, Clancy CM, Nutting PA: Sounding board—Gatekeeping revisited—protecting patients from overtreatment. *N Engl J Med* 327:424–429, 1992.
34. AMA Ad Hoc Committee on Education for Family Practice (Willard Commission): *Meeting the Challenge of Family Practice.* Chicago, American Medical Association, 1966.
35. *Facts About Family Practice 1991.* Kansas City, MO, American Academy of Family Physicians, 1991.
36. Taylor RB: Categories of care in family medicine. *Fam Med* 13:7–9, 1981.
37. Chao J: Evaluation of seven essential family practice concepts. *Fam Pract Res J* 4:152–167, 1985.
38. Taylor RB: *Family Medicine: Principles and Practice, 4th ed.* New York, Springer-Verlag, 1993.
39. Greenfield S, Nelson EC, Zubkoff M, et al: Variations in resource utilization among medical specialties and systems of care. *J Am Med Assoc* 267:1624–1630, 1992.
40. Steinwachs DM, Weiner JP, Shapiro S, et al: A comparison of the requirements for primary care physicians in HMOs with projections made by the GMENAC. *N Engl J Med* 314:217–222, 1986.
41. American Academy of Dermatology: *The Case for Direct Access to Dermatologic Care.* Evanston, IL, American Academy of Dermatology, 1985.
42. Pelligrino ED: The academic viability of family medicine: A triad of challenges. *J Am Med Assoc* 240:132–135, 1978.
43. Poole SR, Schmitt BD, Sophocles A, et al: The family physician's role in school health. *J Fam Pract* 18:843–856, 1986.
44. Rogers DE: Community oriented primary care. *J Am Med Assoc* 248:1622–1625, 1982.
45. White KL, Williams TF, Greenberg BG: The ecology of medical care. *N Engl J Med* 265:885–892, 1961.

46. Saltman RB: Single-source financing systems: A solution for the United States? *J Am Med Assoc* 268:774–779, 1992.
47. Ellsbury KE: Can the family physician avoid conflict of interest in the gatekeeper role? *J Fam Pract* 6:698–704, 1989.
48. Ellwood P: Quoted in: Public and doctors worry about surplus. *Northwest Med Forum* 2:12, 1986.
49. The Omnibus Budget Reconciliation Act of 1989. Public Law 101-239, Section 6102:68.
50. Perkoff GT: Teaching clinical medicine in the ambulatory setting: An idea whose time may have finally come. *N Engl J Med* 314:27–31, 1986.
51. Woodward K: The primary health care model. In: Miller RS (ed): *Primary Health Care: More Than Medicine.* Englewood Cliffs, NJ, Prentice-Hall, 1983, p 54.
52. Peabody FW: The care of the patient. *J Am Med Assoc* 88:877–882, 1927.

SECTION

III
FUTURE DIRECTIONS

COMMENTARY

David B. Nash

While choosing an appropriate specialty or career path in medicine is certainly important, all physicians will need to develop skills in three major areas for the future. These areas are the use of computers, the burgeoning growth in health-care information and its control and assessment and appropriate utilization of new technologies.

Dr. Jay B. Krasner has made many original contributions to the literature on computers in medicine. He has authored several unique software packages for treating patients in critical care units and those with severe nutritional deficiencies. He describes the history of computers in medicine and explains how they will impact on the future practice of medicine. This chapter does not concentrate on the business applications of computers in medicine but, rather, on the use of computers in diagnosing and managing major illnesses. His expert speculation about the future of computers in medicine reads like a believable science-fiction novel.

How can we possibly continue to manage the explosion of health-care information? Which conference should we attend? Which journals should we read? As the past director of continuing medical education at the George Washington University Medical Center in Washington, D.C., Dr. Allen Douma gives us his recipe for mixing journals, videotapes and audiotapes to create the perfect continuing medical education pie. Surprisingly enough, many continuing medical education programs are not reviewed for content and scientific rigor. Dr. Duoma helps readers decide which programs are worthwhile, using generic criteria.

The explosive growth in new technology is probably as threatening as the burgeoning growth in medical knowledge. Dr. Alan L. Hillman and Dr. Mark Fendrick, both at the University of Pennsylvania School of Medicine, trace the impact of technologic developments on the practice of medicine. They also examine the diffusion and adoption of new technologies, such as computerized tomography and magnetic resonance imaging. They provide an outline of cost/benefit analysis and cost-effectiveness analysis as additional tools to aid physicians in their assessments of new technologies. We will all be called on to use new technologies before their true effectiveness can be assessed. Dr. Hillman's and Dr. Fendrick's prescriptions for technology assessment will be exceedingly useful.

This section also provides the reader heretofore unexplored career paths in computers,[1,2] continuing medical education and technology[3] assessment. These fields will continue to attract physicians with interests in engineering, mathematics and the basic sciences.

REFERENCES

1. Winslow R: Patient data may reshape health care. *The Wall Street Journal,* April 17, 1989.
2. Corcoran E: Robots for the operating room. *The New York Times,* July 19, 1992.
3. Greengard S: The physician's new care companion. *AMA News,* June 29, 1992.

CHAPTER 11

COMPUTERS AND MEDICAL PRACTICE:

An auspicious union

Jay B. Krasner

Computers have gradually become an integral part of modern medicine. Many of the roles computers have are not readily apparent on casual reflection. On closer examinination, the myriad of functions they serve and their indispensability become obvious. This statement will only become truer in the future. It behooves all members of the medical community to be aware of the current roles of computers in medicine as well as future developments in this area.

There are many factors involved in this ongoing computer revolution that will allow it to progress at the astounding rate it has demonstrated to this point. The most prominent factors are listed in Table 1. To illustrate the importance of these factors, consider the following: Currently, for less than $1000, one can purchase a briefcase-sized personal computer, bring it home, plug it in, turn it on and instantly begin to interact with any of a host of useful or entertaining software products. That computer is as powerful as the state-of-the-art system of 40 years ago, which filled a room measuring 30 by 50 feet, cost countless research dollars to construct, required a full-time staff of several people to maintain and could solve only the simplest of problems after many tedious hours of hand-coding programs via entry on banks of switches or punched paper tape. The exponential trends in decreasing cost, increasing power (speed and memory) and ease of use have yet to abate. In fact, as a rough rule of thumb, the "computer power" readily available to and usable by a person at any point in time is approximately equal to that of the most

TABLE 11.1
FACTORS ALLOWING CONTINUATION OF THE COMPUTER
REVOLUTION

Physical (hardware) factors
   Miniturization
   Speed of calculation
   Memory capacity
   Physical reliability
   Creation of and adherence to industrywide standards
   Cost
Cognitive (software) factors
   Use of natural language
   General familiarity with the use of computers
   Adaptive systems (programs that alter themselves on the basis of previous experience)
   Metasystems (programs that automatically write user-requested applications)
Combined factors—enhancement of the human/machine interface
   Speech recognition and synthesis
   Optical scanning
      Handwriting
      Bar codes
      Text/graphics
   The "Graphical User Interface" (e.g., Windows [TM])
   Touch-sensitive screens, X-Y digitizers, mice, etc.

powerful system in worldwide existence only 15 or 20 years ago. If one projects these trends to 2000, the computing power available will be incredible. The probable impact of this phenomenon will have on our lives cannot be measured; it far exceeds the fanciful speculations of science-fiction writers of generations past. On one hand, the simplest household items, such as dinnerware and doorknobs, may be driven by microprocessors. On the other hand, certain complex and dangerous tasks, such as construction deep beneath the sea or in outer space, may be accomplished without the physical presence or even direct intervention of human beings. Last, the equivalent amount of information as might be found in a medium-sized public library might be available in an easily portable and instantaneously accessible form. There are clear implications here for health-care professionals.

It is the goal of this chapter to familiarize readers with the current roles of computers in medicine as well as to speculate on what innovations we can reasonably expect that will be applicable to the practice of medicine in the future. These speculations probably lean toward the conservative side, given the rate of technologic advance mankind has witnessed over the past few decades.

Before proceeding, a few definitions for the novice are in order. A computer, as the term is used here, is a device composed of hardware, software and peripherals. Hardware refers to the physical equipment that performs the computing (the central processing unit), a means of input and external control (usually including a keyboard), a means of data storage (e.g., a tape or floppy disk) and a means of output (usually including a cathode-ray tube screen). Software, or programs, are sets of instructions that tell the hardware what to do. Peripherals are other pieces of equipment (which may be input and output devices) that are operated under the auspices of the hardware and software. A frequently used peripheral is the modem, which is a device that allows one computer to communicate with another computer over conventional telephone lines.

A computer system is a combination of hardware, software and, possibly, peripherals that perform a specific task. Occasionally in this chapter and elsewhere, the term *computer* may refer only to the hardware, but this use of the term should be obvious from the context of the discussion.

The references cited in this chapter have been limited for the most part to the noncomputer medical literature to which physicians would generally have access. For readers who wish to commence a more serious study of the field, work of greater depth and detail can be found in the references of the cited publications.

COMPUTERS AND THE BUSINESS OF MEDICINE

Perhaps the first widespread application of computers as a practical tool rather than as an academic curiosity was in the business world. As a natural consequence, the first uses of computers in medicine dealt with their business aspects. Many systems designed for general business were usable as is or easily adaptable for use in private offices, clinics or hospital business offices. The functions that such systems possessed included accounts receivable, general ledger, payroll, cash accounting, charge processing, statement generation, management reports, inventory and check writing. Subsequently, office-practice computing has evolved to encompass a multitude of functions specific to the medical-office environment. Examples of such functions are patient registration, patient recall, insurance-form processing, claims submission to third-party payers, appointment scheduling and form-letter generation.

Simultaneously, the financial world was developing more sophisticated computer applications for financial productivity, for example, word processing, spread-sheet analysis, mailing-list management and local area networks. These applications, too, are now readily available and are utilized by those concerned with the financial aspects of medicine. Medical management is becoming increasingly dominated by persons formally trained in this area. Unlike the physician-managers who preceded them, health-care executives generally have training in and make extensive use of computers for various financial tasks. For this reason, it seems logical to assume that nearly any new development in the use of computers in business will be applied to the business of medicine shortly after its introduction.

In the future, market factors will doubtlessly extend the degree to which computers are used for financial processing in medicine. Analyses by management of hospitals' (or large-scale practices') costs of services and profit margins have already become imperative in today's atmosphere of price regulation; only computer-aided information processing can cope with the amount of data that must be manipulated to perform such analyses satisfactorily. The competitive environment of the early 1980s led to widespread consolidation of hospital providers to take advantage of economies of scale.

The latter 1980s saw the proliferation of HMOs, PPOs, IPAs and a plethora of other alphabet soup ingredients. To track the performance of any of these organizations as well as the performance of their individual member providers, computerized data management is necessary. Finally, looming over the health-care services horizon are such entities as practice guidelines, clinical outcome inquiries and on-the-fly adjustments to the Resource-Based Relative Value Scale (RBRVS) system now in place for Medicare reimbursements. All these will require computer systems for effective administration.

COMPUTERS IN PRIVATE OFFICES

A common question that has been asked by practicing physicians over the past few years is, "Should I computerize my office?" At the time of this writing, cost-benefit analyses of all except the smallest and least complex practice situations would provide an affirmative answer to this question, at least for certain components of the practice. The more appropriate questions would be, How? and Which aspects? The general purpose and business applications of computers to the private office are little different from those relevant to any business of similar size. Most clerical personnel have at least a rudimentary familiarity with and training in the use of such applications. Most vendors of such products provide specific training in the use of their products as well; the net result is that most office personnel can efficiently use such systems after only a few hours of instruction. The standard business functions in an office-practice system are listed in Table 2. All these functions (and more) are available in currently existing medical-practice-management software packages from a variety of vendors and should be found in any contemplated office-practice system. However, it should be noted that these functions merely represent an adaptation of existing business software to the needs of medical offices without any creative, innovative or clinical use of computer technology.

TABLE 11.2
FUNCTIONS COMMON TO IN-OFFICE COMPUTER SYSTEMS

General business functions
  Patient (client) information files with demographic analysis
  Charge processing, statement generation, accounts receivable
  Inventory, accounts payable
  General ledger, cash accounting
  Reports: summary, productivity
  Payroll
  Collection processing, dunning notices
  Mailing labels, form letters
  Word processing
Functions unique to a physician's office
  Procedure pricing
  CPT procedure codes
  ICDA-9 codes
  Clinical patient profiles
  Third-party claims processing
  Practice analysis
  Insurance analysis
  Reminder notices for checkups, etc.

Scheduling Appointments

An important aspect of computers in private practice that begins to take them out of the realm of general business is their capability for scheduling appointments. The current state of the art in automated scheduling goes far beyond "electronification" of the traditional appointment book. Several office locations, examination/procedure rooms, health providers and pieces of equipment can be easily manipulated, as can various types of scheduling, such as flow, wave, pulse and automatic. Vacations and other reserved periods can be accounted for. Various types of printed schedules can be generated. Other features that may be implemented in a particular software product include chart-pull lists, next-day lists and visit histories. Some systems that are integrated with other elements of the overall office system are capable of automatic recall, visit reminders and rescheduling. Finally, time/usage studies and other types of analysis can be performed.

The major benefit of currently existing appointment-scheduling systems is their ability to optimize efficiency in patient flow. This benefit becomes greater as the complexity of scheduling requirements increases. As the growing competition among private physicians intensifies, the ability to minimize patient waiting time provides a distinct advantage. Physician productivity and resource utilization can be enhanced, while scheduling errors (e.g., gaps and overbooking) can be minimized.

Of more interest, however, is the potential addition of intelligence to such systems. Intelligence in this context denotes the capability of the software to generate conclusions based on logical rules built or entered into it (e.g., two patients cannot be scheduled for the same examination room at the same time). For example, if a given health provider or equipment setup was needed for a certain group of patients who required appointments within a certain period, an intelligent scheduler could group those patients together on a certain day. Conversely, if a given room or piece of equipment was needed for a certain group of patients, that scheduler could avoid placing those patients together. Periodic health screening, perhaps one of the most important interventions that practitioners can make on behalf of the community as a whole, could be automated so that health-care providers would not have to depend on themselves to remember which procedures was indicated for a given patient at a given visit.[1] Alternatively, the system could generate a reminder that a procedure was indicated and an appointment could be made. All these capabilities could be realized with minimal involvement by scheduling personnel or practitioners except for setting up the initial retrieval organization.

Searching the Literature

Another use of computers that is bound to have a major effect on the private practice of medicine is on-line literature searches. One traditional dichotomy between physicians in academic medical centers and practicing physicians has been the difference in their ease of access to the medical literature. Most physicians in academic settings are a few steps away from a medical library. In addition, they often have a medical librarian at their service to perform literature searches on specific topics, either manually or through a literature-retrieval system whose use was reserved for a library-search specialist. Private practitioners, on the other hand, have had to rely on whatever journals they subscribed to, the most recent editions of textbooks in their possession and supplementation of these resources by trips to a medical library when time permitted. To compound this dilemma, medical librarians were not allowed to conduct literature searches for private physicians in many cases, or prohibitive fees were charged. The circumstances necessary for perpetuation of such a dichotomy have ceased to exist. Any physician can obtain a personal computer, modem and printer for less than $2,000. There is an everincreasing number of on-line search services that allow physicians to access large and comprehensive medical data bases through commercial telecommunications networks.[2] The mechanics of the search process for desired information are easy to learn with presently existing software, even for physicians who are unfamiliar with computers.[3,4] Searches can be conducted according to subject, words in the title or abstract of an article, range of publication dates, author's name or any combination of these descriptors. The cost of subscribing to a search service is relatively low, and the per-minute fee charged for hookup time to this type of data base is also relatively inexpensive, especially during off-peak hours.

Originally, only the title of an article and the text of the abstract were available on line. After determining whether an article was relevant, a physician had to go to a library and retrieve the article or order it through a commercial retrieval service. More recently, however, the full texts of most major medical journals, textbooks and newsletters have become available on line.[5-7] Thus, the breadth of medical literature has, for the most part, become available to every physician with scant seconds of delay in access time, even in the most remote rural areas or busy office-bound practices.

There are problems with such systems, however. For one thing, the systems in their current form are unable to transmit video images, such as graphs, charts, diagrams and reproductions of photographs. The amount of memory and speed of transmission required to perform this task make it impractical with current technology. Computer screens and the hardware/software that drive them have not been standardized as thoroughly for video as they have for text. It is likely that these problems will be overcome by the general advance of technology in this area. Also, "electronic page turning" is still too expensive to replace its printed counterpart, although its cost may decrease as the potential size of the market and number of vendors increase. Finally, there are always delays in signing on to a data base, equipment malfunctions and other sources of failure to obtain access that might cause users to procrastinate or omit a search of less than paramount importance. Once again, these problems may be resolved by market factors and improving technology.

The advent of the CD-ROM drive at an affordable price takes literature searching one step further. With this technology, mass storage of data of this type becomes available in the office or at home, obviating the factors of cost, delay and equipment malfunction. Currently, the entire contents of several years of the Index Medicus can (and do) fit on to a compact disc indistinguishable from that used in a home audio system. Popularity of the CD-ROM drive will undoubtedly improve access of nonhospital-based practitioners to the medical literature and improve the general standard of medical care.

The major impact that the phenomenon of inexpensive, easy-to-use, literature searching and retrieval will have on the practice of medicine will be to improve the quality of health care. No doubt, the next generation of private practitioners will grow up using such systems and will rely on them as an integral part of their practice rather than as a novelty or luxury, as many physicians now mistakenly regard them to be.[8] In fact, it is likely that on-line literature searching will come to constitute a portion of what is legally termed "reasonable standard of care" and thus become a necessity for practitioners from a malpractice insurer's point of view.

Electronic Mail

A closely related issue is that of electronic mail. Because any type of text can be converted to a standardized form of signal, it is now possible to transmit personal communications from computer to computer over telephone lines in a manner similar to that which occurs with a literature-search interaction. This is a rapid means of information transfer that may prove useful to physicians, as in the transfer of electronic patient records (discussed in the next section) or any other information that requires physical transfer of paper. Commercial networks that provide this service are now commonly used in many other businesses; as the concept becomes more popular, its cost should drop, and many physicians will find it advantageous to avail themselves of this service. Similarly, "teleradiology" is now a reality. A clinician can have a radiographic image transmitted to a remote location to view and act upon. The quality of the image transmitted is faithful to the original near the resolution of the human eye, although this cannot be effected in "real time" yet; several seconds are required to transmit.

Keeping "Paperless" Medical Records

Electronic, or paperless, charting is rapidly becoming a reality. Until recently, the size and cost of systems that could handle the volume of data at a useful processing speed were prohibitive for all except the largest facilities. It should be clear from other sections of this chapter that this situation has changed or is changing. Although commercial examples of electronic patient-charting systems for a typical private office are still rare, the widespread use of such systems is not far off.

What are the benefits of such systems? Obviously, time and cost savings are important factors in determining whether such a system is useful. Virtually all the physical and personnel costs of chart handling can be eliminated by such a system because no space-occupying storage arrangements are needed and chart retrieval is basically instantaneous.

Another benefit is the possibility of enhancing the quality of care. Protocol-based reminders, as described earlier, can be implemented easily on an electronic charting system. The general medicine clinic of a university teaching hospital has been studied in a randomized clinical trial. In this study, reminders from an electronic computer record concerning indicated actions for health problems requiring attention (as determined by a committee of general-medicine faculty and appropriate consulting subspecialists) were furnished to physicians in the study group. The study demonstrated a much higher rate of response to indications in the study group than in the control subjects, thereby providing strong evidence that such reminders can indeed have an impact on health care.[9]

Along with protocol-based reminders, an automated medical record can be configured to detect potential drug interactions, to adjust drug dosages based on individual pharmacokinetic variations, to detect adverse drug-disease interactions and to adjust drug therapy to achieve its stated objectives. Diagnoses can be inferred from information in the chart, and the proper outcome measures to follow up and assess therapy can be assured.[10]

As Barnett[11] pointed out in an article that describes one of the oldest and most extensive computer-based medical-record systems in existence, an ambulatory-care record may contain entries from a variety of health-care providers that must be integrated into a common record. There are growing strains on the capabilities of any manual system, including requirements imposed by governmental agencies, legal issues, the reimbursement process and nearly every health-care provider's desire to assess and improve the standards of care for patients. There are also inherent disadvantages to a manual system that remain practically insurmountable, such as the possibility of physical unavailability, loss or destruction of a record, poor organization, illegibility of handwriting and the need for duplication of data recording. Assimilation of information from a group of records, as would be done in quality-of-care or clinical studies, is exceedingly burdensome when each record must be searched manually to retrieve the desired information. A computer-based medical-record system by its nature obviates a substantial portion of each of these problems.

There are disadvantages to a computer-based medical-record system as well. First is the structural problem. With a manual record, the text is entered free form without regard to content or choice of terms. For any meaningful amount of intrarecord organizing to occur, a computer-based system requires a predefined vocabulary and a predefined set of rules for manipulating the information. Imposing such constraints on physicians might well defeat the purpose of automation because the clerical burden would be merely transferred from the clerical staff to physicians (e.g., memorization of the vocabulary) instead of disappearing. There will always be a trade-off between the depth or detail of clinical information and the degree to which it can be processed as other than free text (e.g., as a clinical data base), at least until computer interpretation of natural language is far beyond its current state of the art.

At present, the difficulties with coding can be partially overcome by providing the stored clinical information in the form of a compact summary that makes liberal use of tables, graphic charts and flow sheets. With this configuration of a medical record, a physician can merely fill in blanks to provide much of the information generated by a given patient encounter. The remainder can be written directly on the summary as a short progress note to be entered into the electronic record by a clerk at a subsequent time. It appears that the amount and type of data furnished to and supplied by a physician in this format do no harm to the flow of information and may even improve the quality of care by making it possible to arrange and summarize information in a concise and legible manner.[12]

Confidentiality and security are perhaps greater problems with electronic records than with paper ones, mainly because the latter require only prevention of physical access to a chart. Conceivably, electronic-chart information can be retrieved from a remote location without any member of an office staff being aware that the information was accessed if proper safeguards are not in place. Even more importantly, it is much easier to tamper with the contents of an electronic chart than with the contents of its paper counterpart because information can be altered electronically without any visible evidence, such as erasures or crossing out. The consequences of such actions can obviously be grave. However, these problems can be partially overcome by impending technologic advances. Security systems are being developed that will recognize users by means other than a password typed in from the keyboard, and such safeguards will eventually become commonplace on systems of this type. Systems may eventually be equipped with transactional recorders conceptually similar to the flight recorders found on commercial aircraft. Such devices provide a sequential and physically permanent log (on paper, magnetic tape or both) of all keyboard entries from a given terminal as well as the identity of the person who made them, in this way providing a virtually permanent and verifiable audit trail. It would then be possible to locate entries on the basis of time of entry, user, terminal or record. Alteration of the tape or paper log would be much more difficult than alteration of an electronic data file, especially if the log were removed or recorded to a remote location. This feature would safeguard both patients (against unauthorized changes to or access of their records) and physicians (against claims that a record was intentionally altered for legal reasons).

Also, again borrowing from general technologic advances, data encryption techniques have advanced to the point where anyone without the proper "key" can be assumed to be prohibited from access to encrypted information. In the current environment of risk-pool exclusion as well as the general augmentation of consumer demand on health-care providers, the significance of this advance cannot be underestimated. Encryption, of course, is not practical in a paper-based system.

For the sake of efficiency, it may be worthwhile in many situations to create systems designed specifically for the setting in which they are to be used. Because storage of fewer data may be necessary, customized systems can be smaller. Any sorting tasks that are requested of such a system will be accomplished more quickly. They would be easier to use because the number of possibilities for data entry would be smaller, and complete operation via a series of menus would be much less cumbersome than in the generalized systems just discussed. Systems of this type have been created for tumor registries[13] and hospital-based dialysis units.[14] More germane to the office practice of medicine, computerized medical records in outpatient hypertension clinics were found to enhance retrievability, assure completeness and allow some degree of standardization.[15]

Automated History Taking

It is a generally accepted notion among clinicians that part of their daily responsibilities consists of rote mechanical tasks. An example is the gathering of data that occurs on a physician's initial encounter with a patient as well as during the initial part of subsequent encounters. One approach that has been tried in an attempt to circumvent this time-consuming process has been the creation of forms for patients to fill out before being seen by physicians. The results from the form-filling method have been largely unsatisfactory.[16] To obtain the amount and detail of data required for a clinically useful history, a large and unwieldy form, typically many pages in length, must be used, with most questions seemingly irrelevant. There is no opportunity to focus on areas where additional information may be important, as occurs in most models of clinical reasoning, where information and testing of intermediate hypotheses begin early in the history taking process. Also, the doctor-patient relationship commences during the history-taking process, when both persons have a chance to "size each other up." The way in which questions are responded to may be as clinically important as the responses. Clearly, the most exhaustive form that could be created would not compensate for these deficiencies.

It should be obvious from the previous sections of this chapter that computerized history may overcome some of these problems while still saving physicians' time. User interfaces can be simplified to the point where any patient capable of seeing (or even hearing) could successfully transmit his or her responses to a computer with minimal instruction. Software products can (and have) been designed that simulate direct history taking by a physician,[17] so the brute-force approach taken by form filling need not be duplicated. In fact, such a system is likely to be more comprehensive than direct history taking by a physician if it is thoughtfully designed. An added advantage is that such a product could be integrated with the electronic patient-record schemata previously discussed, thus providing physicians with the beginning of an organized chart before they even meet their patients!

The personal interaction between physician and patient that occurs during the history-taking process cannot be replaced by automated history taking. Undoubtedly, physicians obtain much subjective, undocumentable information whose value, nonetheless, cannot be discounted. However, in the changing health-care marketplace, where profit is directly related to efficient use of physician time, automated history taking may become commonplace.

COMPUTERS IN HOSPITALS

The operation of a hospital requires the skills and varied abilities of numerous types of personnel. It follows that the applications of computer technology to the hospital setting are also diverse. As noted earlier, hospital depend on the financial and record-keeping capabilities of computers in many areas, such as the billing office, medical-records department, admissions office, personnel office and supply department. Many hospital pharmacies now have computerized inventory control, patient data pertaining to past and present medication histories, electronic drug and drug-interaction data bases and pharmacokinetics calculation capabilities.[18] Nursing departments are beginning to use fully or partially computerized histories, progress notes and problem-solving software. The medical libraries of most hospitals have on-line, or CD-ROM-based literature-searching systems; many of them have electronic card catalogs as well. Radiology departments can and often do register patients, keep track of films and even enter interpretations by computer,[19] with verified cost effectiveness.[20] Hence, computers are already viewed as integral components of midsized or large hospitals, as is electrical power—hospitals theoretically could function without electrical power, but at an undesirable level. Bleich and colleagues[21] have proposed in a recent review on the subject that the keys to optimal use of computers in the hospital setting are integration of the various elements into a hospital-wide system, immediate availability of data via terminals instead of having to wait for printed reports, a rapid response time to on-line user queries, reliability, protection of confidentiality, user friendliness (minimal instruction necessary) and a common registry for all patients. The computer systems of few hospitals would now meet these specifications. However, it is reasonable to predict that these features will be standard in the hospital computer systems of the future.

Laboratory Systems

An illustrative case in point concerning the potential for improvement in hospital health-care delivery by use of computer systems is the laboratory service of a large hospital. Consider the following scenario, still painfully true in many less well-funded institutions. A physician decides to order a laboratory test on a specimen of blood for a patient whom he is caring for. He writes the order in the chart. After some variable delay, the written (often illegibly) order is transcribed by a ward clerk, who generally possesses a high-school education or less, onto a multilayered slip, one copy of which is brought down to the laboratory by a member of the escort service. The order is logged onto a form by yet another clerk with a similar level of education and, theoretically at the appropriate time, a copy of the form or slip is given to a phlebotomist. He then obtains the sample, attaches the slip or a corresponding label to it and brings it back down to the laboratory. Here it is logged in again and then brought to the appropriate area of the laboratory for the test to be run, generally in a batch with a number of other specimens. The operator fills in all the results of the testing on that batch onto still another form, which then goes to a person who transcribes the results back onto another copy of the original slip. A member of the escort service then brings the slip back to the ward clerk, who places it back into the proper chart.

This scenario serves to point out the numerous opportunities for loss, error, inaccuracy and delay that are possible in a manual laboratory system. However, this type of system is simply not necessary. If available technology at reasonable cost were used, the scenario might be as follows: A physician decides to order a laboratory test on a specimen of blood for a patient whom he is caring for. He goes to the computer terminal at the nursing station or other convenient location, enters his identification number, his security password, the patient's name, the requested time for the test to be drawn and the type of test to be run. The computer then determines whether a similar test was recently done; if so, it furnishes the result as well as the cost to the patient and inquires whether cancellation is desired. If cancellation is not desired, the as-yet-unobtained specimen is assigned an identification number. Because the system is tied directly into the laboratory through the main hospital computer, the terminal at the phlebotomists' station immediately assigns the sample to a phlebotomist and prints out labels readable not only by hand but also by optical sensors similar to the bar-code readers now found at the checkout counters of many supermarkets. The computer also arranges for specimens to be drawn in batches to optimize use of the phlebotomist's time; a work list is generated that the phlebotomist takes up to the floor. The blood is drawn and brought back to the laboratory (small robots now exist which could perform this function adequately). Labeled specimen tubes are read and logged in according to identification number by an optical sensor and automatically routed, either by a message on a video screen or by direct mechanical means. The specimen arrives at the proper equipment, where the test is run. All the laboratory instruments are tied into the computer, so the test results are immediately transferred into the patient's electronic record and are obtainable by the physician as soon as the testing has been done, usually in a format that places the result in a table with results of the same and related tests obtained on that patient previously. Alternatively, the physician can view the information graphically, obtain interpretations of the test result in the context of differential diagnosis or methodologic considerations or even receive advice on how best to pursue or rule out possible diagnoses. In addition, summary reports are printed at appropriate intervals and placed in the charts for a more global view of the patient's progress. With this system, at any point in the process from request to reporting, information on the location and status of a specimen can be obtained, and delays are minimized. Many opportunities for human error, especially those on the part of less well trained personnel, are eliminated. In addition, the information is returned in a more usable, and possibly clinically annotated, form.

Few physicians would disagree that the latter scenario is infinitely preferable. In fact, it will someday be commonplace if not ubiquitous, given the trend toward hospitalization of only the sickest patients with the recent consolidations and consequent centralization of resources. As the "level of sickness" rises in a hospital, so do the number of tests required per patient and the importance of timely reporting of test results. These "hospital-wide intensive care units" of the future will certainly rely on computer technology for their laboratory systems.

COMPUTERS IN ACADEMIC MEDICAL CENTERS

Research

Computers are of inestimable value in the execution of clinical research. It is, of course, possible to perform a profusion of statistical calculations on massive quantities of data on paper. It is far more practical to employ a computer in one of its more pedestrian roles to perform the calculations, thereby saving vast amounts of time and ensuring arithmetic accuracy. Statistical software packages that perform virtually all the statistical calculations commonly used in clinical research are easy to find for nearly any computer currently being marketed and are well within the budget of most research projects. Many software packages also have the capability to generate professional-quality tables, figures, graphs and other diagrams directly from the data and derived statistics.

The clinical data base is the foundation of most endeavors in medical research and has benefited greatly from the introduction of computers. A clinical data base, on a computer or otherwise, can be thought of as a stack of identical forms. Each form corresponds to a patient, and each entry on the form corresponds to a piece of clinical data about the patient, arranged so that the same place on each form corresponds to the same piece of clinical data (a category). For instance, a clinical data base about trauma in the emergency room might have such categories as location of injury, type of injury and mechanism of injury. The data can be sorted according to category or combination of categories, and statistics can be generated on a formal or an informal basis. A clinical data base can be designed not only around a specific protocol but also with the expectation that future retrospective analyses with respect to other variables may be performed, thus saving repetitive, laborious and inaccurate reviews of charts. A clinical data base can easily be integrated with the electronic medical-record systems previously discussed, culling the appropriate data when desired directly from storage. A moderate degree of standardization will allow for pooling of data from more than one physical location, enhancing the feasibility of multicenter studies. All these functions can be realized on an interactive basis, which is markedly impractical with a paper-based system.

The net result of the employment of clinical data bases in research protocols is immeasurable savings in time and money, increased assurance of accuracy and of true randomization and the ability to reuse the data for other studies. In the future, most clinical research will be conducted with the aid of such advanced systems.

Bibliographic Assistance

Another welcome aspect of the availability of computers to physicians in academia is bibliographic assistance. Consultants in every specialty and subspecialty are continually called on to give an opinion in complex cases. Often, giving an informed opinion requires a review of the relevant literature on the subject, much of which is in the form of journal articles. The number of articles that most academicians feel they must have at hand becomes unmanageable at an early stage in their careers, so some sort of manual filing system is instituted. Such a system may work well initially, but most manual filing strategies fail sooner or later. Failure may be related to the degree of motivation a physician has for maintaining files, but even a motivated physician may experience difficulty in maintaining well-organized files due to the nonhierarchic nature of medical information. In other words, an article might properly be filed under more than one heading. The traditional solutions are to make sufficient copies of each article so that one can be filed under each of the pertinent headings or to create and constantly update a cross-reference list for each heading. Both solutions take time that is most likely better spent in other pursuits.

A better solution is to use a commercial data-based program on a personal computer for referencing articles. There are many such programs being sold, both specifically for journal articles and generally for a multitude of data-based applications. Although general data-based programs may require more time to learn, they tend to be more powerful and flexible in what they can do in terms of sorting, indexing, generating printouts and otherwise manipulating the contents of the data base.[22] The reference list for this chapter, for example, was created by use of a data-based program. With the advances discussed under "Searching the Literature," a personal bibliographic section may become necessary, however.

COMPUTERS AND MEDICAL EDUCATION

Patient Education

The potential for the use of computers as an aid in patient education remains to be exploited. In ambulatory adults, certain health problems are extremely common; examples are hypertension, diabetes mellitus, coronary-artery disease and degenerative joint disease. Most physicians would agree that all these health problems are at least partially amenable to therapy, especially if a patient has a basic understanding of his or her problem and its consequences and complies with the recommended therapy. However, most physicians and health-care facilities lack the resources for providing the comprehensive patient education that makes this understanding possible. Automation could be a viable solution to this problem. A microcomputer work station could serve as the primary educator for any patient if the material to be learned was presented at an appropriate level and in a format designed to maintain interest. Such a feature of an office or clinic would take advantage of the widespread curiosity and fascination with computers in American society. It would provide an opportunity for the public to experience the hands-on access to a computer that so many people crave but remain tentative about pursuing. It would also take advantage of the public's recently acquired obsession with health, allowing them to take a greater amount of control over and responsibility for, their health. Such a system could largely function independently from health-care personnel after initial setup and may even become a source of revenue in certain situations, not to mention the possible benefits derived from upgrading a person's health, decreasing morbidity from chronic disease (including the need for hospitalization) and prolonging life.

Professional Education

Computers have already been used in all phases of professional medical education, from premedical science to continuing education in the subspecialties. Computerized medical education has met with varying degrees of success, affected not only by the audience for whom a given program was intended but also by the format used. On the simplest level, there are a large number of commercially available programs that present material in a form that resembles that of the National Board of Medical Examiners questions with which nearly all physicians are familiar. Such programs offer little or no advantage over the traditional printed workbooks. In fact, they may be even less desirable because the visual aspect of the materials is far inferior to printed illustrations, unless an accompanying picture book (unwieldy) or videodisk system (expensive and rare) is used. Another type of program is a case presentation followed by a list of management options, one of which the user selects. The program then informs the user whether the choice was correct or incorrect, should provide some insight into why this is so and if an incorrect response was given, and prompts for another response. After the correct response is entered, the program proceeds to the next question. The concept works well in theory only. It is difficult to identify all the possible reasonable responses that a physician would have given to a problem. Failure to list an option that a physician might request rapidly leads to antipathy toward the program. Selection of the correct answer in and of itself gives no assurance that the material was properly understood—the user may have guessed at the answer. Also, situations in clinical practice for which there is only one correct answer (or the answer is not complex) tend to be trivial ones, so an educational experience with problems of that type are for the most part irrelevant. For these reasons, much of what is available today for computerized medical education is simply not worth the trouble.

This is not to say that computers could not add in a major way to the process of medical education. There are certain educational formats that lend themselves well to computerization. There are other formats that actually necessitate computerization. An example of the first type is a programmed learning text; an example of the second type is a critiquing system. Both types will be discussed.

The educational process as realized in a programmed learning text is an entity with which many physicians will be familiar. For physicians who are not familiar with programmed learning text, it functions as follows: A certain amount of information to be learned, heretofore referred to as an educational unit, is presented. The unit is small, usually a few sentences in length, and self-contained. After presentation, several questions are asked about the unit. The questions are most often in a fill-in-the-blanks, true/false or multiple-choice format and can be answered by inspection of the unit in conjunction with material learned from previous units. After the questions are asked, correct answers are provided. The next unit is then presented, and the procedure is repeated. Full comprehension of the material that any unit provides requires comprehension of the material in previous units. Therefore, the text builds on itself and education takes place.

There are several disadvantages to programmed learning texts as an educational method. The disadvantages stem from the inherent lack of feedback in a teacher-pupil relationship. One is the "bogging down" problem. If a learner does not understand a unit, the educational process comes to a screeching halt. The associated questions cannot be answered, and the learner has no choice except to back up through the text until a point is reached where he or she is assured of comprehension and once again goes through the previously experienced units. This process can be tedious; there is nothing to ensure that a better understanding of the material would be obtained on successive attempts. In a more traditional educational setting, a teacher would supply alternative ways of looking at the same material. This approach is simply not possible when a programmed learning text is used. A related problem is the lack of any sort of ongoing evaluation of the learner. Finally, education via a programmed learning text requires motivation, which means the material must maintain the learner's interest. Maintaining interest may be an insurmountable obstacle with certain types of information.

A computer-based programmed learning environment could furnish a distinct improvement over a programmed learning text. The foundations of this improvement lie in a computer's ability to perform branching logic and maintain a record of a learner's previous responses. To illustrate: If the learner responds incorrectly to the questions associated with a unit, the program could explain why the response was incorrect and prompt for another response. Subsequently, that unit could be presented again in another way and other pertinent questions asked. This sequence could continue until a point where the hypothesis was made (by continued incorrect responses) that the previous material was not learned sufficiently well. At that point, the program would return to the previous unit, perhaps presenting that unit in a number of different ways. An additional degree of sophistication would have the program attempt by selective questioning to assess where the deficiency in understanding lay. When the deficiency was ascertained, the program would then return to the appropriate unit for review by further alternative modes of presentation and more questions. In this way, bogging down can be completely avoided if the material is at a suitable intellectual level for the learner. To combat the motivational obstacle, use of a computer is far superior to use of a printed page. Most systems now have video and audio capabilities. Unlike illustrations on a printed page, a computer-generated video image can have alluring kinetic aspects. It can change size, color and apparent spatial orientation practically instantaneously. Cross-sections of an object can be created, viewed and rotated; various aspects of cross-sections can be easily highlighted. The value of these capabilities in such a subject as anatomy is unquestionable. Audio, too, can aid in keeping the attention of a learner. Portions of recognizable melodies can be played when correct responses are given or at fitting junctures during a learning session. Discordant tones can sound for an incorrect response. Finally, frivolous interludes can be provided to break up the intensity of a prolonged learning session. All these aspects allow a programmed learning environment to resemble an amusing game without detracting at all from its content, purpose or efficacy.

In time, as artificial-intelligence programming techniques evolve and as user interfaces, such as speech recognition/synthesis, become standard features of computer hardware, such a programmed learning environment will serve as an adequate replacement for a human teacher. Given the eventual inexpensiveness of these developments, the decreasing governmental funding for medical education at all levels and the ongoing desire on the part of many medical educators (with influence on policy) to make much of medical education universal, it seems that programmed learning environments will be an important and widely used educational tool in the future.[23]

Another innovation in medical education made possible by computers is automation of the Socratic method by means of a critiquing system.

A critiquing system is a clever adaptation of the medical-expert systems discussed later in this chapter. In an expert system, the user enters some information about a patient. By logic and calculation and from stored information, the system draws conclusions about the patient and then generates diagnostic or therapeutic advice (or both) about the patient. A critiquing system possesses the same logic, calculation and stored information but reverses this sequence. The system furnishes information about a hypothetical patient. The learner is then prompted to enter conclusions. The conclusions are compared to the conclusions that the system would have generated from the information, and the reasons for any differences are discussed by the system. This type of system thereby provides an evaluation rather than a correct/incorrect pronouncement, which is especially useful in problems for which only one correct answer may not exist. Such problems are obviously common in clinical medicine. A working critiquing system has been created to teach the design of an anesthesia regimen for a patient with underlying health problems who is scheduled for surgery.[24]

COMPUDOC: COMPUTERS AS CLINICAL ASSISTANTS

In many fields, one of the major boons brought about by computers was relieving users from the computational burden and monotony of repeated but relatively automatic tasks. Also, computers served well as a repository of readily accessible but hard-to-remember information. Medicine has more than its share of the former types of task, and the memorization of countless lists of differential diagnoses, signs and symptoms of diseases, drug dosages/interactions/adverse effects and anatomic relationships is one of the well-recognized ordeals of medical education. For this reason, a number of workers in various areas within medicine began turning their attention toward application of computers to management of medical information and to its more notorious counterpart—medical decision making. The latter applications take the general medical information or knowledge (statistics, IF . . . THEN . . . ELSE rules, data/disease relationships) available in the first type of program and apply it to a specific patient by using characteristics of the patient (symptoms, signs, laboratory data). This application results in the generation of likely diagnoses, recommendations for therapy, suggestions for management or any combination of this information. In short, they attempt to mimic the process by which a physician makes decisions concerning care of a given patient.

Computerization is not a prerequisite for implementation of a medical-decision system. In fact, the literature abounds with examples of medical-decision systems that exist only on paper.[25] However, all except the simplest models of diagnostic reasoning impose an impression computational or logical burden (or both) on their users. In addition, a computer's ability to accurately retain and quickly manipulate large quantities of data makes automation of such systems a natural phenomenon.

When the information and processing capabilities of a system can accurately simulate the problem-solving behavior of persons who have expertise in the problem areas addressed by the system, the system is considered to be an expert system. A multitude of programs that purport to be expert systems have been created to provide diagnostic considerations or therapeutic strategies (or both) in a diverse number of clinical areas. We will examine this field in some detail because it is the area that may have the greatest impact on the practice of medicine in the future.

Medical Decision Systems

Smart Calculators

Medical-decision systems are by no means a homogeneous group. The simplest medical-decision systems began to appear in the 1960s. Such systems basically employed a computer as a smart calculator, where "smart" denotes the ability to retain constants and formulas. In such programs, the user needs only to enter the values of the variables as input. The output of such systems is a set of output values derived from these input values, which theoretically have clinical relevance. Such programs can not only be time-saving but also are inherently accurate and can spare the user from tedious, error-prone calculation and the need for memorization of a multitude of constants and formulas. Applications that have been published in the general medical literature include temperature correction of arterial blood gases,[26] derivation of important hemodynamic parameters from data obtained via Swan-Ganz catheterization,[27] parameters for nutritional and metabolic assessments[28] and calculation of the probability of an acute myocardial ischemic event in a patient presenting to the emergency room with chest pain.[29]

Algorithmic Systems

An algorithmic-decision system is one that can be uniquely defined by a graphic flow diagram, an example of which is illustrated in Figure 1. It sets forth a stepwise procedure for making decisions about the management of a clinical problem that the designer of the algorithm would use if confronted with the problem.[30] The primary objective of a clinical algorithm is to allow physicians who are functioning at a less than expert level concerning a clinical problem to simulate the behavior of an alleged expert or group of experts in approaching the problem. To use an algorithmic-decision system, one makes certain clinical observations about a given patient when prompted by a computer. Calculations and branching logic are performed as encoded in the program, and advisory messages are produced. The nature of the messages can be diagnostic, therapeutic

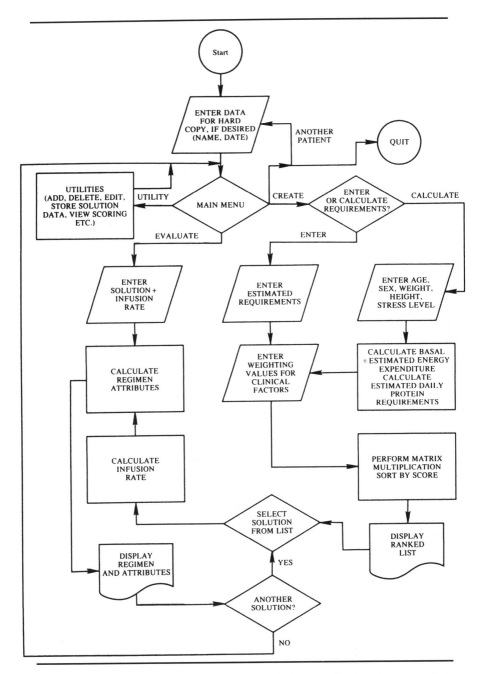

Figure 11.1 An example of a flow sheet that defines an algorithmic approach to a clinical problem.

or both. Such programs are easy to compose when (1) the number of inputs is relatively small, (2) a value for each input is always available, (3) a unique advisory output can be specified (in the real world) for every possible combination of inputs and (4) the logical pathways necessary for design of such a program can be obtained from an authoritative or validated source, such as an expert or the medical literature. Unfortunately, clinically useful algorithmic systems cannot be created for many health problems because these conditions cannot be met. For instance, any clinical information that impacts on the algorithm must be accounted for, which tends to make the number of input variables unmanageable. In the real world, there are often missing or imprecise data corresponding to a program's input values, which makes an output impossible. In clinical practice, one may encounter unusual or spurious clinical data that must be accounted for by the algorithm. Few textbooks or journal articles contain information in a form that can be extracted to construct an algorithm. Experts may often disagree about the outputs derived from unusual combinations of inputs, which detracts from the credibility of the results. There is a well-grounded fear that blind use of algorithms without understanding what went into their creation may undermine the reasoning processes that make physicians more than mere technicians; decisions based on the use of algorithms can be uninformed decisions.[31]

All these problems can be overcome. Careful construction of an algorithm based on well-validated information by physicians whose expertise in an area is unquestionable, flagging of unusual input or output values to inform the user that the results may not be valid and explanation of the thinking behind the decision process at every step of the way are keys to success. The final problem with this type of system cannot be overcome so easily because it is inherent in its design: the calculations and branching logic are encoded in the program itself. The implication is that to incorporate any new information, the program must be rewritten. The information and the manner with which it is used are inseparable, making programs of this type rather inflexible. In the words of experts in this field, such a program is "domain dependent."

Despite these considerations, such programs have been created and can be useful in selected areas. Examples exist for the diagnosis of acid-base disorders,[32] the decision to admit a patient with chest pain to a cardiac care unit,[33] the delivery of protocol-based adjuvant chemotherapy outside academic medical centers to patients with breast cancer,[34] the diagnosis and management of hemodynamic disorders[35] and the creation of parenteral hyperalimentation regimens.[36]

Algorithmic systems are especially useful for providing instruction on handling clinical problems to nonphysician health-care providers, who may be technically competent but have less insight into the rationale behind management decisions and who thus are not qualified to make such decisions but only to carry them out.[37,38] On a large scale, use of algorithmic systems in this setting may prove particularly cost effective. Their computerization and availability on line allow for immediate updating as new approaches to clinical problems become accepted. In this way, the users of the system can provide state-of-the-art care without the lag time associated with the mass production and distribution of printed material.

Decision Analysis

Decision analysis is an approach that is vastly different from the use of clinical algorithms.[39] The emphasis in decision analysis is on validation of proposed clinical algorithms rather than on their use. Thus, decision analysis can be regarded as a meta-algorithmic process. In other words, working with the same type of input data utilized by an algorithmic system, decision analysis attempts to compare alternative management strategies in terms of the probabilities and the costs versus the benefits (known as "utilities" by decision analyzers) of possible outcomes of those management strategies. Costs and benefits are at least in part subjective,[40] both on the part of a patient and on the part of the physician. Actual probabilities of outcomes are often not known. Therefore, decision analysis allows one to add flexibility to an algorithm and in effect custom design it for a given patient.[41]

Decision analysis is generally performed with the aid of decision trees, which are graphic representations of management options. An example of a decision tree is shown in Figure 2. The true power of decision analysis and decision trees becomes apparent when the probabilities and utilities are varied in a stepwise manner over a range of reasonable values. Because the exact probabilities are often not known, and the utilities can at best only be estimated, it is nearly mandatory that they be varied to see how much variation influences selection of management options and where the breakpoints for selection are. These processes of variation are known as threshold calculation[42] and sensitivity analysis,[43] the details of which are beyond the scope of this chapter.

Obviously, the performance of decision analysis necessitates a multitude of calculations, with the attendant potential for arithmetic errors. Fortunately, microcomputer software for modeling and analyzing decision trees have been developed,[44] and the literature abounds with clinical applications relating to complex management dilemmas.[45]

Data-Based Systems (Pattern Recognition)

When we move into the realm of data-based decision systems, we begin to see the separation of knowledge and inference that characterizes true expert systems. Such systems utilize a collection of numeric information that can be conceived of as being in a tabular or matrix form. A typical medical application would have each row of the table correspond to a disease and each column correspond to a clinical manifestation that

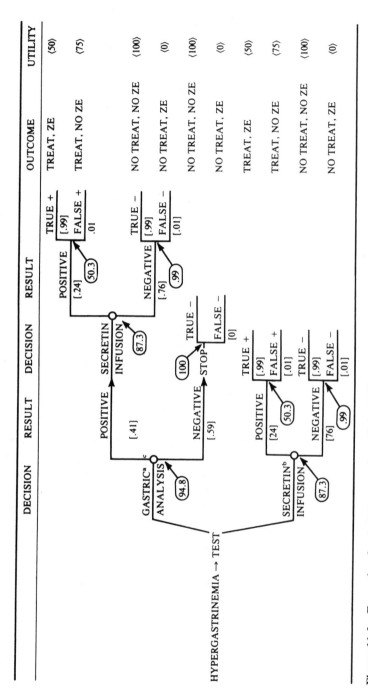

Figure 11.2 Example of a decision tree from Spindel.[25]

may or may not be present in each of the diseases listed in the rows of the table or matrix. Each element of the table or matrix would correspond to a quantitative or semiquantitative measure of the frequency of a manifestation of the disease. These measures could be prevalence rates, numbers of patients or weighted criteria. In any event, when the table or matrix is fully "filled in," it can be used in decision making. More specifically, the user of the program can enter the clinical manifestations exhibited by a given patient. The program can then compare these manifestations against the data base and generate some sort of numeric assessment of the most likely disease. Such numeric assessment can be affected in a number of ways.

SEMIQUANTITATIVE METHODS   In the simplest model of pattern recognition, still using the example of disease diagnosis, a list of manifestations found in a given patient is input. This list is compared serially with a list of manifestations thought to be present in each disease (a row of the table). The diseases whose lists most closely match the patient's list are, in the domain of the system, the most likely diagnoses. This type of system works with raw numbers of manifestations, disregarding the relative weight of manifestations for a certain diagnosis. Hence, it is relatively primitive, and its clinical viability for use with actual patients remains unknown. Nevertheless, such systems exist.[46]

A more sophisticated model for pattern recognition can be quantitatively weighted with a degree of confidence in the absence of actual numeric data. The basis for such weighting may be either statistically unproved assertions from medical textbooks or journals or the clinical judgment of a physician (or group of physicians) with extensive experience in the field of interest. Although in theory actual data would be preferable, such data are not always available. In any event, this semiquantitative approach can result in impressive clinical performance if the information on which it is based is reliable.

The premier system of this type is INTERNIST-1, whose domain is differential diagnosis in internal medicine.[47] Its data base is extensive, containing hundreds of diseases and thousands of disease manifestations. Although INTERNIST-1 searches this data base by use of goal-directed inference methodology more representative of the knowledge-based systems discussed subsequently, its data base is one of the semiquantitative type, consisting of two variables for each disease–manifestation pair: an evoking strength and a frequency. In addition, there is a global import score for each manifestation, which is used to determine the necessity of concluding a second diagnosis to account for manifestations present in a patient (but not explained by the first diagnosis). The scoring schema for this data base is illustrated in Table 3. INTERNIST-1 also makes provision for links between diseases to account for causality and predisposition, which can aid in concluding a diagnosis.

TABLE 11.3
SCORING SCHEMA FOR INTERNIST-1

Raw score	Interpretation, evoking strength	Interpretation, frequency value
0	Nonspecific—manifestation occurs too commonly to be used to construct a differential diagnosis	
1	Diagnosis is a rare or unusual cause of listed manifestation	Listed manifestation occurs rarely in the disease
2	Diagnosis causes a substantial minority of instances of listed manifestation	Listed manifestation occurs in a substantial minority of cases of the disease
3	Diagnosis is the most common but not the overwhelming cause of listed manifestation	Listed manifestation occurs in roughly half the cases
4	Diagnosis is the overwhelming cause of listed manifestation	Listed manifestation occurs in the substantial majority of cases
5	Listed manifestation is pathognomonic for the diagnosis	Listed manifestation occurs in essential all cases—i.e., it is a prerequisite for the diagnosis

The data-base values, import values and links in INTERNIST-1 are used in a complex inference strategy designed to stimulate diagnostic reasoning. Its performance when applied to the Clinicopathological Conferences of the Massachusetts General Hospital as reported in the *New England Journal of Medicine* appears to be quantitatively similar to that of the hospital clinicians but inferior to that of the case discussants, who presumably are among the most qualified experts in the world to discuss a given case. There are a number of proposed reasons for this shortcoming, but the fact that the performance of a computer system can even be compared on the same level with an "average" clinician at a well-known university teaching hospital is of profound importance and demonstrates the viability of semiquantitative data-based decision systems.

Less-involved systems that use purely semiquantitative methodology also exist, for example, to aid in selection of an enteral hyperalimentation product for a patient with multiple health problems.[48]

CLINICAL DATA-BASE INTERROGATION When actual patient data are available, a more quantitative approach to pattern recognition can be used because a clinical data base can be created. To use the clinical data base to obtain information, the user enters characteristics of a patient that are available for all patients in the data base. The software then searches the data base for all patients with those characteristics and provides a summary of some type of output information for that group. The other information could be final diagnoses, prognoses or other features of the group provided numerically or graphically (or in both ways), as was appropriate. In theory, the user can extrapolate this information for application to the patient. The major methodologic difficulties with interrogation of clinical data bases in this manner are (1) whether the patient under consideration is statistically equivalent to the patients in the data base (transferability), (2) whether patients in the data base are themselves statistically equivalent or whether factors not available in the data base exert as strong or stronger influences on the output and (3) whether samples are large enough to produce statistically valid outputs. Nonetheless, if extrapolation of outputs is subject to critical clinical scrutiny, a clinical data base can be a helpful adjunct to clinical decision making.[49-51]

BAYESIAN DATA BASES   A common and easily understood aid to clinical decision making that can be and is used in data-based decision systems is Bayesian analysis. In this straightforward method of analysis, the necessary types of quantitative data are often readily available. The prevalences of various diseases, the relative prevalence of each clinical manifestation of each disease and the overall prevalence of the clinical manifestation in the population under study are all taken into account. A form of Bayes' theorem applicable to the situation under discussion is illustrated in Figure 3.

Many classical statisticians take issue with the use of Bayes' theorem in a number of the cases where it has been employed.[52] Their main objection stems from the fundamental requirement that conditional independence must exist for Bayes' theorem to be applicable. Conditional independence implies that the presence or absence of any manifestation

---

$$p(D/M) = \frac{p(D) \cdot p(M/D)}{p(M)}$$

Where:

$p(D/M)$ = probability of disease D given manifestations M

$p(D)$ = A priori probability (prevalence, clinical suspicion) of disease D

$p(M/D)$ = probability in disease D that manifestations M are present (sensitivity)

$p(M)$ = overall prevalence of manifestations M for all diseases in the data base

---

Figure 11.3 Bayes' theorem as used in making predictions concerning the likelihood of a disease.

in a certain disease has no effect on whether any other manifestation is present or absent. Obviously, this condition can be a difficult criterion to fulfill. Symptoms and signs tend to occur in clusters; in most instances, large numbers of cases and an involved multivariate analysis are needed to determine which manifestations are truly independent. A further objection is that any patient under consideration by the system must have only one disease as defined in the data base. All clinicians are aware of the frequency with which patients have more than one disease that may share the same manifestations as presenting features. This situation may further limit the clinical utility of Bayesian decision systems.

Perhaps a better measure of the validity of a decision system based on Bayesian analysis is its testing in a prospective manner. Demonstration that the system can produce accurate results when compared against a "gold" standard is sometimes more important than its mathematic verification with classical statistics.[53] Indeed, such systems have been created and shown to produce accurate results in a number of situations. Among the first programs ever in medical decision making was one that aided in the differential diagnosis of congenital heart disease by means of a Bayesian approach.[54] A variety of subsequent programs developed by Bayesian data bases have followed, for application to such clinical problems as the diagnosis of solitary pulmonary nodules,[55] acute abdominal pain,[56] jaundice[57] and coronary-artery disease.[58]

A decision system based on a Bayesian data base has several advantages over the algorithmic systems previously discussed. In an algorithmic system, a set of input conditions produces only one output state, or outcome. There is no indication of the "confidence" that the system has in its output; that is, the likelihood of outcomes other than the principal one. In contrast, inherent in the structure of a Bayesian data base is the ability to predict the probability of every outcome. The difference between the highest and the second highest probabilities can be seen, and an intuitive measure of confidence is present. Also, as mentioned previously, the decisions in an algorithmic system are encoded into the system. On the other hand, a Bayesian data base developed by use of actual patients, diagnoses and manifestations can be constructed. As new information in the form of more patients is obtained, their diagnoses and manifestations can be entered directly into the data base. As a consequence, this type of system can be automatically updated to account for new information without rewriting the program. The methodologic difficulties encountered with the number-of-patient clinical data bases previously discussed are also present in a Bayesian data base, however, which should be kept in mind when clinical use is envisioned.

Knowledge-Based Systems

The most sophisticated type of medical-decision system currently available and being studied is the knowledge-based system. A knowledge-based system is built around a collection of rules or frames, which are statements that define the knowledge contained in the system. Rules are represented in the "IF conditions, THEN consequences (ELSE other consequences)" form in most knowledge-based systems. An example of a typical rule would be: IF (tendinous xanthomata AND coronary-artery disease), THEN likely diagnosis is hypercholesterolemia. Frames deal with many types of relationship in a more descriptive manner. For example:

Hypercholesterolemia

IS CAUSED BY	Acute intermittent porphyria
	Anorexia nervosa
	Familial hypercholesterolemia
	High-cholesterol diet
FINDING	Tendinous xanthomata
MUST HAVE	High serum cholesterol
MUST NOT HAVE	High serum triglyceride
MAY BE COMPLICATED BY	Coronary-artery disease

A collection of such rules or frames constitutes a knowledge base. Unlike the data bases discussed previously, a knowledge base does not need a specific structure; it can be a list of rules or frames in no particular order. It is important to note that the content of all the previously described types of decision system can be represented as rules or frames. Calculations, algorithms and data bases all reduce to subsets of a knowledge-based system.

In addition to a knowledge base, a knowledge-based system must have some means of searching the knowledge base. The software that accomplish this task are known as an inference engine. There are various conceptual types of inference engines; their details are beyond the scope of this chapter. Simply, the process underlying all of them is the generation of intermediate hypotheses. In rule-based generation of intermediate hypotheses, when the conditions on the left side of the IF . . . THEN rule are satisfied, the consequences of the right side can be used as conditions on the left side of another IF . . . THEN rule. With frame-based hypothesizing, the system attempts to assert whether the frame heading (hypercholesterolemia in this example) can be concluded on the basis of the descriptors, then uses the just-concluded frame's associations to find a higher-order (final diagnosis) frame in an attempt to satisfy the conditions necessary to conclude a highest-order frame. In principle, at least, these processes simulate clinical reasoning.

The final component of a knowledge-based system is the user interface, wherein the clinician enters information about a given patient. In some respects, this interface is similar to the input prompting of the previously mentioned types of system. There is one important difference, which has to do with the knowledge-based system's ability to generate intermediate hypotheses. Due to this ability, it can be useful for the system to query the user for information not initially entered to reach a conclusion, in contrast to the other systems, where all information was entered at the outset. As a consequence, the number and nature of the inputs need not be fixed, as is the case with the other types of system. The added information is used in conjunction without previously generated intermediate hypotheses and therefore more closely simulates a medical expert.

The prototypical medical knowledge-based system is MYCIN, which is concerned with presumptive diagnosis and initiation of treatment in patients with life-threatening infectious diseases (bacteremia and meningitis). MYCIN has been shown to perform not significantly differently from infectious-disease experts in its domain.[59] At the time MYCIN was created, its structure was considered so innovative that it has been applied successfully in a diverse collection of medical as well as nonmedical fields. INTERNIST-1, discussed at length previously, is a knowledge-based system whose rules are derived from a disease-manifestation data base and strategies for using that data base.[47] Its real-life performance is also credible.

More recent work has focused on systems with broader knowledge domains that more closely simulate the breadth of expertise that might be possessed by an academically oriented subspecialist. ONCOCIN is a knowledge-based system that functions on the level of an expert oncologist in the management of an ambulatory clinic for patients with lymphoma being treated with complex chemotherapy protocols.[60] It considers all factors relevant to the timing and dosages of chemotherapeutic agents in complex protocols, markedly improving compliance to such protocols in an outpatient oncology clinic staffed by relatively inexperienced oncologists in training.

There are drawbacks to knowledge-based systems. They are difficult to create, both conceptually and physically. In most instances, higher-level programming languages, such as LISP or PROLOG, are used to maintain comprehensibility and structure. There is much less familiarity with these languages than with the BASIC or FORTRAN most programmers employ. Furthermore, complete dialects of these higher-level languages often exist only for mainframe computers or minicomputers. Only abridged versions, if any at all, are available for personal computers. Another problem is that of overkill. The degree of complexity inherent in a knowledge-based system is simply not necessary for certain clinical problems, especially those for which decisions are based mainly on numeric values. For instance, although a knowledge-based system has been created for arterial blood gas interpretation,[61] It is unclear whether it provides any true advantage over its algorithmic counterpart. Lack of structure in the knowledge-based system may lead to redundancy, paradox or both in the outcomes generated. These outcomes are impossible with a properly designed algorithmic or data-based system. Similarly, varying methods of searching the knowledge base may yield different outcomes. Finally and most importantly is the philosophic issue. It has never been satisfactorily proved that human expertise can always be represented by a set of rules or frames, no matter how many and how detailed. Nevertheless, it has been shown that knowledge-based systems can furnish advice on complex clinical problems that compares favorably with advice furnished by experts.

Discussion

It would seem that there would be few problems with acceptance of a program whose informational content and algorithmic approach to a problem were furnished by a physician knowledgeable in the field. Nonetheless, perhaps no area within the application of computers to medicine generates as much controversy as the use of computers as an aid in diagnosis or therapy. For the most part, physicians can accept computers as an aid to bookkeeping, scheduling or education. However, decisions concerning patient care are considered sacred ground by most physicians. The concept that a machine could do as well or even better in making such decisions is a source of fear, resentment and jealousy. This view of computers as potentially malevolent entities is not limited to physicians, as evidenced by an abundance of popular books and movies. A logical examination of the facts need to be done before an informed judgment can be made about the usefulness or danger (or both) of the so called expert or consultative systems. First of all, such systems are by no means homogeneous. As an illustration, we can observe the following: At one end of the spectrum, there are programs mentioned in this chapter that function as little more than calculators. At the other end, there is a program that alleges to replace an expert oncologist in one of his or her major functions—running an outpatient oncology clinic at an academic medical center where clinical trials are under way. Few physicians would take issue with the conclusions arrived at by the former type of program, no more than they would question arithmetic done on a calculator as being more suspect than that done with pencil and paper. Most physicians would agree that a computer was superior to a human being for that type of task because the output consists merely of information that they may use as a small part of the care of a patient. However, the level of acceptance of the latter program and others of its type is likely to remain low for some time, as definitive management decisions with possibly profound implications are being made.

The variable that seems to correlate best with physicians acceptance is the level of mathematical and logical explainability. Programs of the first type can easily be "dissected." That is, a physician can easily trace the steps gone through to arrive at the conclusions. It does not take a great leap of faith to accept computer-generated interpretations or even recommendations for therapy based directly on quantitative or simple logical data. Programs of the second type are based on relationships rather than on numeric and logical information. When such a program attains a level of sophistication that approaches clinical usefulness, the number of relationships necessary to mimic clinical practice becomes large. Therefore, it becomes nearly impossible to trace through the logical pathways in a similar manner.

All these programs reduce to simple mathematical or logical operations in binary arithmetic, even when higher-level languages are used. Any rule, frame, calculation or logical statement contained in a "working" program would be considered valid by most physicians when examined on an individual basis. It is only when combined in large quantities to form conclusions drawn from large numbers of outcomes that acceptance declines. Paradoxically, it is at this point where the ability of the human mind to simultaneously remember, use and work with large quantities of information becomes overtaxed, that a computer system is of the greatest potential use. Computers are, by their nature, highly accurate and reliable, work extremely quickly and possess (barring equipment mishaps) infallible memories. A program can, by brute computational force, go through every single disease process that afflicts the human race and match the characteristics of a given disorder against the symptoms, signs and available data on the patient under consideration. A physician simply does not have the time for this task. Fortunately, given the level of training and the innate level of intuitive pattern-recognition skill possessed by most physicians, the end result in most cases is a desirable one. Of course, all computer programs are, in the final analysis, created by the human mind and are only as good as their design and the data entered, but those arguments are separate from whether computer programs can potentially generate clinically viable conclusions.

The preceding discussion should not give the idea that the power of a computer is in all respects superior to the human intellect. For one thing, computers are notoriously poor at relating incomplete or partially erroneous data to those that exist in their memory. For example, a human being can recognize a familiar face in a photograph taken years ago, even if out of focus or with part of the face missing. No computer program has yet been written that can mimic this ability because such data cannot be put into rules, frames or any other representation available with current artificial-intelligence techniques. A computer may be programmed to come up with the correct diagnosis for a patient with acute abdominal pain, but it has no way of deciding when to attempt such a differential diagnosis, rarely an issue when a physician is involved. In short, there are many capabilities of the human mind that cannot now, and probably never will, be duplicated by a computer.

What, then, are the present and future roles of computer-aided decision making in medicine? As Blois[62] pointed out, the clinical-judgment process in any situation begins with an extremely large universe of possibilities for "proper" care extending to common sense and acquaintance with the everyday world. As the judgmental process proceeds, the cognitive span required of a physician shrinks, often to a point where the problem can be reduced to a well-defined and structured task that can be represented in one of the formats illustrated previously. Physicians perform better in the initial stages of this process, whereas computers perform better in the final stage. The current thrust of work in computer-aided clinical decision making is to move back the point at which computers can be shown to function as well as or better than physicians. Naturally, the programs that are found at every point along the way require rigorous testing by comparison with human experts before their clinical use is contemplated. As physicians become more comfortable with use of computers in the most well structured types of problem, and the performance of computers in such tasks is shown to be superior, their level of acceptance of programs that deal with problems of a higher degree of difficulty will gradually increase.

The Future

What does the future hold for computer-aided management systems? The answer is obviously complex. Evidence is accumulating that such systems can serve as "medical experts." Medical students are receiving increased exposure to computers, not only during training, when they may be exposed to systems of this type, but also during their daily lives outside medical school. We have a generation of physicians on the way who will be brought up with a better understanding of the abilities and limitations of such systems and who will be more receptive to their use than their predecessors have been. These two observations taken together speak for the eventual widespread acceptance of expert systems as a clinical tool.

The other question that should be asked is how such systems will evolve. One possibility is the development of "intelligent textbooks," as described by Reggia and colleagues.[63] Such systems are like traditional textbooks, containing a collection of knowledge about a given subject, but the information is encoded in a form that can be interpreted by artificial-intelligence programs, thus generating useful patient-specific information. Presumably, the information such systems contain (the knowledge base) as well as the rules or statistics (or both) used to generate patient-specific conclusions (the inference engine) will be accessible, modifiable and appendable by a nonprogrammer. In fact, in their purest form, such systems will be capable of being created from a general shell by nonprogrammers without regard to the information, rules or statistics that they contain (domain-independent systems) by use of natural language. Other variations on this theme include similar systems that use as their information base actual groups of patients seen by a physician or group of physicians and that change as new patients are entered into the data base. In this type of system, the rules or statistics (or both) will change automatically to account for the new data. All these capabilities can be available to physicians on line in a form analogous to the on-line literature data bases discussed previously. Such systems can be considered public-knowledge bases rather than public-information bases in that concepts and rules rather than key words can be searced for. Prototypes of such systems already exist.[64]

There will be methods of getting medical informtion and clinical judgment out of the minds of a medical expert or experts and into machine-usable form (knowledge engineering) that are better than the "brain-picking" now commonly in use. Methods of computer representation of the graphic and morphologic data so vital to the process of medical reasoning will be developed, refined and standardized. Finally, user interfaces will improve with hardware innovations, increasing acceptance and utilization even further. Such systems are with us to stay, and no amount of inertia or dislike will prevent their eventual widespread deployment.

GADGETS AND TOYS—HARDWARE INNOVATIONS

Current technology allows for miniaturization of an entire computer to the size of a single microchip. This capability makes it practical to install computers in an impressive array of electromechanical devices. Many late-model automobiles have on-board computers; so do a wide variety of household appliances and consumer electronic goods. It naturally follows that this kind of computerization has become a prominent part of the world of medical electronics as well.

Space does not permit a comprehensive discussion of the myriad applications of computers to medical instrumentation. Indeed, such a discussion would be outmoded soon after it was written. Rather, an illustrative example will furnish readers with some insight into how advances in medical technology not only benefit from, but are made possible by, computerization.

Most physicians are now familiar with such imaging modalities as computerized tomography and magnetic resonance imaging. In both modalities, images are obtained of a transverse section of the body at various beam angles. A computer performs a spatial transformation on the data thus obtained to generate a visual representation of that transverse section. When such transformations are performed on serial adjoining sections, a three-dimensional data representation of an anatomic space has been created. By means of graphic techniques, the computer can then generate visual representations that correspond to sagittal and coronal sections as well. Consequently, an area of interest deep within the body can be accurately localized. Demonstrations of the diagnostic power of this technology continue to accumulate. "Real time" dynamic images may someday be available which will replace contrast studies.

Above and beyond the diagnostic capabilities of computer-assisted imaging is the implication for therapy. Specifically, the combination of these techniques with the precision of a laser allows for selective removal of tumors deep within the body with minimal trauma to surrounding tissue. This approach has already been used successfully for removal of intracranial intra-axial lesions, a procedure for which hand-eye coordination and three-dimensional orientation are poor.[65] Undoubtedly, this approach will eventually be used in other parts of the body, perhaps proving superior to traditional surgical procedures in certain circumstances.

Another important therapy-related potential advance in patient care relates to the current proliferation of laparoscopically performed surgical procedures. The surgeon performing a laparoscopic procedure makes decisions about what do "do" based not on direct observation of the patient's anatomy, but on a video representation of that anatomy, which is easily encoded into a form that can be stored, manipulated, retrieved and transmitted by a computer system. Thus, theoretically, another surgeon hundreds of miles away could view the image, and, with only minor modifications to the equipment, perform part or all of a surgical procedure by *remote control*. The implications, of course, are quite startling.

CAREERS IN MEDICAL COMPUTING

Medical computing already exists as an informal subspecialty of sorts. Several organizations are concerned exclusively with the applications of computers to medicine, including the Society for Computer Applications in Medical Care and the American Association for Medical Science and Informatics, to name two of the largest. These organizations hold annual scientific meetings that allow for exchange of ideas and provide for some degree of quality control in the field. There are at present no formal credentialing or accreditation bodies associated with these organizations or others. However, there exist a number of opportunities for training in this area. Of special note, Tufts University School of Medicine offers a postresidency fellowship in clinical decision analysis.* Stanford University has a degree program leading to a doctor of philosophy in medical computer science.† In addition, most fellowship programs in general internal medicine offer at least some exposure to computer applications in medical care, especially in the areas of statistics, bibliographic retrieval and decision support. As interest, awareness and need grow, the numbers of both formal and informal programs will certainly increase.

Outside the applications taken directly from the business world,

---

*Interested readers should write to Steven G. Pauker, M.D., Division of clinical Decision Making, New England Medical Center, 171 Harrison Avenue, Boston, MA 02111.
†Interested readers should write to Edward H. Shortliffe, M.D., Ph.D., Medical Computer Science, TC-135, Stanford University Medical Center, Stanford, CA 94305.

most early work in computer applications to medicine was done by "physician-hobbyists," persons whose primary training and orientation were medical but who had a background in computer science by virtue of previous training or close contact with computer scientists (or both). As the field became more sophisticated, it became apparent that few persons possessed sufficient expertise in both areas to produce state-of-the-art work. Thus, most major advances since the mid-1970s have been made by teams consisting of both computer scientists and medical personnel with some degree of interest in computer applications of their work.

It is unlikely that this situation will change for some time. There will always be a need for computer scientists who understand enough *about* medicine that they can model the thinking processes of physicians well enough to simulate them or perceive the nature of possible means of computer assistance. However, at this stage of development of this field, nearly any physician who becomes immersed in such endeavors will not have the time to maintain medical expertise. Although "pure" physicians may not single-handedly be able to contribute to research advances, there is a vast amount of work that needs to be done to implement the kinds of prototypical systems discussed in this chapter to areas of medicine outside those dealt with by the prototypes. This work can and will be done by physicians by use of "authoring systems" specifically designed to allow them to build expert systems without an understanding of the theory of expert systems; computer scientists need only refine such authoring systems so that this work may proceed. In years to come, it is likely that systems will be developed to deal with nearly every variety of medical-management problem, for the most part using as models the systems discussed in this chapter. It should be possible, after attaining medical expertise in a given area, to create a career out of automation of that expertise.

CONCLUSION

As stated at the outset, this chapter provides not promises but educated expectations. It should be clear that more computer applications to health care currently exist than most physicians are aware of but that their actual use does not extend far beyond the institutions where they were created and may not for some time. The factors presumably responsible for this situation will eventually disappear—the real questions concern the time the process will take and what as yet uncontemplated advances will occur in that time.

In the meantime, physicians would be well advised to pay attention to the applications of computer systems discussed in this chapter because there is little doubt that computers will someday have a major influence on the practice of medicine, perhaps sooner than most of us think. Widespread use of computers should be welcomed by physicians because the only possible results in the long run will be improvements in patient care and more stimulating and enjoyable work for physicians. The relationship between a computer and a physician is like an arranged marriage—it may start off on shaky ground, but it will continue to get better as the parties get to know one another better.

REFERENCES

1. McDonald CJ: Protocol-based computer reminders, the quality of care, and the non-perfectability of man. *N Engl J Med* 295:1351–1355, 1976.
2. Haynes RB, McKibbon KA, Walker CJ, et al: Computer searching of the medical literature: An evaluation of MEDLINE searching systems. *Ann Intern Med* 103:812–816, 1985.
3. Collen MF, Flagle CD: Full-text medical literature retrieval by computer: A pilot test. *J Am Med Assoc* 254:2768–2774, 1985.
4. Horowitz GL, Jackson JD, Bleich HL: Paperchase: Self-service bibliographic retrieval. *J Am Med Assoc* 250:2494–2499, 1983.
5. Elia JJ: Another medium for the journal. *N Engl J Med* 311:1631, 1984.
6. Harris DK: MEDIS: A new strategic option for acquiring medical information—Electronically. *J Am Med Assoc* 254:2801, 1985.
7. Huth EJ, Case K: "Annals" available in new online service. *Ann Intern Med* 102:707–708, 1985.
8. Singer J, Sacks HS, Lucente F, et al: Physician attitudes toward applications of computer data base systems. *J Am Med Assoc* 249:1610–1614, 1983.
9. McDonald C, Hui S, Smith D, et al: Reminders to physicians from an introspective computer medical record. *Ann Intern Med* 100:130–138, 1984.
10. McDonald CJ, Murray R, Jeris D, et al: A computer-based record and clinical monitoring system for ambulatory care, *Am J Public Health* 67:240–245, 1977.
11. Barnett GO: The application of computer based medical record systems in ambulatory practice. *N Engl J Med* 310:1643–1650, 1984.
12. Whiting-O'Keefe QE, Simborg DW, Epstein WV, et al: A computerized summary medical record system can provide more information than the standard medical record. *J Am Med Assoc* 254:1185–1192, 1985.
13. Hokanson JA, Costanzi JJ, Smith MS, et al: Design considerations for a medical school hospital cancer patient data system. *Cancer* 51:1556–1561, 1983.
14. Gordon M, Venn JC, Gower PE, et al: Experience in the computer handling of clinical data for dialysis and transplantation units. *Kidney Int* 24:455–463, 1984.
15. Bulpitt CJ, Beilin LJ, Coles EC, et al: Randomized controlled trial of computer-held medical records in hypertensive patients. *Br Med J* 1:677–679, 1976.
16. Mayne JG, Martin MJ, Taylor WF, et al: A health questionnaire based on paper-and-pencil medium, individualized and produced by computer: III. Usefulness and acceptability to physicians. *Ann Intern Med* 76:923–930, 1972.
17. Pauker SG, Gorry A, Kassirer JP, et al: Towards the simulation of clinical cognition: Taking a present illness by personal computer. *Am J Med* 60:981–996, 1976.
18. Gorry GA, Silverman H, Pauker SG: Capturing clinical expertise—A com-

puter program that considers clinical responses to digitalis. *Am J Med* 64:452–460, 1978.

19. Leeming BW, Simon M, Jackson JD, et al: Advances in radiologic reporting with computerized language information processing (CLIP). *Radiology* 133:349–353, 1979.
20. Arenson RL, London JW: Comprehensive analysis of a radiology operations management computer system. *Radiology* 133:355–362, 1979.
21. Bleich HL, Beckley RF, Horowitz GL, et al: Clinical computing in a teaching hospital. *N Engl J Med* 312:756–764, 1985.
22. Kunin CM: Managing bibliographic citations using microcomputers. *Am J Med* 78:627–634, 1985.
23. Manning PR: Continuing medical education: The next step. *J Am Med Assoc* 249:1042–1045, 1983.
24. Miller PL: Critiquing anesthetic management: The ATTENDING computer system. *Anesthesiology* 53:362–369, 1983.
25. Spindel E, Harty RJ, Leibach JR, et al: Decision analysis in evaluation of hypergastrinemia. *Am J Med* 80:11–17, 1986.
26. Andritsch RF, Muravchick S, Gold MI: Temperature correction of arterial blood gas parameters: A comparative review of methodology. *Anesthesiology* 55:311–316, 1981.
27. Krasner JB, Marino PL: The use of a pocket computer for hemodynamic profiles. *Crit Care Med* 11:826–827, 1983.
28. Agarwal NR, Savino JA, Feldman M, et al: The automated metabolic profile. *Crit Care Med* 11:546–550, 1983.
29. Pozen MW, D'Agostino RB, Selker HP, et al: A predictive instrument to improve coronary care unit admission practices in acute ischemic heart disease. *N Engl J Med* 310:1273–1278, 1984.
30. Margolis CZ: Uses of clinical algorithms. *J Am Med Assoc* 249:627–632, 1983.
31. Ingelfinger F: Algorithms, anyone? *N Engl J Med* 288:847–848, 1973.
32. Goldberg M, Green SB, Moss ML, et al: Computer-based instruction and diagnosis of acid-base disorders. *J Am Med Assoc* 223:269–275, 1973.
33. Goldman L, Weinberg M, Weisberg M, et al: A computer-derived protocol to aid in the diagnosis of emergency room patients with acute chest pain. *N Engl J Med* 307:588–596, 1982.
34. Wirtschafter D, Carpenter J, Mesel E: A consultant extender system for breast cancer adjuvant chemotherapy. *Ann Intern Med* 90:396–401, 1979.
35. Marino PL, Krasner JB: An interpretative computer program for analyzing hemodynamic problems in the ICU. *Crit Care Med* 12:601–602, 1984.
36. Krasner JB, Marino PL: An analytical approach to the creation of parenteral feeding regimens: Implementation on a microcomputer. *J Parent Ent Nutr* 9:226–229, 1985.
37. Sox HC: Quality of patient care by nurse practitioners and physician's assistants: A ten year perspective. *Ann Intern Med* 91:459–468, 1979.
38. Strasser PH, Levy JC, Lamb GC, et al: Controlled clinical trial of pediatric telephone protocols. *Pediatrics* 64:553–557, 1979.
39. Kassirer JP: The principles of clinical decision making: An introduction to decision analysis. *Yale J Biol Med* 49:149–164, 1976.
40. McNeil BJ, Weichselbaum R, Pauker SG: Speech and survival: Tradeoffs between quality and quantity of life in laryngeal cancer. *N Engl J Med* 305:982–987, 1981.
41. Schwartz WB, Gorry GA, Kassirer JP, et al: Decision analysis and clinical judgement. *Am J Med* 55:459–472, 1973.

42. Pauker SG, Kassirer JP: The threshold approach to clinical decision making. *N Engl J Med* 302:1109–1117, 1980.
43. Pauker SG, Kassirer JP: Therapeutic decision making: A cost benefit analysis. *N Engl J Med* 293:229–234, 1975.
44. Pauker SG, Kassirer JP: Clinical decision analysis by personal computer. *Arch Intern Med* 141:1831–1837, 1981.
45. Plante DA, Lau J, Pauker SG: Microcomputer-based medical decision making: Echocardiography for ventricular thrombus. *Semin Ultrasound* 4:308–322, 1983.
46. Weed LL, Hertzberg R: Clinical application of medical software for problem solving in ambulatory care. *J Amb Care Manage* 8:66–83, 1985.
47. Miller R, Pople H, Myers J: INTERNIST-1: An experimental computer-based diagnostic consultant for general internal medicine. *N Engl J Med* 307:468–476, 1982.
48. Krasner JB: A technique for optimization of enteral feeding regimens: Implementation on a microcomputer. *J Parent Ent Nutr* 10:208–212, 1986.
49. Feinstein A, Rubenstein J, Ramshaw W: Estimating prognosis with the aid of a conversational mode computer program. *Ann Intern Med* 76:911–921, 1972.
50. Fries J, Weyl S, Holman H: Estimating prognosis in systemic lupus erythematosus. *Am J Med* 57:561–565, 1974.
51. Heyman A, Burch J, Rosati R, et al: Use of a computerized information system in the management of patients with transient cerebral ischemia. *Neurology* 29:214–221, 1979.
52. Feinstein AR: Clinical biostatistics XXXIX: The haze of Bayes, the aerial palaces of decision analysis and the computerized Ouija board. *Clin Pharmacol Ther* 21:482–496, 1977.
53. Weintraub WS, Madeira SW, Bodenheimer MM, et al: Critical analysis of the application of Bayes' theorem to sequential testing in the noninvasive diagnosis of coronary artery disease. *Am J Cardiol* 54:43–49, 1984.
54. Warner HR, Toronto AF, Veasey LG: Experience with Bayes' theorem for computer diagnosis of congenital heart disease. *Ann NY Acad Sci* 115:558–567, 1964.
55. Templeton A, Jansen C, Lehr J, et al: Solitary pulmonary lesions. *Radiology* 89:505–513, 1967.
56. De Dombal FT, Leaper DJ, Horrocks JC, et al: Human and computer aided diagnosis of abdominal pain: Further report with emphasis on performance of clinicals. *Br Med J* 1:376–380, 1974.
57. Girardin MF, Le Minor M, Alperovitch A, et al: Computer-aided selection of diagnostic tests in jaundiced patients. *Gut* 26:961–967, 1985.
58. Melin JA, Piret LJ, Vanbutsele RJM, et al: Diagnostic value of exercise electrocardiography and thallium myocardial scintigraphy in patients without previous myocardial infarction: A Bayesian approach. *Circulation* 63:1019–1024, 1981.
59. Yu VL, Fagan LM, Wraith SM, et al: Antimicrobial selection by a computer: A blinded evaluation by infectious disease experts. *J Am Med Assoc* 242:1279–1282, 1979.
60. Hickam DH, Shortliffe EH, Bischoff MB, et al: The treatment advice of a computer-based chemotherapy protocol advisor. *Ann Intern Med* 103:928–936, 1985.
61. Wiener F, Fayman M, Teitelman U, et al: Computerized medical reasoning in diagnosis and treatment of acid-base disorders. *Crit Care Med* 11:470–475, 1983.

62. Blois MS: Clinical judgement and computers. *N Engl J Med* 303:192–197, 1980.
63. Reggia JA, Tabb R, Price TR, et al: Computer-aided assessment of transient ischemic attacks: A clinical evaluation. *Arch Neurol (Chicago)* 41:1248–1254, 1984.
64. Bernstein LM, Siegel ER, Goldstein CM: The hepatitis knowledge base: A prototype information transfer system. *Ann Intern Med* 93:169–181, 1980.
65. Kelly PJ, Kall BA, Goerss S, et al: Results of computer assisted stereotactic laser resection of deep-seated intracranial lesions. *Mayo Clin Proc* 61:20–27, 1986.

CHAPTER 12

THE FUTURE OF CONTINUING MEDICAL EDUCATION

Allen Douma

PREFACE

When I was first asked to write this chapter, I thought about doing an erudite and scholarly tome. In it, I was going to trace the historical trends and research in continuing medical education and extrapolate to the future. I am sure the reader will be happy to know that is not what I ended up doing.

The historical developments are interesting to anyone who enjoys understanding social policy, and I highly recommend two books: *Continuing Medical Education*[1] and *The Social Transformation of American Medicine*.[2] However, the changes that will take place in medicine in the lifetime of a physician now entering practice, especially over the next decade, will make the past 40 years of the history of continuing medical education only marginally useful in predicting the future.

Research in continuing medical education has been minimal, and what has been done has not been that helpful. Not only has there been little evidence that any one way of learning is any better than any other, but most studies have not even measured what physicians should be concerned about: changes in their behavior during patient care. Even this is only a proxy for improved patient outcomes.

Because I could not justify the need for or usefulness of an erudite approach, this chapter is composed simply of thoughts and options that the reader may use to choose a course of action toward becoming a knowledgeable and experienced health-care professional.

INTRODUCTION

> If the license to practice [medicine] meant the completion of his education how sad it would be for the practitioner, how distressing to his patients! More clearly than any other the physician should illustrate the truth of Plato's saying that education is a life-long process. The training of medical school gives a man his direction, points him the way, and furnishes him a chart, fairly incomplete, for the voyage, but nothing more.
>
> William Osler in 1900[1]

Continuing medical education is much more important than almost all physicians suspect when coming out of training. However, to understand its importance, one needs to begin by defining what continuing medical education is. There are two definitions, one narrow and one broad, each of which is equally valid. In its narrow definition, continuing medical education is any program or experience that was developed to teach physicians and for which credit is given to the participants. According to the broad definition, continuing medical education is any experience that improves the ability of a physician to be a health-care professional. The broad definition will be used in this chapter.

How important is continuing medical education in the life of a physician? Although the answer to this question is to a large extent a function of a physician's motivations (which will be discussed in detail later), all physicians have a burden and responsibility, and, hopefully, joy and enthusiasm, to maintain and improve their level of competence.

One way to put the question, and therefore its answer, in perspective is to ask another question: How important are undergraduate and graduate medical education in the process of becoming a physician? They are so obviously, profoundly and completely important that the question may seem rhetorical or even silly. What if I told the reader that 50 percent of what he or she now knows will be superseded by better or more precise information within the next five years? Also, what if I told the reader that within the same period, the total amount of medical knowledge will have more than doubled? A great deal of ongoing learning will be needed simply to keep up. The reader should remember that it is more difficult to unlearn something and replace it with something new than to learn it the first time.

I hope these simple statistics have impressed the reader enough to continue to explore this chapter without causing too much anxiety. Physicians will need to be hardworking, lifelong students to maintain their competence. Nonetheless, much of this learning can take place as a natural part of day-to-day practice, and much of it will be fun.

MOTIVATIONS

How much time, energy and resources are committed to the educational process will always depend on the level of motivation. Throughout the training of physicians, a primary motivating force is testing, formal and informal. That won't be true any more, except if you are changing specialties or specialize further.

Without periodic testing (examinations and tutorial feedback), physicians continue to push themselves to learn so they can provide quality care and maintain a position of respect with their peers. Many physicians are also required to document continuing medical education to retain their licenses to practice and obtain certification.

Two dynamic forces in the professional environment that will have an increasing influence on the behavior of all physicians are marketing and malpractice. These forces have been changing so rapidly that it would be presumptuous of anyone to make hard and fast predictions. In the sections that follow, the author will try to create an awareness of the present and potential importance of marketing and malpractice in the professional careers of physicians.

The types of practice opportunities for newly trained physicians are constantly shrinking. Society has decided that physicians charge too much for their services and are increasingly being perceived as mercenaries who care little about their patients. An increasing number of patients are questioning the judgment of physicians and seeking out other health-care professionals for advice and care. In addition, medical information continues to accumulate at a phenomenal pace.

One reaction to this information overload has been an increasing amount of specialization and subspecialization. However, physicians who choose this option may come to know more and more about less and less until they end up knowing everything about nothing. The author predicts that this trend will abate as information-storage and -retrieval technology becomes ubiquitous. Superspecialists may well become obsolete.

Quality Patient Care

There is nothing more satisfying in life than to be able to embrace a person who is in pain and afraid and to help his or her body heal, and fear subside. Being unable to help such a person is gut-wrenching and frustrating.

If physicians were always operating on that high emotional level of awareness combined with the knowledge that medicine is composed of a vast array of changing information, it would be all the motivation they would ever need. It serves the profession well that these motivators continue to be so powerful. However, to ensure that "extra edge," it is worthwhile to consider other factors that motivate physicians.

Peer Standing

Throughout training, the standing of a physician among his or her peers is a major influence. Comparison of one's performance with that of others is the primary feedback on adequacy of performance as a student of medicine. Depending on how feedback is used, it can be helpful in guiding the learning process or it can be a source of frustration.

Because our culture puts so much emphasis on one's professional role in determining a person's worth and because medicine emphasizes this concept, how well physicians perform has tremendous influence on how they feel about themselves. A physician's perception of his or her performance depends on feedback from formal tests and co-workers because there are no absolute measures of performance. After training has ended, feedback comes solely from other physicians, one's peers.

A physician's standing among peers may therefore become the major determinant of his or her sense of self-worth. Relying solely on the opinions of peers in this regard is not a healthy attitude, but assessment of one's performance by peers can serve as a strong motivator for maintaining and improving one's performance.

A physician's standing among peers has strong influences on malpractice and marketing in intuitively obvious ways.

Malpractice

Malpractice, or the threat of it, has a tremendous impact on the way physicians practice medicine and on their enjoyment in practice. Increasingly, juries are defining malpractice as any diagnostic or therapeutic action that, for a given patient, was not the optimal pathway from his or her current state of health to a future state of health. Also, more patients are filing claims simply because "things didn't turn out right."

Although the current malpractice climate has a severe negative impact (defensive medicine being a prime example), it also has the potential to have a positive influence on the way physicians practice. This positive influence relates to clinical knowledge and its application as well as to the way in which physicians deal with their patients.

The legal system and peer physicians judge competence on the basis of a concept called the "community standard" of practice. Simply put, this standard is the way that health care is provided within "one's community." In the past, this standard has protected physicians from the unrealistic demand that all of them should know everything. This situation is changing because the definition of community is being expanded to encompass all information that is reasonably obtainable, including through access to computerized medical data bases.

The second major influence that the professional liability crisis has on the practice of medicine is the changing way physicians relate to patients. Many physicians respond to the threat of malpractice by becoming more suspicious and withdrawn from their patients. Unfortunately, this response may only aggravate the situation. Perhaps a major reason that patients file malpractice suits, whether or not malpractice occurred, is a lack of communication and rapport with their physicians. Maintaining and improving communication skills should be an important part of continuing medical education.

Marketing

Although the delivery of health care has always been a business, physicians have been largely insulated from the business aspects of the profession because the demand for services has outstripped the supply of physicians. This situation is rapidly changing. Over the next 20 years, the ratio of physicians to total population will continue to rise, and the willingness of society to pay an increasing percentage of their earnings for health care will continue to decline.

For physicians just entering practice to thrive, they will have to become more aware of competitive forces in the marketplace and learn how to cope with such forces by means of effective marketing strategies. Marketing is distasteful to some physicians, probably because they equate it with advertising, much of which they think is dishonest or simply in poor taste. Marketing is actually a much broader activity, and it can be useful for purposes other than sales.

Marketing can be defined as assessing the need for a product or service and selling that product or service by providing the highest quality possible at the right time, place and price. Marketing can be beneficial to physicians and also to patients.

Physicians who are skilled at marketing not only assess the needs of the community for their services but also determine their patients' concerns. The public is increasingly concerned about the quality of health care, which depends not only on a physician's knowledge but also on a caring approach to patients.

The public's concern about the quality of care means that physicians not only will need to maintain their knowledge base (perhaps with special attention given to items that receive wide coverage in the media) but also will need to demonstrate it. Making patients aware of one's interest in continuing medical education is helpful in this regard.

The hectic nature of the typical busy practice and the increasing cynicism of patients are making it increasingly difficult for physicians to demonstrate a caring approach to their patients. No matter how much one cares, a patient cannot sense a caring attitude unless it is demonstrated. A caring approach can be demonstrated only if a physician's communication skills are good, and this aspect of medical practice is where continuing medical education can have a strong impact.

CONTENT OF CONTINUING MEDICAL EDUCATION

Not infrequently, when a physician is asked what material his or her continuing medical education should cover, the response is: I'm an X specialist, so, of course, I'll attend programs on X. Even if X is a subspecialty, there are many choices to be made from the plethora of programs available. Also, limiting one's choices to one's specialty may not be a wise decision.

The text that follows discusses a number of generic issues that can be useful in planning continuing medical education.

Clinical as Opposed to Nonclinical Material

Young physicians are entering practice in a volatile era. The time is past when physicians needed to be mere data banks; the public now wants physicians who are more caring and communicative. The growing oversupply of physicians and the consequent escalation in competition for patients make it necessary for new physicians to assess their future educational requirements by first determining how adequately undergraduate education and graduate medical education have prepared them for the health-care marketplace.

Throughout training, physicians are told that medicine is as much an art as it is a science. Some physicians have an awesome ability to perceive things that other physicians, even more knowledgeable, do not perceive. The physicians with such insight are the same ones who have a wonderful rapport with their patients. In fact, it is the interaction and communication with patients that differentiate the medical profession from many other fields of endeavor.

Not only are rapport and communication central to the role of a physician, they are crucial to quality patient care. As all physicians would agree, accurate diagnosis is the key to quality care, and the key to an accurate diagnosis is a thorough patient history. A thorough history can be obtained only if a physician is able to create an environment and a dialogue with a patient in which the right questions are asked (by both the physician and the patient). The style and level of communication should be geared to accomplish this goal.

In addition, all the diagnostic acumen and treatment measures in the world will be of little benefit if a patient does not follow instructions. Compliance depends on the doctor-patient relationship, which, in turn, depends on the ability of a physician to communicate.

Good communication skills not only improve the quality of patient care but also are helpful to a physician in his or her personal life. Physicians communicate with other health-care professionals, not just with patients. Good communication skills make a practice more efficient and more enjoyable.

In the years ahead, competition for patients will be more fierce than ever before. Perhaps the most important criterion people use to choose physicians and medical institutions is their perception of the level of caring and compassion. This perception is almost totally determined by the ability of a physician or personnel at an institution to communicate. Sadly enough, many caring physicians do not make one feel that they care.

The art of medicine involves the ability of physicians to communicate. Yet, there is a profound lack of formal educational experience in this area provided to physicians in training.

Physicians can begin to evaluate their communication skills by self-assessment. However, self-assessment of such skills can be threatening. Therefore, if a physician's ego allows it, he or she could begin by asking co-workers for feedback on an ongoing basis about both the substance and the style of his or her communications. It is also helpful to have a communications specialist evaluate one's skills.

If a physician determines that his or her communication skills need improvement, a good way to begin would be talk with the director of public relations for his or her specialty society or the American Medical Association. The association offers a course that helps physicians become "media docs"; the course incorporates techniques that also help one become a better communicator in general. Alternatively, the physician could talk with the person in charge of public relations at the local medical society, hospital association or hospital with which he or she is affiliated to find out about the availability of local resources. If none are available, the physician could consider working with other persons to set up such programs.

Selection of Information

New physicians just entering practice should ask themselves a very important question *now* and periodically in the future: Do I want to work as a _____ (whatever specialist you are) for the rest of my professional life? Not until physicians are practicing do they understand how different their specialty can be from what it appeared to be when they were in medical school studying it.

Many physicians who change their specialty do so because they find that the practice style required of their specialty does not afford them the satisfaction or enjoyment that they desire. Unfortunately, many other physicians who feel that way do not change to another specialty, probably explaining why personal problems, such as alcoholism and drug abuse, are common among physicians.

Physicians made it through the grinding system of acceptance to, and graduation from, medical school because they were able to delay gratification and pleasure for some distant goal. However, denial can sustain a person only so long. In fact, people who do not genuinely enjoy their work are likely to become less competent at it over time. Enjoying the practice of medicine is becoming increasingly dependent on internalized and personal satisfaction as external reinforcement diminishes.

Let us assume that a physician is satisfied with his or her specialty and simply wants to acquire more knowledge. Such a physician will pursue further education of two types. The first is based on the need or desire to update one's knowledge base and learn about new procedures; the second is based on the development of skills that will make one a leader in a specialty as it changes in the future.

The degree of interest one has in becoming a leader will influence one's selection of sources of information that may not have (for practical or legal reasons) applicability to current health care. Leaders have foresight. It would also be advisable to seek out gurus for advice about trends in one's specialty. Although these pursuits may be rewarding and certainly stimulating, they will take time away from maintaining and improving one's ability to care for today's patients.

Even when the physician has narrowed down the selection process to determining the information needed to care for today's patients, he or she will still have to choose from a plethora of subjects. No matter what the degree of specialization, there is always more information available than any one physician can assimilate. Another major decision point now arises. To what degree should one rely on "educators" in one's specialty to select and synthesize the body of knowledge that is appropriate?

Even though there are many similarities among patients in any given specialty, there are also important differences. The differences depend on the location of a practice, a physician's personality, referral patterns and other variables. Ideally, a physician would review his or her patients' diagnoses and determine educational needs on this basis.

When a physician's patient population reaches several hundred or a few thousand, it becomes difficult to maintain such a patient profile. Having a formal procedure for patient review on a weekly or monthly basis makes it much easier to continue to know the type of practice one has. As will be discussed later, a computerized medical-records system is helpful in this regard.

Once the physician has this information, he or she will still have to decide how much emphasis to place on what occurs frequently and how much emphasis to place on what occurs rarely. This decision will be based on one's memory processing and approach to clinical decision making. However, the author finds the following rule of thumb to be a helpful guideline: emphasize treatments that are instituted more frequently and diagnoses that are less common.

Knowing or Knowing Where to Go

As was mentioned earlier, the biomedical sciences are witnessing an information explosion. Although medicine is becoming more specialized, there still is an endless amount of information for each physician to know. Or is there?

The answer to this question depends on what one means by "to know." Much of our thinking in this regard has been strongly biased by what may be an inappropriate portrait the profession has painted of itself.

Over the past 50 years, not only has the practice of medicine become based on scientific evidence, but all the information used to substantiate and guide decisions made by physicians has had to be stored in their brains. Storage of information is important and valid if one needs it in an emergency or wants to impress other persons about how smart physicians are (especially during teaching rounds). The latter reason is always an important dynamic of any person or profession, especially one that is striving to improve its image. But how important is it, for example, to memorize all the treatment protocols for every chronic disease if that information is readily available at one's fingertips?

Academic institutions, by their nature, naturally demand that students become data banks crammed with as much information as possible. This attitude has been accentuated in medical training centers for a variety of reasons. One important reason has been the use of the multiple-choice test as an evaluation tool, regardless of whether there is any relationship between test scores and quality patient care. Once this type of test becomes the standard, one simply adds more and more facts to the data base that the student is required to memorize until the bell-shaped scoring curve is statistically defensible.

These two forces continue to drive the learning machine down the road to cortical overload while many physicians are questioning its usefulness and some are concerned about its negative effects. Are we being forced to select students based primarily on their ability to perform on memory tests? Are we neglecting the extremely important areas of communication skills and a caring attitude in the selection and training of physicians because of an artificial need to be memory banks? The answer to both of these questions is yes, but it appears that there are going to be major changes over the next 20 years.

The real motivation for the profession to change will be the expectations and demands of patients. All patients want to believe that their physicians know all there is to know about medicine and will always give them the best recommendations. However, many people are aware of the enormity of the task of keeping up with every development in medicine. Patients are also rapidly coming to understand that every recommendation carries a risk and a benefit and that it is in their best interests to be involved in the decision-making process.

For patients to be truly involved, physicians must share information with them. Of course, the information will have to be translated into layperson's language and it will have to be completely up to date and specific. The only way to retrieve current and specific information from the vast amounts in existence is through a system that physicians have been highly trained to use. In the decades to come, the most efficient and respected physicians will be those who know where to go to find answers and how to get them rapidly.

LEARNING ENVIRONMENTS

While I was in medical school, there was much discussion in the medical literature and even in the lay press about the possibility of learning while sleeping. Of course, sleeping seemed to be the ideal situation for learning, but this approach to learning is not too effective. Consequently, where continuing medical education takes place is an aspect of the learning experience that requires continual consideration.

In this section, a number of learning environments will be discussed. Their qualitative and quantitative features will be addressed to assist the reader in selecting the right mix for him or her. One's present allocation of time, to the variety of learning environments that are available, is based on one's particular requirements, which can change dramatically. Also, available learning technologies influence one's choices.

Experience with Patients

The learning that takes place during the care of a patient is probably the most powerful educational experience in medicine. Not infrequently, physicians vividly remember intriguing cases that they dealt with years ago. They may even remember minute details from a few cases for the rest of their lives.

Because physicians spent almost 100,000 hours of their lives caring for patients, the learning that takes place (planned or incidental) in the practice of medicine is obviously substantial. To put this learning in perspective, if the learning efficiency of patient care were only 10 percent of that for attending a lecture (a low figure for many physicians), the learning value of patient care would be four times that required by the most demanding recertification regulation.

This kind of powerful memory etching obviously is extremely effective but also potentially dangerous. The information collected from an encounter with a patient is anecdotal, and it may not be transferred in whole, or in part, to the next patient. Each patient therefore should be used to reinforce clinical norms or prompt the physician to explore why that patient was outside the norms.

An interesting and unfortunate transition that most physicians make when entering practice is a change in attitude (an appreciable diminishing of importance) toward learning from patient care. There are many understandable reasons for this change in attitude; inadequate time as one's patient population expands, lack of a requirement to do so, difficulty in obtaining feedback and difficulty in admitting that patient care is always a learning experience.

Of all these reasons, probably the most important is the lack of adequate time to follow up a patient or group of patients with an eye toward incremental learning. The availability of computerized medical-record systems, combined with the rise of consumerism and malpractice allegations, will not only make this learning much easier in the future but will even force physicians in that direction.

Feedback from Experts

What is an expert? In the context of this chapter, an expert is best defined as anyone who knows or understands something about a particular issue in a particular situation that you do not. This definition, and purposely so, means that every health-care professional is an expert for you sometime. Believing so and acting on that belief will greatly increase the likelihood that other persons will be willing to be an expert for you when the need arises.

A physician's utilization of the expertise in his or her environment depends on so many variables that a general discussion would be of little value. However, it is helpful to examine some changes that will be taking place in the generalist/specialist and specialist/subspecialist relationships in the future. The changes are a good-news/bad-news story.

The good news is that electronic technology will provide an opportunity to use normal medical referral patterns of care as a teaching aid in continuing medical education. To illustrate the potential of this technique, the author will give an example from the area in which electronic technology has advanced the furthest—radiology. The scenario that follows makes use of currently available technology.

You are called to see a diabetic patient who recently suffered head trauma and has a rapidly deteriorating state of consciousness. The community hospital to which the patient was admitted has a nuclear magnetic resonance machine, but no one is at hand to interpret the results of testing with the machine. You have had some training in reading such test results but do not feel that you have enough knowledge in this area to rely on your own interpretations. The challenge and fun now begin.

First you order the study to be performed. Next you alert the radiology specialist on call (who is at home) by transmitting, via electronic mail, the history of the trauma and deterioration of consciousness that you took, a medical-record summary called up from your office computer, your tentative problem/diagnosis list and the time when the study will be completed. Because of the clinical severity of the case, you also alert a diabetologist and a neurosurgeon, giving them the same information.

As the nuclear magnetic resonance study is being done, the pictures are transferred electronically to the intensive care unit, where the patient is having a marginal response to medical therapy. As the pictures roll up the screen, you get this uneasy feeling, because of changes in the posterior fossa, that make you suspect compression of the brainstem. You immediately transfer the information to the three specialists with your impression.

Within minutes, a teleconference call is set up in which you and the specialists are communicating simultaneously on computer screens and audiophone links. You were wrong. The radiologist indicates that you were mislead by a rare congenital malformation. To reassure your lingering doubts, he sends readings through your electronic grapevine from the Nuclear Magnetic Resonance Case Library for your comparison.

A possible ending to this story (fairytale now, but not in the near future) would be the diabetologist checking with the hospital pharmacy's computer, finding that the insulin being given to the patient is from a batch that was put on a national alert within the past hour because of impurities and the possibility of an allergic reaction thus arising.

Now the bad-news side of the generalist/specialist and specialist/subspecialist relationships of the future. Pressures will mount not to refer patients to health-care professionals with more narrow fields of expertise. Because of the increasing oversupply of physicians (specialists and subspecialists in particular) and the relative decrease in available health-care dollars, primary-care physicians will provide more health services to more patients.

Although the public's concern about quality care and physicians' fear of malpractice will continue to make referral to experts desirable, it will take concerted effort by the medical community to ensure that enough trust exists to make quality care the overriding concern. Otherwise, it may be that the only experts called for consultation in the future are those residing in the memory banks of computers.

Individualized Instruction

In reality, all instruction is individualized from the perspective of the learner. However, in this context, individualized instruction is used to distinguish from learning environments in which a group of people are involved. Almost all the education of a physician is based on some form of individualized instruction. Even so, most of the discussion about continuing education and mandatory continuing medical education is based on group instruction.

In addition to learning from caring for patients and through feedback from experts, a physician spends a great deal of time reading journals and monographs as well as a smaller amount of time with audiovisual self-instructional learning programs. These learning modalities all have advantages and disadvantages, and each one is most effective as a learning tool if a physician assesses when, where and how to use it. The text that follows should be considered only as guidelines to assist the reader in making choices most appropriate for him or her.[3]

For the sheer volume of information that can be presented, reading has no parallel, largely because people can read five to even 50 times faster than they can listen. However, assimilation of material that has been read depends on a person's motivation during the act of reading. An esoteric article in the *New England Journal of Medicine* loses much of its esoterica and becomes more relevant and interesting if a physician has just treated a patient with the same or a similar problem.

Physicians do spend a lot of their valuable time reading medical literature. How can they improve their ability to assimilate material that has been read by increasing their motivation? One way to strengthen motivation in this regard is to spend more time reading about medical problems similar to those of patients one has recently cared for or expects to care for in the future. That would seem to be what most physicians do—read journals only in their specialties. But not exactly.

To more fully understand how to become better at selecting appropriate reading material, consider the following example that is presently possible and will become commonplace in the future. The medical practice in this example has a fully computerized medical-record system that contains the diagnoses and treatments for all the patients as well as a category called the uncertainty index.

The uncertainty index is a physician's designation (e.g., yes or no or on a scale from 1 to 5) of how certain he or she is of a particular diagnosis or treatment. This index can be incorporated into a computerized record system without being part of official patient records.

On a periodic basis, the computer automatically scans the records for diagnoses or treatments for which the physician had some degree of uncertainty. With this information, the physician can make appropriate entries to the medical data bases[4] and search for the latest information on such entities. In doing the search, the physician can preselect not only what kind of information he or she would like to have retrieved (e.g., review articles as opposed to research reports) but also which data bases he or she would like to have searched for each problem.

For example, a physician has diagnosed two-vessel atherosclerotic coronary-artery disease and recommended surgical intervention. However, he or she knows that the risks and benefits of surgical therapy in this setting are being studied intensively in long-term clinical trials and that there is a high degree of uncertainty regarding such therapy, particularly in certain subgroups of the population. Because the physician entered an uncertainty value, the computer looked through 20 journals preselected from the NLM data base, five textbooks from the BRS data base and the newly created National Institutes of Health Flash Consensus Conference Reference File (the latter is fictional at this time). While searching through this material, the computer looked only for information published since the last time it made such a search and limited its retrieval to review articles in the English language. This search, which took less than two minutes in each of the three data bases, cost less than five dollars and involved none of the physician's time.

As such "educational" searches are conducted and the retrieved material is entered into a physician's data base for reading at leisure, he or she is creating an important resource for reviewing the practice. Because no person's memory is infallible, one probably would ask the computer to check the results of previous searches every time a new search is initiated.

Although many mechanisms exist for storage of information, the future will see electro-optical storage used universally. Exactly how storage will be accomplished electro-optically is not known, although some form of videodisk will be used, a type that can be erased and rerecorded easily and inexpensively. Electro-optical technology will allow encyclopedias of information to be stored, updated and retrieved through elaborate cross indexes within seconds.

To continue with the story we started earlier, after the physician's computer completed its search as designated, the requested material was retrieved and stored so that when he or she began work the next day, the information was available. During lunch, when she or he sat down to review it, he or she was pleased to see that the newest consensus conference findings demonstrated that surgical intervention was indicated for his or her patient because she belonged to a subgroup of the population for which surgical therapy is recommended in this setting. He or she also noted that the recommended surgical procedure is a modification of standard surgery and a modification with which he was unfamiliar.

He or she then immediately used the electronic mail system built into the office computer to order an interactive video package that would take him or her step by step through the modification. The package would also include programmed instruction for operating-room nurses and an educational lesson for the patient. The package was transmitted over the telephone lines and was ready for the physician to study that evening.

Most of the technologies needed to carry out the preceding scenario are available and can be incorporated into any medical-record system. However, many such systems do not have this capability automatically built in. If a physician is contemplating purchasing such a system or already has one, he or she should talk with the vendor about this capability. It is also advisable to talk with a medical librarian at a large hospital or the nearest medical school about the requirements for searching medical data bases. The requirements change too rapidly to give meaningful advice here.

Conferences

There is little about conferences as a learning environment that the reader probably does not already know; the teaching formats used in that setting are like those in the academic learning environment. The reader may wonder whether going to lectures is worth the time and expense (even if the cost is a deductible business expense). In the past few years, some physicians have been questioning the usefulness of conferences and deciding not to attend. This attitude will be reinforced as learning technologies improve and time and monetary pressures increase.

In addition to providing an opportunity for travel, attending conferences has several advantages. The latest technologic advances are often described by researchers at conferences before they are published and may be demonstrated in exhibitors' booths at large conventions. Exhibitors, in particular, teach not only about new technology but also about how advances may affect clinical practice in the near future. Obviously, exhibitors are biased about their products, but they give honest answers to specific questions.

Another advantage of attending conferences is the opportunity it provides to talk directly with speakers and other attendees with similar concerns. The socioeconomic aspects of medicine and health care are a common topic of discussion. Such issues may have more importance to practice than any clinical issue. Also, because socioeconomic changes can have a global impact, physicians need advanced warning to enable them to adapt to such changes.

Attendance at conferences is most helpful when one participates actively. Medical students may benefit solely by listening to the presentations. However, physicians greatly benefit by participating actively and not being shy.

How does one decide which conferences to attend? The best approach is to sample conferences firsthand and then let experience act as a guide. Over time, going to certain meetings year after year will become a habit. Nonetheless, one should always explore new conferences as well.

Many journals present long lists of available conferences. One can use such lists to find a learning experience in a subject area that fits in with one's schedule and is in an interesting place. However, conferences are not reviewed in regard to their quality as learning experience's. A national review mechanism simply verifies whether basic procedures have been followed in the development of courses in continuing medical education; content of courses is not approved or disapproved.

A good way to start is to attend annual or scientific meetings of one's specialty organizations. Information presented at such conferences is at least relevant, and the speakers are reputable members of one's specialty. If the presentations do not provide a good learning experience, however, this problem should be communicated to the appropriate person in an organization's staff.

ELECTRONIC TECHNOLOGIES

Just for a moment, put aside this excellent book and try doing something else. Because the weather is beautiful and because your environment is oversaturated with random noises, you decide that you would prefer to absorb the information you are now reading while walking along a bicycle path.

You pick out a disk on the future of medicine and attach a WOK-PERSON to your belt (this device is made by a company created by the merger of a Japanese food company and an American high-tech firm). You decide not to wear teleglasses, instead putting on a quadraphonic sunvisor, and head out the door. When you reach the bicycle path and notice that almost everyone is doing the same, you realize how competitive the world has become as the economy continues to slide.

As you start walking, you activate the hand-held touch control pad. Because the disk you have selected is new to you and has just skyrocketed to first place on the health sciences charts, you activate the preview section in the audio mode. After hearing a brief overview and running through the index, you are so intrigued that you cannot decide where to begin. However, because you had a hard week in the clinics, you know that you want an exciting and uplifting place to start. Therefore, you enter the word EUREKA and within a few seconds you hear. . . .

Over the next 40 years, there may well be such quantum leaps in the capabilities of electronic learning technologies that we will have to completely rearrange our thinking about their use.

There are many capabilities of such technologies that are used only marginally, and in many cases the technologies are not used appropriately. In understanding how to use or not to use electronic learning technologies, it is helpful to group them into three categories: tapes, teleconferences and computer-based learning.

Tapes

Audio and video educational programs are similar as well as dissimilar to one another in a number of ways. Each type of program has advantages and disadvantages. As with any other learning technology, it is important to maximize learning by matching the technology with one's needs.

Both audio and video programs can be used as part of a learning experience that is conducted by a live instructor, but the discussion that follows is based on their use as "stand-alone" learning tools. This approach to learning provides greatest flexibility for time and place of learning. The stand-alone approach, however, requires greater motivation than does a learning environment that involves a teacher and other students.

In deciding whether to use audio or video programs, one should begin by comparing each modality to reading. Because the pacing of both modalities is based on audio information, they are two to 20 times slower than reading in providing factual information. Audio and video programs also run in a continuous linear fashion, so that pacing and quick review are more difficult. It is not possible to underline or employ some other means for designating important material for future review.

Although listening is much slower than reading, one may wish to learn at a slower pace. The tone of voice in audio recordings can be effective in distinguishing important information in a program. The tone of voice may also be the best or only way to communicate the emotional aspects of a topic or problem.

Audiotapes have been the unsung heroes of the electronic learning technologies. Probably more than 85 percent of medical knowledge can be completely conveyed without the use of pictures. Much of what remains can be well communicated through the pictorial memory of a trained professional without visual reinforcement every time. Some people would even argue that relying on one's memory is the best approach because it makes more complete use of all the senses, not just sight.

The major advantage of audiotapes is their potential convenience. In some settings, such as while jogging or driving a car, audiotapes are the only practical learning modality. Listening to tapes may simply be a relaxing way to learn while watching the grass grow.

Audiotape programs can be enhanced by the addition of visual material on slides or paper. However, the advantage of convenience is lost when visual material is added. Nonetheless, programs in this combined format are less expensive to produce and modify.

The addition of slides to audiotape programs should be considered in relation to patient education. Patient education is important not only in providing quality care but also in marketing a physician's services. Inclusion of oneself in slides is helpful in both regards. The best approach for this purpose is "pictorial" presence, either in person or on screen. Personalizing slides in an audiotape program is easier and less expensive than the use of other technologies.

Videotapes were first employed as a learning modality for physicians in the 1950s when television became available to the public. However, only during the past decade has this technology become widely used at all levels of training, including continuing medical education. At the time of this writing, videotape programs for educating physicians and patients are available in almost all hospitals and medical libraries; they can be ordered from national distributors or provided by local or national television networks.

As was noted previously, learning by means of videotapes is much slower than learning by reading unless "live action" enhances the learning process. Obvious examples of live action are the demonstration of a manual skill or a procedure and the showing of cineradiographs. In addition, a well-produced videotape program not only teaches but also motivates learners to apply what has been learned.

Videotape programs are the best modality, other than personal interaction, to teach communication skills. Such skills will become increasingly important in the near future for improving quality of care and marketing and for avoiding malpractice allegations. Learning communication skills is an important aspect of continuing medical education because such skills are largely ignored by most medical school curricula.

Video is the only medium that can portray all the nuances of communication in a way that best elicits learning at the cognitive and emotional levels. Videotapes can be used to present role models through dramatic reenactments; better yet, a learner can be videotaped and critiqued as the playback is watched. Using video as a medium for learning can also be enjoyable, an advantage that is laudable in itself.

Interactive videodisks are beginning to be explored as a major educational tool for health-care professionals. A single videodisk can store not only full-motion video but also tens of thousands of pages of text. The real educational power of this technology, however, resides in its capability for accessing any information on a disk within a few seconds. This capability makes it possible to develop computer-driven programs that can fully interact with a learner.

It is likely that this technology or a similar one (see the discussion about CD-ROMs later) will be the backbone of continuing medical education in the future. Until now, the limited availability of hardware to play such programs has been a major impediment to the widespread use of this technology.

Teleconferences

Before discussing the uses and abuses of teleconferencing technologies, it would be helpful to provide some definitions. In the context of this chapter, a teleconference is defined as the linking of people at two or more locations in which there is the capability to transmit audio to all participants. In its most trivial form, a telephone conversation is a teleconference. Except for reading, teleconferences are the most important learning technology for physicians.

An audio teleconference connects people at two or more locations by means of speaker phones over standard telephone lines, with or without on-site visual enhancement. A video teleconference involves the broadcasting of a television signal and connecting participants at all locations via telephone lines for question call-in. Although most teleconferences currently make use of one of these two formats, with the emergence of slow-scan technology (which allows the transmission, over telephone lines, of still pictures) and electronic mail, there will be a blurring of the classic teleconferencing parameters and a potential for tremendous enhancement of effectiveness.

Teleconferences have two major advantages, both of which hinge on reaching a number of participants at several locations. Therefore, an obvious advantage to physicians is being able to participate close to home. This advantage is, in fact, the major selling point made by people who produce and sell teleconferences. Teleconferences also make it possible to enhance small group-learning sessions by bringing in outside experts without the burden and expense of having them travel to several locations.

Teleconferences also have disadvantages. It is much more difficult for a teacher also to be a motivator, and motivation may be the most important aspect of a formal learning experience. The reader may not have been exposed to many great teachers who also provided motivation. Many experts do an excellent job in person but, because of the constraints of the technology and their lack of experience and training, fall flat over electronic media. Another disadvantage of teleconferences is that learners who are shy about asking questions or who have detailed questions about specific cases find it difficult to have their questions addressed in this learning format.

A major determinant of the use of teleconferences as part of continuing medical education is their availability. Over the past few years, there has been a ten-fold increase in the number of locations that provide access to teleconferences, hospitals making up the majority of such locations. Teleconferences have so far been used most often by nonphysician personnel, however, and have not garnered the financial support that is expected for continuing medical education for physicians.

How teleconferencing technologies survive and in what form are open to debate. The future of such technologies will be greatly influenced by the degree to which electronic media will be capable of transmitting information and educational programs from various sources into a single system.

Computer-Based Learning

Programmed learning is an educational technology in which the learner is guided and directed through the material as a function of his or her responses. Although this approach is the basis of the tutorial method, the term is usually reserved for cases in which programmed texts are used. With the availability of relatively inexpensive computing power, programmed text takes on new meaning and the potential for teaching is increased by an order of magnitude.

Educators and students alike should direct much effort to the development of programmed learning technology. It is important to point out that a major reason for placing increased emphasis on this technology is that more interactive testing will be occurring in the future. Historically, it has always been true that whither go the tests, so goes the teaching (see Chapter 11).

To understand better the benefits and power of this technology, the reader should recall the best attending physicians under whom he or she trained. Important characteristics of such physicians are their breadth and depth of knowledge, their ability to communicate at a student's level of understanding and their patience, especially when a learner does not "get" something that turns out to be simple once it is understood. Imagine something that may seem incredible: attending physicians that are available 24 hours a day and always with a smile, on fully developed computer-based learning programs.

The author will present a scenario that will more fully illustrate how a completely computerized environment can be used to provide the optimal learning experience in continuing medical education. Some of what will be discussed here will overlap with the text of the preceding chapter, but it will be presented with the author's educational bias. All the hardware described in this scenario is available from a number of vendors at reasonable cost. The software and educational programs needed to take full advantage of the hardware are in the developmental stage.

Imagine a hypothetical practice that has computerized medical-record and accounting systems. Patients' records are stored so that the computer can be asked to search all of them (or any part of them) to find every diagnosis and tabulate its frequency in the patient population. These data are the best basis on which to develop an educational strategy.

How a physician would respond to the data is an individual decision, but the following thoughts should help the reader decide. Look at the frequency distribution of the diagnoses and try to partition them into three categories. The first group consists of 25 or fewer that occur most frequently. This group probably accounts for more than 80 percent of all diagnoses in the practice. The second group consists of diagnoses that were made only once during the period being studied; the third group is all remaining diagnoses. This partitioning can usually be done by simple eyeballing, but one could also program the computer to partition the diagnoses automatically.

In looking over the diagnosis lists, it became obvious that there is a need for a library and an educational service that fit your needs precisely. Consequently, you decide to subscribe to the CD-ROM-MED educational service, which provides quarterly updates to your computer-stored medical library, based on the diagnoses that you specify. This service was created in 1985 when the cost of a CD-ROM was only $25. That CD-ROM can store and retrieve from 250,000 pages of text anything you want within a few seconds, but in 1986 it cost about $1,000.

In addition to the "normal" text materials in the CD-ROM, there are many different comparative tables that help in the thinking process. One example is the DRUG-DRUG SPEEDCHK system, which looks at all the potential negative and positive interactions of the medications that you have prescribed based on the particular characteristics of a given patient. Another example is the DXCUE system. When a diagnosis is entered into this system, it presents the ten diagnoses most commonly confused with the one entered (based on your practice demographics) and the ways to differentiate one from another. The DXCUE system would be used most frequently for patients whose diagnoses fell in the third partition described previously.

If you are thinking that the last two examples are diagnostic or therapeutic aides and not educational tools, you are half right. They are both. As was discussed more fully in the section titled "Experience with Patients," much of education takes place within the context of patient care, and this statement will become increasingly true when computer technologies are developed that can easily wed and improve both functions.

Although there has been rapid growth in the availability of computer-based learning programs, relatively few such programs exist. Whether companies now producing such programs will be doing so in the future is unknown. If the reader's sources of information about continuing medical education are not helpful in locating such programs, he or she could attend a Symposium on Computer Applications in Medical Care.[4]

Planning Continuing Medical Education for the Future: Whose Crystal Ball?

Physicians have a tremendous responsibility to keep up with a rapidly growing body of knowledge in the midst of a rapidly changing environment for the delivery of health care. Whereas during training students are told what they need to know and when they need to know it, practicing physicians must make such decisions on their own. Also, such decisions must take into account the issues of communication and marketing skills.

Like anything else, the first step is the hardest, and the longer one delays in deciding where to begin, the more difficult the decision becomes. If the reader decides right now to take continuing medical education seriously as a major determinant of the success and enjoyment of a professional career, he or she will be ahead of many colleagues. Hopefully, in making this decision, the reader will be looking forward to the pleasure of learning as well.

Many colleagues and peers can help select what one needs to learn. However, a physician must be the final judge and will be making the right decisions as long as he or she is matching educational needs with the types of patients he or she is seeing or hopes to be seeing in the future.

After determining what skills and knowledge areas one wants to emphasize, the best educational methods or programs must be selected for each skill or area. Again, these decisions can be made only if the physician takes into account his or her individual learning patterns. However, one would probably find, for example, that learning better communication skills can be best accomplished through videotape or one-on-one tutorial instruction, whereas improving differential diagnosis skills can be best accomplished through use of a computer-interactive program.

Because there are so many variables with regard to what one wants to learn and how one wants to learn it, keeping track can be greatly facilitated by developing a continuing medical education matrix. A matrix is simply a sheet of paper as presented here (or a computerized spread sheet) on which all important skills and knowledge areas are listed across the top and the various learning environments and technologies are listed along the left side (Figure 1). The box at the intersection of each row and column is divided in half diagonally, with the upper portion for marking the number of hours one thinks is needed during the next year and the lower portion for recording how many hours were actually spent in that activity.

The first step in this process is to select the total number of hours that one thinks should be spent on each skill or knowledge area. The number of hours are then divided among all the learning modalities listed across the top. This approach may seem tedious, and the numbers marked down may not be followed exactly. This process is nonetheless helpful in formulating an overall picture of one's educational needs. Over

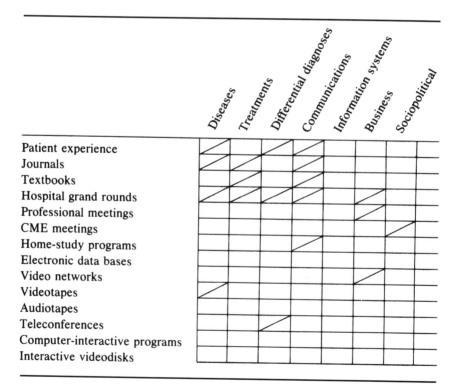

Figure 12.1   Continuing medical education matrix.

time, this process will take less time and will more closely reflect one's activities.

The reader should take time to assess his or her learning activities, whether an organized conference or learning from encounters with patients, and record an assessment immediately. This approach is just like keeping a record of anything; however, if an assessment is not recorded immediately, it will never be recorded.

An alternative would be to consider the continuing medical education matrix outlined previously. The numbers, instead of being hours, are an evaluation scale (e.g., 1 to 5) of the efficacy and appropriateness of each learning technology or environment for learning what one had intended to learn.

The reader will be able to keep pace with the changing opportunities, technologies and requirements for continuing medical education if continuing education is a routine and important part of his or her professional life. To help ensure that continuing medical education remains an important objective throughout one's career, it would be worthwhile to become a member of a national continuing education organization[5] or of a hospital or medical society committee for this purpose.

Although we are witnessing a tumultuous period for medicine, it is also an exciting time. Unlike in the past, when almost all physicians seemed to come out winners, in the future there will be more losers balancing out the winners. Where the reader will fall in this sociologic equation will depend on his or her commitment to continuing medical education and ability to adapt to change and adopt new technologies to reach his or her goals.

REFERENCES

1. Richards RK: *Continuing Medical Education.* New Haven, Conn, Yale University Press, 1978.
2. Starr P: *The Social Transformation of American Medicine.* New York, Basic Books, 1982.
3. Haynes RB, McKibbon KA, Fitzgerald D, *et al:* How to keep up with the medical literature: Deciding which journals to read regularly. *Ann Intern Med* 105:309–312, 1986.
4. American Medical Informatics Association
   4915 St. Elmo Ave., Suite 302
   Bethesda, MD 20814 (301-657-1291)
5. CONTINUING-MEDICAL-EDUCATION ORGANIZATIONS
   Alliance for Continuing Medical Education, †265 Purchase Street, Rye, NY 10580 (914-967-2944).
   Association of Hospital Medical Education, 1101 Connecticut Avenue NW, Washington, DC 20036.
   Society of Medical College Directors of Continuing Medical Education*
   (address changes with current president).

---

*Jointly publish *Mobius,* University of California Press, Berkeley, CA 94720.

CHAPTER 13

THE TECHNOLOGIC IMPERATIVE

Alan L. Hillman
A. Mark Fendrick

> Medical tradition emphasizes giving the best care that is technically possible; the only legitimate and explicity recognized constraint is the state of the art.[1]

The message of this chapter is that the practice of medicine is changing. Whereas most physicians were imbued with a technologic imperative during their training, they now must contend with more cost-conscious use of drugs, devices and procedures and with the moral choices that such economic realities imply. A shift to ambulatory care and other forces in the health-care environment also require adaptability by physicians. The rapid pace of change in health care requires active effort to avoid obsolescence. Health-care technology has contributed to many of these challenges; it also may be used to help physicians adapt to future practice alternatives.

Medicine is a technical trade. Practitioners must have a technical mastery of a myriad of drugs, devices and procedures in addition to a conceptual understanding about how they work. This repertoire of skills constantly must be updated and modified as the context for their use shifts and the techniques evolve. In this way, medicine is distinct from other professional endeavors, such as law, which necessitates mastery of a dynamic body of knowledge and a "way of thinking" but which requires expertise in far fewer technical skills.

During their training, physicians learn how to use technology in a "learning-by-doing" process. When challenged with a health problem, physicians slowly discover the appropriate role of technology: when to order a test, how to perform a procedure, what advantages alternative tests might offer, how to draw blood and perform an operation, how to interpret test results, how to resuscitate a patient during a cardiac arrest. Often, training is rapid—"see one, do one, teach one," for example, in the case of a lumbar puncture or components of the physical examination. At other times, training is prolonged and intense, for example, in the case of surgery or invasive radiology. Always, a trainee's technical skills must develop in parallel with his or her basic fund of medical knowledge.

Medical school and specialty training do more than teach these skills and knowledge. They also socialize medical trainees to an acceptable way of behaving and thinking. The "technologic imperative" is part of this socialization process. Because most education and training take place in technically sophisticated acute-care settings under the supervision of specialist physicians, practitioners often are trained, both actively and by emulating others, that more is better. Use of technology becomes a means for translating knowledge into action; its mastery separates physicians from the lay public, and it becomes the source of social authority. Active intervention is preferred over passive observation, even if both approaches have similar outcomes. Patients reinforce this inclination to active intervention because many of them are more satisfied with a doctor-patient interaction if a drug has been prescribed or a test performed.

Practitioners emerge from training with a body of knowledge, a group of technical skills and certain values and beliefs about the use of technology in medical practice. More often than not, however, they have not been fully informed about the variety of forces in the health-care environment that will influence their practice of the trade. Rather than operating in a "more-is-better" fashion, as in the past, modern practitioners face shrinking reimbursement, increasing competition and important challenges to their authority as decision-makers about what is best for their patients.

This chapter seeks to orient young physicians to the complex and dynamic interplay of forces operating in the health-care environment that will influence the technologic imperative. As in the rest of this book, the emphasis will not be on "how to" keep up with new drugs, devices and procedures. Rather, the goal is to convey an understanding of how the health-care environment operates and of what the future holds, so that young practitioners can learn to use technology to their and their patients' best advantage.

The next two sections explore health-care technology. The first of these sections describes the process by which technology is developed and addresses shortcomings in the technology-assessment process. Often, new technologies are deployed before their usefulness has been fully documented. The section that follows, "Rapid Change—A Historical View," places health-care research and development in a historical context. Technology begets technology—the fast pace of change in diagnostic and therapeutic approaches further challenges the technology-assessment process. It also threatens physicians with obsolescence, if they do not keep current.

The remainder of the chapter shifts the focus of the discussion to explore the interface between technology and the important forces and issues that are operating in the turbulent health-care environment. The section titled "Health-Care Technology and the Evolving context of Medical Practice" shows that cost containment, cost effectiveness, manpower trends, demographic shifts, competition and waning autonomy are forces with which practicing physicians must contend. These forces are changing and shaping health care in important ways. The next section shows that, as a result of these forces, the technologic imperative that clinicians bring to the practice of medicine is clashing with the exigencies of the economic, political, legal, ethical and social environments. The section that follows examines an issue of fundamental concern to the practice of medicine: will physicians continue to be patient advocates first and foremost, or will they increasingly become agents of society, as society attempts to control health-care costs and allocate scarce resources?

DEVELOPMENT OF HEALTH-CARE TECHNOLOGY

The Office of Technology Assessment defines health-care technology as

> . . . the drugs, devices, and medical and surgical procedures used in medical care, and the organizational and supportive systems within which such care is provided.[2]

Such a broad definition subsumes most of what we know as modern medicine—from the pharmaceutical agents, devices and procedures used to the hopsitals, clinics and personnel who use them. Because other chapters in this book are concerned largely with organizational and supportive systems in health care, this chapter will focus mainly on the technical substance of the trade—drugs, devices and procedures—and the issues they raise in the modern health-care environment.

The President's Biomedical Research Panel[3] defined seven steps in the development, diffusion and use of health-care technology:

1. Discovery, through research, of new knowledge and relation of this knowledge to the existing knowledge base;

2. Translation of new knowledge, through applied research, into new technology and development of strategies for moving the technology into the health-care system;
3. Evaluation of the safety and efficacy of new technology through such means as controlled clinical trials;
4. Development and operation of demonstration and control programs to confirm feasibility for widespread use;
5. Diffusion of new technology, beginning with trials and demonstrations and continuing through a process of increasing acceptance into medical practice;
6. Education of professional and lay communities in use of new technology;
7. Skillful and balanced application of new technology to the population.

This formulation represents the ideal situation in which useful, quality-enhancing innovations are introduced and accepted into medical practice after careful evaluation. In reality, the assessment and diffusion process often is a difficult one that occurs in fits and starts. The evolution of health-care technology depends on feedback from its clinical use. Specific indications for new drugs, additional or changed applications of new devices and modifications to procedures often occur as experience accumulates. Many times, the formal technology-assessment process—based largely on slow, expensive, controlled clinical trials—falls behind the pace at which new technologies evolve. As a result, innovations become "moving targets" with anything but a "skillful and balanced" deployment. Although the goal is to develop and promote only quality-enhancing technologies, substantial clinical experience often is required before quality can be assessed. Moreover, only 10 to 20 percent of health-care procedures have been documented to be beneficial by controlled clinical trials.[4]

Medical innovation emerges from research and development (R&D) centers supported by the government, private nonprofit organizations and private sector. Spending on biomedical R&D totals about $12 billion, about two thirds of which is funded by the federal government, with most of the remainder being spent by pharmaceutical firms and instrument and supply companies. Private, nonprofit foundations contribute a relatively small amount of funding. The federal component is made up largely of funding from the National Institutes of Health (NIH), with smaller contributions from other agencies, such as the Veterans Administration and the Department of Defense.

The R&D effort involves substantial interaction among government, academia and private firms. For example, whereas many new drugs result from internal research by pharmaceutical companies, such firms also increasingly rely on research breakthroughs by organizations in the nonprivate sector,[5] including academia. Moreover, pharmaceutical companies are additionally wed to academic institutions, where much of their clinical testing is performed to satisfy requirements of safety and efficacy as mandated by the Food and Drug Administration (FDA). Similar FDA requirements exist to cover newly-introduced health-care devices as well. Unlike pharmaceuticals, which all must be tested, devices deemed "equivalent" to those already available are not required to undergo separate controlled trials.

The heavy reliance on federal funding of medical R&D efforts raises the question of how the medical-research agenda will change as current trends toward diminished federal support of research take hold. Will proprietary organizations delay progress by an unwillingness to disclose the results of their R&D efforts? Will an increased reliance on corporate R&D efforts and corporate funding of academic endeavors bode ill for such initiatives as "orphan" drugs and other potentially unprofitable R&D undertakings.

New pharmaceutical agents are subjected to stringent, formal clinical trials under the authority of the FDA. Manufacturers must show that new devices perform as claimed. By contrast, there is no formal review of new health-care procedures that make use of approved drugs and devices. After approval by the FDA, the theoretic pattern by which new drugs and devices diffuse into medical practice follows a sigmoid (S-shaped) curve. Early, slow adoption during which the medical community conducts clinical trials is followed by more rapid adoption after clinical usefulness has been documented. However, as was mentioned before, this theoretically optimal pattern more often is the exception than the rule.

The research, development and diffusion process emphasizes high-use, high-tech, acute-care technologies. There are a number of reasons for this preference for high-tech curative interventions. First, successes in the 18th and 19th centuries in controlling communicable disease epidemics by sanitation and development of vaccines created a legacy of an ability to find "cures" for acute diseases. Ironically, although it was preventive technologies that generated these early "cures," society focuces on outcomes and did not acknowledge their scientific basis. Second, many insurance plans developed in the 20th century were conceived to protect middle-class beneficiaries from catastrophic illnesses that were infrequent, unpredictable and costly to manage. Insurance is now considered essential to prevent certain economic ruin in the event of a medical catastrophe. The increasing acceptability of insurance is linked to technological advances.[6] Coverage for prevention and primary care became supplemental. Third, federal initiatives, such as the Hill-Burton Act, augmented these trends toward a curative emphasis by pouring money into acute-care facilities after World War II. Finally, the training of physicians in such hospitals, and the development of technology to meet the needs of acute-care hospitals, ensured that practitioners were socialized to value acute care over prevention and that they had the tools and skills to practice in that fashion. Recent trends toward the use of seat belts, reductions in smoking and alcohol use, dietary modifications and increased levels of exercise may signal changes in social values to which medical practice may need to respond.

Technology assessments attempt to document how innovations were accepted into practice, despite appreciable uncertainty about their appropriate uses. The emergence of percutaneous transluminal coronary angioplasty (PTCA) as an alternative treatment to coronary artery bypass grafting (CABG) for severe coronary artery disease exemplifies the assessment, adoption and diffusion process.

This first PTCA procedure was performed by Gruentzig in 1977. By 1983, 32,300 operations were being performed annually in the U.S. The effectiveness of PTCA in relieving angina pectoris and the ineffective constraints on health-care spending at that time encouraged the rapid diffusion of this procedure. In 1987, 175,000 procedures were performed at a total cost of about $7 billion. This rate of increase over the decade is estimated to be up to ten times as fast as occurred in England. (Reasons for such a lower rate of diffusion of technology in England will be discussed later.)

While the effectiveness of PTCA in providing relief from angina is well accepted, this less-invasive procedure became widely used despite a lack of documentation of any advantages in safety or efficacy over available treatment strategies. In fact, recent studies have shown that all three approaches have nearly equivalent effects on survival in the management of most cases of one- or two-vessel atherosclerotic disease.[7-8] A number of factors played a role in the rapid adoption of the procedure: patient demand, high reimbursement rates and industry's ability to supply an expanding market, to name a few.

This analysis points out some difficulties in assessing exciting new health-care innovations that appear to be effective at first glance. Encouragement for their adoption and use comes at a much faster pace than do results of clinical studies. Physicians, indoctrinated with the technologic imperative, like active new interventions: Hospitals know that patients are attracted to institutions with the latest technical gadgetry, although recent reform in reimbursement policies have not favored acquisition of new technologies. This is not to say that the diffusion of new drugs, devices and procedures occurs with anything but patients' best interests in mind. Physicians promote new technologies because of a genuine desire to improve quality of life. Nonetheless, the system of checks and balances often promotes diffusion before adequate assessment of technology can take place.

On the other hand, assessment of technology is exceedingly difficult. As was mentioned before, conclusions about how best to use an innovation depend on accumulated clinical experience. At least partial diffusion must occur to facilitate adequate assessment. Also, the slow and tedious technology-assessment process may produce results that are outdated as soon as they are available. "Moving-target" technologies rapidly evolve and are refined to a new state of the art. This was the case with many PTCA clinical trials. For example, some such trials did not make routine use of adjuvant antithrombotic agents. These drugs (i.e., aspirin) clearly prevent subsequent myocardial infarction and decrease mortality in patients with atherosclerotic coronary-artery disease. Because use of such drugs has become standard practice, the results of clinical trials comparing PTCA to medical therapy to surgical therapy for such patients cannot be generalized unless those treated with PTCA received the benefits of full standard care, including use of antithrombotic agents.

There is constant conflict between the impetus to apply new technologies and the need to temper this enthusiasm until some assessment of how best to use them can be made. Therefore, a delicate balance between diffusion and assessment should be maintained. These difficulties point out the need for a greater number of better-funded, better-organized, more-powerful and more-timely assessments of technology. Although the FDA has authority to review new drugs and devices, it is concerned only with safety and efficacy (defined as the ability of a drug or device to do what is claimed). There is no coordinated effort to oversee assessments of technology, especially the need to determine cost effectiveness and how innovations compare to traditional, accepted practices. A myriad of governmental and nongovernmental agencies attempt some assessments; examples are the American College of Physicians, the Institute of Medicine, the National Center for Health Services Research, the Health Care Financing Administration, the NIH, the American Medical Association, health-insurance companies and technology manufacturers.[9]

Another difficulty is to determine the appropriate risk/benefit trade-off for various drugs, devices and procedures. In the case of a disease or disorder with an especially poor prognosis, an intervention with a higher risk might be more acceptable than it would be if the problem had a favorable prognosis. People with metastatic cancer often choose a risky intervention, such as bone marrow transplantation, whereas those with only localized disease do not. Efforts directed toward assessment of technology, therefore, must consider this risk/benefit tradeoff.

Assessment of technology may have several objectives. Although definitions vary, evaluating the *efficacy* of an intervention generally involves assessing whether it works under optimal circumstances. The *effectiveness* of an intervention is a measure of whether the intervention is successful in practice. The *efficiency* of an intervention measures outcome per unit input, and thus is an economic assessment.

Shortcomings in the difficult technology-assessment process require that practitioners maintain a constant vigilance against haphazard, unrestrained use of new and unproved drugs, devices and procedures until their mature clinical roles have been documented. An open mind, a willingness to adapt to new standards of care as they are developed, and an effort to keep abreast by reading the literature and becoming involved in continuing medical education are already of paramount importance. As will be shown in subsequent sections, such behavior becomes obligatory as physicians are forced to practice under new incentives brought to bear by cost containment and other evolving trends in the health-care environment.

RAPID CHANGE—A HISTORICAL VIEW

Technology begets technology. Health-care advances build on prior ones in an accelerating fashion. This section explores the underpinnings of the technologic imperative from a historical perspective. A view of the past may provide insight into health-care technology of the future and the challenges that await us.

The pace of progress in health-care technology over the past two or three generations has been astounding. Consider health care at the turn of the century. The diagnostic capabilities of radiology were in their infancy, antibiotics were not available for managing bacterial infections, modern chemotherapeutic approaches had not been devised, effective pharmaceutical agents were uncommon, and prostheses were primitive. Often, a physician's only recourse were carefully rehearsed words of consolation and sorrow. The prognosis for most patients with chronic diseases was a painful, uncomfortable and incontrovertible one.

In the relatively few years that have transpired, progress in diagnosis and therapy has substantially changed the outlook for many health problems. Countless drugs, devices and procedures have contributed to this progress; even the most forward thinking physician at the turn of the century could not have forecast synthetic antibiotics, magnetic resonance imaging, artificial organs, sonography and fiberoptics, to name only a few important innovations.

However, progress has not affected all diseases equally. The battle against cancer is illustrative. Hodgkin's disease, childhood leukemia and testicular carcinoma, for example, respond to combinations of chemotherapy and radiation therapy. These modalities offer significant chances of cure. Unfortunately, these cancers are relatively uncommon, and many of the common cancers (e.g., those of breasts, lungs and colon) have not yet yielded to medical therapy. Although most patients with cancer can obtain palliative therapy or, at least, be assured a more comfortable existence, progress in cancer therapy has been uneven.[10]

Even the luckiest patient with cancer often suffers discomfort, time lost from work and side effects of therapy, such as nephrotoxicity, leukopenia, radiation fibrosis and alopecia. Many of these problems stem from the lack of specificity of therapeutic agents that attack both malignant and healthy tissue. Yet, the evolution of health-care technology is far from finished. If the pace of recent progress is sustained, the practice of medicine will continue to change in remarkable ways. For example, new cancer therapies with substantially enhanced specificity may minimize toxicity to normal tissue. Already, experimental approaches have linked chemotherapeutic agents to monoclonal antibodies specific for tumor antigens. Once injected, such ligands concentrate at tumor sites, thus minimizing exposure of healthy tissue to toxic agents. If the genetic code that triggers uncontrolled mitotic activity can be broken, molecules may be designed to turn off or prevent growth of malignant cells. Many other innovative approaches may be on the horizon.

The rapid rate of technologic change in medicine renders practitioners especially vulnerable to obsolescence. The explosion of information and technical progress is one important event that has encouraged physicians to specialize and subspecialize. Physicians feel more secure and less pressured if they are obligated to keep abreast of one narrow, but deep, aspect of medicine, instead of taking a more general approach. Nonetheless, all practitioners must establish good habits early to keep apprised of technologic change. Attendance at medical meetings and reading the literature are helpful, yet the most important requisite is intellectual flexibility. Especially troubling will be newly trained physicians who spend years learning a special technique only to find their ''bread-and-butter'' skills rendered obsolete by some new device or procedure.

Another threat to physicians is political in nature. Funding and reimbursement decisions by policymakers influence the health-care armamentarium. Congress' decision to pay for dialysis as part of the Social Security amendments, for example, created a substantial need for dialysis technology (and for nephrologists to run the dialysis units!).

Laparoscopic cholecystectomy (LC) is a recent example of a new technology that may have a major impact on the practice of medicine and that may stimulate the need for a modification in manpower and training of certain specialists. LC permits the surgical removal of the gallbladder without a large abdominal incision to directly visualize the operating field. Instead, a fiberoptic camera projects the field into a large video monitor, allowing the surgical team to perform complicated maneuvers. It may substantially reduce the number of open cholecystectomies performed, as well as the number of surgeons required to be skilled in this procedure. Such vulnerability to obsolescence may be minimized by the maintenance of a portfolio of skills and a willingness to learn new ones.

There are numerous examples of obsolete or worthless technology: pneumoencephalography (replaced by computerized tomography), gastric-freezing surgery for ulcer disease (shown to lack efficacy and to be associated with the development of gastric cancer) and antiarrhythmic suppression of ventricular premature beats (shown to increase cardiovas-

cular mortality).[11] Although many obsolete medical and surgical procedures were accepted practices for only a brief period, their impact on the
cost and quality of health care may only have been a negative one.

The challenge to keep current is a formidable one. A more detailed
perspective on three eras of progress in health-care technology may offer
insight into what the future holds and how fast it may evolve.

Pharmaceutical Agents

Since World War II, there has been a burst of productivity from
pharmaceutical companies that have been using traditional organic and
inorganic chemical procedures. Many discoveries, such as Fleming's observation that bread mold inhibits growth of certain bacteria, were made
fortuitously by keen observers. Other discoveries, for example the finding
of H_2-blockers, emanated from the tedious testing of numerous compounds—a search for one that behaved as predicted by theory. The list
of pharmaceutical agents produced during this period includes some of
the most common and useful drugs, many of which altered life-styles
dramatically.

Antibiotics, starting with sulfa drugs and penicillin, transformed
health care. Consider such common problems as ear infections, pneumonia, urinary-tract infections and strep throat. These ailments can be cured
by merely filling a prescription and complying for several days with a
simple therapeutic regimen. Anyone with children would find it difficult
to imagine how parents coped with their children's ear infections before
the advent of antibiotics. Antibiotics also are integral to the success of
surgical procedures and cancer chemotherapy and to the cure of many
common parasitic infections. Current research is addressed toward extending these successes to viral infections, overcoming the problem of
induced antibiotic resistance and designing synthetic drugs with less severe side effects, such as nephrotoxicity.

Several important vaccines emerged from this era. For example,
the polio vaccine conquered epidemics of the disease and ended a generation of fear among parents of bringing their children to public places
where the chances of encountering and contracting polio were increased
during certain seasons. Another product of this era, psychotropic medications (e.g., chlorpromazine) enabled many people to return to productive
lives and allowed many institutional asylums to be closed. Steroid pharmaceutical agents, leading to the development of birth-control pills,
helped revolutionize sexual values. Diuretics and nitrates offered victims
of heart disease the first relief from symptoms of their affliction.

In 1962, the Kefauver amendment empowered the FDA to review
and approve all new pharmaceutical agents. The FDA approval process
is a long and tedious one. Many observers feel that this legislation has
been responsible for the precipitous drop in the number of new pharmaceutical agents introduced since that time. Other observers feel that this

legislation has protected the public from many unproved, useless or dangerous compounds. Nevertheless, traditional pharmaceutical approaches continue to result in the development of useful new drugs, although at a slower pace than before (see Chapter 7).

Devices

For the past two to three decades, technologic advances have focused on instrumentation. Automated blood tests have been refined to the point where many are found in physicians' offices. Prosthetic organs, such as joints and optical lenses, now commonly replace the original body parts when they fail. Other organ replacements, such as artificial hearts, are in earlier phases of development. Diagnostic imaging techniques, such as sonography, computerized tomography, magnetic resonance imaging and fiberoptics, have had a special impact on the practice of medicine.

The case of magnetic resonance imaging (MRI) illustrates how fast technology evolves and is accepted into practice. This imaging modality is based on the principle that hydrogen ions absorb and then emit energy pulses applied at the appropriate frequency (the resonance frequency). The emitted energy is detected by special coils. Three-dimensional data about hydrogen density and the way in which the atoms return to the resting state (the "relaxation" characteristics) are recorded. Computers can then reconstruct images from such data. Although nuclear magnetic resonance has been used for several decades to help characterize test-tube samples of various molecules, its first two-dimensional imaging application did not take place until the 1970s. By 1980, the first clinical prototypes of imaging units were available, although image quality was poor. Since then, the rate of improvement in image quality has been striking. This technique currently provides far better views of certain parts of the body than does computerized tomography (in the posterior fossa, for example, MRI images are not plagued by bone artifacts as are images obtained with the latter technique) and has become by acclamation the modality of choice for such structures. New hardware and software applications become available on a monthly basis. The number of MRI devices in place in hospitals and clinics has increased dramatically as well. By the end of 1984, there were 151 units in use[12,13] and, by 1991, approximately 2,700 units. Thus, in a decade, an entirely new imaging modality, and a resultant multimillion dollar market, was conceptualized, designed, refined, produced and disseminated. This process also required the training of technicians and diagnosticians to process the images and the indoctrination of clinicians about its potential usefulness.

Magnetic resonance imaging is not yet a mature technology. In fact, many critics maintain that it represents another example of how technology is often deployed before its legitimate usefulness has been determined. Nonetheless, it is a good example of how fast health-care technology evolves and how difficult it often is to keep abreast. As MRI matures, physicians will be required to assimilate it into their practice. What can MRI accomplish? In what settings have good studies been performed? Is it cost effective? Are there complications or side effects? What tests and procedures can it replace? These are some of the relevant questions that a thoughtful practitioner would ask. Given the rate at which MRI and other technologies are evolving, such questions must be asked in a timely fashion.

Biotechnology

New biologic techniques, such as therapy with monoclonal antibodies and recombinant DNA experimentation, are opening new vistas in diagnostic and therapeutic approaches. Gene-splicing techniques someday may permit scientists to understand genetic codes and to replace defective or absent genes in malfunctioning cells. These techniques, outgrowths of Watson and Crick's elucidation of the molecular structure of DNA in 1953, are totally new conceptual approaches to the conquest of disease. The aforementioned use of monoclonal antibodies to target specific cancer cells for destruction by chemotherapeutic agents is only one of many potential applications of such antibodies. They also can be used by themselves to fight specific types of bacteria, they can be linked with paramagnetic contrast agents to highlight MRI images, and they can be used to purify synthetic vaccines. In fact, monoclonal antibodies and recombinant DNA techniques offer new ways to create pure and effective synthetic hormones (i.e., insulin and growth hormones and vaccines, thus avoiding some potential hazards of conventional agents.

Even space has been exploited for medical purposes. In the absence of gravity, substances can be separated by electrophoresis with much greater purity and volume than can be achieved on earth. Also, a gravity-free environment may be used to grow crystals of protein-cell receptor ligands that can then be analyzed and duplicated for medical purposes.

This brief historical perspective on technologic progress in medicine conveys the rapid pace by which innovations build on one another to advance diagnosis and therapy. Drugs and devices combine to generate new procedures, understanding and further progress. Such advances often represent moving targets. That is, they evolve so quickly that assessments of potential usefulness made at one time are no longer applicable to more refined, subsequent generations.

Table 13.1 summarizes a survey conducted by the Office of Technology Assessment in which knowledgeable medical spokesmen were asked in 1984 to list clinically useful innovations that may be forthcoming in the next five to 15 years.[14] Some are already in clinical use, others are emerging and few remain in the development phase.

TABLE 13.1
FRONTIERS OF BIOMEDICAL TECHNOLOGY

- Transplantation: Kidneys, liver, pancreas, heart/lungs, pancreatic islet cells, endocrine organs, limbs, bone, small bowel, cloned skin
- Prostheses: Heart, lungs, pancreas, kidneys, bladder, improved joints, blood substitutes, intraocular lenses, skin, ligaments/tendons, ventricular assist devices, implantable sensory aids, myoelectric limbs, robotics
- Biotechnology: Monoclonal antibodies (in vitro and in vivo), hybridization probes, home diagnostic testing, gene therapy, new vaccines (e.g., viral, bacterial, parasitic and "anti-cancer"), in utero therapy, genetic screening
- Imaging: Ultra-high-speed computerized tomography, digitalization of radiographic system, MRI, magnetoencephalography, filmless radiology, PET scanning
- Computer and information technology: Medical decision making, case-specific data bases, ambulatory monitoring, robotics
- Surgical advances: Advanced replantation microsurgery, somatosensory evoked potential monitoring during neurosurgery, electroanesthesia, chemical modulators of wound healing, increased outpatient surgery
- Laser therapy: Photodynamic cancer therapy, angioplasty, surgery in conjunction with fiberoptic scopes
- Miscellaneous: extracorporeal shockwave lithotripsy for nonurolithiasis patients, extracorporeal membrane oxygenation, electromagnetic bone growth stimulator

The innovations listed in this survey will shape the practice of medicine over the next generation, but they are not likely to solve all health problems, nor are they likely to obviate the need for maintaining good basic skills in patient history taking, physical examination and clinical decision making. Office-based computers, for example, will assist physicians in retrieving data, listing differential diagnoses, recording patient information and keeping track of some administrative and billing aspects of their practices. Computers will not replace good judgment, sensitivity to the human aspects of the doctor-patient interaction or the "art of medicine"—that exclusively human ability to detect important, but subtle, clinical clues (see Chapter 11).

Similarly, biotechnology will improve clinical testing, but cancer vaccines may not be available in the next five to 15 years.[15] Prostheses (e.g., sensory aids) and imaging techniques (e.g., MRI spectroscopy) hold special promise,[15] although they also require much research and development.

The history of health-care technology is one of accelerating change. Certainly, the future promises further exciting innovation. Taking full advantage of this burgeoning knowledge base will require effective technology-assessment programs, good clinical judgment and compassion concerning its appropriate use.

HEALTH-CARE TECHNOLOGY AND THE EVOLVING
CONTEXT OF MEDICAL PRACTICE

The preceding two sections looked at how technology is developed and introduced and examined the technologic imperative from a historical perspective. In this section and the two that follow, the focus of the discussion shifts to explore how the turbulent health-care environment is influencing the use of drugs, devices and procedures. First, we examine specific forces that are shaping the practice of medicine. Understanding how such forces influence the technologic imperative will provide practitioners with insight into future practice alternatives.

Cost-Containment

Health-care technology is helping shape the context of medical practice. It is extending the frontiers of medical knowledge. Yet, the explosion of technology has been blamed as a major cause of the rapid escalation of health-care costs.[5] Both the number of new technologies and their frequency of use have increased in recent years. Studies have shown the effect of new technology on per diem hospital costs, ranging from 33 to 75 percent.[16-18] Regardless of the exact number, it is clear that technical capabilities are expensive.

Both high usage of "little-ticket" technologies, such as blood tests, and less frequent use of "big-ticket" technologies, such as MRI or organ transplantation, have been implicated as important factors in the skyrocketing costs of health care (now almost a $900 billion annual enterprise accounting for 12 percent of the gross national product).[19] Innovations are expensive because the private sector incurs substantial R&D costs in identifying and refining new tests and procedures and in documenting their safety and efficacy to comply with the requirements of the FDA. Also, the costs of marketing innovations must be passed along, as must a profit margin sufficient to compensate for past R&D failures. Even a simple in vitro assay for home use, for example, is the culmination of years of expensive, sophisticated microbiologic R&D.

Health-care inflation is exacerbated because new drugs, devices and procedures lead to further innovation. For example, fiberoptic technology generated such new procedures as laparoscopic cholecystectomy and thoracoscopic lobectomy; drugs developed to inhibit the immune response have opened the door to new, more complex transplantation procedures; such biotechnologies as monoclonal antibodies and recombinant DNA have facilitated the design of new diagnostic assays and therapeutic agents. Further, as these new technologies penetrate the practice of medicine, they engender a self-perpetuating situation in which the findings of one test lead to the application of other interventions.

Although the potential of health-care technology somtimes seems infinite, resources certainly are finite. Only recently have physicians begun to feel the impact of this economic fact. In the past, health-care expenditures were reimbursed retrospectively; payments by insurers were made for all "usual, reasonable and customary" costs. This system insulated physicians and patients from the direct effects of the cost of care. Such cost-based reimbursement provided a stimulus to the technologic imperative, and physicians performed more and more services. Indeed, their own pecuniary interests were advanced by such an arrangement.

These reimbursement incentives exacerbated health-care inflation until the government and other third-party payers demanded that costs be brought under control. As a result, the "blank check" is being replaced by new systems of reimbursement that limit the amount of resources a practitioner can employ in the care of a given patient. Capitation payments, in which a set fee is paid to a physician to provide for all a patient's health-care needs for a given period, reverse prior incentives. Under this system, a physician prospers only by the use of minimal technologic resources. Moreover, the physician's style of practice may change; the prevention of severe disease, or at least its early detection, becomes more important to avoid allowing an ailment to progress to a stage where more costly resources must be employed. Limits are also set in other ways. Medicare's system of using diagnosis-related groups for paying hospitals only a set fee per Medicare inpatient admission stimulates hospitals to shorten length of stay and to perform as many services as possible in the unregulated outpatient setting, where overhead is less, and, at least for now, services are still reimbursed in a retrospective fashion.

The impact of these new payment mechanisms are discussed in detail elsewhere in this book. For the purposes of this chapter, the goal is to understand that they reflect a new emphasis on cost consciousness that is changing how, when and what services are performed. This philosophy will dominate health-care reimbursement mechanisms are more settings become affected (e.g., Medicare is considering the use of diagnosis-related groups for payments to physicians).

Cost containment also has implications for technology R&D by the private sector as physicians choosing between two alternative tests or procedures learn to consider their respective cost effectiveness. For example, the new reimbursement incentives encourage physicians to use tests and procedures that provide the best information or outcome at the lowest cost. Manufacturers will respond by developing products that have some advantage in terms of cost or quality but that do not compromise safety. A characteristic of the development and marketing of laparoscopic cholecystectomy, for example, has been an emphasis on the convenience to the patient and lower cost per gallbladder removal to the hospital due to a reduction in length of stay and the ability to return to work sooner.

Cost-containment is affecting how practitioners use technology. Physicians who think in terms of cost effectiveness and who can implement cost-effectiveness principles in their practices will have an advantage over those who continue to operate as though past reimbursement incentives remained. Remember the concept of choosing future clinicians by market-relevant criteria!

Formal analysis of cost effectiveness in assessment of technology compares the cost of a service to its effect on health. In general, the more desirable of two interventions has a lower ratio of cost to effectiveness, as long as the outcome of each intervention can be measured in similar units. For example, if a throat culture provided by company A costs less than one provided by company B but has the same operating characteristics (sensitivity and specificity) in detecting group A beta-hemolytic streptococci, company A's product obviously should be used. Although this conclusion may seem obvious, practitioners were formerly insulated from such sensitivity to cost and may have elected company B's product on the basis of considerations unrelated to price, such as a preference for one pharmaceutical company's detail person over another's or the belief that higher cost means better quality. Now, sensitivity to cost and effectiveness are paramount.

Also, practitioners must plan work-ups with special care. A single expensive test must not be overlooked because of cost alone, if it is likely to be cost effective in the long run by substituting for a variety of other tests whose aggregate cost is higher. On the other hand, tests or procedures that provide only minimal or marginal information must be avoided. Although the costs of tests are not the most important consideration in planning patient care, they are becoming more important as diagnosis-related groups, capitation plans and other cost constraints infiltrate medicine. The challenge is to sustain the quality and safety of health care as new incentives take hold.

Demographic Changes

Our society is aging. We are barely replacing ourselves. Other health-care technologies—sanitation, nutrition, prevention and curative measures—have substantially lengthened the average life span over the past century. The result is a growth in the elderly population (people over age 65), especially those over age 85. Because the elderly tend to have more chronic, debilitating diseases, the epidemiologic characteristics of disease in the population are changing. As a higher proportion of young people move into the work place, fewer offspring are left to help at home and the chronic disabilities of the elderly become even more challenging to practitioners.

As these trends evolve, so will the focus of health-care technology. Products and services will be designed to meet the special needs of the elderly who are struggling to remain ambulatory and independent. Iridectomy with lens implantation and joint replacement in degenerative disease are two examples of the specialized services that are increasingly improving the quality of life of the elderly. Preventive measures, such as screening and vaccination, and rehabilitative programs after coronary or cerebrovascular events are also important, as is merely the access to adequate follow-up for chronic disease.

The special needs of the elderly clash with the need for cost containment. Already, some critics have challenged the advisability of performing outpatient iridectomy in elderly patients, whose other health problems often require in-patient perioperative management. If reimbursement is not adjusted to match the intensity of resources used by the elderly, providers will have a strong disincentive to specialize in geriatric care.

The locus of care will also change. Health-care technology and its underlying support services will be designed to enhance home care and nursing-home care. Already, some mobile dental services that feature fully equipped, self-contained vans travel among various retirement villages to provide high-quality dental care to retirees with limited mobility.

Corporatization of Health Care

American medicine increasingly is becoming the domain of the private-sector corporations, and even private nonprofit institutions are acquiring a corporate structure and values. Physicians increasingly are working in managed groups, whether as salaried staff members of health maintenance organizations or hospital corporations or as members of looser affiliations of physicians under contract to provide care at a discount. (Preferred-provider organizations, independent-practice associations, health maintenance organizations and other organizational entities are discussed in detail elsewhere in this book.) In addition, entrepreneurship and competition are increasing, as practitioners seek investment capital to open out-patient diagnostic imaging centers, urgicenters and other profit-oriented entities. Although these trends are occurring partly in response to the new emphasis on efficient health care, they are reflect an overall trend toward privatization in the economy, as public interests withdraw from the provision of many services. Nonetheless, in medicine, these phenomena are both new and controversial (see Chapters 8 and 9).

These trends are helping shape health-care technology. They enhance the stimulus from cost-effective (i.e., profitable) devices that can be delivered in the less expensive, and currently better reimbursed, out-patient setting. As mentioned, manufacturers of PTCA supplies exemplify this emphasis on profitability as they compete largely on the basis of costs, quality and service. Already, most cardiac catheterization laboratories have the ability to perform this procedure.[12,13]

The insinuation of corporate values and market incentives into the development and use of technology raises troubling questions about its long-term impact. Will drugs, devices and procedures become increasingly tailored to the diseases of the rich or well insured who can compensate technology manufacturers and health-care providers? Already, some proprietary companies are using monoclonal antibodies directed against specific tumor antigens to design individualized cancer therapies for patients who can afford them.[20] What will happen to rare diseases, the cure or management of which might never serve a substantial and, hence, profitable market? Will equitable access to technology be sustained? Although corporate incentives may not be inherently inconsistent with moral social objectives, society must remain viligant that uninsured patients have access to health-care technology and that uncommon diseases are not neglected by a profit-oriented R&D establishment.

Physician Manpower, Waning Autonomy and Malpractice

There are too many physicians. Past federal policies in response to the perception of a physician shortage have augmented the number of medical school graduates over the past two decades, creating a manpower glut, except in rural and inner-city areas. This oversupply places physicians in direct competition with one another for shrinking resources. In the past, competing physicians could enhance their income by performing an unlimited number of reimbursable procedures and services. In the future, they will prosper only through cost-effective behavior (see Chapter 10).

Simultaneously, physicians who were once revered without question and granted autonomy from oversight are now finding their authority questioned. Patients are becoming more savvy medical consumers, less likely to accept what one physician says. Symptomatic of this trend is the growing number of malpractice suits against physicians and the large dollar amounts awarded by juries for settlement of claims.

These forces are changing the context in which technology is used by practitioners. Competing physicians are subject to the influence of group-practice managers about what are appropriate uses of specific tests and procedures. Although physician managers may have more sympathy than nonphysician managers toward use of technology, increasingly both types of manager will be interested in cost containment and the avoidance of litigation. The extremes of this trend—guidelines by which physicians must practice—contrast sharply with historical antecedents for use of technology by practitioners. In the past, physicians largely practiced alone with the freedom to develop their own styles of medicine, including when and how long to hospitalize, which medications to use and which tests to perform. And yet, guidelines may help practitioners solve the conflict between the need to conserve technologic resources for cost-containment purposes and the need to employ technologic resources to satisfy the technologic imperative. Guidelines could also help document a practitioner's careful attention to a patient for medicolegal purposes.

Whether clinical treatment protocols foreshadow a trend to "cookbook" medicine or whether such protocols will allow physicians to practice high-quality, cost-effective medicine is an issue that warrants investigation. It is clear, however, that the trend to standardization of care will continue.

The extent to which these forces will influence physicians' use of technology in the future is to a large extent already programmed. Nonetheless, understanding these trends will enable physicians to optimize their practice patterns, grapple with broad social issues and, perhaps, establish a collective voice that will influence future practice alternatives.

HEALTH-CARE TECHNOLOGY—SOCIAL ISSUES

Physicians need to understand the broad social implications of health-care technology. The aggregate actions of practitioners and hospitals create a global pattern that society judges and regulates, if necessary. If physicians and hospitals are to affect their practice environment in a constructive fashion, they must not only understand but also anticipate the broader social implications of their actions. In *Future Shock,* Alvin Toffler describes a world in which technologic advances proceed at a rate that overwhelms society's ability to assess, control and use them to their best advantage.[21] He forecasts many of the social problems that will now be described. Modern physicians, too, are prone to medical "future shock."

Economic Issues

The collision between technologic advances and cost-containment efforts requires that choices be made about which tests and procedures should be made available and about who should receive them. Not all patients can have access to all health-care technology. Imagine the immediate costs, for example, if a week-long battery of diagnostic and screening services were available to this country's population. Patients might undergo a number of fiberoptic screening procedures (e.g., colonoscopy), blood tests (complete blood count, SMAC-12, thyroid functions), magnetic resonance scans, radiographic studies, Papanicolaou smears of sputum, urine and cervical secretions and other procedures. The costs of the procedures and services would be augmented by the economic loss of the extra time off from work (an automatic 2 percent decrease in the gross national product if the entire work force took an additional week off). Of course, we have not even mentioned the additional cost of intervening in the case of positive findings. Acknowledging that "not everyone can have everything" is the essence of economic choice. The consequence is the need to decide how available resources should be used.

The limitations of health-care resources are set at the broadest level by social priorities. The gross national product is a measure of all the goods and services a society can produce with its manpower, technology and natural resources. Currently, the United States devotes more than 12 percent of its gross national product to health care. The federal government's contribution, approximately 40 percent of the total, is slightly less than that devoted to defense spending (approximately 5 percent of GNP). This priority of "missiles over medicines" is mandated by society through its elected officials and policymakers. This priority sets constraints on how much health-care technology can be produced—for example, the number of hospital beds, radiographic machines, surgical suites, research grants, physicians, nurses and ambulances.

Health-care costs were not perceived to be a crisis until the proportion of the gross national product devoted to health care underwent a rapid rise over the past two decades. However, what is the "correct" amount to spend on health care? Less than 10 percent of the gross national product? More? Although this question is difficult to answer, scarcity of health-care resources is, in the broadest sense, a function of social choice at the macro level. Physicians' organizations with effective collective voices attempt to sway public opinion and congressional votes regarding health-care spending.

Once social priorities set constraints on total health-care spending, choices must be made about how available resources should be allocated. This necessity is true whether decision-makers actively identify and consider such choices or whether they make them indirectly or subconsciously. At the macro level, two dichotomous decisions must be made—whether to emphasize curative or preventive technologies and whether to emphasize high technology or low technology. The curative/preventive dichotomy is illustrated by the dilemma of whether to concentrate health-care spending on technology-intensive surgical and chemotherapeutic options to deal with lung cancer when it is detected or whether to spend more on educational programs to prevent and stop people from smoking. An intermediate approach (secondary prevention) would be to facilitate the earlier detection of disease. The high-tech/low-tech dichotomy is illustrated by the choice between conducting experiments to isolate the gene responsible for atherosclerotic coronary-artery disease and educating the public about ways to minimize atherosclerosis through nutrition and exercise programs.

Although preventive practices often involve the use of resources that are less technology intensive than curative approaches, this is not always the case. Many new vaccines, for example, are derived from sophisticated biotechnologic advances, such as gene-splicing and monoclonal antibody techniques. Vaccine development is one example where sophisticated and expensive programs may be the most cost-effective and appropriate level of technology, even for developing countries. The concept of "appropriate" technology depends, then, on social, cultural and economic variables indigenous to different environments.

Whereas a balanced approach between these two sets of extremes is probably appropriate for a sophisticated society such as ours, as was mentioned before, we tend to value high-tech curative interventions over prevention. This emphasis has evolved incrementally over the years, instead of resulting from active consideration of the alternatives and choosing such a path. As we come to terms with difficult economic decisions regarding the allocation of scarce medical resources, practitioners and policymakers have difficult decisions to make. Should traditions continue or should we consider a shift toward technology that will augment our ability to conduct effective primary-care and preventive health practices?

Ethical and Legal Issues

Technology generates ethical and legal dilemmas that affect the practice of medicine with increasing regularity. Such issues receive ample attention in the media and are most pressing at the extremes of life. Technology has enabled physicians to sustain fetal life outside the womb at an earlier stage and to lengthen the life span of our population. Yet, the drugs, devices and procedures that accomplish these biologic miracles do not provide answers to moral questions about when human life begins and ends, when abortion and euthanasia are appropriate and how quality of life should be valued over longevity. As more organs become available for transplantation, the same moral challenges become relevant to people who are between these extreme ages.

Practitioners become increasingly involved in such decisions as they attempt to balance family wishes, unclear legal requirements and personal beliefs with a need to protect themselves from litigation. Physicians have been sued for "pulling the plug" too soon and also for not pulling it soon enough. Ironically, that plug, symbolic of the technologic armamentarium of skill and knowledge possessed by physicians, augments both their ability to fight disease and their confrontation with moral ambiguity.

Certain mechanisms developed to deal with the problem of life-sustaining technology have sometimes created more problems than they address. "Advanced directives" for example, are signed by persons who wish to convey in advance their feelings about life-sustaining technology in case they become incapacitated and such technology is considered. The courts often have difficulty interpreting such documents, except in the most obvious cases of brain death. How can a person know what his or her preference will be before a life-threatening illness is encountered?

The rapid and accelerating pace of technologic advances in health care will continue to propel physicians into the uncertainties and ambiguities of moral dilemmas. These challenges add a new dimension to the practice of medicine—that of deciding when to avoid, or even to terminate, the use of drugs, devices and procedures. Humane, quality health care will necessitate such choices in the future.

Political Issues

The U.S. political system is a pluralistic one in which the lobbying powers of many divergent interests converge to set policy. American medicine reflects this eclectic approach as well. There is no comprehensive system of health insurance, no single central planning authority (even certificate-of-need laws were left to the states to enact) and, importantly, no coordinated technology-assessment effort. The absence of such coordinated systems partly stems from periodic shifts in governmental priorities. The changing political milieu alters perceptions about what is the appropriate level of governmental regulation on the development and diffusion of drugs, devices and procedures. Should the federal government closely monitor and supervise how health-care technology is used, or should it permit market forces to operate to a great extent? Shifting political ideologies between these alternatives have influenced incentives for adoption of technology over the years.

For example, computerized tomography was introduced in the early 1970s when skyrocketing health-care costs were first becoming a concern. Legislators felt that this technology would make a good test case for their new certificate-of-need requirement. At the time, such laws consisted of a federally mandated, state-administered requirement that all new capital purchases by hospitals be subject to review and approval by a regional authority (usually local health-systems agencies). This authority was responsible for ensuring a rational diffusion of new technology and, ultimately, containment of costs.

The impact of certificate-of-need laws on the diffusion of computerized tomography was problematic.[12] Because such regulations were not fully operative during the early years of computerized tomography, they actually may have stimulated early adoption of this technology, as many hospitals acted quickly to purchase equipment before effective laws could be enacted. Also, because certificate-of-need regulations never covered outpatient settings, many units were placed outside hospitals. Finally, because this technology was perceived as such an exciting, useful new innovation, regulatory agencies were never fully capable of restricting its deployment (however, certificate-of-need laws have been shown to have influenced the dissemination of other health-care technologies). Adoption of computerized tomography became widespread despite the enactment of such regulations, and before its efficacy could be well documented, because the health-care market demanded access to this important device.

In keeping with the political ideology of a minimalist government, the Reagan administration implemented a deregulation trend, allowing states to decide for themselves whether certificate-of-need legislation was necessary. As a result, several states have no such regulations, whereas others review the use of technology in in-patient and out-patient settings.

The introduction of MRI in 1981 permits a comparison of the impact of governmental policies in different eras. This technology is similar to computerized technology in that both modalities are expensive, diagnostic imaging procedures. Although there are important differences in the technologies that affect their relative diffusion patterns, MRI is being deployed in a different political milieu. Prospective reimbursement on the basis of diagnosis-related groups and the recent introduction of entrepreneurial and corporatized influences in the health-care environment have conferred competitive forces on the adoption and diffusion of new technology. Now, consideration of cost effectiveness becomes paramount: How much will an MRI device cost to purchase and operate, how many patients will it attract because of its prestige, and how will the device impact on a purchaser's bottom line—will it raise costs of caring for specific patients or lower them?

Magnetic resonance imaging has been deployed to a much greater degree than has computerized tomography in freestanding, investor-owned imaging centers. This trend can be partly explained by the increasing competitive and entrepreneurial health-care environment and by the fact that reimbursements based on diagnosis-related groups (as well as the review mechanisms provided by certificate-of-need laws in most states) do not yet cover out-patient use of technology. Thus, political decisions that influence reimbursement policies and regulations affect how new technology is adopted and used.

Currently, manufacturers are struggling to produce cost-effective technologies suitable for use in out-patient settings. Theoretically, under prospective reimbursement, regulators need not worry about the economic impact of specific new technologies—competitive pressures will force the market to promote the economically most appropriate dissemination and use of technology. The desirability of relying on market forces to allocate health-care resources is another ethical dilemma.

Of course, specific political decisions can have other profound effects. For example, by adding payment for hospital-based dialysis to the Social Security amendments, Congress ensured access for all kidney patients to this life-sustaining technology. However, in addition to raising health-care costs, this decision may have suppressed the development of other, more cost-effective approaches, such as home dialysis or kidney transplantation. Similarly, waning congressional enthusiasm for subsidizing the procurement of other organs for transplantation will impede the refinement and deployment of such interventions. In this way, the thrust of medical R&D can be affected by the political process. Sometimes, an effective congressional lobby is the most important determinant of the ultimate success of a particular medical tool.

Economic, legal, moral and political issues challenge social decision-makers and physicians. As potential technologic interventions increase in number, cost and moral ambiguity, the need to distinguish the cost-effective, quality-enhancing drugs, devices and procedures from less useful ones becomes paramount. Avoiding further medical future shock in this way requires consideration of the broad social implications of health-care technology. Hopefully, informed and effective decision making will be championed by physicians.

PHYSICIANS' USE OF TECHNOLOGY—PATIENT ADVOCATE OR SOCIAL AGENT?

In the preceding two sections, we outlined the specific forces that are shaping the future of health-care technology and considered broad social implications of such advances. Use of drugs, devices and procedures will involve medicolegal and moral dilemmas, and physicians will be subjected to guidelines and supervision by managers, affected by changing reimbursement incentives toward cost-effective practice and offered little assistance by an uncoordinated system of technology assessment. In this section, we consider a special challenge that is complicating the use of technology and the practice of medicine.

Physicians increasingly are finding themselves in the awkward position of serving two masters—their patients and society.[22,23] In the past, when technology was characterized by salves, kind words and concern, it was simple to adhere to the Hippocratic vow of putting a patient first and foremost. Health-care resources in that era were scarce only in the sense of efficacy, not quantity. A physician was a patient's advocate pure and simple. However, as the health-care armamentarium becomes more costly and resource intensive, there is a danger that practitioners will be called on to serve as society's agents—the means of implementing social constraints on the level of health-care spending.

This evolving conflict is well illustrated by considering the situation in Great Britain, where constraints on health-care spending are more institutionalized, having had a longer time to impact on physicians. In Great Britain, general practitioners (GPs) are gatekeepers to sophisticated interventions.[24] They are expected to decide, for example, who are reasonable candidates for dialysis and to refer only patients who meet the criteria. In this way, British physicians are the vehicle for the expression of social policies, and their responsibilities to patients must be tempered with practical realities. British GPs resolve this conflict by translating economic decisions about allocating scarce resources into medical ones.

For example, rather than saying a patient is "too old for dialysis" (economic criteria), the decision is rationalized in terms of dialysis being "too painful" or "not likely to help" (medical criteria). Of course, Great Britain's socialized health-care system is vastly different from ours, as are the sociocultural values of the British people, who submit to medical authority more than do Americans, possibly in return for a "cradle to grave" system providing universal access to care. Nonetheless, the predicament that British physicians confront as middlemen between social policies and patients' needs illustrates an extreme to which we may be headed as well. As was mentioned before, dialysis in this country is not a scarce resource because of congressional appropriations. In the setting of cost containment, future policies toward sophisticated, expensive, new interventions cannot be expected to be as generous in every case. Unless society sets specific standards and criteria to guide physicians, decisions about "who gets what" will fall to practitioners, placing their role as patient advocate in jeopardy.

This conflict is further illustrated by the notion of the statistical patient versus the identifiable patient. Consider, for example, that you are a social decision-maker, such as a congressman faced with the issue of whether to provide funding so that artificial hearts could be made available to any eligible patient. For the purpose of discussion, assume that current technology has improved to the point where the device can be used reliably without making complications as a temporary support while a permanent heterologous transplant is found or as a permanent prosthesis for up to 18 months. The cost for each procedure is estimated to be approximately $100,000. Should every person who may potentially benefit be eligible? These diseases are relatively common, and even quick calculations reveal a requirement for billions of dollars of yearly appropriations. As a social decision-maker in an era of cost-containment, it might be easy to conclude that a blanket endorsement of this technology is not justified. Perhaps only limited support is appropriate—for certain types of disease, only as a temporary device or only in certain age groups. This conclusion is acceptable to a social decision-maker because he or she is considering unidentified, statistical patients, never to be known personally.

On the other hand, consider a practitioner who is confronted by a 60-year-old woman whose death from idiopathic cardiomyopathy is imminent. It is much more difficult for physicians to withhold potentially helpful interventions from known, identifiable patients with whom they interact. That is why British physicians cloak economic criteria in medical parlance. To the extent that society sets standards and criteria for the allocation of health-care resources, the dilemma for physicians is less problematic. To the extent that society does not set specific standards and criteria, the dilemma of whether to act as patient advocate or as social agent becomes magnified.

A poignant example of how physicians respond when called on to adhere to social policies occurred in 1984, when physicians were asked by the federal government to conserve dwindling supplies of pertussis vaccine. Many pharmaceutical companies had stopped producing the vaccine because of the increasing frequency of litigation brought by parents whose children suffered from rare, but severe, neurologic complications of vaccination. Physicians were asked by policymakers (considering statistical patients) to limit their use of pertussis vaccine to fewer than the three recommended vaccinations per infant. Many physicians did not do so. When confronted with identifiable patients for whom they felt responsible, such physicians administered all three shots (of course, only after careful informed consent was obtained and documented for medico-legal purposes).

The conflict between identifiable and statistical patients is another reason that the medical profession has favored curative approaches over preventive ones. We have a natural proclivity to favor the identifiable, known, present problem over the statistical, unknown, potential future problem, even when preventive measures, such as eliminating smoking, are simple and more cost effective (of course, political and economic interests championed by the tobacco lobby also need to be considered). Thus, "while one death may be a tragedy, 1,000 deaths is merely a statistic."

Some practitioners may feel comfortable serving two masters; they may not experience the ethical or practical conflicts that other physicians associate with the obligation to interpret and implement social policies regarding the allocation of health-care resources. Nonetheless, all physicians will be better off with an awareness and understanding of the potential for conflict. Such awareness and understanding also may enable physicians to interact more effectively with their patients and, for physicians who feel compelled to do so, to respond both individually and collectively with an effective political voice.

Perhaps the optimal solution would be for society to structure the foundations or resource-allocation policy, for example, to decide basic age, health and prognostic criteria for the use of drugs, devices and procedures (as has recently been experimented with the Medicaid population in the state of Oregon).[25] Hospitals and community committees of physicians, philosophers, clergy, family members, attorneys and other interested parties could then monitor physicians' interpretations of such criteria and mediate or advise in unclear situations. Such a combination of guidelines and sounding board might assist physicians in the decision-making process, as well as rescue them from sole legal and moral responsibility.

CONCLUSION

Health-care technologies—drugs, devices and procedures—are the tools of a physician's trade. Although physicians are instructed in the use of these tools during the intense and prolonged medical-education experience, they are usually not apprised of what to expect thereafter. Unfortunately, the health-care environment is undergoing such rapid change that the future bodes poorly for physicians who lack an appropriate perspective about what is in store. They will enter practice with a strong technologic imperative—the inclination to apply health-care technology; they will not understand why more circumspect use of the constantly changing technologic arsenal will be a precondition to optimal health care.

This chapter has attempted to alert modern practitioners to how the complex and dynamic interplay of social, economic, political, historical, legal, demographic and technical forces in the health-care environment will impact on their future use of drugs, devices and procedures. We have not discussed formal assessment of technology; that is, how to compare the sensitivity, specificity and predictive values of various tests, how to design epidemiologically sound, randomized, controlled clinical trials and how to perform formal decision analysis to optimize the use of health-care technology. Although these skills are helpful in the process of deciding how to use new technologies, they exceed the scope and objective of this book.

Instead, we have taken a more global view of technology to illustrate the issues relevant to future medical practice. A recurrent theme has been the clash between expensive new technologies and trends toward cost containment, as exemplified by capitated reimbursement, a conflict that obligates economic choices about a patient's eligibility for treatment. These choices occur both at the societal level, in terms of percentage of gross national product devoted to health care, and at the practitioner level, in terms of pecuniary interests, which now depend increasingly on rational and circumspect use of only quality-enhancing and cost-effective technologies. Even more troubling is the potential for decisions about the allocation of health-care resources to devolve onto practitioners, placing in jeopardy their responsibility to be their patients' advocates first and foremost.

Another theme has been the rapid rate at which the technologic armamentarium evolves and the inability of current technology-assessment mechanisms to keep up. Future shock places an increased burden on practitioners to keep up to date and to avoid accepting innovations as standard practice before their mature role has been documented. The rapid evolution of technology makes subspecialists especially vulnerable to changing standards, if their livelihood depends on one special test or procedure.

Shifting demographic patterns, increasing corporatizations and competition and medicolegal challenges also are influencing how technology is developed and used. A shift in the locus of health care to outpatient settings has important ramifications. These forces will continue to affect the practice of medicine.

By maximizing the cost-effective use of drugs, devices and procedures, keeping up with rapidly changing technical capabilities and maintaining intellectual flexibility, physicians can optimize their future practice alternatives. By maintaining an effective political voice, they can help influence the political process, for example, by garnering increased support for technology-assessment efforts.

In the final analysis, however, technology will always remain an adjunct to the doctor-patient interaction—to be applied humanely, precisely and carefully. It should not be allowed to take on a life of its own. Drugs, devices and procedures are tools to *aid* in effective health care—they will never be ends in themselves.

ACKNOWLEDGMENTS

The author is indebted to Drs. Bernard Bloom, Jack McConnell and J. Sanford Schwartz and to Ms. Marie Jaskel.

REFERENCES

1. Fuchs V: The growing demand for medical care. *N Engl J Med* 279:190–195, 1968.
2. U.S. Congress Office of Technology Assessment: *Medical Technology and the Costs of the Medicare Program.* Washington, DC, Government Printing Office, 1984.
3. President's Biomedical Research Panel: Report. DHEW Publication (OS) 76–500. Washington, DC, Government Printing Office, 1976.
4. White K: International comparisons of health services systems. *Milbank Mem Fund Q* 46:117–126, 1968.
5. Banta HD, Behney CJ, Willems JS: *Toward Rational Technology in Medicine—Considerations for Health Policy.* New York, Springer Verlag, 1981.
6. Weisbrod BA: The health care quadrilemma: An essay on technological change, insurance, quality of care, and cost containment. *J Econ Lit* 29:523–552, 1991.
7. Coronary Artery Surgery Study (CASS): A randomized trial of coronary artery bypass surgery: Survival data. *Circulation* 68:939–950, 1983.
8. Coronary Artery Surgery Study (CASS): A randomized trial of coronary artery bypass surgery: Quality of life in patients randomly assigned to treatment groups. *Circulation* 68:951–960, 1983.
9. Iglehart JK: Health policy report: Another chance for technology assessment. *N Engl J Med* 309:509–512, 1983.
10. Bailar JC, Smith EM: Progress against cancer? *N Engl J Med* 314:1226–1232, 1986.
11. Hiatt HH: Protecting the medical commons: who is responsible? *N Engl J Med* 293:235–241, 1975.
12. Hillman AL, Schwartz JS: The diffusion of CT and MRI: A comparative analysis. *Med Care* 23(11):1283–1294, 1985.
13. Hillman AL, Schwartz JS: The diffusion of MRI: Patterns of siting and ownership in an era of changing incentives. *Am J Roentgenol* 146:963–969, 1986.
14. U.S. Congress Office of Technology Assessment. *Compilation of Responses to 1984/1985 Survey on Future Health Technology.* Washington, DC, U.S. Congress Office of Technology Assessment, 1985.
15. Behney CJ: The role of technology in future care. *Internist* May-June 1986, 21–23.

16. Waldman S: The effect of changing technology on hospital costs. *Social Security Administration Research and Statistics Note, # 4*. Washington, DC, Government Printing Office, 1972.
17. Feldstein M, Taylor A: *The Rapid Rise of Hospital Costs*. Washington, DC, President's Council on Wage and Price Stability, 1977.
18. Klarman H: Observations on health care technology: Measurement, analysis, and policy, in Altman S, Blendon R (eds): *Medical Technology: The Culprit Behind Health Care Costs?* Hyattsville, Md, National Center for Health Services Research and Bureau of Health Planning, 1979.
19. Moloney TW, Rogers DE: Medical technology—A different view of the contentious debate over costs. *N Engl J Med* 301:1413–1419, 1979.
20. Lind SE: Fee-for-service research. *N Engl J Med* 314:312–315, 1986.
21. Toffler A: *Future Shock*. New York, Random House, 1970.
22. Levinsky NG: The doctor's master. *N Engl J Med* 311:1573–1575, 1984.
23. Fuchs VR: The "rationing" of medical care. *N Engl J Med* 311:1572–1573, 1984.
24. Aaron HJ, Schwartz WB: *The Painful Prescription: Rationing Hospital Care*. Washington, DC, Brookings Institution, 1984.
25. Packwood R: National policy perspectives: Oregon's bold idea. *Acad Med* 65:632–633, 1990.

INDEX

DAVID B. NASH, M.D., M.B.A.

Dr. Nash is Director, Health Policy and Clinical Outcomes, Thomas Jefferson University Hospital and Clinical Associate Professor of Internal Medicine at Jefferson Medical College, Philadelphia, Pennsylvania. He previously was Medical Director of the Health Evaluation Center at the Hospital of the University of Pennsylvania and a full-time faculty member in General Internal Medicine at Penn Medical School. He also has been Deputy Editor of *Annals of Internal Medicine,* at the American College of Physicians, where he was responsible for health economics, medical education, and health care policy.

Dr. Nash received his bachelor's degree in economics (Phi Beta Kappa) from Vassar College, Poughkeepsie, New York; his medical degree from the University of Rochester School of Medicine and Dentistry; and an MBA with honors in Health Care Management from the Wharton School, University of Pennsylvania. He served his internship and residency in internal medicine at the Graduate Hospital of the University of Pennsylvania and was a Robert Wood Johnson Foundation Clinical Scholar at the University. Dr. Nash is a Diplomate of the American Board of Internal Medicine.

Among Dr. Nash's professional memberships are the American College of Physician Executives (ACPE); the American College of Physicians (ACP), of which he is a Fellow; the Association for Health Services Research; the American Society of Internal Medicine; and the Society for General Internal Medicine. He is the editor of three books on medical management topics and the author of more than 30 journal articles. He serves on the editorial boards of five national medical publications. His research interests include health care financing, medical public policy, physician behavior and the impact of cost-effectiveness on the pharmaceutical industry.

Nationally, he is the Chairman of the American Medical Review Research Center (AMRRC) in Washington, D.C.—a not-for-profit research organization interested in the quality of medical care, a member of the Joint Commission's (JCAHO) National User's Advisory Board, and the Chairman of the Clinical Evaluative Sciences Council of the University Hospital Consortium in Oak Brook, Illinois.

Dr. Nash is married to Dr. Esther J. Nash, Director of Quality Assurance and Medical Education at Bryn Mawr Hospital. Dr. Nash lives in Lafayette Hill, PA, with his twin five-year-old daughters, and two-year-old son.